Selected
Readings in
the Philosophy
of Education

Selected Readings in the Philosophy of Education

FOURTH EDITION

EDITED BY

Joe Park

Northwestern University

MACMILLAN PUBLISHING CO., INC.
NEW YORK

Earlier editions © 1958 and 1963, copyright © 1968
by Macmillan Publishing Co., Inc.

Macmillan Publishing Co., Inc.
866 Third Avenue, New York, New York 10022

Collier-Macmillan Canada, Ltd., Toronto, Ontario

Library of Congress Cataloging in Publication Data

Park, Joe, comp.
Selected readings in the philosophy of education.

Bibliography: p.
1. Education—Philosophy—Collections.
I. Title.
LB7.P26 1974   370.1'08   73–1039
ISBN 0–02–391650–8

Printing: 1 2 3 4 5 6 7 8   Year: 4 5 6 7 8 9 0

Preface

The purpose of this collection of readings is to help philosophy of education students to apply some of the tools of philosophy to problems in education. Stated more specifically, the purpose is threefold:

(1) To analyze some of the more significant concepts commonly used by educators such as teaching, knowing, indoctrination, education, and equality, i.e., to search out how such concepts are employed in the language of education.

(2) To learn how to analyze, resynthesize, and evaluate a philosophy of education.

(3) To identify some of the more significant problems in education about which doubt, confusion, and dispute arise in regard to means and ends, and to learn how one goes about generating the best and wisest solutions to such problems.

In preparing this book, I have sought to achieve the aforementioned purposes by arranging the material in the following order. The first and the briefest part, by way of introduction, is addressed to the place of philosophy of education in the study of education. Part Two shows how some of the techniques of contemporary language analysis can be and have been applied to education. Part Three raises the problem of inference (which has always been troublesome for those who believed the aims and practices of education somehow could be deduced from certain metaphysical presuppositions), provides a model for analyzing philosophies of education, and supplies two philosophical viewpoints as means for applying the model. Part Four sets forth criteria for identifying significant normative problems in education and illustrates the ways in which philosophers have attempted to supply tentative answers for several such problems. The last two parts of the book are necessarily longer than the first two.

This anthology has been designed to serve as a textbook or a source book. The first three editions served in one or both of these capacities in many colleges and universities.

In compiling this collection, I have tried to choose from the writings of some of the foremost men in the field selections that reveal the most significant points of view. My policy has been to quote each author at considerable length in order that the methods or position he uses or advocates becomes as understandable and coherent as possible. Introductory statements appear at the beginning of each part of the book. An extensive annotated bibliography of recent works in philosophy and education is provided at the end of the book.

Students will discover that the selections in this book require critical reading and careful discussion. The serious student should take time to think through the selections deliberately and thoroughly. Insofar as possible, each student should re-examine his current views on education and compare and contrast them with those of men who are distinguished in the field. This procedure is recommended with the hope that the student will develop those critical philosophical skills that will enable him to deal more effectively with some of the problems in education and, if he wishes, to formulate for himself a tentative philosophy of education which he will be able to articulate intelligently. He should try to find time to read in its entirety each of the books from which selections have been taken—first, to get a more comprehensive view of each author's position, and second, to get from many of the sources a number of very important ideas that could not be included in this collection because of the limited space available.

I should like to acknowledge the cooperation of the various authors and publishers whose permissions to quote made this collection possible. I am grateful for the aid and suggestions offered toward the improvement of the volume by those who advised Macmillan, Inc., as the manuscript was being prepared. Most especially, I am indebted to Lloyd Chilton of Macmillan, Inc., for his tolerance, advice, and support during the past ten years. He has been more than an editor. He has served both as a counselor and as a trusted friend.

A number of others have aided in the preparation of this and previous editions. Everett John Kircher, Ohio State University, and Paul Schilpp, Southern Illinois University, encouraged the editor from the very beginning. Allan Hart Jahsmann, The Lutheran Church—Missouri Synod; Robert Browning, Northwestern University; Meir BenHorin, Dropsie University, Philadelphia; and Hugh Petrie of the University of Illinois are but a few of the many persons who have been especially generous with their time and suggestions.

My former students must be thanked for helping me clarify some of my thoughts. Among those who immediately come to mind are Joel Auble, Western Georgia College; Eric Beversluis, Capital University, Columbus, Ohio; Gary Cox, State University of New York; William Duffy, University of Iowa; Daniel Coffey, Central YMCA College, Chicago, Illinois; Ron Podeschi, University of Wisconsin, Milwaukee; Ken Strike, Cornell University; Marc Briod, Oakland University; Warren Strandberg, Commonwealth

University of Virginia; Ward Weldon and Eli Krumbein, University of Illinois, Circle Campus, Chicago, Illinois; Judy Gottsegen, The Community School, Evanston, Illinois; Sonja Stone, Northeastern Illinois State University, Chicago, Illinois; and Bill Barron, presently a graduate student at Northwestern. All these persons, and others far too numerous to mention, taught me more than they may realize. But most of all, I wish to thank my son, Joe Charles Park, University of Wisconsin, Whitewater, for the hours he has spent in trying to re-educate a reluctant father; my daughter, Diane, for the editorial services rendered on occasion; and her husband, Mr. Evan Hammond, for the many pleasant philosophical conversations; and above all, my wife for her continued love and care.

J. P.

Contents

PART

One

The Place of Philosophy in the Study of Education

Introduction to Part One

The term "philosophy" (*philos*, "fond of," and *sophos*, "wise") has varied considerably both in meaning and in scope throughout history. Plato used the term in the most general way in his *Republic*, ". . . describing philosophers as those who see the absolute and eternal and immutable . . . those who love the truth in each thing." Plato thus fused all knowledge into a semireligious synthesis. It remained for Aristotle, with his methodic intellect, to separate the vast field of philosophy into the disciplines we recognize today as logic, psychology, ethics, aesthetics, metaphysics, and the like.

Philosophy, however, has not remained the grand subject it was in ancient times. It has been rocked to its very foundations by the advance of knowledge and by natural science in particular. Much of what was once epistemology has become the chief concern of the physiologist and the psychologist. Cosmology has yielded to research in astronomy and physics, and logic has been greatly modified by the work of the mathematical logicians. Metaphysics and ethics too have not gone unscathed. Many modern philosophers completely reject all metaphysical statements as nonsense, believing these statements to be unverifiable, at least as the term is commonly used. These same philosophers are likely to point out that ethical statements are not empirical facts but are imperative sentences that cannot be verified, although reasons may be advanced to justify them.

Even though not all philosophers are as skeptical as some of these comments would indicate, philosophy is, nevertheless, no longer the pretentious and all-inclusive subject it was in the days of Plato, for much of its subject matter, as well as the absolute, eternal, and the immutable, has been eroded away, even for those who are not skeptics.

The philosophy of education has also undergone, and is now undergoing, profound changes. In the past, a philosopher would usually stake out a claim in some systematic school of philosophy such as idealism, realism, or progmatism, and infer, or attempt to infer from the general tenets of that philosophy, the ends and means for education. Today a philosopher is much less likely to undertake anything on such a grand scale. Indeed he may repudiate eclectic and synoptic efforts in the philosophy of education as

3

fostering social engineering and spawning vagueness, ambiguity, pseudo-problems, pseudoexplanations, vacuous principles, and impractical prescriptions.[1] In order to avoid these kinds of evils the modern philosopher is likely to concentrate his efforts upon the logic and language of education.

We have moved from the study of a body of literature about the philosophy of education, from which it was supposed that each person could readily infer the proper ends and procedures for education. Instead, we are now moving toward the development of philosophical procedures and methods that can be used to work on certain kinds of problems in education, and most specifically, problems of the language and logic of education.

As a consequence, we have become better informed about concept usage in education and more sophisticated with regard to the logic of education. Perhaps what is most important is that we have begun to fashion specific tools, such as models for analyzing philosophies of education, methods for studying concepts, and criteria for identifying the kinds of problems that confront us. Thus we are no longer dealing in such broad and general ways with education, but we are focusing on specific problems and issues.

Part One is designed to give the reader a general idea of what philosophers of education do and the place they see for philosophy in the study and practice of education. This part may be studied first, or it may be initially omitted and returned to later, by those who are eager to get on with philosophy.

---

[1] Reginald D. Archambault, *Philosophical Analysis and Education* (New York: The Humanities Press, 1965).

1

The Uses of Philosophy
and the
Problems of Educators

ARNOLD B. LEVISON

When this topic was first suggested to me, "In what ways can philosophy be of use to educators?", my inclination was to reply "None," or at least "None that would be relevant to the educator in his professional capacity."* But when I set myself to work out the implicit considerations which had led me to make this judgment I found that the conditions were more complex than I had envisioned. I found that although there was one sense at least in which it would be wrong to claim that philosophy could be of special help to educators, there were other senses in which it would not be so. For originally I had thought of the educator as a professional person whose primary interest was in education as a "practical" science, that is to say a science which seeks knowledge of what to do in the teaching situation. But upon reflection I found that the notion of "teaching situation" was ambiguous and that there were at least three senses in which the teaching situation could present itself according as the educator was (1) an educational theorist, (2) a planner of curricula, and (3) a classroom teacher. And the way in

Arnold B. Levison is Professor of Philosophy at the University of Maryland. Arnold B. Levison, "The Uses of Philosophy and the Problems of Educators," Educational Theory, Vol. XI, No. 4, April, 1961, pp. 123–128. Used by permission of the author and Educational Theory.
    * A paper read at the 12th Annual Meeting of the Philosophy of Education Society (Southeastern Section), February 5–6, 1960.

which philosophy could or could not be of assistance to educators, I found, was similarly no univocal matter but depended on whether philosophy was conceived as (1) an autonomous activity, (2) a certain type of institution, or (3) an expression of a broad human concern. This last category is vague but not necessarily insignificant. In view of this complexity, I have revised my original opinion so that it now seems to me that there are definite ways in which one *can* speak of philosophy being of help to educators, provided that the sense in which philosophy *cannot* be of such assistance is first clearly comprehended. For it must be kept in mind that philosophy is a field of study in its own right, and is not especially oriented to education any more than it is oriented to the problems of other special fields outside its own province. The same, of course, is true of education; and in the sense in which both philosophy and education are independent, autonomous areas of study with their own standards, goals, ends, and requirements, it is downright impertinent to speak of one being of any special help to the other. But recognizing the integrity and independence of each as a branch of human knowledge and concern, it is permissible to speak of ways in which they can be of help to one another. In this paper, I shall speak from the side of philosophy only, and of how I conceive that it can and cannot be of assistance to educators.

To begin, I must devote some space to telling you what, in my opinion, philosophy is. I should observe, first of all, that to me philosophy is something that one "does," as opposed to something that one merely "talks *about*" or "reports," i.e. philosophy is first of all an activity of a certain kind and only secondarily a subject-matter consisting of a definite body of literature. But it is an activity which is accomplished through talking and writing, and for this reason is regarded by many people, who view all talking as "just talking" and never see that talking can be a kind of doing, as a rather silly or idle preoccupation. They take this attitude because they see philosophy only from the outside. From the inside, a different picture emerges. Here philosophy reveals itself as the analysis or systematic interpretation of general problems such as meaning, truth, perception, proof, knowledge, and so on. It seeks to say what can be said, logically and evidentially, about such general problems *as* general. It is thus, professionally regarded, a highly circumscribed activity, but one with an intense intrinsic value and interest for those who practice it.

Now philosophy in this sense, as an activity in its own right, is of no earthly use to educators or anyone else except those whose whole interests happen to be for that time philosophically engaged. Thus it would be absurd for a public school teacher to undertake to establish the reality of the external world prior to deciding how to discipline a recalcitrant pupil. In the same way, it would be ridiculous for an educator planning a curriculum for a system of public schools to concern himself with the question whether, if Hume is right, tomorrow will be like today or indeed whether there will be any schools at all in which to apply his program. These things are absurd and silly, but they would not be absurd and silly if the activity of philosophizing *were* directly relevant to the activities of an educator. It would be logically just as absurd to judge on the basis that philosophizing is of no value to educators that it has no value or use *whatever*. The usefulness and value of philosophy as such is to be judged wholly by those whose interests are philosophical, and not by those whose interests are in something else. Philosophy is essentially to be conceived, then, as an activity in its own right, cognitive, yet distinct from science and art, and in this sense the activity of philosophizing is wholly irrelevant to the activities of the educator.

But this way of viewing philosophy, as a certain distinctive type of human activity, is not the only one. Thus philosophy conceived as a certain type of institution *can* be of assistance to educators. I shall argue that philosophy in this respect is of assistance not so much to classroom teachers as to educational theorists and program planners. I will now proceed to elaborate this point.

Philosophy, I have said, is essentially to be conceived as an activity in its own right, cognitive, yet distinct from science and art. But the use of the word "philosophy" is not limited to this sense. There is another sense of the word "philosophy" in which what is referred to is an institution belonging to a complex social nexus of institutions. Philosophy conceived as an institution among institutions is an ill-defined community of diverse activities, some of which are not distinctively philosophical in the sense in which I have defined the philosophical activity. The philosophical community, as it exists today, contains many activities which I should call essentially "scientific", but I do not wish to say that they are for that reason out of place in that community. One of the peculiar characteristics of the philosophical activity is that it can be practiced on subjects not themselves distinctively philosophical. There is always room for the activity of probing into our deeper perplexities, in the very general way that is characteristic of philosophers, even when such perplexities are "philosophical" only because they are not sufficiently well-defined to be amenable to scientific treatment. Many of the problems of educators are of this nature, that is to say they are "scientific" in character and yet not sufficiently well-defined to be amenable to scientific treatment. Consequently, these problems come to rest for the present in the roost of the philosophers.

So far as we have any knowledge, it seems that there will always be such perplexities, however far back the frontiers of positive scientific knowledge are pushed. The general activity of probing into ultimate perplexities, some of which may be amenable to eventual scientific investigation and some of which may not, forms a large part of the activities and concerns of people operating within the institution of philosophy. Taking first those problems which may never be amenable to scientific treatment, it is still possible to attempt to come to some kind of systematic conclusion with regard to them, the best that one can, logically and evidentially. These are the problems that philosophers concern themselves with under the titles of epistemology, metaphysics, cosmology, etc. But, and this is the point, *other* problems presently occupying the attention of people within the philosophical community may eventually prove so productive as to develop into new sciences or at least contribute substantially to the improvement of an existing science. In this way the philosophical community may function as the mother of new sciences, as an influential force in the development of existing sciences, or as the permanent home of problems which will never be anything but philosophical.

Thus, people working within the philosophical community, whether we call them scientists or philosophers, can be of help to educators, especially educational theorists and program planners, in the following ways. 1. They can undertake to conduct, at least in the preliminary stages, the necessary empirical investigations which will establish the basic concepts of an educational theory. 2. They can assist in the development of tests for judging the truth and adequacy of any hypothesis which is advanced in educational science. 3. They can develop and supply the techniques for analyzing the words or concepts of educational discourse, in order to remove verbal conflicts and resolve inconsistencies in the language of education.

Since the philosophical community functions as the natural harbor and refuge for problems, whatever their real character, which are homeless and wandering, and since many of the problems of educators at the present time are of this nature, it is natural for educators to look to philosophy and philosophers for aid, especially in the matter of offering sound hypotheses and general programs for educators to try out in the teaching situation, in the manner of John Dewey. But it must be pointed out that when philosophers function in this way, they are functioning not as people whose interests are wholly absorbed in philosophical activities as such, but as scientists, offering hypotheses and formulating objective tests for validity. I have not tried to develop for you the concrete ways in which philosophy conceived as an institution can be of help to educators. I have concentrated rather on specifying the ways in which philosophy *logically* could and could not be of help to educators.

There is yet a third way, it seems to me, in which philosophy could be of help to educators, this time not to the educational theorist or program planner, but to the classroom teacher. And this involves the conception of philosophy not as an autonomous professional activity, nor as an institution among other institutions, but as an expression of a broad type of human concern. In this broader or vague sense philosophy is of peculiar importance to the classroom teacher because it typifies a kind of concern which is common to all mankind. The classroom teacher, whose profession is practiced on human beings as subjects, is peculiarly in need of a strong dose of philosophy in this sense. In order to bring out my meaning, however, I must take some space to develop an aspect of philosophizing which has not so far been made explicit.

I have said that philosophy is essentially to be conceived as an activity, cognitive, yet distinct from science and art. Its distinction from art may be assumed, but I have not yet made clear for you how it is to be distinguished from science. You will understand that I am here using the word "science" in a somewhat limited sense, that is, merely to denote such sciences as mathematics, physics, biology, anthropology, and so forth. They are sometimes called the "special sciences". In what way, then, is philosophy distinct from these special sciences? The answer to this question lies, I believe, in the fact that the philosophical activity incorporates as a part of its methodology the peculiar limitations of the human condition, that is to say, the fact that our results in an investigation must be affected by the presence of an observer or desirer such as man. The notion of complete non-intervention in the facts, or of maintaining an attitude of stolid passivity in the examination of pure data, which has been rendered sacrosanct by the special sciences, has really no place in philosophy.

You will tell me, of course: "Yes, but scientific results are testable by observation, and are therefore perfectly objective and imply no subjective intervention which might distort their character." But this seems to me to involve a false conception of "observation". What you say may well be true in the sense that it describes, for all practical purposes, the way in which a biologist or chemist goes to work, but it is not true as a theoretical statement about "observation". Observation is *not* an utterly passive activity. It is not merely the confrontation of a set of pre-labeled facts by a passive perceiver. The analogy of the man watching the behavior of the goldfish in the goldfish bowl is only one kind of observation, and a rather trivial one at that. The results of scientific investigation have their peculiar status and value not merely because they can be tested by observation but because large groups of human beings, namely, those whom we call scientists, know what to take them for. There are, of course, important reasons why a significantly large group of human beings *can* know, in that precise sense of "knowledge", how to take the results of a scientific investigation. It is because the whole sense of a "scientific" investigation is that it creates perfectly general standard conditions under which any scientist can follow out the specified procedure and arrive at the same results. But though there are analogues between this scientific procedure and the philosophical one, the essential difference remains that a purely philosophical investigation cannot proceed in ignoration of the fact that it is undertaken by man. The fact that the person conducting the philosophical investigation may affect the results is not considered as an unhappy chance to be avoided so far as possible, but *as itself something that requires investigation and explanation.*

It is for this reason that a philosophy, from the time of Socrates, has always been in part the views of a certain individual, and since the time of

Socrates, society has never been quite unambivalent in its feeling for such an individual. Socrates felt that it was the peculiar office of the philosopher to be a goad or "gadfly" in relation to his fellow citizens. You all know the story in the *Apology*. My contention is that philosophers continue to fulfill this social function as defined by Socrates, especially in their own classrooms. They still administer the paralytic shock to those of their pupils who imagine that their "knowledge" rests on perfectly secure foundations.

It is part of the distinctive function of philosophy, as opposed to science, to get out into the open this aspect of cognition, on which our beliefs are so largely founded, namely, what we claim to know through personal experience and through the personalities of important individuals in our lives, such as classroom teachers. We all know that classroom teachers have an enormous influence over the choices made by their pupils as the latter mature in life. Yet this type of knowledge, namely, that which we claim to have through personal experience, though precious, is probably the most precarious and the least secure of all our forms of knowledge. This fact does not preclude its being the most often used. In most of the practical and important decisions we make in life, we cannot call upon the disclosures of science to back us up. What we normally rely upon are the personalities of influential people in our lives, such as our teachers. We come to regard certain people as arbiters of taste and right conduct, and attempt to guide our lives according to their approvals and disapprovals. Teachers are certainly high on the list of those who influence us in this way.

Teachers, therefore, even more than most people, have the responsibility of freeing themselves from prejudice and from irrationally formed opinions. The relation of a teacher to a classroom filled with pupils is symbolic of the tremendous danger in the human situation. There is no way of eliminating the type of danger inherent in this situation and preserving the distinctive character of human society, as opposed, for instance, to insect society or a society of perfect automatons. Now of course if people could be persuaded to form their opinions on the basis of expert testimony exclusively, except where they could through investigation formulate their opinions directly on the basis of evidence, this particular danger would be greatly averted. And that in a sense is the goal towards which we here are striving. But in the meantime the facts are otherwise. One of the facts about our human nature appears to be that we would rather have our beliefs vindicated, whatever the consequences, than to examine them to see whether or not they are worthy.

The responsibility of the teacher is at least in part not to pass on to his pupils the prejudices and unanalyzed, subconscious desires of his own generation, so far as he can help himself. And philosophy, it seems to me, is peculiarly apt to be of help to the teacher in gaining the requisite self-knowledge to discharge this responsibility. For how can a teacher fulfill this responsibility if he himself is not aware of the danger? Now in contrast to all other forms of cognitive activity, philosophy begins not by filling a person's mind full of propositions which he must take for granted, but by emptying his mind (ideally) of *all* uninvestigated and unanalyzed beliefs. The rule in philosophy is that no belief, however indispensable to practical life, is to be regarded as *true* without supporting evidence. It is this fact that makes some philosophical questions appear so peculiar, such as questions about the reality of an external world. But in no better way, it seems to me, than through the study of philosophy, can a teacher come to realize the lack of secure foundation for most of our beliefs. And the insight thus gained into the lack of justification we have for many of our beliefs naturally results in a disposition to be cautious with respect to stating those beliefs which, though held, cannot be securely supported. Furthermore, by coming to appreciate the way in which personality *can* affect results, the teacher is less likely to be dogmatic about anything, even science.

To come to the point at last, philosophy can be of help to the classroom teacher by the fact that it is training in the activity of evaluating our beliefs, and thus, in effect, training in the art of self-knowledge. Philosophy instructs us in that knowledge of one's own ignorance generally which is indispensable to the improvement of the human mind, and since the professional task of classroom teachers is this improvement, a philosophically cultivated habit of thought can greatly assist a teacher, it seems to me, in the discharge of his responsibilities.

I will end with a note of reassurance. Human beings, and that includes philosophers and educators, are entitled to a degree of prejudice. Prejudice is a luxury, and one of which it would be unwise, I think, to seek to deprive ourselves altogether. Some prejudices are silly because they are plainly refuted by the evidence. Others are harmful, at least when practiced on a social scale. But many of our prejudices are quite harmless and it would be inhuman to expect anyone to be completely free of them. I think that the teacher, like the rest of us, is entitled to his measure of prejudices, but it is one thing to be the victim of a prejudice in ignorance of its true nature, and another thing to give expression to a prejudice in awareness of the fact that it is, or may be, nothing else.

To sum up, I have tried in this paper to make clear for you the major ways in which philosophy logically could and could not be of help to educators. Philosophy as an institution can be of practical and concrete assistance to educational theorists and program planners; and as an expression of a broad human interest in the foundations of our beliefs, it is of help to the classroom teacher in the discharge of his most fundamental responsibility. But as an autonomous activity, demanding complete absorption in the philosophical problem for its own sake, philosophy is of no special use or assistance to educators or anyone else outside its province.

2

Analytic Philosophy and Theory of Education

GEORGE L. NEWSOME, JR.

For better or worse, analysis, logical and linguistic, is being offered by some of its advocates as a theory of education, or possibly even as a theory of educational theories. What are some of the distinguishing features of analytic philosophy? What are the pitfalls in relating analysis to education? Is analytic philosophy a second order theory of education? How may analytic philosophy contribute to the development of theory in education? Can analytic philosophy adequately meet the demands of a practical discipline such as education? For the purposes of discussing and clarifying these kinds of questions, an analytic approach will be taken in this paper.

DISTINGUISHING FEATURES OF ANALYTIC PHILOSOPHY

Although analytic philosophy may be termed a "school of thought," it is not a system of philosophy. Indeed, from the analytic point of view, systems of philosophy are repudiated.[1] Within the school of analytic philo-

George L. Newsome, Jr., is Professor of Education at the University of Georgia. George L. Newsome, Jr., "Analytic Philosophy and Theory of Education," *Proceedings of the Sixteenth Annual Meeting of the Philosophy of Education Society,* published by the society, June, 1960. Used by permission of Ernest E. Bayles, editor of the *Proceedings,* and George L. Newsome, Jr.

[1] Herbert Feigl, "Aims of Education For Our Age of Science: Reflections of a Logical Empiricist" in *Modern Philosophies and Education.* Chicago: The University of Chicago Press, 1955, p. 304; Israel Scheffler (ed.), *Philosophy and Education.* Boston: Allyn and Bacon, Inc., 1958, p. 7; and Richard W. Dettering, "Philosophical Semantics and Education," *Educational Theory,* 7: 143–149, July 1958, p. 146.

sophy there are numerous differences of opinion concerning matters philosophical. It seems to make little difference, however, whether one looks to the group stressing informal logic and common language or to the group emphasizing symbolic logic and philosophy of science, philosophical analysts seem to agree on one major function of philosophy: clarification. By and through philosophical analysis (logical and linguistic) what men say (statements, sentences, or propositions) can be clarified and made meaningful or exposed as nonsense.

The statements that men make are, of course, sometimes clear and meaningful, but because of the "open texture" of language, ambiguity, vagueness, and other linguistic difficulties, confusion arises. Furthermore, and probably even of greater concern, because of "improper" philosophical training, common sense notions, or just plain ignorance, emotive and metaphysical statements worm their way into discourse. Lest such emotional expressions and "nonsense" pass for statements of fact or "profound insights," language must be subjected to a thorough and dispassionate scrutiny loosely termed "analysis."

Just how one performs analysis, the particular methods and techniques by which language is analyzed, and the various tests or criteria of meaning are matters of major concern and debate among analytic philosophers. Although analytic philosophers disagree about many aspects of analysis, they do seem to be in general agreement concerning several ways in which analytic philosophy differs from the traditional philosophies of Western culture.

1. Analytic philosophers strongly contend that truths about human experience and the universe cannot be discovered by philosophical means.[2] Matters of empirical fact and truths about the world are discovered or established by science—not by philosophers.

2. Analytic philosophers seriously question (many completely reject) the idea of logical unity of truth, goodness, and beauty.[3] Many, if not most, analytic philosophers maintain that statements concerning matters of fact and statements of value are radically different kinds of statements which require entirely different means for verification.[4] Some analytic philosophers seriously doubt that statements of value can have any meaning beyond that of personal preference.[5]

[2] Alfred Jules Ayer, *Language, Truth and Logic*. New York: Dover Publications, Inc., n.d., pp. 71–72; Arthur Pap, *Elements of Analytic Philosophy*. New York: The Macmillan Company, 1949, p. 6 and p. 478; and D. J. O'Connor, *Introduction to The Philosophy of Education*. New York: Philosophical Library, 1957, pp. 5–6.

[3] Ayer, *op. cit.*, pp. 102–103; Dettering, *loc. cit.*, p. 147; and Charles L. Stevenson, *Ethics and Language*. New Haven, Conn.: Yale University Press, 1944, p. 173.

[4] Pap, *op. cit.*, pp. 23–26; Henry D. Aiken, "Moral Philosophy and Education," *Harvard Educational Review*, 25: 39–59, Winter, 1955, p. 51; and John Hospers, *An Introduction to Philosophical Analysis*. Englewood Cliffs, N.J.: Prentice-Hall, Inc., 1953, pp. 476–482.

[5] Reference here is made to those who view ethical statements as purely emotive expressions. For example, see Hospers, *op. cit.*, pp. 471–476 for discussion of this view, or Ayer, *op. cit.*, pp. 102–113 for a classic argument by one of the chief exponents of the emotive theory of ethics.

3. Analytic philosophers strongly maintain that language does not give us a true picture or copy of reality.[6] Verbal expressions have only such meanings as we give them, and hence do not derive their meanings from objects in the world. We relate words to the world, and the relationship is not a " one-to-one " relationship that makes language exactly correspond to reality.

4. Analytic philosophers prefer to deal with the problems of man one by one and strongly resist the urge to construct broad, general, and speculative theories.[7]

5. Analytic philosophers, since they construct no general and speculative theories, do not consider analytic philosophy to be composed of metaphysical, ethical, or epistemological theories. To them the subject matter or analytic philosophy is thought of as theories for the clarification of language, and such concepts, methods, and presuppositions as might be found in most sciences.[8]

6. Since analytic philosophy is concerned only with clarification of language, most often the language of science or some other discipline, one can philosophize about almost anything, because to philosophize is to analyze language.[9]

Analysis, both logical and linguistic, has always in some form or other characterized philosophy. It was the stock in trade of Socrates, Plato, and Aristotle.[10] From the time of Socrates to the present, analysis has frequently been employed as a means for ushering in synthesis and speculation, or philosophy in the " grand manner." Whatever analysis reduced, separated, or exposed, *a priori* metaphysics promptly restored, unified and justified as an ultimate reality, a transcendental entity, a state of mind, or as some kind of unobservable, unknowable reality beyond the corrupting influence of linguistic analysis and the positive verification of science. Furthermore, *a priori* philosophers have, in spite of Ockham's Razor or the Principle of Parsimony, often multiplied entities beyond necessity. By assuming much, *a priori* philosophers sought to prove much, but their proof was no better than their assumptions, and frequently no more than the assumptions.[11] It is against this synthetic and speculative philosophy that analytic philosophers rebel.

---

[6] Max Black, " Language and Reality," *Proceedings and Addresses of The American Philosophical Association*, 1958–59, Yellow Springs, Ohio: The Antioch Press, 1959, pp. 16–17; Ayer, *op. cit.*, p. 42; and O'Connor, *op. cit.*, pp. 39–40.

[7] Scheffler, *op. cit.*, pp. 6–7; and Dettering, *loc. cit.*, pp. 146–147.

[8] Pap, *op. cit.*, p. 1.

[9] *Ibid.*, p. 478, and O'Connor, *op. cit.*, p. 4.

[10] Pap, *op. cit.*, Preface vii.

[11] Philosophy is not a system for proving by axiomatic methods truth about the universe in a metaphysical fashion. Logic, of course, does contain methods for proving, but such proofs are logical not metaphysical. For further discussion, see O'Connor, *op. cit.*, pp. 29–35.

PITFALLS IN RELATING ANALYSIS TO EDUCATIONAL THEORY

Educators, when confronted with the problem of relating analytic philosophy to education, are likely to find analytic philosophy to be "strange" and different, and the usual ways of relating philosophy to education not very rewarding. Analytic philosophy seems to be lacking in the "systematic niceties," ideological, doctrinaire, and moralistic canons, and the more immediate practical applications to education to which educators seem to be accustomed. Analytic philosophy also confronts the educator with a new and strange terminology, with a "frightening calculus of language," with "distinctions too subtle for the practical minded," and with an alarming restriction upon treasured emotive and metaphysical statements. Moreover, in attempting to relate analytic philosophy to education, educators should be careful not to make one or more of the following mistakes: (1) Attempting to construct an analytic philosophy of education modeled after traditional systems and ideologies,[12] (2) Attempting to derive implications for education from analytic philosophy,[13] and (3) Becoming so fascinated with language games, logic, or philosophy of science that the relation of analysis to education becomes superficial.

The fact that philosophical analysis is analysis of language rather than analysis of feelings, mental states, or concrete situations, indicates that it is a second or third level order of analysis. Consideration of this fact suggests that instead of constructing an analytic philosophy of education or deriving educational implications from analytic philosophy, all one need do is employ analytic methods and techniques in analyzing statements about education.

ANALYTIC PHILOSOPHY AS SECOND ORDER THEORY OF EDUCATION

Education as a practical activity is a process which should not be confused with education as a discipline and body of knowledge. Education as a discipline is related to the process of teaching and learning, but it differs from the process in that it is composed of statements, rules, directives, principles, and the like about various aspects of practice. The discipline of education then is verbal and linguistic; it is knowledge that purports to be in a considerable measure propositional and cognitive in character. Frequently this discipline of education is termed "theory of education" although it might more appropriately be termed "pedagogical knowledge."[14]

---

[12] Scheffler, *op. cit.*, p. 2.
[13] Feigl, *op. cit.*, pp. 304–305.
[14] Paul Komisar, "*Pedagogical Knowledge and Teacher Education*," *Proceedings of the Fifteenth Annual Meeting of the Philosophy of Education Society*. Lawrence: The University of Kansas Press, 1959, pp. 15–22.

The body of pedagogical knowledge contains many statements which do have genuine philosophical connotations. They appear on their face to be propositions which assert something significant about education. For example, such statements as "real and life-like activities produce more learning than assign-study-recite procedures," and "education is the process of self-realization in which the self realizes and develops all of its potentialities," appear to be genuine and significant propositions about education. How may these statements be verified? What kind of evidence would be needed for verification? What cognitive meanings do the propositions have? What matters of fact do they assert? What do such terms as "real," "life-like," "self," and "potentialities" mean? What does it mean to say a self realizes itself? When is a self, self realized? Questions of this sort suggest that neither of the two statements is clear or cognitively meaningful. Suppose a teacher were asked to implement either or both statements, how could one determine empirically the result or consequence? Are these statements metaphysical (necessary and synthetic), purely analytic (tautologies), emotive; or are they commands, questions, or resolves?

It is precisely questions of this sort about statements, as ambiguous and meaningless as those just cited with which analytic philosophy deals. By and through analysis, both logical and linguistic, educational philosophy as a second order of analysis can clarify and make meaningful or expose as nonsense many statements about pedagogy. When one carefully explores the meaning, the means of verifying, the semantics, the structure, and the context of such statements, he is playing the role of analytic philosopher. Furthermore, he is dealing with education at the second level of abstraction; namely, the level of clarifying statements of pedagogy.

How May Analytic Philosophy Contribute to the Development of Theory in Education?

Those who deal with pedagogy and philosophy of education frequently feel considerable pressure to provide, if possible, and justify, if necessary, a theory of education.[15] Can criticism and analysis meet the more positive challenge of helping to construct an integrative theory of education? Does not the discipline of education, since it is a hodge podge of facts and theories derived from other disciplines, need a unifying theory? Is not the chief function of philosophy that of constructing generalized theories (philosophies), be they metaphysical or not, as a prerequisite to a critical and analyti-

---

[15] Example of such concern for a "defensible theory" of education are "Symposium: The Aims and Content of Philosophy of Education," *Harvard Educational Review*, Vol. 26, Spring, 1956, and "A Symposium: What Can Philosopy Contribute to Educational Theory," *Harvard Educational Review*, Vol. 28, Fall, 1958.

cal approach to theory?[16] Or is it that philosophy only needs to be clear about the more general relations that exist between and among matters of fact; or what one philosopher has termed "synoptic clarity"?

If a synoptic clarity be admitted, then can analytic philosophy clarify statements concerning the more general relations of matters of fact, and can it clarify the more general features of a theory of education? In certain respects analytic philosophy, if it be conceived relative to the task, can meet this demand. Analytic philosophy need not be viewed merely as sentence editing, or as lexicography, or as literary censorship.[17] Analytic philosophy can help to develop a defensible theory of education in the sense that it can help analyze and clarify language, provide models of theory, state criteria for meaning and verification, and in general, help unsnarl the logical and linguistic tangles in pedagogical knowledge.[18] The degree to which analytic philosophy can actually bring about a unity of knowledge in education similar to that undertaken by some logical empiricists in the unified sciences movement remains to be seen.

Some of the characteristics of pedagogical knowledge present genuine difficulties for analytic philosophers. Many of the so-called "principles and theories" of teaching, learning, and curriculum are merely descriptions of practices, summaries of case studies, matters of opinion, or application of certain concepts such as democracy, socialization, or creative expression to educational practice. Pedagogical knowledge contains very few, if any, general laws under which individual facts can be adequately subsumed and explained. The so-called theories and principles of pedagogy are not only descriptive, but they frequently are directive as well. Descriptions and directives (prescriptions)[19] point to consequences rather than to logical conclusions.[20] Yet, somewhere between description and prescription, dealers in pedagogical knowledge apparently make some kind of logical inference. Such inferences are not deductions because no conclusions follow necessarily from established premises. Similarly, the inference is neither a valid inductive causal inference, nor a statistic inference in terms of probabilities. The only alternative left is that it is a probable inference, in some cases an inference based on reasoning by analogy.[21]

---

[16] For example, see Harry S. Broudy, *Building a Philosophy of Education*. Englewood Cliffs, N.J.: Prentice-Hall, Inc., 1954, and J. Donald Butler, *Four Philosophies and Their Practice in Education and Religion*. New York: Harper and Row, Publishers, 1957.

[17] Ayer, *op. cit.*, p. 59 ff.

[18] Probably with the exception of a few articles and O'Connor's little book, not much seems to have been done along this line.

[19] Technically speaking, directive and prescriptive language is not the same and do not have the same meanings. Directions are, however, frequently put in persuasive form. For example, see Bernard Rabin, "Teachers Use of Directive Language," *Educational Leadership*, 17: 31–34, October, 1959, for various forms in which directive language appears.

[20] P. H. Nowell-Smith, *Ethics*. Baltimore: Penguin Books, Ltd., 1954, p. 149.

[21] *See*, Irving M. Copi, *Introduction to Logic*. New York: Macmillan Publishing Co., Inc., 1953, Chapter 11, pp. 311–326.

Probable inferences and reasoning by analogy, though weak, are not always false or unproductive. The major problem is to be found in evaluating such arguments and explanations. Though such arguments and explanations can be logically evaluated in part, ultimately one must appeal to some more fundamental explanation such as one finds in the sciences.[22] But, probable inference cannot always be so tested and verified. The prescriptions which come from the inference might be rather significant, in the opinion of many competent judges. The problem-project method of teaching and the core curriculum, for example, are frequently thought to be more productive than more traditional methods of teaching and curricula designs, yet empirical testings have not shown them to be decidedly superior. Educators, however, must make decisions; they must choose methods and curricula designs in terms of the best evidence and logical arguments available. They cannot postpone action until some remote future when scientific inquiry will have confirmed some one particular method or curricula plan. If choice must be made in absence of decisive evidence, then the educator would at least like to know as clearly as possible the probable consequence of his choice. Analytic philosophy can help the educator clarify statements of probable inference and help him clearly and logically state the probable consequences of choosing one course of action over another.

Since pedagogical knowledge is often prescriptive, practical, and not logically precise, one of an analytic persuasion might be tempted to dismiss too quickly pedagogical statements as emotive, cognitively meaningless, unanswerable, or the like. This however, might be a serious mistake based upon an untenable separation of thought from action, language from language function, ends from means, and logical and linguistic clarity from empirical consequences. Many of the significant statements in pedagogical knowledge do not seem to fit into the neat classifications of logic and language.[23] Facts do appear to color values and values do apparently influence choice among facts. Actions have consequences and consequences of actions seem ultimately to relate back to the logic and language of inquiry and deliberation which led to choice.

Pedagogical prescriptions are not all as illogical or emotive as one might suspect. Some prescriptions are much like those of the physician who, for example, might prescribe certain medicines and a diet as a remedy for some particular physical condition. Surely the prescription and its predicted consequences are not emotive or unscientific. Similarly, when the educator prescribes: "to promote interest and facilitate learning, employ life-like activities that meet the felt needs of the learner and come within the learner's

---

[22] *Ibid.*, p. 322.

[23] For example, *see* Gilbert Ryle, *Dilemmas*. Cambridge University Press, 1954, Chapter 8—"Formal and Informal Logic," pp. 111–129.

range of experience"—he is providing a prescription and predicting consequences of its employment. Such a prescription with its stated consequences is not beyond empirical confirmation. If the kinds of evidence needed for confirmation can be specified, then the statement has meaning and can be clarified.

Many pedagogical statements are not as logically and linguistically "pure" as the foregoing illustration. Some are rather moralistic in character and their consequences, if any, "intangible." For example, if one should prescribe that "students ought always be treated as ends and never as means only," then a moralistic imperative has been introduced, the consequences of which seem to defy empirical confirmation. What is an end? How does one treat a student as an end? What meaning, if any, does the statement have? Similarly, many statements about educational aims and values and a wide variety of value judgments, when subjected to analysis reduce to statements of preference or emotive expressions of the form " I like such and such and so should you " or " hurrah for X."[24]

Mere preference, as a simple expression of desire or a " I like it," and intellectual preference based upon experience and anticipated consequences of action are quite different.[25] To be sure, some educational moralisms and value preferences are statements of simple preference which have little or no cognitive meaning. An intellectual preference, however, may be discussed in terms of experience, evidence, and probable consequences. Not only may it be intelligently discussed, but statements about it can be clarified.

Analytic philosophers who dismiss intellectual preference (moralistic or valuational) seem to hold to a rather narrow and truncated view of analysis. Such a narrow view might result from a confusion of substantive ethics with analytic ethics.[26] Substantive ethics deals with first-level problems of deliberation and choice. In pedagogical knowledge statements of substantive ethics serve as practical modes of communication, the main function of which is direction and control of conduct, not prediction of empirical fact.[27] Analytic ethics, on the other hand is a second-level analysis of the language of ethics and hence is concerned largely with problems of logic and meaning.

[24] Many statements in educational discourse are purely statements of personal likes and dislikes. Arthur P. Coladarci and Jacob W. Getzels, *The Use of Theory in Educational Administration*. Stanford University Press, 1955, pp. 10–14, claim educators are afraid to theorize, have an inadequate professional language, and frequently tend to become emotionally identified with their own views.

[25] The distinction which is being made here is John Dewey's distinction between *desire* and *desirability*. *See*, John Dewey, *Democracy and Education*. New York: Macmillan Publishing Co., Inc., 1916, p. 279.

[26] Aiken, *loc. cit.*, p. 42.

[27] *Ibid.*, p. 51.

CAN ANALYTIC PHILOSOPHY MEET THE DEMANDS
OF A PRACTICAL DISCIPLINE?

So far, in the short history of modern analytic philosophy its major successes have been in the fields of science and mathematics.[28] It is rather paradoxical, however, that modern natural sciences achieved their preeminence without analytic philosophy, indeed, often in opposition to philosophy. A philosophical analysis of science is somewhat like a chemical analysis of a known solution, neat, easy, and according to the rules. Philosophical analysis of the newer applied and practical disciplines, on the other hand, is more like the chemical analysis of an unknown solution; very necessary, perhaps, but very difficult and uncertain. In natural sciences and mathematics a rather "firm" language has been developed along with precise methods, techniques, proofs, and verifications. Evidence counts for much more than opinion (even informed opinion), moralisms have been rooted out, and psychological factors reduced to a minimum. Furthermore, the particular things which are studied are frequently material things or abstractions. In either or both cases, statements about such things are much more easily adapted to analytic dichotomies such as synthetic or analytic than are statements about the things studied by the behavioral sciences and practical disciplines.[29]

Some of the particular distinctions, techniques and methodology of analysis, particularly of the logical empiricist kind, though apparently well suited to analysis of scientific language might not be equally appropriate for analysis of the language of pedagogy or social sciences. One might suspect then that the informal logic and common language approach might have more to offer.[30] On the other hand, the languages of education are not common languages, and the logic of educational discourse and argument is a practical logic rather than an informal logic. It may be suggested then that an analytic philosophy of the social sciences and practical disciplines is needed. There seems to be no reason why the logical and linguistic methods of analysis cannot be modified so as to be more applicable to the kind of logical and linguistic problems found in the social sciences and practical disciplines. To this end, educational philosophers of an analytic persuasion might well devote considerable attention.

---

[28] Pap, *op. cit.*, Preface viii.
[29] *See*, Nowell-Smith, *op. cit.*, Chapter 7, pp. 95–104, for explanation of the functions of Practical Discourse and how the Analytic-synthetic dichotomy breaks down.
[30] Reference here is to the John Wisdom-Gilbert Ryle school of analysis.

3

Philosophy of Education— Directive Doctrine or Liberal Discipline?

EVERETT JOHN KIRCHER

Like most cultures, American democracy has evolved to its present state without benefit of any single formal system of philosophy. This is not to deny that the philosophic mind has been present nor that the general character of our culture has benefited at one time or another from a rich diversity of both formal and informal philosophies. It is rather to deny that our culture has been self-consciously constructed along the lines of any one comprehensive system of thought which was first theoretically formulated and subsequently actualized into a whole way of life. In other words we have not built our American democracy deliberately according to any pre-selected system of philosophy. Conversely, modern Russia is an example of a culture in which it was belatedly decided to do just this.

Marx was a philosopher with a disposition toward philosophy which has become more and more popular throughout the world. He was a philosopher who inclined to the notion his disciples wholly embraced that the discipline of philosophy could recover itself only if it largely abandoned its role as one of the liberal disciplines and became literally directive of human affairs. Since the teaching of philosophy, like other of the liberal

Everett J. Kircher is Professor Emeritus at Ohio State University. Everett J. Kircher, "Philosophy of Education—Directive Doctrine or Liberal Discipline?" *Educational Theory*, Vol. V, No. 4, October, 1955, pp. 220–229. Used by permission of the author and *Educational Theory*.

studies, has often been unimaginative and sterile and has failed to function as an intellectual leaven in our common culture, it was easy for him to conclude along with many another in other systems of thought that philosophy fell into either one of two categories. Either it was ivory tower and irrelevant to the moving concerns of men or it was an ultimate commitment, doctrinally conceived, and effectively directive of the practical affairs of the market place. Faced with these two alternatives, he concluded that philosophy should be changed from its esoteric status and be made to bake bread. Such a proposal was not only congenial to the Marxist reformers who followed him, it has been congenial to the academic reformer in America. The idea has intrigued us. Preplanned systems in the large, theoretically formulated world views, inspire the imagination with a high hope. And reformers respond to the notion that a system of philosophy can be used as a reliable referent in the conduct of the confusing, inconsistent and conflicting forces of the human enterprise.

One in this mood looks at the social scene and asks what it adds up to other than over-all, meaningless and incoherent confusion. One sees only a welter of disparate and conflicting social forces in the fields of religion, economics, and politics. One senses that the gods looking down from the Olympus see us running helterskelter like ants at cross purposes with one another in a state of endless frustration and conflict. What any culture and finally the world desperately needs, we are then told, is an over-all system of thought, an integrating world-view, which would establish a common purpose for mankind and mutually consistent subordinate goals. Some all-comprehending philosophy within whose generous circumference men could find themselves at peace; a common way of life in which social forces were harmonized and the culture convincingly integrated is what is required. Then men would enjoy a community of mind and spirit, social harmony would be approximated and the brotherhood of man would become a reality on this earth. Such is the philosopher's dream, and all it would take to realize this cultural millennium would be the long-sought discovery of the philosopher's stone.

This is a noble dream which the over-agitated and the over-eager recurrently discover that they are destined to fulfill in reality. In other words, men who seek the philosopher's stone too expectantly soon find it. There is a compulsion in their quest which guarantees its premature discovery. And upon such an occasion they look down upon struggling man and know what he must do. This is where Hegel finally stood. It is where Marx stood. And it is where every philosopher-reformer is destined to stand who lays claim to the exclusive adequacy of his philosophy for any culture or for the world. This evil role in which knowledgeable man succumbs to the temptation to play God because he is surrounded by men without sufficient knowledge to controvert his system of thought does not pertain only to philosophies we have come to look upon as evil. It pertains alike to those philosophies we have come to look upon as good. The evil and the suffering ultimately entailed derives from misrepresentation on the grand scale. Philosophic man presumes to an adequacy of systematic knowledge that he does not have, and other men follow in an unwarranted faith eternally destined to disaster.

Yet men in the large hold themselves perennially prepared to believe again that the philosopher's stone has been found. Consequently there is a social climate conducive to the notion that a philosophy of freedom has been found, a philosophy that is inherently not susceptible of subversion to evil ends. What is so alien to our thought is that the very claim to have found such a philosophy makes that philosophy inimical to human freedom. To claim that one has found the true or the ultimately adequate philosophy is to claim that one has found the philosophy of philosophies, that the philosophic quest in the large has been completed. The philosophy of Marx speculatively projected and creatively entertained would not have jeopardized the philosophic enterprise nor human freedom on this earth. The Communist institutionalization of this system of philosophy as a wholly adequate world doctrine is the point at which the philosophic enterprise and all human freedom was cast into jeopardy. The evil is not inherently in the speculative system but in the disposition of those who would universalize it. It is therefore unfortunate that so many of us have been so preoccupied with the notion that the Russian error was in the selection of a wrong philosophy that we have neglected to note their more fundamental error; namely, that they embraced the inhumanity of attempting to integrate their social order, and finally the world, in accordance with some one pre-planned and elaborately conceived philosophy. Their fatal error in judgment revealed itself in their uncompromising conviction that a distinguished system of thought could be made so logically adequate that it could be put into practice without fundamental modification. Their error did not seem greater to them than ours does to us when we also incline to the notion that a comprehensive and carefully conceived theory could be made reliably adequate to the conduct of human affairs. We too indulge, from time to time, in the unwarranted faith that the academic mind at its best is equal to the task of providing a system of philosophy that will prove itself adequate to the complex exigencies of fact. And the systematic academic mind is understandably susceptible of this persuasion whenever reforming zeal runs high. Conversely, the creative and dedicated scholar is uniquely impervious to this profane presumption himself and always suspicious of it in the many varied forms it takes in others.

EDUCATION AND THE ONE PHILOSOPHY

There have been many theorists and some formal philosophers in the history of American culture who have periodically proposed to involve us in the same error. It is the common aspiration of theorists, and their recurring presumption, to have worked out a system of ideas that would adequately harmonize and integrate the American social order. It is to the credit of our own culture that it has largely resisted persuasion in this matter up to the present time. Not only in the culture at large have we resisted the temptation to be wholly logical according to some one system of logic, we have largely resisted this temptation in the public school systems of the state. Consequently, our educational program shows neither the theoretical benefit nor the actual deterioration which would result from the adoption of the central doctrine of a one-philosophy state. In other words, public education in the United States is not, and never has been, conducted according to any one system of philosophy. *It is significant to note, however, that it has become the prevailing mode of our time to lament this fact.* The past generation of educational theorists have been at great pains to show that this has been unfortunate in the past and promises to be disastrous in the future. We are told that the welter of prevailing philosophies and theories in conflict can logically result only in general confusion, cultural disintegration and the ultimate frustration of both the American teacher and the rising generation. To many academic minds intent upon effecting logical coherence and cultural integration, this is self-evident.

Since it is the primary function of the intellectual to knit the desparate and disarrayed tag ends of things into clear and consistent meaningful wholes in every area of learning, nothing could be more natural than for each to envision the whole as finally organized, integrated and explained in terms of the generalized insights of his own distinctive philosophy, religion or academic discipline. Not only is this natural, to a certain degree it is inevitable, and there is a sense in which it is proper. It is proper as forever unfinished aspiration.

The social and educational theorist is faced in a more dramatic way with the same paradox which faces every man and every culture. For his own sanity, he must hold to the somehow rightness of his own personal-intellectual point of view. He cannot be forever qualifying, denying and doubting himself. And yet, in any free society, and in the world at large, every man's carefully intellectualized outlook on life is in fact qualified, denied or doubted by men and cultures of equal intellectual equipment and equal intellectual integrity. To believe in one's self and yet to honor the person and the thinking of those who find it necessary to deny one's own beliefs, presents finite and inevitably biased man with a dilemma he does not have the cosmic mind finally to resolve. All extant theories for the resolution of this problem end in one more theory which attempts to persuade man that he actually is intellectually competent to resolve this dilemma after all. And the native presumption of men is always prepared to rise once more and to believe again that a new device has been created that will allow him to transcend those limits of his finitude that it is not reasonable to believe he can surmount with any distinctive point of view or any unique system of logic. Indeed, to be distinctive and to be unique is to be *other than* other forms of distinction and uniqueness that forever rise to confound the intellectual resolution of uniqueness.

One must grant that there is no more adequate evidence of learning and personal culture than the progressive enlarging of one's own understanding of the world from his own unique perspective. One's coherent distinctiveness is doubtless the greatest contribution one has to make to the world. But the all too human tendency to universalize this uniqueness and presume to assimilate all relevant diversity into one inclusive perspective, the fatal end toward which all systematic rationality inclines, fails to recognize the strategic limits of intellection and robs a diversity of men of the only real freedom in the world, the freedom to engage life with integrity each on his own terms.

GROWTH OF ANY ONE PHILOSOPHY

There is no open-minded philosophy in the sense that each often boasts that it is. No philosophy is open to other than its own assumptions, its own methods, its own distinctive pattern of meanings and, above all, its own ultimate propagation. No philosophy frees a man in all directions for any or all assumptions or values. Every philosophy releases man into the full and generous arena of the only universe there is—the materialistic, the idea-istic, the realistic or the empirical—but the only universe there really is; and it is designed to explain all the others away. If there is anything characteristic of any system of philosophy, it is that it is sufficient unto itself. Of all the things it logically does not need in the world, it is the conflicting and denying assumptions and propositions of other philosophical systems. Or if it does need these, it needs them as the materials for its own assimilation and development. It needs them as the negative to its own positive, the error to demonstrate its own truth. It needs them as food upon which to feed, a process which results in the disintegration of the food and its assimilation into a growing body of thought which is designed to prevail through the disintegration of its opposition.

In a sense, a system of philosophy is like a cat in the forest. It grows by what it feeds upon and by transforming what it feeds upon into itself. It has no way of doing justice to other forms of life except from its own point of view. And from this point of view, other forms of life look like a means of growth and development for itself. Its promise of the good life to what it regards lesser forms is a promise to assimilate them into a nobler structure that is more glorious in the sight of gods or men. Sometimes they are promised that this will be a painless transformation. Sometimes they are promised a special place of residence that will not do violence to their own distinctive form. And yet it seems to be the fact with both the organic system of the cat and the organic system of a philosophy that undigested foreign matter must ultimately be assimilated or be passed off, and this on pain of death. Regardless of high promises on the part of any system of thought to protect the distinctiveness of other organic forms within its own system, we would do well to recall that no matter how many birds a compassionate cat may eat, it never becomes more birdlike. Rather, it becomes a bigger cat. A philosophy lives upon the assimilation into its own organic system of the facts of life, the problems of men and the relevant aspects of all other philosophies. It is modified in this process but not in a way congenial to the forms assimilated.

There is a fundamental sense in which all philosophies are, therefore, philosophies of growth. Each struggles to grow into a state of universal explanation of the only real world it acknowledges. Anything not yet assimilated into the organic structure of any philosophy leaves it still hungry and growing. Philosophies which would distinguish themselves as philosophies of growth have a doubtful distinction for they are as ungenerous in the large as any other philosophy. They are always characterized by growth toward their own fulfillment through a disintegration of other logical forms and by a digestive process distinctively designed to this end. It is consequently the dilemma of all systematic intellection that it is carried on in such a way as to perpetuate its own distinctive form and proceed from its own perspective whereas it aspires to enfold a variety of forms and it wishes to appear inclusive of a wide diversity of perspectives. The implicit denial of this which occurs when any philosophy aspires to universalization and to becoming directive of a whole way of life sounds the knell of philosophic thought, makes a mockery of the liberal university and introduces into any culture the rational conditions for the denial of freedom to all who choose to define it differently from the prevailing rationale.

In simple point of fact, a philosophy can no more afford to assimilate the total complex of life into its own system than a cat can afford to assimilate the total complex of forest life into its own system. For a philosophy to explain the world, and finally all other philosophies, a not uncommon presumption of comprehensive world-views, is literally to embrace self-extinction. The ongoing life of both philosophies and cats depends upon the continuing existence of other organic forms. In the case of the cat, these other forms must be both an abundance of birds and other cats. No matter how many of the former are consumed and the latter bred or killed in combat, cats die from this earth when they assimilate into themselves all that they prey upon, fertilize or engage in mortal combat.

Remarkably similar observations can be made of integral and organic systems of philosophy. In order to keep healthy, vital and growing, they need what they commonly hasten to deny; they need an abundance of as yet unexplained problems, aspects of the natural world and of the human enterprise that they have as yet been unable to assimilate into their own organic structure. Moreover, they need cross-fertilization with other systems of philosophy which they commonly attack with the intention of annihilation. The perennial claim of exclusive adequacy for any philosophy is the expression of an unwitting presumption calling for the abandonment of the philosophic enterprise. Contests of explanation among the philosophies and creative engagements over the problems that beset us result both in health and procreation of a rich diversity of philosophies. But the determination, once and for all to win the field results in a declaration of war. The philosophic temper and intention is abandoned; and if the war is successful, the winner will have devasted the field in which he was wont to forage. Yet there are educational philosophers reminiscent of such cats, for they leave the survival of the philosophic enterprise not to intention but to chance. Like the forest tom, many a philosophy would have annihilated the condition of its being except that it was not able to assimilate the whole field.

We must conclude, therefore, that no system of philosophy, not even the presumed right one should be allowed to gain the uncontested status of being the exclusively adequate philosophy of free men. Freedom resides not in a system of philosophy but in the acceptance of a state of consciously maintained diversity which thereupon becomes a state of ethical diversity. In saying this, we have dealt only with the ought; no philosophy ought to aspire to universal and exclusive adequacy. We may go on to say that any philosophy uniquely designed to guarantee freedom among men not only ought not be universally adopted, it probably cannot be universally adopted. The complex enormity of the world appears to protect the philosophic enterprise from self-annihilation. There is just too much in the world for any one organic structure to assimilate. Even in Soviet Russia the original Marxist philosophy has not only been grossly modified in process of Communist application but there is reason to believe that large and silent sectors of the people have never accommodated themselves to its fundamental assumptions. In the attempt to translate any one system of philosophy into a whole way of life, we are therefore confronted with an aspiration that not only ought not but cannot finally be realized. A very real evil and much suffering results from the attempt and the partial success that is attained.

It is probably safe, then, to say that no philosophy has ever fully realized itself in any culture without fundamental compromise. Moreover, it is probably true that no formal system of philosophy has ever taken up unqualified residence in the life of any single man. A man, like a culture, is forever more than any theory about him. Each encompasses not only a logic but a mystery beyond the logic. Consequently, while it is apparently possible for both a man and a culture to identify themselves with some comprehensive rational theory, it is not possible for them to conduct their lives strictly in accordance with any such theory. The whole man is never encompassed by any rational theory but suffers unaccountable modification and growth out of the mysterious heart of him. Whether the intellectual system is

Christian, Marxist or pragmatist, it appears impossible to fulfill the theorist's dream and strategically or forcefully to actualize any formal theory either in the free society or in the totalitarian state.

There is, of course, some basis for believing that the integration of a social order in terms of some one philosophy of life can be more fully attained in the totalitarian state. Certainly this is widely assumed. Yet there is reason to doubt that the overt conformity to the state philosophy is expressive of the vital and living principles of that philosophy. It is doubtful if the philosophy lives as philosophy in the hearts and minds of those it appears to motivate and direct. Perhaps in such seemingly monolithic states philosophy is largely dead and only the philosophic skeleton remains to give the appearance of philosophic structure to the social body. In such cases, conventions, ritual, habit and formal directives take the place of action enlightened by philosophic principles. However this may be, no one philosophy can endure indefinitely in any culture without stimulating alternative and conflicting systems of thought. The formal regulation of life according to some rational system cannot finally bring about the stultification of the human spirit. It would therefore behoove us in all of modern culture, but in the schools of the state particularly, to ask ourselves whether or not we are incorporating into our teacher training the assumption that one of the formal systems of philosophy in our time holds the promise of freedom for the human spirit. In other words, we must ask whether we are openly or subtly imparting the notion that there is one wholly adequate philosophy of democracy.

DEVELOPMENT OF DISCIPLESHIP

There is reason to believe that creative philosophers themselves tend to divide on this issue even though the great majority of them have long made the assumption that the freedom and vitality of the philosophic enterprise depended, among other things, upon a rich diversity in philosophic speculation. Yet it appears that some philosophers are more content than others simply to bring into being a new perspective on life for the general enlightenment of men. Others incline to the notion that they have conceived a theoretical formulation of such adequacy that it merits universal acquiescence. Santayana was typical of the former and therefore finds it natural to say in the preface to his *Skepticism and Animal Faith,*

> Here is one more system of philosophy. If the reader is inclined to smile, I can assure him that I smile with him. . . . I think that common sense, in a rough dogged way, is technically sounder than the special schools of philosophy, each of which squints and overlooks half the facts and half the difficulties in its eagerness to find in some detail the key to the whole.[1]

---

[1] George Santayana, *Skepticism and Animal Faith.* New York: Charles Scribner's Sons, 1923, p. V.

Conversely, Friedrich Hegel is widely known to have grown congenial to the notion that his dialectical system of thought finally led to the possibility of an ultimate synthesis on its own terms in the German state of his time.

Between these two extremes there rests the great majority of philosophic minds about whose location on the scale we may only speculate. This much may be said however; the character of some systems of philosophy appear to solicit followership in ways almost too subtle to define. Others seem to effect the conditions which make discipleship next to impossible. Of the former, the disciples are characteristically unphilosophic and essentially doctrinal in their thinking. And one of the hidden sources of their power and of their cruelty is that they are oblivious to this fact. The doctrinal mind of the disciple who is following the authority of a pre-fabricated system of thought finds what he calls freedom in this enterprise, and he would like to enroll as many others as possible into this kind of freedom. In speaking of his commitment he often refers to it as the philosophy of freedom. But the genuinely philosophic mind is of an entirely different order. It finds its freedom in creating distinctive modes of thought out of the philosophic heritage and the occasion of its time. Former systems of thought are reconstructed rather than simply followed, implemented and applied. Any philosopher worthy of the name is therefore the beneficiary of the philosophies of the past but never the victim of any one of them.

The transition from the creative thinking which results in a system of philosophy to a doctrinal acceptance of the system is very subtle. One lives through the creative process with the original mind, knows the delight of an unfolding organization of thought and discovers life more richly meaningful than he had known it before. In this state of intellectual excitement it is a very great temptation to identify one's self with the master and with his system of thought, envision one's self as a co-partner in the evolution and the extension of his ideas and become a champion of his views. If one's distinguished mentor is living, it is common to be desirous of his public approval and deeply enthralled by his expression of endorsement and affection. The long struggle to be worthy of discipleship then follows. The rewards for acceptance are very great, for the disciple himself becomes an authority through his identification with an undeniable authority. Competition for favor among the disciples always sets in and much bitterness attends every followership. Among such disciples every face is turned toward the central philosophy; their teaching and discussion centers upon philosophy; they are primarily concerned with philosophy—and yet natively philosophic minds look upon them in wonderment, for the philosophic enterprise has mysteriously been abandoned. A cult has developed, and the cult struggles in vain to fill the philosophic vacuity left by a great and seminal mind.

Much good work is done by disciples and much necessary work but much evil ensues from the very deception that they are philosophers who have inherited the authority that originally attached to an intellectual enterprise of great scope and integrity. They do not know how to wear the authority, for their power stems from their commitment and their commitment denies them the privilege of fundamentally reconstructing the philosophic source of their authority. Yet it was this privilege that kept the original philosophers free and philosophic. He was free to abandon or rebuild anything he constructed; he was free to indulge in doubt about his most fundamental premises; he was free to wonder about the adequacy of his system. Consequently, he was free to listen to other competing and conflicting philosophies and, across the bridge of his wonderment and his doubt, meet other philosophic minds also stepping out to the precarious edge of their thought. He was free to join in the transcendent community known to all philosophic minds of integrity, the key to which is the qualified commitment to what one has rationally proved to be true and necessary. The qualified commitment to one's own rational system and an unqualified faith in an undiscovered future or an unknown God that transcends systematic rationality—these are the conditions of the philosophers' community of mind in the midst of their inevitably diverse rational systems. Yet these freedoms and this transcendence are characteristically what the disciple abandons. He is, therefore, not only not a philosopher, he is not free. He is the victim of his appropriated system and he is the uncompromising enemy of those systems of thought which are in conflict with his own. With him literal rationality takes precedence over the philosophic temper and the philosophic quest. He cannot say with Whitehead that at its best all philosophy becomes poetry. Refusing to admit poetic transcendence over literal rationality at the higher levels of insight, he wages unremitting war over literal and exact differences in doctrine. This is the common fate of the man who goes through life on the ultimate authority of another. And it is thus that he makes the transition from freedom to slavery through a philosophy of freedom.

DEWEY'S PHILOSOPHY OF FREEDOM

One is constrained to believe that this is essentially the transition that has taken place between John Dewey, the philosopher, and many of his disciples. Their native presumption in the face of other social, religious and academic philosophies must derive from an essentially unqualified commitment to their naturalistic empiricism. The arbitrary denials of other philosophies of life can hardly mean other than that they really believe Dewey found the philosopher's stone and passed it on to them. This allows them the presumption that their philosophy is different in the sense that it is the only truly democratic, the only truly adequate philosophy of freedom. Over the last generation unnumbered students have been given to believe that this philosophy is so exclusively adequate, in this sense so universally true, that a democratic society has no need to sponsor and teach other conflicting systems of philosophy. Consequently, in a largely Christian-Hebraic culture, this nontheistic philosophy is commonly spoken of as THE democratic philosophy. It implies, we have been told, a whole *Weltanschauung* waiting for explicit realization which may properly be thought of as the only adequate conception of the democratic way of life. Yet what this turns out to be is the implementation of the formal philosophy of Dewey-pragmatism as a whole American way of life. Bode's *Democracy as a Way of Life*[2] turns out to be naturalistic empiricism as a way of life. Such indirection on the part of one of the many formal systems of philosophy in American culture may be strategic and persuasive among American teachers who are not philosophically oriented, but to many professional philosophers in the last generation it has appeared unwarranted and unwise. Indeed, it has appeared inimical to freedom in the name of freedom because the literal identification of freedom with one system of thought violates the most fundamental faith of free men; namely, that no one system of philosophy finally defines freedom in a culture which is dedicated to being inclusive of a diversity of philosophies speculatively entertained.

Progressive education is the educational counterpart of the naturalistic philosophy of John Dewey, and probably William Heard Kilpatrick has been its most celebrated exponent. Gentle, patient and persuasive, Professor Kilpatrick oriented himself steadfastly to this one philosophy of life and in a lovable, temperate, and compromising approach to all his teaching inclined untold thousands of teachers in our time toward a philosophy of life whose fundamental principles he has not compromised. The comprehensive statement of his position in his later years[3] reveals his steadfastness, his dedication and his uncompromising philosophic commitment. The American teacher to whom the book is largely addressed is gently dissuaded from believing in other less adequate philosophical views with an artfulness and sincerity that can hardly offend them even when they wonderingly differ. But the philosophically astute who hold self-consciously to a Christian, idealist, or other system of philosophy may be offended by what they properly take to be caricatures of their philosophical positions. To them, this gentle man is an unfair partisan, and many of them are as gentle and liberal in the entertainment of their views as he. Most of them are also unconditionally committed. And here we are confronted with the human dilemma again. How is a committed man to make good his boast of impartiality in the presentation of views contrary to the truth as he sees it?

Some hold to the proposition, herein denied, that it is the distinguishing character of a certain system of philosophy that is uniquely impartial toward all philosophies. Some hold that their philosophy is inevitably biased toward

---

[2] Boyd H. Bode, *Democracy as a Way of Life*, New York: Macmillan Publishing Co., Inc., 1939.

[3] William Heard Kilpatrick, *Philosophy of Education*. New York: Macmillan Publishing Co., Inc., 1951.

all others but that they have the capacity to stand outside of their philosophy and present all the rest as sympathetically as their own representatives would. Still others incline to the notion that teachers in training can only get a fair presentation by the representatives of each position. There may be one more alternative. From time to time, there are teachers of history, and literature and of philosophy in the tradition of the liberal university who have no ultimate commitment relative to systems of thought. Such men present a variety of philosophies with the kind of sympathy which comes from genuine indebtedness to each and genuine reservations with respect to each. Such a teacher's faith may be of another order. It is the faith of the pilgrim rather than the disciple. It is the commitment to the unending quest in which one's way is enlightened by all systems of thought but not finally directed by any one of them. It is the commitment of the doctrinally uncommitted scholar. It is the faith of liberal learning in which the teacher knows more but learns with his students in a distinctive sense. For about one thing he does not finally know. He does not finally know what really is the best rationalized ultimate commitment for mankind even though he does know more than his students do about what man's ultimate commitments have been and more of the arguments for and against them. In other words, he has much more knowledge than his students do, but his knowledge has led him not to an ultimate dogma but to wisdom. And in a state of wisdom he discovers that, in all his knowledge, he does not finally know. It is the students' sense of this fact, when it is a fact that sets them at one with their teacher in ultimate wonderment. It is this fact that sets them free. And it is dedicated inquiry in this state of disciplined freedom through knowledge in which the liberal university at its best puts its final faith. Qualified commitment at all levels of knowledge may very well be the condition of ethical community in the free society. If so, such teaching would tend to extend it by example and by contagion.

In contrast to the basic motivation of such men, there are those who incline to the conviction that a social order must be integrated along the lines of a comprehensively coherent system of thought. They ask that a philosophy be actualized into a whole way of life, that it become practical and directive of the human enterprise rather than merely enlightening of it. They ask that philosophy abandon its sterile role as one of the liberal disciplines, that it take up residence in the market place and that it become self-consciously the ideological center of reference for the culture. They are asking, in deference to practicality and their highest partisan hope, that philosophy abandon its liberal status for a doctrinal status. This has been the fundamental error of the pragmatist-progressive school of thought; namely, that they would rescue human freedom by substituting one philosophy of freedom for another, in this case the philosophy in which Dewey found his freedom. But they have forgotten to note that he found his freedom both negatively and positively—negatively, by not committing himself to any extant philosophy in his heritage, positively, by constructing his own system of thought out of this heritage and the occasion of his time. His is the kind of freedom we honor and he took the only sure pathway to it. Thus must each philosophic mind and each generation hew its own freedom from the raw rock of life.

PART

Two

The Language
of Education

Introduction to Part Two

It is said, partly in jest, that language is a tool for thinking, except, of course, in politics where, as often as not, it is used deliberately to muddle thinking. Seldom, it is hoped, is language used deliberately in education to muddle thought; however, thought in education is often muddled. Why is this so? In part it is a result of the limitations of language. At best, the English language does not permit ideas to be communicated with complete exactness. Ambiguities creep into and vagueness often characterizes many of our concepts. The concept "teaching," for example, can be used to refer to an *occupation* in which a person called a teacher is engaged. It can also mean a *body of knowledge* and beliefs to be passed on, such as the teachings of Aristotle, or it can be applied to the *activities* employed by teachers in making something known to other persons. Thus the concept "teaching" can be used in ways in which it is difficult, if not impossible, to choose between the alternative meanings of the word.

In addition to the ambiguity that frequently plagues our thinking and communication, many of our concepts are vague, that is, they are characterized by indefiniteness. An excellent example of such vagueness is the term "adolescent." Precisely at what age does adolescence begin? When does it end? No one knows the answer to these questions with certainty, and yet we use the word everyday. Let us return to the concept "teaching." What does it embrace? If one conditions, is he teaching? If one indoctrinates, is that to be construed as teaching? Suppose one beats a child, with the hope of promoting learning, may this too be called teaching?

One can, of course, stipulate definitions for key concepts. Although to do so may occasionally be useful, it may on other occasions stifle meaningful investigations into the usage of concepts or lead unknowingly into programmatic or prescriptive definitions. Thus, instead of terminating discussion by first defining concept, many modern philosophers have wanted to extend their investigations into the uses made of key concepts. In fact these philosophers maintain, as you may have learned in Part One, that the study of the uses of such concepts should be the chief concern of a philosopher. Some philosophers have developed methods for doing this kind of analysis whereas others have done analyses of specific concepts.

In Part Two we begin with an examination of several kinds of definitions and how they are used in education. This is followed by the presentation of a technique for doing concept analysis, which, it is hoped, may be usefully employed by instructors and students in analyzing key concepts in education. Finally, some results of philosophical inquiry into teaching, knowing, and equality are presented for the clarity these inquiries afford and the examples they provide for doing philosophy.

4

Definitions in Education

ISRAEL SCHEFFLER

A general definition is often simply a stipulation to the effect that a given term is to be understood in a special way for the space of some discourse or throughout several discourses of a certain type. Such a definition may be called 'stipulative.' A stipulative definition exhibits some term to be defined and gives notice that it is to be taken as equivalent to some other exhibited term or description, within a particular context. It is a piece of terminological legislation that does not purport to reflect the previously accepted usage of the defined term,—if indeed there is such a predefinitional usage at all. Stipulative definitions may in turn be divided into two groups, depending on whether, in fact, the defined term has such a prior usage to begin with. Where it does not, the stipulative definition may be called an 'inventive' stipulation. Where, on the other hand, the stipulative definition legislates a new use for a term with a prior, accepted usage, it may be called a 'non-inventive' stipulation.

Inventive stipulation may be illustrated by the introduction of a system of arbitrary letters (e.g., 'S,' 'G,' 'E') to denote pupils' examination papers whose grades fall within specified intervals; these letters, having no accepted usage prior to their introduction, are assigned uses by stipulation. They are designated as shorthand labels equivalent to certain complicated descriptions of papers falling within the several score intervals. On the other hand,

Israel Scheffler is Victor S. Thomas Professor of Education and Philosophy at Harvard University. Israel Scheffler, *The Language of Education* (Springfield, Illinois; Charles C. Thomas, Publisher, 1960), pp. 13–14, 15–17, 18–24, 30–35. Used by permission of the author and publisher.

39

the use of a set of "qualitative" terms for the same purpose (e.g., 'passing,' 'fair,' etc.) is often governed by a series of non-inventive stipulations, non-inventive because such terms possess a predefinitional usage.[1]

... There is, however, another sort of general definition, which we here call 'descriptive' in contrast with the stipulative sort. Descriptive definitions, like the latter, may also serve to embody conventions governing discussions, but they always purport, in addition, to explain the defined terms by giving an account of their prior usage. In fact, descriptive definitions are thus often presented in answer to requests for clarification. The question, "What does that term mean?" is typically intended to elicit some explanatory rule or description of the term's prior functioning, that is, something in the nature of a descriptive definition. Every such definition is construable as a formula equating a defined term with other, defining, terms in a way that purports to mirror predefinitional usage. It is such mirroring that, it is hoped, will provide understanding of the defined term's meaning. An illustration is the definition of the term 'indoctrination' as 'the presentation of issues as if they had but one side to them.'[2] This and analogous definitions of 'indoctrination' are frequently presented in an attempt to clarify the term as it is ordinarily and most clearly applied. Such definitions aim at the distillation of a general rule out of the term's prior usage, a rule that may at once sum up such usage and clarify it by relating it to the usage of other, familiar terms, a rule that may thus be employed to teach someone how the term is normally used.

In contrast to stipulative definitions, then, descriptive definitions are not simply abbreviatory devices adopted for convenience and theoretically eliminable. They purport not to economize utterance, but to provide explanatory accounts of meaning. As a result, there is no counterpart among descriptive definitions to the inventive stipulation, inasmuch as the terms defined by inventive stipulation have no prior meanings to be explained. Given, however, a term *with* a prior use, the non-inventive stipulation may put it to unfamiliar uses for the purpose of facilitating communication, whereas the descriptive definition may provide a general account of its prior use. If we visualize the definition as a formula, after the fashion of modern logic, in which the defined term (definiendum) appears at the left and the defining term or set of terms (definiens) appears at the right separated by some special sign ('=df') in the middle, (e.g., 'indoctrination =df the presentation of issues as if they had but one side to them'), then we may also visualize the difference between stipulative and descriptive definitions as a difference

---

[1] Another contrast between inventive and non-inventive stipulation is illustrated by alternative ways of labelling grades in an elementary school. Two fifth grades may, for example, be distinguished as 'Bright' and 'Normal,' or they may be assigned two different letters, initials of their respective teachers' names, precisely in order to avoid the unwanted suggestions carried by their "qualitative" alternatives. For discussion of this point and related questions, I am indebted to Dr. David V. Tiedeman.

[2] This example is taken from Brubacher, J. S.: *Modern Philosophies of Education.* Second Edition. New York, McGraw-Hill Book Company, Inc., 1950, p. 201.

in the *direction* of interest in the formula as a whole. Whereas the interest in stipulation moves from right to left, that is, toward more condensed utterance with increased vocabulary, the interest in descriptive definition moves from left to right, i.e., toward expanded explanatory utterance with a smaller vocabulary.

It is evident that descriptive definitions are not matters of arbitrary choice in the way in which stipulative definitions have been said to be. For beyond formal and pragmatic considerations, descriptive definitions may be called to account in respect of the accuracy with which they reflect normal predefinitional usage. It is not irrelevant to argue against a descriptive definition that it violates such usage. It may indeed be explicitly stipulated that the term 'tree' is to count as equivalent to 'window' for the duration of some particular discussion, but such an equation clearly violates the prior use of the term 'tree' and must hence be judged wrong if it is offered rather as a descriptive definition. This example may, incidentally, serve to underscore the fact that a given definitional equation may serve either as a stipulation or as a descriptive definition, depending on the context in which it is offered and the purposes which it is intended to serve; the difference is thus not a formal or purely linguistic one but relates rather to the pragmatic environment of the definition. If and only if the definitional equation purports to mirror predefinitional usage is it descriptive. . . .

It remains for us now to consider a further, practical rôle of general definitions that is of especial importance in education; it is through this practical rôle that general definitions are often keyed fairly directly into social practices and habits of mind. How may the practical rôle of general definitions be described? Roughly speaking, some terms (e.g., the term 'profession') single out things toward which social practice is oriented in a certain way. (This orientation may be supposed expressible by a general principle of action: Example: "All professions ought to receive privileged treatment.") To propose a definition that now assigns such a term to some new thing may in context be a way of conveying that this new thing ought to be accorded the sort of practical treatment given to things hitherto referred to by the term in question. (E.g., to define 'profession' so as to apply to a new occupation may be a way of conveying that this new occupation ought to be accorded privileged treatment.) Similarly, to propose a definition that withholds such a term from an object to which it has hitherto applied may be a way of conveying that the object in question ought no longer to be treated as the things referred to by the given term have been treated. Even if a definition is proposed that assigns the term just exactly to the objects to which it has hitherto applied and to no others, the point at stake may be to defend the propriety of the current practical orientation to such objects and to no others, rather than (or as well as) to mirror predefinitional usage.

Where a definition purports to do either of these three things, it is acting as an expression of a practical program and we shall call it 'programmatic.'

As in the case of stipulative and descriptive definitions, programmatic definitions are not recognizable as such by their linguistic form alone; reference to the context needs to be made. A definition may, for example, have the effect of implying some practical consequence in *hypothetical* combination with *some* principle of action, but this does not mean it is therefore programmatic. It may not, that is, purport to convey the practical consequence in question; the context may make it clear that the definition is not to serve as a practical premise. Thus it is the practical purport of the definition *on a particular occasion* that reveals its programmatic character. The same repeatable formula, obviously, may be programmatic on one occasion and not on the next. A programmatic definition, in effect, may perhaps be said to convey the practical consequence itself, rather than merely to express a premise capable of yielding it under suitable conditions. It is this practical force of some definitions on particular occasions that is of interest to us here.

Programmatic definitions represent the last sort of general definition that will be distinguished for our present purposes.[3] Thus, together with the stipulative and descriptive sorts, programmatic definitions exhaust the class of general definitions here discussed. The difference between each sort and the others, as has already been emphasized, is not a formal difference. Exactly the same definitional equation may be stipulative, descriptive, or programmatic, depending on the context in which it is offered.

What sorts of consideration are relevant to the appraisal of programmatic definitions? Let us consider a partly schematic example. Imagine a type of work W that has hitherto fallen clearly outside the range of the term 'profession.' Suppose a definition is offered that has the consequence of applying this term to W. From the context, it is evident that the definition is not being used merely to introduce an eliminable, abbreviatory device to facilitate communication. Proposals of other likely abbreviations are, for

---

[3] The treatment of definition in the text is influenced in several respects by the important work of C. L. Stevenson, op. cit., but the use of the term 'programmatic' rather than his term 'persuasive' is motivated by certain substantive considerations marking a difference of approach: Persuasive definitions are interpreted by Stevenson in terms of emotive meaning, that is, in terms of psychological responses, feelings and attitudes, whereas programmatic definitions are here interpreted in terms of the orientation of social practice. The treatment in the present text connects the practical force of definitions with the *references* of constituent terms, and associated principles of action, rather than with the emotive properties of the terms themselves. This practical force is thus not explained as a conscious or unconscious use of definition "in an effort to secure, by this interplay between emotive and descriptive meaning, a redirection of people's attitudes" (Stevenson, op. cit., p. 210) but appears as a "cognitive" effect, a function of the references and logical relations between terms and statements involved. Emphasis on persuasiveness suggests that where a definition goes beyond the explanatory function, its surplus function is not to raise new questions but rather to cause new effects in the hearer. Emphasis on programmatic character, on the other hand, suggests that the bearings of a definition on social practice frequently are expressible as *arguable issues*, though they are not issues of meaning but practical or moral questions. The emphasis on programmatic rather than persuasive definitions is not a denial of the importance of the latter, but, at least in part, an attempt to stress the "cognitive" import of definitions for social practice, which has, it seems to me, been unduly neglected recently despite its significant rôle in general discourse.

example, uniformly rejected. Further, when the objection is raised that the definition fails to accord with prior usage, its author is unperturbed; he wants precisely to depart from such usage. It thus becomes clear that the definition is neither stipulative nor descriptive. The author's point is different; he wants W to be treated as other sorts of work are treated which fall within the predefinitional range of the term 'profession.' This point is one that requires independent, practical evaluation. It would surely be irrelevant to argue that the definition is not a very helpful abbreviatory convention, or that it is unorthodox with respect to predefinitional usage. What needs investigation is the practical or moral question: "Ought W to be accorded the treatment normally given to sorts of work hitherto called 'professions?'" The considerations appropriate to this question are relevant to the appraisal of the definition itself.[4]

From the preceding discussion, it is clear that, though programmatic definitions are like stipulative ones in not being bound by prior usage, they are unlike stipulations in raising moral or practical issues. Even stipulations, we have already remarked, are not *wholly* arbitrary. They may be criticized in terms of formal considerations, such as those relating to consistency, and appraised with regard to their helpfulness as devices of communication, e.g., do they aid memory, do they mislead by introducing irrelevant associations, etc. But they do not raise moral issues which go beyond the immediate discussion; they do not call for evaluation of practice, for appraisal of commitments, for the making of extra-linguistic decisions. In general, it is thus a mistake to suppose that *any* definition is wholly arbitrary, and an even more serious mistake to suppose that all but the descriptive definitions are bound only by considerations of consistency and communicatory convenience. Programmatic definitions, in particular, may be used to express serious moral choices.

Programmatic definitions, it may then be said, are like descriptive definitions in raising questions that go beyond those of consistency and convenience. But the kind of question that is raised by either sort of definition differs strikingly from the kind of question raised by the other. On the one hand, the issue is whether or not the definition before us accords with prior linguistic usage; on the other hand, the issue is whether or not the program expressed by the definition ought to be adopted.

We may now sum up the comparison of our three sorts of general definition by labeling, in a rough way, the interest underlying each sort. The interest of stipulative definitions is communicatory, that is to say, they are offered in the hope of facilitating discourse; the interest of descriptive

[4] For treatment of related questions see Cogan, M. L.: The problem of defining a profession, *Annals of the American Academy of Political and Social Science, 297*: 105, (January) 1955; Cogan, M. L.: Toward a definition of profession, *Harvard Educational Review,* 23: 33, (Winter) 1953; and Lieberman, M.: *Education as a Profession.* Englewood Cliffs, N. J., Prentice-Hall, Inc., 1956.

definitions is explanatory, that is, they purport to clarify the normal application of terms; the interest of programmatic definitions is moral, that is, they are intended to embody programs of action.

There is obviously no point at all in pitting these three sorts of general definition against each other or any or all of them against scientific definitions. The purposes each serves are all perfectly legitimate and there is no call to decide for or against some set or to rank them all in some scale of value. Rather, what is wanted is that the critical appraisal of a definition of any sort be directed to the issues at stake on the occasion of its use, and to this end the foregoing distinctions among sorts of definitions may be helpful.

There are, however, certain complications to be faced in considering the relations among sorts of general definition. It has been stressed above that the same definitional equation or formula may, on different occasions, express a stipulative, descriptive, or programmatic definition, depending on the context. May there, in addition, be an overlapping of definitional sorts on the same occasion, and for the same definitional formula? May the same definition, in context, belong to more than one sort?

If we consider this possibility first for stipulative and descriptive definitions, we find that overlapping is excluded. Descriptive definitions purport to describe predefinitional usage whereas stipulative definitions do not. Thus, no given definitional equation can be both stipulative and descriptive at the same time.

How about an overlap of stipulative and programmatic sorts? If we consider first inventive stipulation, it seems again that the possibility is excluded, inasmuch as the defined term in such a case, having no prior application at all, cannot, *a fortiori*, single out objects toward which practice is oriented in some particular way. Thus, a definition of such a term cannot express a program by suggesting either an alteration or a perpetuation of the practice associated with it. Nor, if the defining phrase denotes objects uniformly associated with some practical orientation, can the defined term serve to suggest an alteration or perpetuation of such orientation. For in order to do that, it should have to possess some initial application of its own that differed from or matched that of the defining phrase. But such initial application is just what is lacking in inventive stipulation.

On the other hand, when we examine the possibility of an overlap of non-inventive stipulation and programmatic definition on a given occasion, it is evident that such overlap does frequently occur. Furthermore, it is evident why it occurs, at least on numerous occasions. Briefly, the expression of a particular program may call for new linguistic apparatus; a given definition may, at one stroke, create such apparatus as well as give voice to the program. Examples abound in writings on social topics, but one educational illustration must here suffice.

We often find, in recent writings on education, that the term 'curriculum' is defined as referring to the totality of experiences of each learner under the influence of the school.[5] Now this definition has been rightly criticized as vague and difficult in a number of respects, but the point that concerns us here is quite different. The definition, it should be noted, has as an intended consequence that no two pupils ever have the same curriculum and, further, that no two schools ever have the same curriculum, each school having as many curricula as it has pupils. These consequences clearly violate the standard predefinitional usage of the term 'curriculum.' For such usage surely allows us to speak truly of the (unique) curriculum of a given school, of a number of schools with the same curriculum, and of the curriculum of a school as enduring for a longer or shorter interval during which its pupil population is completely changed.

This definition is not an inventive stipulation, for the term 'curriculum' does have a prior usage, as we have just seen. Nor is it merely a descriptive definition that happens to be unsuccessful, a defective attempt to mirror predefinitional usage. For if the violations of such usage that we have noted are made explicit, they are not treated as if they were counter-instances to a proposed descriptive hypothesis. Rather, they are typically taken as further symptoms of the definition's intended distinctiveness, which is then usually supported by other arguments. These arguments generally make it plain that the definition is programmatic, that its point is precisely to apply the familiar term in a strange way, in order to rechannel the practice associated with it. In particular, the programmatic point is to extend the school's responsibility, hitherto limited to its so-called formal course of study, in such a way as to embrace the individual social and psychological development of its pupils. The presentation of this programmatic point, however, requires repeated reference to the enlarged domain of responsibility envisaged, and, to facilitate such reference, the same definition stipulates the appropriate novel use of the term 'curriculum.' Thus the definition serves, on the same occasion, both as programmatic and as stipulative, in the non-inventive sense. Indeed, the need for the stipulation in question arises out of the program espoused. . . .

Many thinkers have claimed to possess special insight into the real and unique meanings of social terms, on the basis of which they could decide what ought to be done in controversial social spheres. Knowing the uniquely real definitions of 'the state,' 'society,' 'man,' etc., they have supposed that they could derive therefrom social imperatives governing newly arisen conditions requiring decision. If our previous analysis is correct, their claim is

---

[5] Compare the article 'Curriculum Development,' contributed by O. I. Frederick, in Monroe, W. S., editor: *Encyclopedia of Educational Research.* New York, Macmillan Publishing Co., Inc., 1941, which states that "in recent educational literature and in this report the school curriculum is considered to be all the actual experiences of the pupils under the influence of the school. From this point of view each pupil's curriculum is to some extent different from that of every other pupil. The course of study is considered to be a suggestive written guide for teachers to use as an aid in curriculum planning and teaching." (Passage cited with permission of Macmillan Publishing Co., Inc.)

totally misguided. For, in the first place, there are alternative ways of descriptively defining 'the state,' 'society,' 'man,' etc., all equally accurate with respect to prior usage or meaning, but differing in their legislation of new cases. In the second place, moreover, there is always the possibility of altering even prior standard usage in order to convey a practical program. (We have illustrated this possibility in discussing the overlap of non-inventive stipulation and programmatic definition in the case of the term 'curriculum.') In the third place, finally, definitions of social terms do not in isolation yield practical consequences at all; they require contextual supplementation by principles of action. (In the 'curriculum' case, recall, for example, the principle that the curriculum is coextensive with the school's responsibility.) Only in relation to such principles do social definitions serve to convey practical consequences. There is, then, always the possibility of countering such consequences by accepting the definition as accurate and denying the presupposed practical principles. In short, the jump from definition to action is long and hazardous, even where the definition is unquestionably accurate as an account of meaning.[6]

The above considerations are highly relevant to the use of definitions in discussions of education. To offer a definition of the term 'education,' for example, in non-scientific contexts is quite often to convey a program as well as, at best, to state an equation that may be accurate with respect to prior usage. Even where such a definition is accurate, *such accuracy cannot be used as a measure of the worth of the expressed educational program.* Different programs are compatible with accuracy and the justification of any program is thus an independent matter.

Definitions of terms in education are, to be sure, not generally embedded in as precise a network of practical rules as are legal definitions, but, in combination with broad and informal (though socially fundamental) principles of action, they often serve nevertheless as vehicles for debating new programs of education, new views of method, aims, or content. We have already seen one example in the case of the term 'curriculum.' Definitions in education thus may be said to resemble definitions in art which, though of no legal significance, also serve frequently to express changing conceptions of the artist's task.[7] For example, definitions of artistic innovators often extend the use of the term 'work of art' to new sorts of objects; the counter definitions of conservatives withhold the term from these same objects. Both

[6] Karl Popper, in his work, *The Open Society and its Enemies.* Third edition. London, Routledge & Kegan Paul Ltd., 1957 (First edition, 1945), has strongly criticized what he calls 'essentialism,' the search for essential meanings of basic terms; the present paragraph in the text is indebted to his treatment. Nevertheless, the present text diverges from Popper's defence of the exclusively abbreviatory function of definitions, in that we here allow for descriptive definitions with explanatory force. Essentialism is nonetheless avoided in that an extensional interpretation of descriptive definition is adopted throughout, allowing for different accurate definitions of each notion.

[7] For the points made in this paragraph, I am indebted to Ziff, P.: The task of defining a work of art, *The Philosophical Review,* 62: 58, (January) 1953.

sets of definitions are, furthermore, often consonant with artistic tradition, that is, they are in conformity with prior usage. The dispute can thus not be taken, in such cases, to be a matter of the meaning of terms alone. Rather, it is a question of divergent artistic programs, conveyed by opposing programmatic definitions that are also descriptively accurate. An attempt to define a work of art is not, in the words of Collingwood, "an attempt to investigate and expound eternal verities concerning the nature of an eternal object called Art," but rather to give "the solution of certain problems arising out of the situation in which artists find themselves here and now."[8]

Education, like art, literature, and other phases of social life, has changing styles and problems in response to changing conditions. These conditions require decisions governing our practical orientation to them. Such decisions may be embodied in revision of our principles of action or our definitions of relevant terms or both. In the making of new definitions for such purposes, there is no special insight into meanings that tells us how revisions and extensions are to be made. Not an inspection of the uniquely real meanings of terms (if this were possible) is here relevant, but an investigation in the light of our commitments, of the practical alternatives open to us as well as of alternative ways of putting desired decisions into effect.

The way in which this point is often overlooked in professional writings on education may be illustrated by the following description of a new program for secondary schooling:

> The curriculum was organized around four sorts of activities, story projects, hand projects, play projects, and excursion projects; opportunity was provided for continuing evaluation of activities, and such evaluation was directed by pupils. The organization of this school program proceeded naturally from the belief that the fundamental meaning of the concept of education is to help boys and girls to active participation in the world around them.

The issue is here put in terms of fundamental meanings. But, in fact, what is at stake? Clear cases of the concept 'education' as embodied in usage prior to the advent of modern innovations did not include cases where play and excursions as well as pupils' continuing evaluation characterized the educational program. But some of the clear cases, like the present example, did involve special institutions, overall direction by adults, evaluation of achievement, and so forth. The present educational innovation, as a matter of fact, is both sufficiently like and sufficiently unlike clear past instances to constitute a borderline case.

To propose an educational reform along the lines of the above passage is to say that such a procedure ought to be tried under the aegis of the schools. The proposal may thus be said to assimilate the borderline case to the past clear cases, leaving intact all those principles of action formulating

---

[8] Collingwood, R. G.: *The Principles of Art*. Oxford at the Clarendon Press, 1938, p. vi, quoted in Ziff, Op. cit.

our positive orientation to educational endeavor. The stated definition tries to do just that by, in effect, dwelling on the resemblances, i.e., on the common aim to help boys and girls to active participation in the world around them. It would, however, be easy to concoct alternative definitions that built on the differences, segregating the new reform from previous clear cases of 'education.' The issue, in short, is one of practice, and needs evaluation in terms of our preferences and commitments as well as in terms of expected effects. What is to be done with respect to this proposed educational reform is thus our practical responsibility and cannot be decided by inspection of the concept of 'education.'

Let us now consider a final example of a somewhat more abstract sort. In educational discussions, it is often said that a definition of 'man' provides directions for curriculum making and for evaluation of methods of schooling.[9] It is, indeed, true that the way in which we organize our educational efforts and operate our schools is conditioned by prevalent definitions of human nature. It is not, as we have seen, that practical educational consequences are derivable from accurate definitions taken in isolation but rather that they may be conveyed by such definitions in contexts where relevant principles of action are taken for granted. The conclusion often drawn in educational theory is that we must first decide what the correct definition of 'man' is, and that then practical educational consequences will only need to be inferred by us through the application of pure logic.

This picture is, however, wrong not only in postulating a simple deductive implication between definitions of human nature and practical educational consequences, but also in failing to take account of the several points noted above regarding definitions that are both descriptive and programmatic. There are an indefinite number of alternative definitions of 'man,' indefinitely many ways of dimensionalizing his structure and capacities, all equally accurate. To choose one such dimensionalization on the basis of its accuracy and to proceed to read off curricular counterparts to each dimension, as is often done, is to beg the whole question. One basis of choice of a definition for educational purposes must be a consideration of the very consequences for educational practice to be expected as a result of adoption of such a definition. The programmatic character of such a definition means that it requires evaluation with respect to the program conveyed. Indeed, such evaluation may even lead us to adopt a non-inventive stipulation that clearly violates prior usage; it surely may lead us to differentiate between equally accurate descriptive definitions that convey different programs. It is just because definitions of the latter sort are programmatic that their adoption should follow rather than precede a moral and practical evaluation of

[9] In this connection see, for example, Ducasse, C. J.: What can philosophy contribute to educational theory?, *Harvard Educational Review*, *28*: 285, (Fall) 1958. Ducasse asks what the several dimensions of man's nature are, as a preliminary to determining the chief dimensions of education, which (as he says) "correspond, of course, to those of man's nature."

the programs they convey. Inspection of meanings cannot substitute for such an evaluation.

An analogous point holds for the transfer of definitions from science to education, a transfer whose dangers we have already intimated. We remarked that scientific definitions are continuous with the theories and evidence in their respective domains, and that they may therefore best be treated apart. They cannot be fitted into our stipulative, descriptive, and programmatic categories without serious distortion. They are to be judged, roughly, by their contribution to the adequacy of their respective scientific networks in accounting for the facts. It follows that, to take a scientific definition for programmatic use is not to avoid the need for evaluation of the program such use conveys. The scientific adequacy of a definition is no more a sign of the practical worthwhileness of such a program than accuracy with respect to prior usage.

Finally, note must be taken of the converse truth. Just as, if a definition is accurate it does not automatically follow that its associated program is worthwhile, so if a definition is inaccurate, it does not automatically follow that its program is not worthwhile. We have already seen, in the case of non-inventive stipulative definitions that are also programmatic, the possibility of a worthwhile program conveyed by a descriptively inaccurate formula. Nevertheless, writers occasionally do argue, invalidly, that their definitions are accurate, since their programs are worthwhile, and they provoke the equally invalid rejoinder that their programs cannot be worthwhile since their definitions are inaccurate. The issue thus set up needs cutting through rather than intensified partisanship. It needs to be recognized, in short, that the same definitional formula on a given occasion may be both descriptive and programmatic, and that it thus requires double evaluation.

5

J. L. Austin's Method

J. O. Urmson

Austin, though he admired the methods and objectives of some philosophers more than others, held no views whatever about *the* proper objective or *the* proper method of philosophy. One reason for this is that he thought that the term 'philosophy', without any stretching, covered, and always had covered, a quite heterogeneous set of inquiries which clearly had no single objective and which were unlikely to share a single method. Another reason is that he thought that those inquiries which had continued to be called philosophical and had not hived off under some special name (as have, for example, physics, biology, psychology, and mathematics) were precisely those for the solution of whose problems no standard methods had yet been found. No one knows what a satisfactory solution to such problems as those of free will, truth, and human personality would look like, and it would be baseless dogmatism to lay down in advance any principles for the proper method of solving them.

All philosophers, therefore, are entitled to pursue those problems which most urgently claim their attention and to which their ability and training are best suited; and they are entitled to use any technique that seems hopeful to them, though we cannot expect that every technique will be equally successful. Austin, for his part, thought that he had developed a technique for tackling certain problems that particularly interested him, problems

J. O. Urmson is Fellow and Tutor in Philosophy at Corpus Christi College, Oxford, England.
J. O. Urmson, "J. L. Austin," *The Journal of Philosophy*, Vol. LXII (1965), pp. 499–508. Used by permission of the author and *The Journal of Philosophy*.

about the nature of language. He did not imagine that he had first formulated the problems and he did not imagine that he had discovered the
only possible method of tackling them; but he thought that he had devised a
sort of "laboratory technique" which could be fruitfully used for finding
solutions to them very much fuller, more systematic, and more accurate than
any hitherto. The justification for the use of the technique was its success in
practice; if another technique proved more successful it would be better. In
deserting Austin's technique for this we would not be abandoning one
theory of the nature of philosophy for another, but doing something more
like substituting the camera for the human eye in determining the winners of
horse races. This technique, like other research technique, could not be fully
exhibited in action in the conventional book, article, or lecture. Though
Austin gave some general indications about it in his writings, particularly in
"A Plea for Excuses" and "Ifs and Cans," its details are inevitably less
widely known than his more conventional work, though this clearly drew
heavily on the results obtained by the use of the technique. Yet Austin
himself thought it his most important contribution, and hoped that a
systematic use of it might lead to the foundation of a new science of
language, transcending and superseding the work of traditional philosophers, grammarians, and linguisticians in that field. So a fairly full account of
it by someone (myself) who frequently observed Austin employing it may
well be of more value than any critical comments I might make on his
published writings. Moreover, I think that a knowledge of it does help in the
understanding of the general character of the published writings. In giving
my account of this technique of Austin's I shall make use of some notes by
Austin, too fragmentary, brief, and disordered for publication, characteristically entitled "Something about one way of possibly doing one part of
philosophy."

It will be best to start with as factual as possible an account of the actual
employment of the technique, not searching as yet for a philosophically
helpful account of what it is being used for. Let it suffice at present to say
that the aim is to give as full, clear, and accurate account as possible of the
expressions (words, idioms, sentences, grammatical forms) of some language, or variety of language, common to those who are engaged in using the
technique. In practice the language will usually be the mother tongue of
the investigators, since one can employ the technique only for a language of
which one is a master.

We cannot investigate a whole natural language at a sitting, or series of
sittings; so we must first choose some area of discourse[1] for investigation—

---

[1] I write 'area of discourse'; Austin's notes speak merely of an 'area.' There is little point
in searching for a precise definition of an 'area of discourse'; terms are part of a single area of
discourse if it is of interest to compare and contrast their employment, and if not, not. Some
expressions may usefully be studied as falling into two different areas. There is no certain test of
whether a term falls into a given area or not, prior to our investigation.

discourse about responsibility, or perception, or memory, or discourse including conditional clauses, to mention first areas traditionally of interest to
philosophers; or discourse about artifacts, or discourse in the present perfect
tense, to add less traditional fields of investigation. Austin always recommended that beginners on the technique should choose areas that were not
already philosophical stamping grounds. Having chosen our area of discourse, we must then collect as completely as possible all the resources of the
language, both idiom and vocabulary, in that area. If we have chosen the
field of responsibility, for example, we must not start by offering generalizations about voluntary and involuntary actions, but must collect the whole
range of terms and idioms adumbrated in "A Plea for Excuses"—words like
'willingly,' 'inadvertently,' 'negligently,' 'clumsily,' and 'accidentally,'
idioms like 'he negligently did X' and 'he did X negligently.' In the field of
artifacts we must collect all such terms as 'tool,' 'instrument,' 'implement,'
'furniture,' 'equipment,' and 'apparatus.' In this task common sense is
needed; a useful collection of terms and idioms require art and judgment;
thus it probably would be a mistake to omit the term 'furniture' when
examining discourse about artifacts, but it is unlikely to be necessary to
include all names for all kinds of furniture—'table,' 'chair,' 'stool,' etc.
Moreover, the notion of a field of discourse is imprecise, and we may initially
be unclear whether a given term should or should not be included in it.
Austin's precept was that, when in doubt whether a term was necessary or
really belonged to the field in question, we should start by including it, since
it is easier to strike out later terms that turn out to be intruders than it is to
repair omissions. The most obvious devices for getting a fairly complete list
are: (a) free association, where the investigators add any terms to the initial
few that occur to them as being related; (b) the reading of relevant
documents—not the works of philosophers but, in the field of responsibility,
such things as law reports, in the field of artifacts such things as mail-order
catalogues; (c) use of the dictionary, less ambitiously by looking up terms
already noted and adding those used in the definitions until the circle is
complete, or, more ambitiously, by reading right through the dictionary—
Austin, who must have read through the *Little Oxford Dictionary* very many
times, frequently insisted that this did not take so long as one would expect.

At the stage of preliminary collection of terms and idioms the work is
more quickly and more exhaustively done by a team. Austin always insisted
that the technique was at all stages best employed by a team of a dozen or so
working together; the members supplemented each other and corrected each
other's oversights and errors. Having collected its terms and idioms, the
group must then proceed to the second stage in which, by telling circumstantial stories and conducting dialogues, they give as clear and detailed
examples as possible of circumstances under which this idiom is to be
preferred to that, and that to this, and of where we should (do) use this term
and where that. Austin's two stories of the shooting of the donkey to illus-

trate the circumstances in which we should, when speaking carefully, prefer to say 'accidentally' or 'by mistake' will indicate the sort of thing to be done at this stage ("A Plea for Excuses," *Philosophical Papers*, p. 133). It is also important to tell stories and make dialogues as like as possible to those in which we should employ a certain term or idiom in which it would not be possible, or would strike us as inappropriate, to use that term or idiom. We should also note things which it is not possible to say in any circumstances, though not manifestly ungrammatical or otherwise absurd (Aristotle's observation that one cannot be pleased quickly or slowly is the sort of thing that it meant here). This second stage will occupy several sessions; it is not a matter to be completed in a few minutes.

We have now got our list of terms and idioms (first stage), and a list of circumstantial stories illustrating how these expressions can and cannot occur, according to context. Experience shows that a group, not just a group of Oxford philosophers but, say, a mixed American and British group, can reach virtual unanimity on these matters. Maybe something that seems perfectly in order to all the rest will sound odd to one member, or vice versa. When this happens it can be noted down and it may be of interest. But getting things right up to this stage is a group activity, and it is easy for a single individual to make mistakes initially that he can be brought to see. The device of a statistical survey of "what people would say" by means of a questionnaire is no substitute for the group, (1) because there cannot be the necessary detail in the questionnaire, (2) because the untrained answerers can so easily make mistakes, (3) because we are raising questions where unanimity is both desirable and obtainable. The group is its own sample, and its members can always ask their friends and relations "What would you say if . . . ?" as required.[2]

Austin always insisted that during the work so far described all theorizing should be rigidly excluded. We must make up detailed stories embodying the felicitous and the infelicitous, but carefully abstain from too early an attempt to explain why. Premature theorizing can blind us to the linguistic facts; premature theorizers bend their idiom to suit the theory, as is shown all too often by the barbarous idiom found in the writings of philosophers who outside of philosophy speak with complete felicity. But eventually the stage must come at which we seek to formulate our results. At this stage we attempt to give general accounts of the various expressions (words, sentences, grammatical forms) under consideration; they will be correct and adequate if they make it clear why what is said in our various stories is or is

[2] An illustration: so shrewd an operator as Noam Chomsky says on page 15 of his admirable *Syntactic Structures* that "Read you a book on modern music" is not a grammatical sentence of English. Consider the dialogue: A. "Please read me a book on modern music." B. "Read you a book on modern music? Not for all the gold in Fort Knox!" Chomsky should have been working in a group. The statistical datum that Urmson allows, Chomsky disallows: this sentence is of no interest. Chomsky has made one of his few errors, as a group of us discovered while reading him.

not felicitous, is possible or impossible. Thus it is an empirical question whether the accounts given are correct and adequate, for they can be checked against the data collected. Of course, if we have rushed the earlier stages new linguistic facts may be later adduced that invalidate the accounts; this is the universal predicament of empirical accounts. But though the accounts are empirical, the discovery and formulation of adequate ones is a matter requiring great skill and some luck; there is no rule of thumb available.

We may now, if we wish, go on to compare the accounts that we have thus arrived at with what philosophers have commonly said about the expressions in question (or with what grammarians have said). If one does so one may go on to a further project, the examination of traditional philosophical arguments in the light of the results of the technique. This type of project is illustrated by Austin's *Sense and Sensibilia*; here a thumbnail sketch only is given of the use of the technique on various groups of terms: 'illusion,' 'delusion,' and 'hallucination'; 'looks,' 'appears,' 'seems,' etc.; 'real,' 'apparent,' 'imaginary,' etc.; Austin then tries to show that various traditional arguments depend for their apparent plausibility on the systematic misconstruction and interchange of these and similar key terms. The book illustrates this stage of the inquiry; I do not now ask whether it is a successful illustration. . . .

6

A Topology of the
Teaching Concept

Thomas F. Green

I. The Teaching Continuum

A concept is a rule. When someone learns a concept, without exception, what he has learned is a rule, a rule of language, or more generally, a rule of behavior. But some of the rules we observe in action and speaking are enormously complicated. Some are "open textured" in the sense that they do not specify with accuracy and precision what is permitted under the rule and what is not. These are the kinds of rules which are vague. They circumscribe the limits of vague concepts.

We can imagine what a vague concept is like by picturing a modern painting in which the different colors are blurred, one blending into another in degrees more imperceptible and gradual even than those which we discover in the spectrum. Such a painting, when viewed at a distance, clearly possesses a certain order among its several parts. There is a pattern of light and colors which constitutes the structure of the figures in the painting, but which when seen in close proximity, conceals the order of the painting.

How could we draw a clear and precise representation of what is found in such a painting? Here is a certain place where the colors change from red to orange and thence to yellow. Yet we cannot, with any certitude, point to a place and say at that point the color ceases to be red and becomes orange, or

Thomas F. Green is Professor of Education and Co-Director of the Educational Policy Research Center at Syracuse University. Thomas F. Green, "A Topology of the Teaching Concept," *Studies in Philosophy and Education*, Vol. 3, No. 4 (Winter 1964–65), pp. 284–319. Used by permission of the author and *Studies in Philosophy and Education*.

ceases to be orange and becomes yellow. Any attempt to specify precisely where the colors change, any attempt to eliminate the delicate blending of one color into another, would misrepresent the order or pattern of the painting. There are many points at which such a line can be drawn. They would all be equally right and all equally wrong.

A vague concept is like such a picture. It is a rule which is enormously complicated, and a part of its complication arises for no other reason than that it is not precise. It allows differences of opinion and differences of judgment at precisely those blurring points where people try to specify where one color begins and another leaves off. Nonetheless, the difficulty of making such differences precise does not mean that there is no order, or that we cannot find it. It means simply that we must not insist on too much precision in the order that we find.

We can, in fact, give a description of such a picture without sacrificing anything in the way of a faithful representation. For if we discover that there are two patches of paint which can be cut out and substituted one for another without in any way changing the picture, then we would be justified in saying that these two patches are related in a certain sense, namely, in the sense that they are exactly similar. And if we discovered that the color in the space intervening between them could be reproduced by imperceptibly and gradually blending the pigment in each of these patches with some second color in ever increasing proportions, then we would be justified in saying that we understand, in a different sense, *how* these two patches of color are related. We would have specified the rule which will suffice to relate the two patches of color. In this fashion we could develop a topology of such a canvas, showing by what rule each point on the canvas is related to every other point by the gradual blending of the pigments. Thus we could reveal the structure of the painting without converting it into a line drawing.

The concept of teaching is like such a blurred picture. It is a vague concept. Its boundaries are not clear. However accurately we may describe the activity of teaching there will, and always must, remain certain troublesome border-line cases. In admitting this, the point is not that we have failed to penetrate the darkness and to discover that juncture at which an activity ceases to be teaching and becomes something else. The point is rather that beneath the darkness there is simply no such precise discrimination to be found. There is therefore an initial presumption against the credibility of any analysis which yields precise criteria, which, without a trace of uncertainty assigns to every case a clear identity.

We can, nonetheless, describe the structure of the teaching concept, or if you wish, map its terrain, by standing at a distance and by asking not about teaching itself, but about such patches or parts of teaching as training, indoctrinating, conditioning, showing and instructing. We need not insist that the blur between these patches be removed. We need only show how they are related and how the gradual transition from one to the other may be reproduced. When we have done that, we will have drawn a map of the teaching concept; we will have described a rule or complex set of rules which formulate the structure of the concept.

At the outset, one must recognize then, that the concept of teaching is molecular. That is, as an activity, teaching can best be understood not as a single activity, but as a whole family of activities within which some members appear to be of more central significance than others. For example, there is an intimate relation between teaching and training which can be observed in many ways. There are, for example, contexts in which the word "teaching" may be substituted for "training" without any change of meaning. One reason for this is that teaching is often conceived to involve the formation of habit, and training is a method of shaping habit. Thus, when engaged in training, we may often say with equal propriety that we are engaged in teaching. The two concepts are closely related.

Nonetheless teaching and training are not identical. Training is only a part of teaching. There are contexts in which it would be a rank distortion to substitute the one concept for the other. For example, it is more common, and perhaps more accurate, to speak of training an animal than to speak of teaching him. I do not mean there is no such thing as teaching a dog. I mean only that it is more accurate in this context to speak of training. We can, indeed, teach a dog to fetch, to heel, to point, and to pursue. There is in fact a common saying that you cannot teach an old dog new tricks. The use of the word "teaching" in each of these cases has its explanation. It has to do with the fact that the actions of a trained dog are expressive of intelligence; they involve obedience to orders. Indeed, a well trained dog is one which has passed "obedience trials."

But the intelligence displayed in such cases is limited, and it is this which renders the education of an animal more akin to training than to teaching. What should we think of a trainer of dogs attempting to explain his orders to an animal, giving reasons for them, presenting evidence of a kind that would tend to justify them? The picture is absurd. Dogs do not ask "Why?" They do not ask for reasons for a certain rule or order. They do not require explanation or justification. It is this limitation of intelligence which we express by speaking of training rather than teaching in such circumstances. Moreover, those rare occasions in which animals most clearly display intelligence are precisely those in which they appear to ask "Why?" They are the occasions when they do precisely what they have been trained *not* to do, or when they do *not* do what they have been trained to do. The horse, trained to pull the carriage, saves his master's life in the darkness of the night by stopping at the edge of the washed out bridge and refusing to go on. The dog trained not to go into the street, is killed because he rushed into the path of a truck to push a child to safety. On such occasions, it is as though the animal had obeyed an order which was not given. It is as though he had given himself a reason for acting contrary to his training.

I am not concerned whether this, or something like it, is a correct explanation of such remarkable happenings. I am concerned only to observe that training resembles teaching insofar as it is aimed at actions which display intelligence. In this respect, training has a position of central importance in that congerie of activities we include in teaching. Ordinarily, however, the kind of intelligence aimed at in training is limited. What it excludes is the process of asking questions, weighing evidence and, in short, demanding and receiving a justification of rules, principles, or claims of fact. In proportion as training is aimed at a greater and greater display of intelligence, it more and more clearly resembles teaching, and one of the clues as to how closely training approaches teaching is the degree to which it involves explanations, reasons, argument, and weighing evidence. It is because training sometimes approaches this point, that we can in many cases substitute the word "teaching" for the word "training" without any change in meaning.

This point is strengthened when we consider what happens in proportion as training is aimed less and less at the display of intelligence. In that case, the concept fades off imperceptibly into what we would commonly call conditioning. It is natural to speak of teaching a dog to fetch, to heel, to walk in time to music. It is more of a distortion to speak of teaching a dog to salivate at the sound of a bell. It is in precisely this latter context that we speak of conditioning. Conditioning does not aim at an intelligent performance of some act.[1] Insofar as training does not aim at the display of intelligence, it resembles conditioning more and teaching less. Thus, we can see that training is an activity which is conceptually of more central importance to the concept of teaching than is conditioning. We teach a dog to fetch; we condition him to salivate. And the difference is a difference in the degree of intelligence displayed.

Instruction also must be numbered among the family of activities related to teaching. Instructing, in fact, is so closely bound to teaching that the phrase "giving instruction" seems only another way of saying "teaching." There seems to be no case of an activity we could describe as "giving instruction" which we could not equally and more simply describe as teaching. Nonetheless, teaching and giving instruction are not the same thing. For there are almost endless instances of teaching which do not involve instruction. For example, it is acceptable and even correct, to speak of *teaching* a dog to heel, to sit, or to fetch. It is, however, less acceptable, more imprecise, and perhaps even incorrect to speak of *instructing* a dog in sitting and fetching.

But why, in such contexts, is it more awkward to speak of instructing than to speak of teaching? We need not go far to discover the answer. When we train a dog, we give an order and then push and pull and give reward or punishment. We give the order to sit and then push on the hindquarters

---

[1] There may be circumstances, however, in which it would be intelligent, i.e., wise, to "teach" with the aim of producing a conditioned response.

precisely because we cannot explain the order. We cannot elaborate its meaning. It is precisely this limitation of intelligence or communication which disposes us to speak of training a dog rather than instructing him. What we seek to express by the phrase "giving instruction" is precisely what we seek to omit by the word "training." Instruction seems, at heart, to involve a kind of conversation, the object of which is to give reasons, weigh evidence, justify, explain, conclude and so forth. It is true that whenever we are involved in giving instruction, it follows that we are engaged in teaching; but it is not true that whenever we are engaged in teaching, we are giving instruction.

This important difference between training and instructing may be viewed in another way. To the extent that instructing necessarily involves a kind of conversation, a giving of reasons, evidence, objections and so on, it is an activity of teaching allied more closely to the acquisition of knowledge and belief than to the promotion of habits and modes of behavior. Training, on the contrary, has to do more with forming modes of habit and behavior and less with acquiring knowledge and belief. Instructing, in short, is more closely related to the quest for understanding. We can train people to do certain things without making any effort to bring them to an understanding of what they do. It is, however, logically impossible to instruct someone without at the same time attempting to bring him to some understanding. What this means, stated in its simplest and most ancient terms, is that instructing always involves matters of truth and falsity whereas training does not. This is another reason for observing that instructing has more to do with matters of belief and knowledge, and training more with acquiring habits or modes of behaving. It is not therefore a bit of archaic nonsense that teaching is essentially the pursuit of truth. It is, on the contrary, an enormously important insight. The pursuit of truth is central to the activity of teaching because giving instruction is central to it. That, indeed, is the purpose of the kind of conversation indigenous to the concept of giving instruction. If giving instruction involves giving reasons, evidence, argument, justification, then instruction is essentially related to the search for truth.

The point is not, therefore, that instructing necessarily requires communication. The point is rather that it requires a certain *kind* of communication, and that kind is the kind which includes giving reasons, evidence, argument, etc., in order to approach the truth. The importance of this fact can be seen if we consider what happens when the conversation of instruction is centered less and less upon this kind of communication. It takes no great powers of insight to see that in proportion as the conversation of instruction is less and less characterized by argument, reasons, objections, explanations, and so forth, in proportion as it is less and less directed toward an apprehension of truth, it more and more closely resembles what we call indoctrination. Indoctrination is frequently viewed as a method of instruction. Indeed, we sometimes use the word "instruction" to include what we quite openly confess is, in fact, indoctrination. Nonetheless, indoctrination is a substantially different thing from instruction, and what is central to this difference is precisely that it involves a different kind of conversation and therefore is differently related to matters of truth.

We can summarize the essential characteristics of these differences by saying that indoctrination is to conditioning as beliefs are to habits. That is to say, we may indoctrinate people to *believe* certain things, but we condition them always to *do* certain things. We do not indoctrinate persons to certain modes of behavior any more than we condition them to certain kinds of beliefs. But the important thing is to observe that *insofar as* conditioning does not aim at an expression of intelligent doing, neither does indoctrination aim at an expression of intelligent believing. Conditioning is an activity which can be used to establish certain modes of behavior quite apart from their desirability. It aims simply to establish them. If a response to a certain stimuli is trained or conditioned, or has become a fixed habit, it will be displayed in the fact that the same stimuli will produce the same response even when the person admits it would be better if he responded otherwise. This is an unintelligent way of behaving. In an analogous way, indoctrination is aimed at an unintelligent way of holding beliefs. Indoctrination aims simply at establishing certain beliefs so that they will be held quite apart from their truth, their explanation, or their foundation in evidence. As a practical matter, indoctrinating involves certain conversation, but it does not involve the kind of conversation central to the activity of giving instruction. Thus, as the teaching conversation becomes less related to the pursuit of truth, it becomes less an activity of instruction and more a matter of indoctrination. We may represent these remarks schematically as shown below.

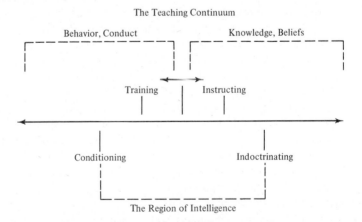

The diagram is not meant to suggest that the distinction between conditioning, training, instructing and indoctrinating are perfectly clear and precise. On the contrary, each of these concepts, like the teaching concept itself, is vague. Each blends imperceptibly into its neighbor. It is as with the well-known case of baldness. We cannot say with precision and accuracy at precisely what point a man becomes bald. There is nonetheless a distinction, clear enough in its extremities, between a bald head and a hairy head. One might say that the difference is a matter of degree. But if the difference between conditioning and training or between instructing and indoctrinating is simply a difference of degree, then one must ask, "What is it that differs in degree?" The fact is that instructing and indoctrinating are different in kind, but the respects in which they differ may be exemplified in different degrees. Thus, we may be uncertain in many concrete cases whether the conversation of a teaching sequence more nearly resembles instructing or indoctrinating. But it does not follow from this that the difference between them is obscure, that we are uncertain about it or that they differ only in degree. It follows only that in such specific instances the criteria that mark the difference though perfectly clear in themselves, are neither clearly exemplified nor clearly absent.

A parallel example may suffice to make this clearer. To lie is to tell a falsehood with the intent to deceive. But now consider the following circumstances. Two brothers go to bed on the eve of one's birthday. He whose birthday is coming wishes to know what in the way of gifts the next day may hold in store for him; and so he questions, prods, cajoles, and teases his brother to tell him. But he receives only the unsatisfactory but truthful answer from his brother that he does not know. And so the teasing continues and sleep is made impossible. The only recourse for the weary one is to invent a lie. It must, however, be a lie that is believable. It must satisfy and yet must be most assuredly a lie. And so he says what is most improbable, "You will get a bicycle." But now suppose they discover on the morning after that indeed the principal gift is a bicycle. The question might arise, did the brother lie or did he not? If the answer is "Yes," the difficulty arises that what he said was in fact the truth. If the answer is "No," the fact will arise that he intended to deceive. A case may be built for both answers, because in this illustration, the criteria for lying and for truth telling are mixed. The case is neither one nor the other. It does not follow, however, that the difference between lying and truth telling is obscure. Such examples show only that the criteria which mark the difference may be in more or less degree fulfilled. It shows there is a degree of vagueness present, a point at which we cannot decide.

And so it is in the present case. The concept of teaching, as we normally use it, includes within its limits a whole family of activities, and we can recognize that some of these are more centrally related to teaching than others. We have no difficulty, for example, in agreeing that instructing and certain kinds of training are activities which belong to teaching. We may have more difficulty, and some persons more than others, in deciding whether conditioning and indoctrinating legitimately belong to teaching. There is, in short, a region on this continuum at which we may legitimately disagree, because there will be many contexts in which the criteria which tend to distinguish teaching and conditioning or teaching and indoctrination will not be clearly exemplified. Thus, there is an area of uncertainty on this continuum, an area of vagueness neither to be overcome nor ignored, but respected and preserved.

Nonetheless, were we to extend this continuum, we would discover another region of agreement. For we would surely stretch a point too far were we to extend the line on the left and include such activities as intimidation and physical threat, or on the right and include such things as exhorting, propagandizing and just plain lying. The continuum is shown in the diagram that follows.

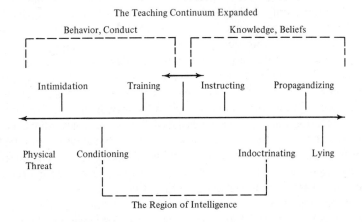

The Teaching Continuum Expanded

We would have to strain and struggle to include within the teaching family such things as extortion, lying and deceit. The point is not that such things *cannot* be included among the assemblage of teaching activities. The point is rather that to do so would require an extension and distortion of the concept of teaching. It is clear in any case that such activities are less central to the concept of teaching than conditioning and indoctrination, and that these are, in turn, less central than training and instruction. Thus as we extend the extremities of this continuum we depart from a region of relative uncertainty and enter a segment within which we can agree with relative ease. Lying, propagandizing, slander and threat of physical violence are not teaching activities, although they may be ways of influencing persons' beliefs or shaping their behavior. We know in fact, that these activities are excluded from the concept of teaching with as much certainty as we know that training and instructing are included. This shows approximately where the region of vagueness occurs in the concept of teaching. It occurs in respect to matters of behavior, somewhere between the activities of training and conditioning, and in respect to matters of knowledge and belief, it occurs somewhere between instructing and indoctrinating. The most central properties of the concept of teaching are revealed, in short, within the limits of what we have called the region of intelligence. Or, to put the matter in another way, we can say that teaching has to do primarily with the relation between thought and action.

It is a matter of no consequence that there have been societies which have extended the concept of teaching beyond this limit of vagueness and have thus included even the most remote extremities of this continuum. That propaganda, lies, threats, and intimidation have been used as methods of education is not doubted. But the conclusion warranted by this fact is not that teaching includes such activities, but that education may. Propaganda, lies, and threats are more or less effective means of influencing and shaping beliefs and patterns of behavior. It follows that teaching is not the only method of education. It does not follow that the use of propaganda, lies and threats are methods of teaching.

The concept of teaching is thus a molecular concept. It includes a congerie of activities. In order to more clearly understand the concept it may suffice to simply describe in schematic form what are the logical properties most central to this family of activities and to display in what respects other less central activities do or do not bear the marks of teaching. In this way we may gain in clarity without doing violence to the vagueness inherent in the concept. At the same time, we may avoid importing some obscure and *a priori* normative definition of teaching.

. . . When beliefs are held without regard to evidence or contrary to evidence, or apart from good reasons or the canons for testing reasons and evidence, then we may say they are held non-evidentially. It follows that beliefs held non-evidentially cannot be modified by introducing evidence or reasons or by rational criticism. When beliefs, however, are held " on the basis of" evidence or reasons, can be rationally criticised, and therefore can be modified in the light of further evidence or better reasons, then we shall say they are held evidentially.

This contrast between holding beliefs evidentially and non-evidentially corresponds closely to a fundamental point on the teaching continuum. It has to do with a conventional contrast between teaching and indoctrinating. This difference has nothing to do with the contents of beliefs. It is perfectly possible that two persons may hold to the same belief and yet one may do so evidentially and the other non-evidentially. It is possible in other words, to indoctrinate people into the truth. The only problem is that they will not *know* that it is the truth. They will only know that it is a *correct* belief. That is to say, they will hold to certain true beliefs, but will be unable to give any adequate reasons for them, any clear account of them, or offer any sound evidence in their support beyond the logically irrelevant observation that they are commonly held beliefs. And yet we cannot be said to *know* that a belief is true, if we cannot give any reasons for it, any explanation of it or any evidence in support of it. In short, even though the beliefs one holds are true, one cannot be said to know they are true, if they are believed in this non-evidential fashion. They can only be known to be *correct* beliefs, and that is one of the features of beliefs held as a consequence of indoctrination.

But this contrast between teaching and indoctrination cuts more deeply. Consider the following context.[2] At some conferences there is a period set aside to lay out the work of the conference, to set the limits to be observed and the methods to be followed. It involves the presentation of decisions already arrived at and now presented as "the ground rules," so to speak, within which the work of the conference shall proceed. A sales conference, for example, may be concerned with the study and discussion of a single method of selling, excluding all others from consideration.

Such a period is sometimes called an orientation period. But it may also appropriately, more accurately, but less wisely, be called a period of indoctrination because of the place and function served by debate. In such a period, persons may raise questions; there may be discussion and a certain amount of disagreement expressed with decisions arrived at. This process overtly resembles the process of debate carried on for the purpose of informing and arriving at decisions. But in this context questions are raised, information given and discussion permitted only for purposes of persuasion, never for purposes of *arriving* at conclusions.

Both teaching and indoctrination may involve debate, questions, discussions and argument. Both appear to involve instruction, and, in that respect, there is a striking resemblance between them. But there also is a great difference. In indoctrinating, the conversation of instruction is employed only in order that fairly specific and predetermined beliefs may be set. Conflicting evidence and troublesome objections must be withheld because there is no purpose of inquiry. The conversation of instruction is adopted without its intent, without the "due regard for truth" so essential to instruction. Not every point on the teaching continuum is, therefore, equally a point where truth is significant. Indoctrination begins precisely where a concern for truth ends. In short, the intent of indoctrination is to lead people to hold beliefs as though they were arrived at by inquiry, and yet to hold them independently of any subsequent inquiry and therefore secure against the threat of change by the later introduction of conflicting reasons or conflicting evidence. The intent, in other words, is to produce persons who hold their beliefs non-evidentially.

. . . This kind of reply would not signal the failure of instruction. It would be evidence of singular success. Instruction is an activity which has to do not with what people believe but with how they believe it. It has to do not so much with arriving at "the right answer" as with arriving at an answer on the right kind of grounds. It is no objection to point out the many areas of

---

[2] The following illustration was suggested by a student of mine, Mr. William Lauderdale.

knowledge in which it is important to lead students to the right answer. For all that is usually pointed out is that there are many areas of knowledge in which the grounds of decision are decisive, and in which therefore there *is* a correct answer which it is important to know. Even in mathematics, however, where a "right answer" is often discoverable, a concern simply to lead students to that answer, or to equip them to find it, is a fundamentally defective kind of instruction. Even in such a formal science where certitude is common, we are concerned that students be brought to an evidential style of knowing. To focus simply upon securing a right solution without understanding the nature of mathematical operations is the mathematical equivalent of indoctrination. Indeed, when indoctrination is seen to involve a certain style of knowing or believing, we can discover the possibility of indoctrination in nearly every area of human knowledge and not simply in those having to do with what we would more commonly call "matters of doctrine." In other words, when, in teaching, we are concerned simply to lead another person to a correct answer, but are not correspondingly concerned that they arrive at that answer on the basis of good reasons, then we are indoctrinating; we are engaged in creating a non-evidential style of belief.

There is one further curious fact to observe about the concept of indoctrination and its relation to a non-evidential way of holding beliefs. It has to do with the difficulty in identifying concrete cases of indoctrination as opposed to teaching. We have already suggested that there is an area of vagueness between instructing and indoctrinating. The difference between them is clear, but the criteria that mark the difference may, in specific instances, be mixed. For example, a person who has received his beliefs by indoctrination will be able to give reasons for them, offer evidence, and in other ways display every mark of holding his beliefs in an evidential way. But this is an illusion, albeit an illusion to which each of us, in some measure, submits. A person who is indoctrinated can sometimes give reasons and evidence for his beliefs, because as a practical matter, reasons and evidence were necessary in the process of establishing his beliefs. The difference, however, is betrayed in his *use* of reasons and evidence. He will use argument, criticism, evidence, and so forth, not as an instrument of inquiry, but as an instrument establishing what he already believes. He will display a marked incapacity to seriously consider conflicting evidence or entertain contrary reasons. That is to say, such a person will hold his beliefs as matters of ideology. It is indeed the characteristic of an ideology that it requires reason and argument, not for inquiry, but for defense. It requires reason as a weapon. This is not required for the defense of a belief held evidentially.

The point is that the differences between instruction and indoctrination, clear enough conceptually, are extraordinarily difficult to detect in specific cases. It requires, in ourselves, the capacity to discriminate between beliefs which are held evidentially and those which are not. To do this, we must not only have the capacity to detect sophistry in ourselves, but the courage to reject it when discovered, and the psychic freedom to follow where the pursuit of truth may lead. The detection of non-evidential beliefs in ourselves, therefore, requires not simply the logical skill to examine and appraise the adequacy of reasons, but the psychic freedom to give up or alter those beliefs which are non-evidential. In short, the distinction between instruction and indoctrination, easy enough to grasp intellectually, is immensely difficult to detect in practice, because it involves nothing less than the most radical examination of our belief systems in their psychological dimensions. To possess such a capacity is a mark of rare courage and honesty.

II. THE TOPOLOGY OF ENABLING BELIEFS

This emphasis on an evidential system of belief is susceptible to misunderstanding in a dangerous way. It could be understood to imply that one should not have *any* passionate convictions. A belief held evidentially is ammenable to examination, and therefore open to change in the light of better reasons and more substantial evidence. Thus the possession of firm convictions seems to conflict with the cultivation of evidential beliefs. He who has passionate convictions is to that extent and at those points no longer open-minded, and he who is at *every* point open-minded must be without any passionate convictions. He is that completely flexible man, whose placid and weak mentality marks him off as dangerous, because he thinks nothing is really very important.
An evidential belief style does not commit us to such a mentality. The problem is rather to seek closure of mind at precisely those points and on those matters which will permit us to be open to the evidence on all other matters of belief. The only beliefs, in short, which must be rejected are those which prevent us from being open to reasons and evidence on all subsequent matters. As Chesterton has put it in another context: "There is a thought that stops thought. That is the only thought that ought to be stopped."[3] He might have added that there are beliefs without which no beliefs can be warranted and these are the only beliefs which at all cost must be affirmed.

Such beliefs, in fact, ought to enlist our most passionate loyalty; for they are the ones which enable us to hold all other beliefs in an evidential way. For example, a thorough skepticism in regard to reason, a kind of complete anti-intellectualism; if held to as a deep conviction, would successfully prevent the examination of any subsequent beliefs. It could lead only to a non-evidential way of believing. On the other hand, a "due regard for

---

[3] Orthodoxy, 58.

truth,"—the belief that truth is powerful, attainable and to be treasured whenever identified—such a belief is indispensable if *any* belief is to be held evidentially. Such a conviction does not commit us to the naive faith that all men have a due regard for truth or are equally moved to dispassionately weigh and consider the evidence on important questions. Nor does it commit us to the truth of any specific belief. It commits us only to a certain *way* of holding beliefs, and that way is an evidential way. Indeed, a "due regard for truth," understood in this way and passionately held to, is indispensable if we are to hold to *any* beliefs in an evidential way. A deep conviction concerning the value of truth is in this sense rationally defensible because without it there can be no rational defense of any belief whatsoever.

It is not, therefore, the aim of teaching to eliminate all passionate convictions. The aim, on the contrary, is to seek every possible assurance that our passionate convictions, our enabling beliefs, are also rationally or evidentially held. Such enabling beliefs may be open for examination, capable of refinement and elaboration, but under no conditions can they be exchanged for others. Their abandonment cannot be warranted on the basis of evidence or reasons, because they are precisely those beliefs without which we could not seriously entertain the evidence.

These comments also are susceptible to a dangerous misappropriation. At the point of enabling beliefs, there is only the most tenuous line between the fanatic and men of less singular devotion. For at this point, the difference between what is believed and how we believe it is obscured. How a person believes something can be reduced, at this point, to an account of what he believes. The actions of the inquisitor, after all, may be defended on grounds of the most passionate regard for truth, a regard for truth so strong, in fact, that it becomes necessary to stamp out every trace of error that the truth may receive the recognition it deserves. The difficulty with the fanatic at every point, however, is that he confuses a due regard for truth with passionate concern to propagate certain *specific truths.*

But it may be answered, "Is not a due regard for truth also a specific set of beliefs?" It is indeed. It is the belief that truth is attainable, powerful, and to be treasured. But the belief that truth is attainable does not entail the belief that we have attained it. Such a regard for truth does not permit us the illusion that we have appropriated more than a fragmentary vision of the truth. It does not permit us with ease to identify the truth. Rather, it places upon us the difficult and tortuous task of weighing with great care whatever beliefs we may regard as true, holding them always as open to challenge, and to change in the light of further evidence and fresh reasons. In short, although a due regard for truth involves a passionate and unswerving loyalty to certain specific beliefs, although it involves a kind of fanaticism, it is an unyielding commitment to just those beliefs which will not permit the fanatic to develop.

Indoctrination, nonetheless, has a perfectly good and important role to play in education. There is nothing in these remarks which would suggest otherwise. Like the development of attitudes, indoctrination may be useful as the prelude to teaching. Just as we need not cut off the hand of every child or thrust one of every fifty into the street in order that they may understand the dangers of knives and highways, and learn to obey the rules established to protect their lives, so we need not offer reasons for every belief we think important for children and adults to hold. On the other hand, we have no warrant to inculcate beliefs for which there is no good reason, or for which we can offer no good reason; and we must be prepared to offer reasons or evidence when they are requested. Though indoctrination may, in many contexts, be both good and necessary, it can never be justified for its own sake. It can only be justified as the nearest approximation to teaching available at the moment. Indoctrination, in short, may be sanctioned only in order that beliefs adopted may later be redeemed by reasons, only that they may be vindicated by teaching.

III. TEACHING, LEARNING, AND EDUCATION

To say that indoctrination plays a legitimate role in education, but is, nonetheless, peripheral to the concept of teaching, is already to strike at an immensely important and powerful distinction. It is already to begin to describe the logical relations that exist between teaching and learning on the one hand, and teaching and education on the other.

Learning is commonly defined as any change of behavior. This definition or one like it, has certain advantages for the science of psychology. It makes it possible to deal with learning as an observable phenomena, which is important if the study of learning is to remain a scientific inquiry. Such a definition, nonetheless, is wholly inadequate to capture what we normally mean by "learning." Ordinarily, we would regard a change of behavior at best as only *evidence* of learning, and we would not regard it as either necessary or sufficient evidence. A change of behavior in many contexts is not evidence that one has *learned* something new, but only that he has decided *to do* something new. A bank cashier who begins to embezzle, has not necessarily learned anything not learned by the cashier who does not embezzle. And this is so, because it is not obvious that learning to embezzle is distinguished in any way from simply learning to keep books. In this case, as in unnumbered others like it, a change of behavior is not sufficient evidence that anything new has been learned. But for exactly the same reasons it cannot be necessary evidence either. A person may learn to do something and yet never in his life decide to do it, or in any other way display his knowledge or capacities. Unless such a supposition can be shown to be absurd or meaningless, it cannot be held that a change of behavior is a necessary part of what we *mean* by learning.

The important point to observe, however, is that regardless of our definition of learning, it must remain true that *every* point on the teaching continuum is *equally* a point of learning. Or, more precisely, every point on the teaching continuum, as much as any other, represents a method of bringing about learning. It is not therefore anything implicit in the concept of learning itself which distributes the teaching activities in certain logical relations along the teaching continuum. They are distributed by the logic of the concept ' teaching' and not by the logic of the concept ' learning.' People can and will learn by propaganda, indoctrination, and lies. They can be brought to adopt certain patterns of behavior by conditioning, by intimidation, by deceit, by threats of physical violence. Indeed, these different methods appear on the teaching continuum *because* they are all ways of bringing about learning, and because it is true *in some sense*, that teaching aims at bringing about learning. It is not true, however, that every method of bringing about learning is equally a method of teaching. Some are more central to the concept of teaching than are others.

It is because of this logical fact that the teaching concept can yield a continuum of the kind I have described. It is an immensely important fact, however, that the concept of learning cannot yield such a continuum, and that it cannot for the following reasons. The concept of teaching includes within its limits a whole assemblage of human activities. Teaching stands related to instruction, training, indoctrination, and conditioning as genus to species. But it is not the relation between genus and species which is represented on the teaching continuum. Every point within the limits of teaching is a species of a certain genus, and *in this respect*, no point is different from any other. The continuum, however, is directional; it is directional in a way that membership in a certain genus would not warrant. What is represented by the direction of the continuum is a logical relation between the *members* of the genus, indicating the extent to which they do or do not instantiate the properties of central importance in the logic of the concept. The concept of teaching is peculiar in the respect that not only does it stand related to certain activities as genus to species, but there is also *between* its species a discernable order.

If we consider learning to be a human activity, then it will also stand related to such things as drill, memorization, practice, and study, as genus to species. But among the species of learning there is *no* corresponding logical order of the kind that exists among activities of teaching. That is to say, the activities of learning fall under the concept as members of a class. It makes no sense to ask whether insight is more central logically to the concept of learning than, say, drill or practice or any other learning activity. But it *does* make sense to ask whether instruction is more central to the concept of teaching than, say, indoctrination. In short, teaching is a vague concept, but learning is not.

We might discover that some activities on the teaching continuum are more efficient or effective than others in bringing about learning, or that some methods of teaching are more appropriate to certain types of materials to be learned. But these distinctions cannot be discovered in the concept of learning itself. They must be discovered by empirical study. And such studies might show that the most effective methods of bringing about learning do not fall within the province of teaching at all. If that were to happen, it would follow that teachers ought *not* to adopt the most effective or efficient means of bringing about learning. In short, teaching and learning are conceptually independent *in the sense that* we cannot discover in the concept of learning, any principles sufficient to distinguish those kinds of learning aimed at in teaching from those which are not.

Now this may sound like an utterly fantastic and unwarranted claim, but it is not. Suppose it is true that by their consequences, we can identify many different kinds of learning. We can discriminate between learning habits and learning to obey certain principles, between acquiring belief sets and conditioned responses, or between learning by insight and by rote memorization. It is quite conceivable that different kinds of learning can be related to different points on the teaching continuum, and therefore, can be ordered in a certain relation to each other and some identified as more appropriate to teaching than others. For example, there may be a certain kind of learning which would result in a non-evidential belief set, and which might therefore be related to the methods of propaganda or indoctrination. Similarly, learning certain habits or skills might be related, more or less, to training or conditioning.[4] If this is so, then different kinds of learning can be placed in an order similar to the order of the teaching continuum. But the point is that this order is imposed upon the phenomena by the logic of the concept 'teaching.' There is no such order discoverable among species of learning. We can, in short, discriminate between kinds of learning and iden-tify which are appropriately aimed at in teaching only if we *bring* to the concept of learning some principles or presuppositions which are derived from the concept of teaching. This is, in fact, what we usually do when we "select" from studies of learning those insights and truths which we think will be of practical use in classroom instruction. The fact remains that no species of learning is more centrally related to the concept of learning than is any other, and therefore when we discover how to bring about learning, it does not follow necessarily that we have discovered how to do anything we are concerned to do in teaching.

---

[4] I do not suppose there is in fact such a correspondence between kinds of learning and methods of enhancing learning. On the other hand, I see no logical reason why there should not be.

But what is the significance of this fact? The most immediate and far-reaching conclusion is a somewhat negative one. It is not clear within what limits or on what grounds we are warranted in deriving a theory of teaching from a theory of learning. To what extent, in other words, can our knowledge of learning be made to yield, in a logically defensible way, some principles which can be normative for the conduct of teaching? Indeed, one may ask whether there is any logically well-founded principle which will suffice to mediate the inference from the management of learning to the practice of teaching.

The problem arises because the concept of learning is of greater dimensions than the concept of teaching described in our topology. But the concept represented in that topology is the one we normally employ when we think about teaching in the setting of the school. How do we know then, that when we study certain phenomena of learning we are concerned with phenomena which fall within the more narrow limits of teaching? The fact is that apart from assumptions or presuppositions concerning the activity of teaching we do not know when our studies are relevant to the activity of teaching and when they are not. The methods of instruction and the techniques of deceit are both ways of inducing learning. On what possible grounds then, are we more concerned to master one than the other? Can it be that at this point we manifest a presupposition that one is in some sense more relevant to the practice of teaching than the other? On what grounds can we justify such a presupposition? Apart from some theory of teaching, assumptions of this kind have no warrant; and yet without such assumptions, we have no grounds for an inference from the principles of learning to the principles of teaching. In order to profit from our studies of learning, the logically prior problem is not to develop a general theory of learning, but to develop a theory of teaching. The topology of teaching described in these pages is a step in that direction.

There are, however, at least two other ways of meeting the logical problem posed by the conceptual relation between teaching and learning. The most attractive alternative is simply to extend the teaching concept so that it has a scope of equal dimensions with the concept of learning. Teaching understood in such an inclusive sense, may be defined as any activity the primary purpose of which is to induce learning. Thus, the concept of teaching can be made to include within its limits all the endless activities which appear on the extended continuum, including the use of deceit, propaganda and outright lies. Such a move would suffice to guarantee that every discovery about the conduct of the learning process would have immediate and valid implications for the conduct of teaching. But the logical problem would not be solved. It would simply be made to appear at a different point. We would then have two concepts of teaching, a very inclusive sense and another more narrow sense. The problem then remains. Apart from some unexamined assumptions or presuppositions, we have no way of knowing when our knowledge of teaching in the wider sense is relevant to the conduct of teaching in the more restricted sense. We are left without any logical principle which will mediate the inference required.[5]

The second method of resolving this logical difficulty has to do less with the relation between teaching and learning and more with the relation between teaching and education. It may be argued that the construction of the teaching continuum is merely the consequence of certain social values which we share. It is because of our liberal-democratic tradition or because of our rational-humanistic inheritance that we do not regard the use of lies, propaganda and deceit as proper instruments of teaching. Apart from certain assumed values, it may be argued, any means of inducing learning, however barbarous they may seem to us, are perfectly bona fide methods of teaching. Thus, what we have been concerned with is not the difference between activities of teaching on the one hand, and other methods of bringing about learning on the other hand. Instead, it may be argued, that we have been concerned only to discriminate between good or socially sanctioned methods of teaching and bad or socially proscribed methods. In short, it might be held that the construction of the teaching continuum is possible only because of certain values which are presupposed in it, and that all we require in the way of presuppositions about teaching is adequately provided by our commitment to these values.

This view, however, is fundamentally mistaken. The teaching continuum is in fact neutral as regards the different options of value from which men may choose. The relation between instruction and indoctrination, for example, has nothing to do with any presupposed values. The relation between them has been described on grounds of logic only. Between the

---

[5] There is a third way of meeting this problem. It could be argued that the kinds of learning aimed at in teaching are only a special case of the wider phenomena of learning. Thus whatever one discovers about the process of inducing learning must A FORTIORI be true also of the activity of inducing learning by teaching. But what is the meaning of the phrase "special case of"? Does it point to a relation of class membership, class inclusion or to some other deductive relation?

Consider the following concepts and the relations of the members of the classes generated by each.

   a. 'activities aimed at inducing learning'
   b. 'activities aimed at inducing learning by teaching'

The class (b) is said to be a special case of (a) in the sense that b < a. Thus whatever is true of every member of the class (a) is true of every member of (b). But the class generated by (b) has a greater intension than the class whose members fall under (a). Thus the members of the class generated by (b) have certain properties NOT shared by other sub-sets falling under (a), and the problem is that in the present case, our concern is with exactly those features of the intension of the class (b) by virtue of which it is a sub-set of (a) and NOT those by virtue of which it is a "special case of" (a). Thus, it may be admitted that (b) is a "special case of" (a) in the sense that b < a. But this observation, though true, is not the kind of observation which will meet the difficulty posed by the relation between teaching and learning. What we need to study about the activity of teaching has to do with those respects which are not relevant to its being "a special case of" activities aimed at inducing learning.

activities of instructing and indoctrinating, there are certain striking resemblances. But there are also substantial differences. They are activities with different purposes. They aim at the development of different kinds of belief systems. They are differently related to a concern for truth. The process of each is differently related to the purpose of each. These relationships have nothing to do with the acceptance or rejection of any social values whatever. The logical relations will be the same whether we approve of indoctrination as a method of education or not. These distinctions will hold whether in our moral sentiments we are inclined to aristocracy, democracy or fascism. In this sense, the constructing of the teaching continuum does not rest upon any prior assumptions concerning what is valuable and what is not. All the difficult questions of values concerning the goals of education remain undecided and untouched by the topology of teaching. In this sense, such a topology is genuinely formal and neutral.

Moreover, the view that instruction is more centrally related to teaching than indoctrination has nothing to do with the relative value of one over the other, or with our preference of one. It has to do simply with the fact that in so far as the conduct of indoctrination possesses certain properties, it resembles instruction, and as it lacks these properties it resembles propaganda. And as this change occurs and indoctrination tends to assume the characteristics of propaganda, it becomes increasingly difficult to substitute the concept of "teaching" for the concept of "indoctrination" without a change in meaning. The topology of teaching therefore is not based upon any value presuppositions, but only on a series of logical distinctions.

From the topology of teaching it does follow, however, that education may be accomplished by other methods than teaching. In short, the idea of education, like the idea of learning, is of considerably larger dimensions than the idea of teaching. Education includes all of the enormously diverse means by which we learn, and these range all the way from the intricate processes of socialization to the rather formal methods of teaching mathematics and grammar. Propagandizing, lying, and intimidating are all methods we may use to educate. Education is therefore like an instrument. It can be used for any purpose men may adopt. It may be used to barbarize or to civilize. It may be used to liberate the heroic capacities of men and make them free or it may be used to make them cowards and slaves. Education is the kind of activity which may be adopted for many purposes. That is why the problem of value is important for educators. We must seek some grounds for determining what shall be our purposes. But though it is true that education can be used to accomplish many different purposes, it is not true that teaching is a method of education adequate to every purpose. One of the most difficult of all questions in educational theory is the question to what extent and within what limits shall we employ or be permitted to employ teaching as the method of education. In the construction of the teaching continuum, no resolution to these perpetual questions of value is presupposed. Education is an adequate instrument for barbarization, but teaching is not. Teaching is that human activity which is preeminently suited to enhance the human capacity for action. It is that activity of men which being engaged in, contains the conditions for the nurture of free human beings.

7

Knowing and Learning

KENNETH STRIKE

It is my purpose in this article to investigate the concepts of knowing and learning and their interrelations, and to suggest some implications for education. Thus, I am concerned with the following three questions:

(1) What does it mean to know something?
(2) What does it mean to learn something?
(3) Assuming that knowing and learning are basic goals of education, what follows from an analysis of these concepts for how we should teach?

The reader should be warned at the beginning that these are difficult and complicated questions, much too difficult to be given adequate treatment in a short article. Thus, although reasons are given for the conclusions reached, it is my intent to be suggestive rather than rigorous and to provide an overview of the problems involved rather than an exhaustive analysis of any one of them. Footnotes are used to indicate where more detailed discussions of some of the problems may be found.

KNOWING

Any discussion of the nature of knowledge must begin with the distinction between *knowing how* and *knowing that*.[1] Although there are some

Kenneth Strike is Assistant Professor of Education at Cornell University. Especially prepared for this edition.

[1] See Gilbert Ryle, *The Concept of Mind* (New York: Barnes and Noble, Inc., 1949), pp. 25–60.

interesting exceptions, the types of things we are willing to call knowledge generally fall into one of these two categories. Since what one knows when he *knows that* is a proposition, *knowing that* is often called propositional knowledge. For our purposes, a proposition can be defined as a sentence that asserts something and is, therefore, either true or false. Thus, claims about *knowing that* typically raise questions concerning truth or error, evidence and argument, and justification and confirmation. As noted later, to correctly claim to *know that* is to believe a proposition that is true and for which one has adequate evidence.

Knowing how, on the other hand, is a matter of possessing some skill. To *know how* is to be able to do something. To justify a claim to *know how*, it is usually necessary only to be able to exhibit the skill under the proper circumstances.

Generally, *knowing how* and *knowing that* are logically independent of one another. That is, it is not necessarily the case that in order to know that something is true, one must also possess some skill; nor is it necessarily the case that in order to know how to do something, one must also know that some proposition is true. Concerning this latter case, it should be kept in mind that knowing how to do something and knowing the truth of some proposition about how to do something are quite different things. People who can provide accurate descriptions of how to do something are often not able to do what they can describe, and people who can perform some skill quite ably may be unable to provide an accurate description of what they are doing. Numerous illustrations can be found for this point in the world of sports. A good coach (who presumably possesses considerable propositional knowledge about a sport) may be a poor player, and a good player (who presumably possesses considerable skill in a sport) may know little about how the game is played.

It does not follow from this, however, that there are not cases where skills do, in fact, depend on the possession of propositional knowledge. An example of this is chess, where a high degree of skill often depends on a substantial propositional knowledge of the rules and strategies of the game. Typically, however, *knowing how* depends more on practice than on propositional knowledge. For a wide variety of skills, practicing the skill is more important in being able to perform it than is being able to describe it. With such skills as knowing how to swim, knowing how to drive, or knowing how to read, propositional knowledge about how the acts are performed is largely irrelevant to actually possessing those skills, whereas practice is all important in their acquisition. The connection between practice and *knowing how* perhaps suggests the point of the emphasis on doing as opposed to telling in some educational theories. With regard to *knowing how*, there is surely considerable truth in the observation that people learn what they do rather than what they are told. It is, however, probably a mistake to generalize from such facts to the conditions for the acquisition of propositional knowledge. Indeed, it is not altogether clear what learning by doing would mean as a prescription for the acquisition of propositional knowledge.

If *knowing how* depends largely on practice, *knowing that* depends (in a somewhat different sense of 'depend') on the truth of one's belief and in having evidence for what one believes. This comment can best be developed by sketching what has been for some time among philosophers the "orthodox" view concerning the nature of propositional knowledge. The question concerning propositional knowledge may be asked as follows: Suppose we are told that some person, let us label him X, knows some proposition labeled P: What are the conditions under which such a claim will be true? The orthodox view holds that there are three such conditions. Thus, 'X knows that P' will be true when:

(1) X believes that P.
(2) P is true.
(3) X has adequate evidence for P.[2]

Let us briefly consider each of these criteria.

Philosophers have traditionally taken the question "What is knowledge?" to concern which of our beliefs we may consider to be knowledge. Plato, in the dialogue entitled *Theatetus* represents Socrates as asking whether it is possible that whatever a person believes is knowledge. When it is noted that this idea has some odd consequences, the question is then formulated to concern how we are to distinguish those beliefs that are knowledge from those that are not. What *kinds* of belief are knowledge? Plato's approach seems sensible. Often the question as to whether or not someone knows something is a question about whether what he believes meets the other criteria for knowledge. Thus, when a person's belief that P turns out to be a true proposition for which he has adequate evidence, we conclude that he knows that P; whereas, if he claims to know that P, but if either P is false or if he does not have adequate evidence for P, we conclude that he only believes that P. These facts suggest that knowledge is a kind of belief. The most conclusive piece of evidence here, however, is the fact that the claim 'X knows that P, but he does not believe that P' seems clearly self-contradictory. Thus, it is reasonable to conclude that belief is one condition of knowledge.

Plato, however, was right when he held that not everything a person believes can be said to be knowledge. What properties must a belief have, then, if it is to count as knowledge? Philosophers have typically wanted to add two conditions. First, a belief can count as knowledge only if the proposition believed is true. Clearly, if we believe that the proposition that

---

[2] This definition of *knowing that* is developed and discussed by Isreal Scheffler, *Conditions of Knowledge* (Chicago: Scott, Foresman and Company, 1965). A less demanding but still worthy discussion may also be found in Thomas F. Green, *The Activities of Teaching* (New York: McGraw-Hill Book Company, Inc., 1971), pp. 65–94.

someone claims to know is false, we will deny that he actually knows it. The claim that 'X knows that P, and P is false' is self-contradictory. But neither, as Plato also pointed out, is knowledge to be identified with true belief. Suppose, for example, we knew someone who believed that the world was round, but who gave as his reason for this belief the fact that only by assuming the world to be round could we explain why the sun god (who is known to have preference for spherical shapes) would condescend to shine on it. We may want to hold that such a person's belief that the world was round was correct, but we would hardly be willing to say that the person knew the world to be round. Neither are we likely to ascribe knowledge where a person has a true belief but is unable to provide any reason for his belief. Here again, a sentence of the form 'X knows that P, but does not have adequate evidence that P' seems problematic. That it does not seem to be as obviously problematic as the claim to know what is false has led some philosophers to distinguish a strong and a weak sense of knowing, identifying the former with true belief for which a person has adequate evidence and the latter with true belief unsupported by evidence. Typically, however, these considerations have motivated philosophers to add a third condition. Thus, it is usual to hold that to know it is necessary not only to possess a true belief but also to have adequate evidence for the belief. It should be noted that this final condition is to be interpreted such that it is not sufficient to be aware of some fact that constitutes adequate evidence for one's belief. It is also necessary to see that this is the case. One must be aware of the line of reasoning according to which the facts that he has are evidence for the truth of the proposition that he claims to know.

LEARNING

Just as one can distinguish between *knowing how* and *knowing that*, one can also distinguish between *learning how* and *learning that*. It is worth noting, however, that learning has a wider range of application than knowing. For example, one can sensibly talk about learning attitudes although it is unlikely that there is any kind of knowing that corresponds to this sort of learning. Although one may learn attitudes, it is unlikely that one can sensibly speak of knowing an attitude. In keeping with the scope of this article, however, it will be necessary to restrict the topic, so that the following discussion is limited to *learning that*.

It has been frequently noted that to claim that a person has learned something does not in most cases commit us to holding that he knows anything. This is most easily seen in that although it is self-contradictory to hold that someone knows something that is false, it is not self-contradictory to hold that he has learned something that is false. Thus, it is wrong to say that Jones knows that the world is flat. Since the world is not flat, Jones cannot know that it is. However, there is no corresponding problem with holding that Jones has learned that the world is flat. If, then, one can learn what is false, but cannot know what is false, then learning does not imply knowing. One can learn that P and not know that P.

It must be added quickly, however, that there are cases in which when we hold that someone has learned something, we commit ourselves to the truth of what he has learned. We would not, for example, say that Jones had learned the solution to some problem unless we thought that the solution that Jones had learned was the correct one. It is conceivable that in such cases we might not only feel a commitment to the truth of what Jones has learned but a commitment to Jones's having adequate evidence for what he had learned as well. If Jones, for example, claimed to have learned the solution to the problem of how to cheaply produce fresh water from salt water, we might expect him to produce reasonable evidence for the adequacy of his solution before we would hold that he had actually learned it, even though we believed his solution to be correct. Here we seem to have a use of 'learn' in which 'learn' approximates 'comes to know.'

These remarks suggest that it may be useful to distinguish between two kinds of learning, separating a kind of learning where learning does not imply coming to know from a kind of learning where learning does imply coming to know. I call these weak and strong learning, respectively. Although this distinction was suggested by some features of ordinary usage, there are other and perhaps more persuasive reasons for making it. Most interestingly, in education we are often appropriately concerned to produce not just learning, but knowledge as well. We would surely not feel ourselves to have succeeded because our students had learned something if it turned out that what they had learned was largely mistaken or if, even when what they had learned was true, they failed to have any appreciation of the reasons for believing it. Thus, even if the distinction between weak and strong learning were not to some degree reflected by ordinary discourse, it would be useful to construct such a distinction for the purposes of a coherent discussion of educational problems.

Thus far, the defining property of weak learning has been expressed negatively. To say that X learns that P in the weak sense does not commit us to X knows that P, and is hardly a sufficient characterization. Telling us what weak learning is not is not very informative about what weak learning is. Thus, I would like to propose the following analysis of weak learning. I shall hold that 'X has learned that P' is true when:

(1) X can recall P (in appropriate circumstances).
(2) X understands P.
(3) X believes P.

The first of these conditions I call the memory condition. It seems clear that we will be unwilling to say that a student has learned P unless he is able to produce P when asked a question to which P is considered an answer. Thus, a student will not be considered to have learned who the first president was unless he can produce the name George Washington in response to the question, "Who was the first president?" or (to suggest a somewhat weaker criterion) unless he can select the name of George Washington from an appropriate list in response to this question. Memory is therefore a condition of learning.

Memory, however, is obviously not a sufficient criterion. Let us consider a case where a student learns to recognize the sentence P as the expected response to a particular question, but does not understand what P means. Suppose, for example, that a student was able to produce the expression $f = ma$ in response to a question about one of Newton's laws of motion, but on further examination was shown not to understand what the expression meant. Although in such cases we might say that the student had learned to make the response $f = ma$, we would be reluctant to say that he had learned that $f = ma$. It follows that the ability to comprehend the meaning of some proposition P is a condition of learning that P.

A third condition is necessary. Although a person may be able to produce the response P to a question for which P is an appropriate response, and although he understands what P means, we are still unlikely to hold that he has learned that P unless he also believes that P. Suppose that some student in response to a test question, "Who discovered America?" provided the response, "Columbus," although he was convinced that the honor was appropriately ascribed to Leif Erickson and that he was merely answering "Columbus" because he thought that this was the answer expected of him. The most reasonable way to describe such a situation is to deny that the student has learned that Columbus discovered America and to hold that instead he had learned that "let's say" the history book asserts that Columbus discovered America. If this is the case, then belief is a condition of learning.

Although these conditions are necessary if we are to say that someone has learned something, they are not sufficient. To have learned that P, it is necessary not only that one be in the states described by conditions 1–3 but also that he has gotten in those conditions and has gotten in them in the right way. For example, to say that someone had learned that P implies that at some previous time he was ignorant of that P. You cannot learn what you already know. To have learned is not only to be in a certain condition but to have gotten there. In addition, it is likely that only some ways of "getting there" will count as learning. If it should turn out, for example, that some kinds of knowledge result from a process of biological maturation, that is, they are acquired like one acquires teeth, it is unlikely that we will speak of learning having taken place. It seems, therefore, that to adequately analyze learning we will not only have to talk about results but also of processes. Indeed, it is likely that a thorough analysis of X learns that P consists of two types of conditions that may be called "result conditions" and "process conditions." The previously listed conditions 1–3 constitute, in my opinion, an adequate analysis of the "result conditions" of learning. Since I am largely concerned with these result conditions, no more is said here about the process conditions except to point out the need of extending the analysis of learning in this direction.

As the label 'strong' suggests, the analysis of strong learning, where learning means coming to know, can be achieved by adding two more conditions to the analysis of weak learning. As the reader might have already guessed, weak learning can be "changed into" strong learning merely by adding the remaining two conditions of knowledge to the analysis. Thus, we have a case of strong learning when, in addition to conditions 1–3 and whatever process conditions are necessary to supplement them being met, it is also true that:

(4) P is true.
(5) X has adequate evidence that P.

The reader should note that since strong learning is coming to know, whatever argument might be needed to justify the inclusion of these conditions in the analysis of strong learning has in effect already been given in the analysis of knowledge. Thus, conditions 1–5 are a sufficient statement of the result conditions that comprise an analysis of the strong sense of learning.

The virtue of this analysis is that it provides a relatively complete statement of the immediate ends toward which any attempt to bring about *learning that* must be directed. Moreover, it can be used to suggest some of the relations between these ends and to make some observations about relative priorities in teaching. Each of these five conditions suggests certain problems with which any adequate theory of education must deal.

THE MEMORY CONDITION

The memory condition suggests what is perhaps the most elemental problem of education. What are the conditions under which information is retained? How can students be helped to remember what they are taught? Such questions can easily lead to the most abstract problems of learning theory and information theory, and to complicated questions concerning the relations between learning and motivation. Among the more interesting questions posed by this condition of learning are those that concern the relation of this condition to the next. To what extent is retention dependent on comprehension? Empirical research and common sense both suggest that understanding in some way facilitates learning.

Having made these fairly obvious comments, it should be emphasized that as far as an adequate philosophy of learning is concerned, the most important thing about memory is to get beyond it. If the way in which we in education talk about and test for learning is an indication, all too often what a person has learned is treated as though it were identical with what he can remember. Learning often is defined operationally in terms of providing the appropriate response to a given question. The analysis of learning developed here reveals such procedure as overly simplifying the concept of learning. Thus, an adequate theory of learning must keep in mind that retention of information is a necessary condition of learning and thus of much else in education, but also that to define educational success overly in terms of retention of information can lead to an impoverishment of educational goals.

THE UNDERSTANDING CONDITION

It is possible to learn to repeat the proposition P in response to some question without knowing what P means. This is possible, but it is presumably not particularly desirable. Thus, an adequate theory of learning will have to address the question as to how students can be gotten to understand as well as to remember.

Often the concept of understanding has been given emphasis in order to point out the inadequacies of rote learning. Rote learning, the repetition of a desired phrase in response to a question to which the phrase is considered the correct answer, is held to be objectionable in that although it encourages the student to associate one phrase with another, it does not provide the conditions under which the student may learn what a phrase says. Rote learning, thus, seems more appropriate to teaching parrots than children.

It is, however, a great deal easier to decide what does not promote understanding than what does. To decide this latter question, it is necessary to answer such questions as "What is it for a sentence to mean something?", "What is it to understand what a sentence means?", and "How does one come to understand?" Some philosophers have held that for a sentence to mean something is for it to say something about how the world appears and that, therefore, to understand a sentence is to know what the world would look like if the sentence were true.[3] This has led to an emphasis on experience in education. Coming to understand a sentence is conceived of as a matter of learning to correctly connect the words with the experiences which they describe. This suggests that learning what a sentence means presupposes a background of experience with the areas of existence which the sentence is about. Conversely, it suggests that an overly "bookish" education, one in which ideas are studied in isolation from those domains of experience which they are ideas about, is likely to result in the learning of little but empty phrases and verbal associations.

---

[3] See, for example, A. J. Ayer's discussion of the verifiability criterion of meaning in A. J. Ayer, *Language, Truth and Logic* (New York: Dover Publications, Inc., 1946), pp. 33–45.

Other philosophers have emphasized that learning what a set of words means is a matter of learning their correct use, i.e., how they are employed by some community of language users.[4] To know what some word 'W' means is to know the rules according to which some things are and other things are not called 'W' and to know the rules according to which the word 'W' may be correctly placed in a sentence. Since learning the meaning of words is a matter of learning how people use them, this view has led philosophers to emphasize the importance of participation in actual social situations. We learn to speak a language, according to this argument, by participating in the activities in conjunction with which the language is spoken. Although this view and the preceding one have received varying emphasis by different philosophers, they are by no means incompatible, and may be found on occasion living happily side by side in the views of the same philosopher.[5] Indeed, both views point to a similar conclusion. Language is most readily learned in conjunction with those situations in which it normally functions and which it normally describes. Thus, to separate a form of discourse from its "usual home" is the first step in teaching the student mere patterns of words and empty clichés, instead of meaningful ideas. It does not follow from this that we should tear down the school walls and involve the student in "real life" situations. It does, however, follow that we must bring enough of "real life" into the school (perhaps in the form of materials, equipment, field trips, sometimes simply illustrations) so that the student can make the connection between the words and what the words are about. The price of failure is meaningless verbal learning.

THE BELIEF CONDITION

This condition poses a paradox. To have learned that P, it is necessary for a student to believe that P. Students are gotten to believe by what I call persuasion, i.e., *any* means whereby belief may be produced. Yet although we are usually quite willing to assert learning to be a goal of education, we are typically reluctant to hold that persuading students of our beliefs is an equally appropriate goal. Is this not inconsistent? If learning entails believing, can we commit ourselves to bringing about learning without committing ourselves to persuading our students to believe something? Three comments will help here. First, there are cases where we are quite legitimately interested in persuading students of something. If we find that we have a student who believes that $2 + 2 = 6$, we must be legitimately concerned to persuade him that $2 + 2 = 4$. There is little reason to treat idiosyncratic arithmetical opinion as anything but a problem to be overcome. Second,

---

[4] This theme is developed by Ludwig Wittgenstein, *Philosophical Investigations* (New York: Macmillan Publishing Co., Inc., 1953).

[5] With allowance for a different vocabulary, both views can be found in Dewey's writings.

there are other cases where it is less obvious that there is something appropriately called "the correct opinion," when we should be more concerned that the student have a *reasonable* opinion than that he have *our* opinion. In many cases it is more of a triumph to have a student hold a mistaken opinion for good reasons than it is to have a student hold a correct opinion for no reasons or for poor reasons. One of the things that may be learned from this example is that it is sometimes not desirable to formulate too precisely what it is that we want a student to learn, particularly that we not formulate our goals in terms of some specific set of propositions. Rather, we should be concerned that the student learn some propositions that meet less specific criteria which can be summed up by the phrase "a reasonable opinion." Third, and most important, is the fact that, with respect to persuasion, the ethical questions raised seem to outweigh questions of technique. We are inclined to think that it is more important to persuade legitimately than efficiently, that the question "How may we rightly persuade?" is more important than the question "How can we effectively persuade?" Thus, the condition of belief raises foremost what may be termed the problem of legitimate influence. We need to know the answers to questions concerning the extent to which and the means by which we may transmit our opinions to others. Here, we should note that the concept of giving reasons looms very large in the ethics of persuasion. Generally, we are inclined to think that it is permissible to attempt to get a student to agree with us by indicating what evidence points to our opinion as being the correct one. Other means of persuasion, indoctrination, punishing, or disagreement are less than ethical.

THE TRUTH CONDITION

This condition differs from the other four in that it does not specify or require some change to be brought about in the student if he is to learn. The truth of what a person has learned or what he believes depends not on how he has learned it or how he believes it. It does not depend on anything about the student. Rather, it depends on the world being the way the proposition learned says it is. Thus, the truth condition does not specify a goal of teaching the same way that the other conditions of learning do; 'truth' is not a name for some state of a person or some capacity in the way that memory is.

It is, of course, desirable that students learn true propositions, not false ones, and a number of educational problems are immediately suggested. How do we know what is true? Who is to decide what is true for purposes of instruction? What sort of atmosphere is most conducive to the pursuit, discovery, and dissemination of truth? Thus, it is at this point that a philosophy of learning becomes involved with the most difficult questions not only of epistemology but also of social and political philosophy. Once we assume the desirability of teaching true propositions and not false ones,

we will be required to answer both the epistemologic.
are to distinguish between truth and error and the poli
is to be empowered to make such decisions when th
what we shall teach. To address ourselves to the forme.
have to decide the respective claims of science, revelation,
ment, insight, and reason to provide the intellectual aut
what we should believe. To address ourselves to the latter
have to examine the question of the respective rights of ec̠   ̣ᴜɪ̣s, parents,
legislators, ethnic and religious subcultures, and governments to decide
whose "truth" shall be taught.

THE EVIDENCE CONDITION

If we wish to transmit knowledge and not just true belief to our students, we will have to be concerned not only in communicating propositions to be believed but reasons for believing them as well. However, if we are to indicate to our students the evidence for what we ask them to believe, then the student will first have to come to understand what counts as evidence for something. Thus, a central ingredient of an adequate theory of learning will be an account of how a student comes to learn what counts as a good reason and of how he comes to be able to recognize a mistake.

Of course, we ought to be interested in more than having our students be able to recognize good evidence for believing something when they see it. We should also be interested in cultivating the student's ability to find out evidence for himself, in creating the student's capacity for independent thought. Thus, we shall also want to ask ourselves the question of how it is that people learn how to think. How can schools be made instruments for the creation of reflective, intellectually independent people?[6]

Whatever else, the answers to these questions may suggest about how to teach, the evidence condition points to the following two comments about good instruction. First, if we are genuinely interested in transmitting knowledge, we must be sure that our teaching goes beyond a mere accounting of the conclusions of inquiry to a concern for the reasons as to why inquiry has reached these conclusions as well as a concern for what may be said for other opinions. It follows that an essential part of good teaching is the giving of reasons and that a condition of good teaching is an understanding of what counts as a good reason. (There is an unhappy tendency to identify expository teaching with the mere transmission of conclusions and to identify letting the student find out for himself as the "other alternative." This has the unfortunate consequence of obscuring the middle ground—a kind of expository teaching that is more concerned with relating evidence than conclusions.) Second, if we are interested in teaching good habits of thought,

---

[6] I know of no better source for a discussion of this question and its implications than John Dewey, *Democracy and Education* (New York: Macmillan Publishing Co., Inc., 1916), particularly Chapters 11 and 12. See the portions reprinted in this volume.

quiry must become a part of classroom activity. Consider that know-
how to think is a kind of *knowing how*. It is essentially a skill or, more
accurately, a set of skills. But skills are typically acquired as the result of
practice. There is no obvious reason to think that this will not hold equally
for learning how to think as learning how to swim, for example, and no more
reason to believe that trying to teach people how to think by describing how
it is done is any more plausible than trying to teach people to swim by telling
them how it is done. Of course, to practice an activity is to engage in it, and
to practice thinking is to engage in it. That suggests that the activity of
inquiry should be a standard part of a student's educational diet.

Thus far, these conditions of learning have been used merely to indicate
the kinds of questions that form a part of an adequate theory of learning and
to indicate my opinion of the general lines of a reasonable answer to some of
these questions. In addition, some general comments may be made about
these conditions and their interrelations.

It is first noted that these criteria as ordered have some of the conceptual properties usually ascribed to need hierarchies. To some extent, the
earlier conditions are necessary for the achievement of the later ones.
Memory is a condition of belief; weak learning is a condition of strong
learning. Moreover, later conditions can be regarded as the end or
fulfillment of the process of learning so that part of the value of the earlier
conditions consists in their being means to the later ones. Thus, our interest
in accomplishing the goals specified by the earlier criteria is largely instrumental whereas we often treat the later ones as being valuable for their
own sakes. The relation between weak and strong learning is, therefore,
somewhat analogous to the relation between the need for food and the need
for love. Obviously, if we are to meet any of our other needs, including love,
the need for food must be met. Food thus plays an essential, but largely
instrumental role in human life. Love, however, is not sought for the sake of
something else, but for its own sake. In the same way we are interested in
weak learning as a means toward strong learning, but whereas strong learning may also be of instrumental value, we are often interested in strong
learning for its own sake. To some extent one can judge the maturity and
success of an educational system by noting where on this scale of criteria
attention is focused. An educational system in which attention is focused
entirely on weak learning is less mature and successful than one in which
weak learning is taken for granted and attention is focused on strong
learning.

We should also note that some of the ethical problems raised by the
belief criterion cannot be successfully resolved unless strong learning is
thought of as the end of the process of learning. At least one reason why
indoctrination is less desirable than giving reasons is that an indoctrinated
belief is unlikely to meet the evidence condition for strong learning. A student who has been indoctrinated to believe that P has not been provided

with adequate evidence for P. However, the contrary is the case where a student is led to believe something by being given reasons. Since in such cases belief is produced as a result of the student's considering the evidence for some proposition, the evidence condition for strong learning is more likely to be met. But if this is the case, then insofar as we are only interested in weak learning to the exclusion of strong learning, a persuasive objection to indoctrination disappears. If our goals do not extend beyond wanting to get our students to remember, understand, and believe something, then there is no reason except simple efficiency in producing belief for preferring one way of inducing belief to any other. One is not, however, likely to find indoctrination objectionable if the only criterion is efficiency.

The distinction between weak and strong learning can be used to suggest other features about an adequate theory of learning. First, the questions raised by the conditions for weak learning belong for the most part to the discipline of psychology, whereas the questions raised by the additional criteria of strong learning are essentially philosophical questions. Thus, questions concerning the conditions that promote remembering, understanding, and believing are largely the property of psychologists, whereas questions concerning the nature of truth and how it is discovered, the rights and obligations of various groups in determining what should be taught, and the nature of adequate evidence are for the most part questions that have been the concern of philosophers. It follows that an adequate theory of learning will require the cooperation of psychologists and philosophers. It also follows that a theory of learning that is overly dependent on psychology will exhibit a tendency to reduce learning theory to a concern with only weak learning, whereas a theory of learning that is overly dependent on philosophy is likely to overly ignore the empirical work on which an adequate knowledge of how to achieve weak learning (and subsequently strong learning) depends. Although one can find both problems in the theoretical research on learning, the former difficulty seems to be more of a real threat to actual educational practice.

The tendency to behave as though weak learning were all there was to learning may be exacerbated by the present demands for empirical rigor in the study and practice of education. Today one is expected to be able to state his goals in empirical terms, to be able to say how he will recognize them when he sees them. Otherwise, it is held that he will not know when he has succeeded, nor will he be able to find out when his teaching techniques work. Perhaps even worse, goals that cannot be empirically defined are meaningless and those who advocate them will turn out on analysis to be advocating nothing at all.[7] I am inclined to think that most of this is true. If we

---

[7] This thesis has manifested itself in what has been called the behavioral or instructional objectives movement. An early example of this sort of thought that nicely exhibits the point of view along with most of its defects is Robert F. Mager, *Preparing Instructional Objectives* (Palo Alto, California: Fearon Publishers, Inc., 1962).

cannot state some empirical criteria whereby we may recognize when we have succeeded, we do not know what we are doing and may actually not be aiming at anything at all. Unless this demand for empirical objectivity is formulated and executed with some sophistication, it can exert a marked trivializing effect on educational goals. It is the case that in principle any meaningful educational goal can be given some empirical content. It is also the case that some goals are more difficult to define this way than others. Weak and strong learning differ in this respect. It is easy, for example, to state behavioral criteria for recognizing when a student can remember something. It is harder, but still (for practical purposes) relatively simple, to translate the notions of understanding and believing into empirical terms. It is much less likely that concepts such as 'has adequate evidence' or 'knows how to think' will be successfully defined by a small number of easily listed behaviors even though such concepts do have behavioral implications. The difficulty is not that such concepts are meaningless, but that they are complicated. Thus, it is likely that an attempt to translate these concepts into a short and simple list of behaviors that would be suitable for classroom use will be most difficult if not quite futile. An excessive demand for such behavioral translations is, therefore, likely to end up ignoring such goals with a subsequent trivialization of educational objectives. Thus, although I do not think that an adequate theory of learning that is suitable for the guidance of most teaching activities has anything to fear from a serious and sophisticated empiricism, it has a great deal to fear from the more mindless empiricism that seems to be widely advocated.

This article has not been directed toward any specific conclusions. Its merit stems from having a reasonable idea of the "ingredients" of some educational goal, in this case, learning. It is hoped that a more sophisticated appreciation of the concept of learning will lead to a more sophisticated view of how learning is achieved. In conclusion, the reader's attention is directed to the central distinction of this article—that between weak and strong learning. This distinction is important, if for no other reason, because our educational ideologies often talk about creating knowledge, but our educational practice seems more oriented toward weak learning. The first step in resolving this tension is to notice it. It is to be hoped that the reader will add some steps of his own.

8

The Concept of Equality
in Education

B. Paul Komisar and Jerrold R. Coombs

This essay addresses itself to the perennial and prodigal question: What is equality in education? Concern with this question is ubiquitous and, according to some authors, particularly germane at the present moment in human affairs. Herbert Thelen's plea is as symptomatic of this concern as any other we might quote:

The imagination of the civilized world has been captured by the concept, pioneered but not perfected in America, of "equal educational opportunity for all." What does this mean? Does it mean, for example, equal opportunity to learn a particular body of knowledge set by the school—regardless of its meaningfulness to students having different capabilities and need? Or does it mean opportunity to learn whatever each child needs to learn in order to profit from his particular capabilities? Does it mean that every child in every state should have the same amount of money spent on him? Assuming that some teachers are better than others, who should get the best ones— the child who learns most readily or the one who learns least readily? What about the "culturally deprived" child, whose "background" has built-in resistance to learning; or the emotionally disturbed child, whose preoccupations keep him from listening; or the physiologically precocious or immature child, whose biological needs are out of step with the social possibilities for those of his age—What does equal opportunity mean here?[1]

B. Paul Komisar is Professor of Education at Temple University. Jerrold R. Coombs is Professor of Education at The University of British Columbia. B. Paul Komisar, and Jerrold R. Coombs, "The Concept of Equality in Education," *Studies in Philosophy and Education,* Vol. III, Number 3 (Fall, 1964), pp. 223–244. Used by permission.

[1] Herbert A. Thelen, *Education and the Human Quest* (New York: Harper & Row, Publishers, 1960), pp. 11–12.

It is to this question we address ourselves, though perhaps not in quite the way Thelen poses it. Thelen's concern is with what the equality principle requires of us in different areas of education. We approach the question obliquely, by way of a linguistic analysis of the *term* 'equality.'

In the course of this paper we advance and try to justify the following claims: There are two concepts of equality—'equal as same' and 'equal as fitting' tied usually to two different uses of language—descriptive and ascriptive.[2] The sameness concept has a determinate definition and a singular meaning in all contexts of application. Equality in the fittingness sense has an indeterminate definition; its meaning shifts across contexts and language users.[3] Since the principle of equal opportunity employs the fittingness concept, it is not possible to give it a unique and definite interpretation without prior ethical commitments. Therefore, the equality principle is a second-order principle, derivative with respect to the necessary first-order ethical premises. Nor can the equality principle itself confer distinctiveness on one philosophy of education *vis a vis* any other philosophy. Philosophies with different commitments can, all the same, champion their own version of equal opportunity.[4]

Though these are the only fish we care to fry here, there is much more to the story. 'Equality' and the equality principle seem always to have been with us in American education, from the classical liberals through the recent humane welfare theories of education. And even our contemporary austere educational Calvinists do not simply pump for a crash program in excellence. They pause to ask almost plaintively, can we be excellent and equal too? Indeed these contemporary educational philosophers, engaging in what has been called, euphemistically, "The Great Debate" have shown concern for only the narrow question of whether equal educational opportunity requires a common curriculum for all students, or variegated curricula in which students with unique clusters "interests, abilities, and needs" will find a clutch of studies peculiarly congenial to them.

But in addition to the areas enumerated by Thelen, we find other areas in which equality plays a disputed role. In the legal context, even before the Supreme Court unanimously supported the words "Separate educational facilities are inherently unequal," there were attempts to broaden 'equality' to cover "intangible" factors of schooling.

---

[2] This apt expression, the Fittingness Concept, was suggested to us by Harry S. Broudy. It is more suitable than our original label, the Fairness Concept. We take this opportunity to express our thanks to Broudy and James E. McClellan for their generously offered criticisms and, as custom would have it, absolve them of further responsibility.

[3] I.e., the sameness concept can be defined in the accepted way—more or less in terms of the necessary and sufficient conditions for applying or assessing applications of the term. The fittingness concept is not susceptible to definition in this way. The difference is roughly analogous to the divergence in definitional strategy one would follow with "brown" and "good" as applied to shoes.

[4] If one educational philosophy proclaims support of equal opportunity and another disavows it, to this extent they differ. But this is a trivial difference of sheer avowal or disavowal. Nothing of significance follows from it.

In the area of school finance, the equality principle has been invoked by supporters and opponents of federal aid. But surer indications of its importance here are the dispute over the variables to be included in equalization formulae and the surprising distinction made between equal expenditures and equal educational effort.

The concept of equality, then, stands astride the path of educational thought as does no other term. Indeed, it is one of the few terms employed in nearly all the departments of educational language. Add to this the presence of disputed meanings, and conceptual analysis needs no further temptation or justification. It may be that our analysis is wrongheaded, but it is honor enough to be part of the search for clarity. When arson is the desideratum, they also serve who only blow.

I. Two Concepts of Equality

A. THE SAMENESS CONCEPT

Let us begin putting meat on these abstract bones by contrasting two speech acts—one descriptive, the other ascriptive. Consider first a common sort of case wherein we say of students that they are of equal height or ability or have read an equal number of books. This we dub the descriptive use of 'equal' and put it on a par with reports of hair color and the like.

What is the sense of the term 'equal' when it is so employed? In these cases 'equal' means 'same' as in 'same height' or 'same IQ.' One forewarning is in order, however. As Chappell[5] has recently noted, the term 'same' has itself a dual use. We can refer to an object as 'the same one we saw yesterday.' Here the force of 'same' is to identify as *one* thing what might appear on hasty, *prima facie* grounds to be distinct things. This is the *identifying* function of 'same.' But the term also serves a comparative purpose, in which it is presupposed that there are multiple objects and a comparison is made of them for this or that purpose (though not all purposes), with respect to certain characteristics (though not all characteristics). It is in this latter role that we take 'same' as synonymous with 'equal.' Now our definition:

To say that X and Y are equal with respect to some characteristic C, is to

(1) *presuppose* that an appropriate (valid) scale for measuring units of C has been correctly applied to X and Y under standard conditions; and to

(2) *presuppose* that the scale applied to X is equivalent or identical to the scale applied to Y; and further to

(3) *presuppose* that the units of measurement employed have a degree of fineness suitable to the context; and, then, to

[5] V. C. Chappell, "Sameness and Change," *Philosophical Review*, LXIX (July, 1960), 351–362.

(4) *assert* that the resultant scores or measurements in both applications are the same.

We need not tarry here very long. Equality as sameness gives us little trouble. Our main reason for specifying this concept is to contrast it with another sense of equality yet to come. There are those, however, who would make all uses of 'equal' cleave to this sameness sense, and the temptation for such a move lies in the sameness concept itself.

Given two speakers sharing the above definition, there need not be *automatic* agreement in recognizing instances of sameness. That is, descriptive claims of equality are not *completely* rulebound. One is given one's head to a limited extent; there is room for individual judgment in even such a hardheaded task as determining whether two characteristics are the same.

The source of this freedom is criterion 3 of the definition. Thus we may say of two students that they fared equally well (or fared the same) in a course of instruction when they received the same letter grade (A or B, etc.), despite discrepancies in their test scores or their dissimilar performance at varying stages in the instruction. But in such a circumstance we could not say that their test scores were necessarily the same. A college admissions officer might want measurements on a finer scale before allowing the two candidates to be "equal in school achievement." A shift to an unexpected level of precision is the stuff of contrived melodrama.

"Yes, but they are not precisely equal," says Villain to Goodheart, who never imagined we were going to use calipers on cauliflower. So Goodheart loses the bet and coughs up his soul, his deed or daughter (for even tastes of Villains run in different directions). Goodheart's intentions were of the best but the moral is not to let your logic slide.

Consequently, there is a place for context, individual perspective to make a difference. Claims of equality are not *just* reports, not "a mere reading off of the facts." They reflect, to some degree, judgments of the speaker that can vary from case to case and speaker to speaker, depending on purpose, seriousness of concern and kinds of scales available.[6] There is a chink here in the wall of complete determinateness, but next we are considering another concept of equality wherein whole sections of this wall are absent. Our concern is that the critic not confuse a chink with a breach.

B. THE FITTINGNESS CONCEPT

Consider a second range of speech acts in which we invoke 'equality' as the operative term.

(a) "The teacher gave equal treatment to both sides of the dispute."

---

[6] In connection with this point and the discussion in the preceding paragraph, see Robert Crawshay-Williams, *Methods and Criteria of Reasoning* (London: Routledge and Kegan Paul, 1957), Chapter 2, especially pp. 22–24, in which he discusses the role of context, i.e., purpose, in the interpretation of statements, including assertions of sameness.

(b) "This school offers equal opportunity to all students."
(c) "Both candidates were given an equal chance of admission to college."

1. These assertions differ from those made with the sameness concept in several respects.

First, note that these assertions have the force of judgments rather than reports. They avow that some practice was proper to the subjects at hand: they are expressions of approval (or disapproval in claims of inequality). Since we usually do not make a judgment of propriety or impropriety without cause, it is not surprising to find that these assertions have another function. This second function is most clearly seen in the negative case. A claim of unequal treatment constitutes a rebuke, censure of the perpetrator of it. It carries with it the presumption that the agent was responsible. Of course the responsibility can frequently be disclaimed ('I was made to change his grade'), passed on ('The school-board mandated this') or its existence denied altogether ('Really, this is the only thing we can do'). But even when such disclaimers are justified, when responsibility cannot be assigned or assigned definitely, there remains what one writer has called the 'evaluative residue.'[7] "All right, the unequal treatment may not have been your fault, but it's a shoddy way to treat the student all the same."

The situation is less simple with respect to a positive claim. For if a claim of inequality (impropriety) is censure, what is the force of a claim of equality (propriety)? Given a suitable contextual plot, the positive claim may exonerate an agent of presumed wrongdoing ("No, he did treat the students equally") or it may give official certification to an alleged propriety ("We find there is equal opportunity here" announced by some suitable committee or office).

We found above that this use of 'equal' has affinities with evaluation. Nonetheless, a claim of equal treatment is not usually praise.[8] "You presented all viewpoints brilliantly" is commendation. "You gave ten minutes to each position" is descriptive. A claim of equal treatment hangs uneasily between. It is not praise because it is a requirement of the *concept* of teaching that the teacher be fair, impartial, just.[9] It is not description for we are passing on the legitimacy of the teacher's behavior.

2. There are two quick forays to make before the undergrowth thickens. Let us preface the first by stipulating that the approving, legitimizing, censuring, etc., acts be called the ascriptive functions of 'equal.' The

[7] V. C. Walsh, "Ascriptions and Appraisals," *Journal of Philosophy*, LV (November 20, 1958), 1,062ff.; and in *Scarcity and Evil* (Englewood Cliffs, N.J.: Prentice-Hall, Inc., 1961), p. 108.

[8] There is always the exception. When a teacher maintains equal treatment at a time and in a place calling for unusual skill, forebearance, etc., then it is praise. It is also unexpected.

[9] We would include it in the "restrictions of manner" made part of the concept of teaching in Israel Scheffler, *The Language of Education* (Springfield, Ill.: Charles C. Thomas, Publisher, 1960), 57f, 68.

sameness concept usually does not have these functions. The report that students have equal grades or read an equal number of books is not of itself approval or disapproval, censure or exoneration. Of course we may take it as such, if we care to, by suitable additions to the context.

This brings us to another point: we do not need additional information to detect that "This teacher treats students unequally" is obloquy. We want to emphasize that it is the word '*equal*' which has the ascriptive functions we are discussing. That is, we are considering the ascriptive uses of the term itself, not the presence of the term in an otherwise ascriptive speech act. '*Equal*' is the operative term making the statement 'This student was not given equal treatment' a rebuke. If the operative term were to be replaced, the whole force of the assertion would be altered. It is easy enough to note that 'You should have players of equal (same) height' is a prescription. But 'equal' does not make it so. It's more discerning to see with Benn and Peters, that:

In social and political theory, however, 'equality' is more often prescriptive than descriptive. In this sense, 'all men are equal' would imply not that they possess some attribute or attributes in the same degree but that they ought to be treated alike.[10]

That is, the ascriptive functions (and Benn and Peters' prescriptive function as well) are built by convention into the very meaning of the term 'equal.' The functions don't simply arise from the syntactical form of the assertion. This is the point that is not grasped by those who analyze the concept of equality: the ascriptive functions *are part of the meaning* and must be accounted for in any definition we give.

So there is no doubt that the sameness concept can enter into ascriptive and prescriptive speech acts. It is likewise clear that the fittingness concept can be used purely descriptively, when its approving, censure, etc. functions have been revoked or neutralized.[11] But in both 'You should group students of equal ability' and 'He said there is equal opportunity here' the term 'equal' is not the operative one regulating the kind of speech act involved.

Our point, put in its most forceful manner, is that the fittingness concept of equality has ascriptive and prescriptive functions built into it. These are not part of the sameness concept. So the differences we have been discussing are truly differences between the concepts themselves. They are not differences between various speech acts in which 'equal' is merely present.

3. It is this last point that is the sticky one, and it is surely time to stop dawdling over the ascriptive *functions* of 'equal' and get to the main question. Granted that when the term is applied in contexts of the sort being discussed, it will have the force of approval or rebuke, etc. However, what is

[10] S. I. Benn and R. S. Peters, *Social Principles and the Democratic State* (London: Allen & Unwin, 1959), p. 108.

[11] E.g., A. H. Halsey, Jean Floud, and C. Arnold Anderson, *Education, Economy, and Society* (New York: The Free Press, 1961), pp. 209–214.

the *sense* of the term in these contexts? This sense of 'equal' is *fittingness*. To say that certain treatment is equal treatment is to be saying that it is fitting to the subjects exposed to it. It is difficult, however, to pin this sense down with a definition; for the criteria of fittingness, unlike those for sameness, shift with the ever-moving sands of context. We will offer a general defining formula to fix the concept in place. But it should be borne in mind that it is the ascriptive functions, not the criteria for application, that are common to all contexts in which the fittingness concept is applied.

Skipping further preliminaries, we offer this definition of the fittingness of equality:

(a) The provisions or practices being adjudged equal be in accordance with rightful rules, properly applied.
(b) The rules employed be selected with reference to the appropriate characteristics of the subjects, correctly described.

4. The definition stands in need of further explication. But criticism being more delightful than explanation, we will postpone discussion of our own definition in order to give protracted attention to an alternative view of the meaning of the fittingness concept. The view we refer to goes something like this:

When I say "This teacher gave equal treatment" I may very well be approving the teacher's demeanor and what not, but nonetheless I am approving the treatment (of X and Y) because it is the same treatment (X and Y). So we can say that 'equal' has the *sense* of sameness despite differences in *functions* or *use*. On this view there is one concept of equality not two, albeit in some speech acts the single concept has ascriptive and prescriptive appendages. But even with a full complement of barnacles and weeds, a boat is a boat for all that.

We want to oppose this single-meaning view, which we call the sameness thesis. 'Equal,' we will say, has not only taken on new functions but shifted its sense as well; and it is false to claim that sameness is identical with or essential to equality in the fittingness sense.

(Two points of procedure. Since our main interest in the next section is with the fittingness concept, it seems useless to reiterate the designation. Hence we simply write 'equal' when we mean the 'fittingness concept of equal.' However, those who are already disenchanted with the single meaning view of 'equal' are advised to skip the next section and proceed to part III where we return to the problem of definition.)

II. Critique of the Sameness Thesis

There have been varied attempts in education to make sameness a defining characteristic of equality. Philip Phenix supplies us with one recent and notable example:

Equal opportunity means the distribution of schooling in such a way that the interests of each are served to the maximum, consistent with the equal claims of others. This general principle is not easy to apply in practice because different interests are not truly comparable and thus no definite meaning can be attached to their equality. Perhaps equality of educational opportunity in the last analysis means simply that the distribution of education shall be determined through discussion and agreement within the democratic community, where each person has the same right of voice and the same standing before the law.[12]

Why should Phenix be concerned whether the students' interests (or even the curricula catering to them) are comparable? Presumably because he assumes that equal opportunity requires sameness. But since the interests cannot even be compared, we are in no position to assert their sameness. So Phenix, in the grip of the sameness thesis looks elsewhere—to the procedures followed in establishing school programs—for the necessary aspect of sameness. And here in the midst of democratic decision processes, he finds the desired identical element, *viz.*, that each person's voice and vote count the same, i.e., as one! This is surely a desperate price to pay for retaining sameness in equality.

Myron Lieberman also champions the thesis, but by more labyrinthian paths:

At this point, it becomes important to recognize that complete equality of educational opportunity is impossible. Not everyone can have the same teacher or live in the same home environment or travel the same distance to school, to mention just a few things that could be the basis of inequality of educational opportunity. The impossibility of complete equality tells us something about what people do not ordinarily mean when they say that there is equality of educational opportunity. They do not mean that there are no inequalities whatsoever. Rather, they mean that some inequalities can be disregarded in judging whether there is or is not equality of educational opportunity.

Minor inequalities are thus disregarded in common usage. But at what point does an inequality cease to be minor? How much equalization is necessary before we are willing to say that there is equality of educational opportunity?

And farther along:

equality does not mean that every student receive the same grade, but that every student be graded according to standards which apply to all. When we think of equality before the law, we do not suppose that there can be no equality unless all persons on trial are acquitted or all convicted. . . . The "equality" involved is not one of outcome but of procedure to determine the outcome.[13]

[12] Philip H. Phenix, *Philosophy of Education* (New York: Holt, Rinehart and Winston, Inc., 1958), p. 144.

[13] Myron Lieberman, "Equality of Educational Opportunity," *Harvard Educational Review*, XXIX (Summer, 1959). Also reprinted in B. O. Smith and R. H. Ennis (editors), *Language and Concepts in Education* (Chicago: Rand McNally and Company, 1961), pp. 133, 137.

Lieberman is so insistent in his asseverations concerning the practical limits on the amount of sameness that is possible, that we are apt to overlook the fact that he makes sameness—*some* sameness to be sure—the defining element in equality. Thus the problem (to Lieberman) in equal opportunity is determining *which* conditions must be the same. His prejudice in favor of sameness forces him to overlook the obvious: *viz.*, that it is the presence of dissimilarity which *constitutes* equal opportunity in certain circumstances.

Others are less clearly supporters of the sameness thesis, but their ambiguous definitions are as susceptible of this interpretation as of any other:

In practice it [equal opportunity] means an equal chance to compete within the framework of goals and the structure of rules established by our particular society. . .[14]

Education, we now say, equalizes when it matches equally well the variant needs, wants, and abilities of individuals.[15]

Although the quotations above do not reveal the fact clearly, the sameness thesis may take any one of several forms. We will consider each of these seriatim even though some forms are without supporters at present. However, it is likely that even the most neglected bastion, once under attack, will be found bristling with defenders.

We begin by distinguishing two general ways of construing the sameness thesis. Consider the claim 'A and B were given equal treatment.' The first approach holds that however sameness enters the picture, it obtains between A and B, the explicit subjects of the utterance. This approach we will dub the *explicit comparison*. The alternative approach is, as you would expect, more covert. It assumes that the intended comparison is 'A and B treated equally' is not between A and B as explicitly stated, but between A and other presumed A's; B and other presumed B's. The equal treatment, then exists between the asserted subjects and their respective, but unmentioned, kinsman. This naturally, we label the *implicit comparison*. What the implicit comparison does is to interpret the single claim about A and B into two separate utterances, one about A's and the other about B's.

A. SAMENESS THESIS: EXPLICIT COMPARISON

This approach itself comes in a variety of forms. These are best exemplified through consideration of the elements found in a context in which we make some claim of equal treatment: There are five such elements.

---

[14] John Gardner, *Excellence* (New York: Harper & Row, Publishers, 1961), p. 12.
[15] M. H. Willing, *et al.*, *Schools for Our Democratic Society* (New York: Harper and Row, Publishers, 1951), p. 139.

(a) *Subjects:* implicitly or explicitly involved; not only students but competing hypotheses, theories, recipients of funds or other specifiable characteristics; who are exposed or subjected to some treatment.

(b) *Rule(s)* mandating how the subjects are to be treated, called often the treatment-generating rules.

(c) *Justification:* principles invoked to defend the use of rule(s) on certain subjects in particular circumstances.

(d) *Treatment:* the practices or provisions the subjects are exposed to, or the course of action taken in connection with the subjects.

(e) Finally, the *results*, in some relevant sense, of the treatment given.

1. *The Identity Form.* In this form the thesis holds that there is equal treatment of subjects if and only if the treatment (d) is literally similar or identical for each subject. This is the form we sketched earlier as the single-meaning view of equality. It posits only one concept of equality fitting all applications of the term, *viz.*, the sameness concept defined earlier. (Recall that this does not deny that some uses may have ascriptive functions. However, it is the *sense* of the term that remains the same.)

Clearly, in some cases we do require that the treatment of A and B be the same before we say that it is *equal* treatment. But this covers only those cases in which the relevant characteristics of the subjects are the same. Our use of 'equal' seems to follow the rule: when there is identity in element (a) the subjects, a judgment of equality requires sameness with regard to element (d) the treatment.

But the sameness thesis can't settle for this limited victory; it aspires to hold for all cases, including those in which subjects differ in relevant traits. Simply as a matter of fact we see that it does not hold. If two students are given the same penalties for the same misdemeanor we say that they have received equal treatment. But we judge it to be inequality of treatment to give the same penalties for dissimilar infractions. Here our use of 'equal' follows a second rule to the effect that differences in subjects require differences in treatment in order for the treatments to be judged equal.

At this juncture the sameness thesis might take one of two paths: one is to keep the identity between equal treatment and same treatment, but withdraw from the explicit to the implicit comparison. The other is to drop the identity of 'equal' and 'same' but retain sameness in some other defining capacity. We will follow up on this latter possibility first.

2. *Essential Aspect Form.* In the face of the criticism directed at the identity form, the supporter of the sameness thesis might seek some other omnipresent feature of the context as the ubiquitous element of sameness in all claims of equality. The likely candidates are the elements listed above.

(a) It might appear plausible to choose the rule(s) (element b) as the necessary element of sameness. Now we can recast our definition of 'equality' in this manner.

For treatment of A and B to be equal requires that the treatment of each be mandated by rules which are the same for each.

Now the defining element is not found in the disparity of treatment accorded but in the identity of the rules invoked to determine it.

But this definition will not hold for all uses of 'equal.' The following counter example, wherein the treatment is admittedly equal, yet not generated by the same rules, is illustrative. Imagine a teacher presenting controversial views of a topic. One side is a long, necessarily detailed inductive argument and the other a deductive, nearly stark defense (Hutchins vs. Dewey on curriculum; Catholic vs. humanist on birth control). Equality of treatment here requires not only that the actual treatment be dissimilar (in time, type of presentation); but, more relevantly, it also demands that the treatment of each alternative position be derived from rules which are *different* for the respective sides. That is, the treatment of each side will be mandated by explanatory regulations fitting to arguments of the type at hand, not by any common set of rules for all sides.

(b) In the quotation from Philip Phenix, he seems to select the justification (element c) as the necessary element of sameness in the definition of equality. However it is not clear which of the two definitions he would favor.

Treatment of subjects is 'equal' when the treatment-generating rules are justified *either*

(1) on the basis of a principle containing an element of sameness in it (e.g., same number of votes for each man principle); or
(2) by reference to one principle which covers the disparate treatment-generating rules in the situation.

Position 1 fails whenever we offer a justifying principle with no mention of sameness within it. Phenix's illustration *happens* to be a justification of type (1), justifying a rule of curriculum on the basis of the one man—one vote principle. But certainly it is not this principle, nor any other mentioning sameness within it, which justifies, say, the use of deductive rules in presenting deductive arguments or the rule that applicants for college admission exceeding a certain standard will be admitted.

So it is not the one man—one vote principle which makes an arrangement *ipso facto* an arrangement of equality. The decision, for example, made by the one man—one vote procedure, to treat *all* arguments by deductive rules, would be a violation of equality! There is a limit to the number of actions for which democracy can be conscripted as warrant.

It is the second (2) position which is the more plausible, but not so much so that another clear instance of usage does not refute it. Consider two boys applying for admission to college (or two school districts for subsidies). One applicant with below average qualifying scores is rejected (cut-off rule); another with the same scores but a religion under-represented on the campus is admitted (proportionate representation of social groups rule).

Here we find different treatment; different rules and a *different justification for each rule*. For the cut-off rule, there is the usual one about the low probability of success in such cases; in support of the other rule we are regaled with stories of the educational advantages of encountering a "balanced" college environment. Yet here is equality of treatment all the same.

It might be objected that there is more to the justification process in these cases. If the justification is pushed to its limits, the critic avers, then all justifications of presumed equal treatment consist finally in one general principle: *all treatment generating rules be appropriate to the subjects being treated*.

But this simply will not do. To defend the sameness thesis on these grounds is suicide for the thesis. For it is precisely this claim, *viz.*, that equality means fitting, we are defending *against* the sameness thesis. It trivializes the thesis to claim that the equality requires sameness because equal treatment must always be fitting treatment!

So much for the use of the element of justification as the essential aspect of sameness in ordinary claims of equality.

(c) There are probably other elements, increasingly inscrutable, more esoteric, which might be invoked as the desired element of sameness. We will consider but one more. It might be contended that equality requires that the *results* of the treatment be the same in any case of equal treatment.[16] We need not linger here long. The plausibility of the position arises in a case, for example, wherein a teacher may give different coverage to each side of a controversial topic. When charged with giving unequal treatment, the teacher might report that students were very familiar with one alternative, thus requiring less exposure to it to reach a level of understanding commensurate with their understanding of the other side. But what if this "identity in level of understanding" did not come to pass in a case where two sides to a controversy are given divergent, yet proper, presentations? Would this render the presentation unfair? Or what if the "level of understanding (or development or achievement, etc.)" is not detectable, are we then unable to judge the fairness of the teaching? Surely not. We would judge such cases by the rules for correctness that apply to the presentation itself, regardless of outcome, known or unknown. This fact is even clearer in a case of college admissions. Equal opportunity here does not require that all candidates be admitted (same result) but that all be handled appropriately (fitting procedure).

In summary, then, we conclude that for every element that is posited as providing the sameness in a claim of equality, we can find legitimate cases where that element is not the same yet the case is a genuine and legitimate application of the expression 'equal treatment.'

[16] See Gregory Vlastos, "Justice and Equality" in Richard B. Brandt (ed.), *Social Justice* (Englewood Cliffs, N.J.: Prentice-Hall, Inc., 1962), 41ff. for a discussion of equality in terms of results of treatment.

B. SAMENESS THESIS: IMPLICIT COMPARISON

In the face of objections raised thus far, the defender of the sameness thesis might claim that the thesis has failed because we are seeking the comparison in the wrong place. In utterances of the form 'A and B, were given equal treatment,' the intended contrast is not between A and B, but between A and other A's; B and other B's. When so interpreted 'equal treatment' will mean 'same treatment' (the identity form), albeit not sameness between A and B.

But if this position is correct, then it must follow that every demand *for* equal treatment must be a demand for identical treatment. Consider, however, such a demand in these different contexts.

Here we can retain the sameness thesis in its pure identity form. For, as shown, 'equal' has the sense of 'same.' But this later virtue marks the fall of the sameness thesis. We need only show that *not* all demands for equal treatment are intended as demands for same treatment. This is easily done, for to interpret all such demands as claims for identity is to miss the point of the assertion in many cases and to trivialize the concept of equality.

Consider the following contexts in which demands for equal treatment can arise from different intentions.

(a) A person is correctly grouped, i.e., admitted to be an instance of X, but from oversight or intention is not actually treated as an X. For example, a community is admittedly one of a certain tax classification, but fails to receive the state funds earmarked for communities with that classification.

(b) A subject is treated as others with whom he is grouped but claims to have been wrongly grouped. E.g., a candidate for college admissions is classified as *low* in entrance examination results and rejected along with others in the group but argues that his relation to an alumnus has been overlooked. He should be *low-alumnus*.

(c) A subject is admittedly grouped properly but claims that this treatment is unfair to the entire group. The examples here are profuse. All students who would have once been rejected for further education now demanding it are illustrative.[17]

Case (a) marks the apex in the career of the sameness thesis. The request here, clearly, is to be treated the same as other members of a given group. Identity seems to hold for case (b) as well. But proponents will have to admit the fit is looser. For there are two ways of construing the claim made in (b): (1) as a demand to be treated the *same as* others of like characteristics or (2) as a demand to be treated with respect to one's *proper* characteristics. It

---

[17] These types of challenges are freely adapted from Isaiah Berlin, "Equality," *Aristotelian Society Proceedings*, LVI, 1955–56, 307ff.

seems to be a matter of choice as to which is the relevant description of the situation.

But the (c) type situation is a pickle from a different barrel. The issue here is *not* one of identical treatment, for that condition has already been fulfilled. The issue here is whether the treatment is the rightful, i.e., fitting way to treat the group. This shift from (b) to (c) marks the last extremity of the sameness thesis. For what has just been demonstrated is that even when the subjects and treatment are the same, it still makes sense to ask whether the treatment is equal, i.e., fitting. If "equal" literally *meant* "same," such a claim would be redundant, absurd.

Now certainly sameness is involved even in the (c) case, but only in the secondary sense that once rightful treatment is established, it should apply to all members of the group. But the sameness thesis celebrates this secondary characteristic into an intellectual way of life. To the supporter of sameness, for example, the Negro demand is to be treated the same as the white, not a demand to smash down improper differentiating characteristics. But the misconception is revealed when we realize that evidence of superior intellectual characteristics in the colored race would justify, in the name of *equality*, a demand for education superior to that given to whites.

And this reveals a deep truth about ordinary use of "equal." When we judge A and B to have fared equally, part of what we are saying is that each was managed according to his kind. But more importantly we are claiming that this is the proper kind, and that it is *right* to treat subjects of this kind in this way. This is the moral element involved in type (c) cases (which will be discussed in the next section).

Both Lieberman, explicitly, and Phenix, by implication, want to include type (c) cases into the class of claims of equality. The reason is apparent. To restrict the concept of equality to (a) and (b) cases is to trivialize the concept. The term would only operate, then, in cases of simple error and apparent corruption. As such the concept would be a fraud, considering the weight it is asked to carry in social and political philosophy, as well as philosophy of education. The trick is to retain the significant scope for the concept while holding fast to the sameness thesis. But when the former is done, the latter is already a dead thesis. The way to keep the horse from escaping the barn is never to bring him in.

SUMMARY

So much for the attempt to wed equality to egalitarianism by reportive, not persuasive, definition. Generally we have tried to show that to interpret 'equal' as 'same' (*in any way*) is to distort the meaning of the term in some ordinary contexts. On the other hand, to interpret 'equal' as 'fitting' retains the ordinary sense of the term in all contexts. We do not deny, of course, that same treatment may constitute equal treatment *in some contexts*, as a special case of fitting treatment. Or to put the matter differently: we are contending that 'equal' is *defined* as 'fitting' and that same treatment may on occasion be equal treatment *as a matter of fact, not definition.*

Why be concerned with this issue—so concerned that we follow the sameness thesis through its tedious convolutions? The reason is that a definition in terms of sameness offers the last best hope for a determinate, single interpretation for such a ubiquitous educational ideal as equal educational opportunity for all. To this topic we now turn.

III. The Fittingness Concept and the Equality Principle

Having assayed and rejected varied attempts to define equality in terms of sameness, we turn now to an explication of our own definition. Earlier we cited the following rules as constituting a definition of 'equality' in its fittingness sense:

(a) The provisions or practices being adjudged equal be in accordance with rightful rules, properly applied.
(b) The rules be employed with reference to appropriate characteristics of the subjects, correctly described.

A. INDETERMINACY

Ponder now the state of our system. If equality were defined in terms of sameness, then there would be at least one constant criterion for the application of the term in each and every context. But the upshot of our discussion in the previous section was negative with respect to this hope. The definition offered here in place of sameness is indeterminate. It is indeterminate with respect to the content of the rules to be followed and the characteristics of the subjects that are relevant.

Furthermore, the definition stands in constant danger of redundancy on the score that relevancy of subject characteristics and propriety of rules are functions of one another. That is, whether a candidate's religion is relevant in college admissions is dependent on the presence or absence of a rule about treatment of candidates with respect to this characteristic. And whether we have such rules is dependent on the importance we attribute to the characteristic.

B. PRIMACY OF ETHICAL JUDGMENT

This indeterminacy in the definition of the fittingness concept is apparently analogous to that encountered in connection with the sameness concept. With regard to the sameness concept, the selection of a suitable scale for gainsaying measures of things to be compared is a matter of practical judgment. In applying the fittingness concept, however, one is choosing the morally right rules to adhere to in a given case. This is a *moral* judgment.

It is commonly recognized that assent to equality is a moral act. What we here assert is that the decision as to what *constitutes* equality in concrete cases is likewise a moral decision and a logically necessary one. Allegiance to the equality principle as such is an empty gesture. The principle is a secondary one, depending on logically prior moral commitments to make it meaningful. For example, it is meaningless to support the idea that school subsidies should be distributed to communities on an equal basis. It is not until a commitment is made as to what constitutes rightful allocation that assent to the equality principle becomes significant. Therefore no philosophy of education is identified or made controversial by its belief in educational equality. What is distinctive about an educational philosophy is the particular way it interprets this belief, the judgments and commitments it makes along the way. For to round out this topic on a note of redundancy, the definition of equality does not dictate our educational preferences. Rather it is the case that our educational preferences constitute *our* meaning for equality.

C. ESSENTIALLY CONTESTED

Thus it is that the specific criteria or rules by which we determine a treatment to be equal are not part of the definition of the concept. As illustration, consider the distribution of state funds to local districts on an "equal" basis. A rule (read 'formula') which allocates funds on the basis of local tax *effort* is no more or less "true equality" than rules which dispense moneys to compensate for deficiencies in local tax resources or which give the same amount to each local district or which reward districts manifesting greatest educational improvements; or any combination of these. Any of these can be defended as the right, and hence fitting, way to distribute subsidies. The same holds true for, say, the allocation of teaching talent to students of differential ability. The best teachers might be allocated to the most able students; to the least able, or assigned on some compromise basis. There is nothing in the linguistic conventions which render any one rule as the "real" or "true" meaning of 'equal treatment.'

We would borrow from Gallie at this point and speak of 'equality' in its fittingness sense as an essentially contested concept, i.e., as one of the "concepts the proper use of which inevitably involves endless disputes about their proper uses on the part of their users."[18]

---

[18] W. B. Gallie, "Essentially Contested Concepts," *Aristotelian Society Proceedings*, LVI (1955–56), 169. Our borrowing of this designation does not adhere to the strict requirements for the employment of this term as set down therein.

This does not apply, however, to the ascriptive functions of the concept depicted earlier. These functions (approving, assigning responsibility, etc.) are invariant from one context to another, and from one language user to another. However, what particular criteria a person will use will depend on that to which his moral commitments will allow him, justifiably, to apply these functions.

D. CONSEQUENCES OF THE SAMENESS THESIS

Thus it should be clear why a definition of the fittingness concept in terms of sameness is to be so vehemently rejected. For if the concept is so defined *and made to retain its ascriptive force*, the result is the thoroughgoing egalitarianism, so well depicted by Berlin:

In its simplest form the ideal of complete social equality embodies the wish that everything and everybody should be as similar as possible to everything and everybody else . . . I doubt whether anyone has ever seriously desired to bring such a society into being, or even supposed such a society to be capable of being created. Nevertheless, it seems to me that demands for human equality which have been expressed both by philosophers and by men of action who have advocated or attempted to reform society, can best be represented as modifications of this absolute and absurd ideal. In this ideal egalitarian society, inequality—and this must ultimately mean dissimilarity—would be reduced to a minimum.[19]

Even to hold to a less strict form of the sameness thesis is still to give priority to uniformity over variety.

So as a *reportive* definition of the fittingness concept, the sameness thesis is not only factually incorrect; it is also morally wrong. The results are no less severe if the sameness thesis is offered as a stipulated definition. For if the ascriptive force of the term is retained, then the "stipulated definition" becomes an ethical recommendation. If the ascriptive functions are dropped, then the stipulation is pointless. We would still need a term to perform the ascriptive services of the fittingness concept.

E. OTHER MISCONCEPTIONS

1. Even those who realize that 'equality' cannot be defined in terms of sameness fall into the error of supposing that it still has a determinate definition. This is probably the source of the crude circularity in the definitions by Willing, *et al.* and Gardner, cited earlier, and in the following definition:

[19] Berlin, *op. cit.,* 311f.

equality does not mean identity. . . . Let me suggest again that equality in our sense involves an *equal right* of every child, . . . to achieve excellence, to excel. This is what equality means . . .[20]

It is quite conceivable for someone to adopt "right to achieve excellence" or "right to compete" or "right to express judgment" as criteria for determining equality of treatment in appropriate contexts. Of course, it is understood that these are not *definitions* of the term, since different and even contrary criteria might also be justified. What is fostered here is the illusion that 'equality' has a determinate sense which modifies in some way the criterion of application. But 'equal right to achieve' means no more than 'right to achieve.' One's equality with others, then, consists in the right one shares with others to achieve. It consists in no more than this, because there is nothing beyond having the right. Adding 'equal' to the right is a redundancy.

　　To sum up. Being given equal opportunity does not consist in being given a *special* right, viz., an *equal* right; it consists in being *given* the right. The point in saying that this right is a criteron of equality (what equality means) is that it is morally justified to employ this as a criterion to apply in appropriate contexts.

　　2. Still another definition of the fittingness concept misconstrues the moral element in the concept and suppresses its essential contestability.

the expression "equality of educational opportunity," as it is used, refers. . . . to the environmental circumstances that influence the growth and development of the individual. No reference to equal intellectual capacity or to any other native endowments is intended. The intended reference is the *chance* to get an education, *of whatever amount and kind one's* endowments make possible. It is the chance that is to be equalized.[21]

　　The illusion is created here that the criteria specifying what is equal treatment in some context are simply "read off" from the facts of the

[20] Peter H. Odegard, "Education and American Values," in *Foundations for Excellence*, Fifteenth Yearbook of the American Association of Colleges for Teacher Education, *Proceedings of the 1962 Annual Meeting* (Washington, D.C., 1962), p. 39. Italics added.
　　Dewey appears to have gone down this path also: "Belief in equality is an element of the democratic credo. It is not, however, belief in equality of natural endowments. Those who proclaimed the idea of equality did not suppose they were enunciating a psychological doctrine, but a legal and political one. All individuals are entitled to equality of treatment by law and in its administration. Each one is affected equally in quality if not in quantity by the institutions under which he lives and has an *equal right to express* his judgment, although the weight of his judgment may not be equal in amount when it enters into the pooled result to that of others. In short, each one is *equally an individual* and entitled to *equal opportunity of development of his own capacities* . . ." John Dewey, *Problems of Men* (New York: Philosophical Library, Inc., 1946), p. 60. Italics added.
　　[21] William O. Stanley, B. Othanel Smith, Kenneth D. Benne, and Archibald W. Anderson, *Social Foundations of Education* (New York: The Dryden Press, Inc., 1956), p. 228. Some italics added.

environment and student's characteristics. (As, for example, equal right can be "read off," merely from the facts.) But a student's endowments make different kinds of education possible. Which should we give the student a chance to get? And which of his endowments do we judge to be appropriate to encourage? The authors state that fair play is the sense of equal opportunity,' but they ignore the fact that this is a moral notion. What is equal treatment is a matter of moral choice, not factual reporting, and this yields contesting, not uniform views.

Three

Analyzing and Synthesizing Philosophical Positions

Introduction to Part Three

Although the kind of philosophical endeavor discussed and illustrated in Part Two is commonly found in the United States, Great Britain, Canada, and Australia, a number of philosophers have expressed their displeasure with it and do not wish to restrict their work to such narrow parameters. Although they may concede that the analysis of concepts has contributed to the clarification of the language of education, they are unwilling to settle for this alone. They concur with Morton White that some philosophers have concentrated so intensively upon what is meant by certain words that they have little time or inclination for anything else, and have thus failed to address themselves to the equally pertinent problems of means and ends in education.

Those philosophers who have expressed their dissatisfaction with the narrowness of concept analysis may or may not hold to a philosophical position such as realism, idealism, or existentialism, or to a theological grounded philosophy of education. They are, however, disposed to think that the philosophy of education should be concerned with ends and means, and they are prone to believe that these ends and means are in some manner logically connected with a set of philosophical presuppositions, particularly concerning the nature of man. So prevalent is this kind of philosophical activity along with the notion that ends and means are directly inferred from philosophical stances, especially among philosophically unsophisticated educational administrators and practitioners, that several prior questions are often overlooked. For example, are all philosophical presuppositions true? Do the ends and means of education necessarily follow from metaphysical and epistemological presuppositions? Or, putting the question in a slightly different way, is one's philosophy of education the cause for one's selection of certain ends and means for education?

If means and ends can be inferred, then we have sufficient reason for studying synoptic philosophies of education for what they may teach us about these matters. If on the other hand, we encounter difficulties in inferring ends and means for education from philosophical presuppositions, as some hold, then we might well be advised to become knowledgeable of these difficulties and prepared to be more cautious in drawing inferences, especially dogmatic ones, from philosophical presuppositions.

The purposes of this part of the book are to learn to note the difference between empirical and normative matters, to examine the problems of inferring ends and means for education from philosophical presuppositions, and to learn how to analyze philosophies of education by the use of a model designed for that purpose.

9

Philosophy of Science
and Educational Theory

ERNEST NAGEL

A certain part of educational theory is, undoubtedly, empirical in content, and can be evaluated in the light of evidence obtained by factual inquiry. I'd say this is so for those things that fall into theories in the second sense, and also for certain statements that are made in educational theory that belong to the third component, as I have distinguished it: when somebody offers a proposition which says that a certain objective is to be achieved through the use of certain means, this is a conditional statement which in effect says, if one adopts certain instrumentalities and proceeds in a certain way, then certain end-products are going to be realized. This is clearly an empirical proposition, and it is, in effect, a proposition which falls into my second category of theory.

So, there are propositions which are empirical in content, which constitute a part of educational theory. But, then, as I have indicated, insofar as part of educational theory is concerned with conceptual analysis, this is not empirical at all. This is an attempted clarification. And to the extent that the conceptual analysis involves, not so much a reproduction of what ordinarily is meant by certain terms, but an attempt at reconstructing them, this is in effect, a recommendation for the adoption of certain extensions or certain

Ernest Nagel is John Dewey Professor Emeritus of Philosophy at Columbia University.
Ernest Nagel, "Philosophy of Science and Educational Theory," *Studies in Philosophy and Education*, Vol. 7, No. 1 (Fall 1969), pp 16–23, 26–27. Used by permission of *Studies in Philosophy and Education* and the author.

limitations, if you will, of certain familiar terms. And to the extent that this is so, these are recommendations of norms. These are, if you like, a kind of a value judgment. And so, by and large, this part of educational theory cannot be regarded either so much as conceptual analysis, but as a set of propositions which recommend certain linguistic uses, allegedly on the ground of their fruitfulness or what not.

But, then, in addition to this, certainly there are statements of educational ideals or aims. These are of a distinctive kind, since they are neither descriptive statements nor, I take it, are they derivable from factual statements. I don't mean to say, of course, that these statements of educational ideals are necessarily arbitrary, or that they cannot be evaluated in the light of factual data, but I would want to maintain the view that it is not possible strictly speaking, to derive statements which involve some educational ideal, or some recommendations as to what should be done, that statements of this kind are not derivable, and general norms are not, strictly speaking, derivable from any propositions which are allegedly descriptive in character. And that to the extent to which you can use factual information in order to evaluate proposed norms, either of educational practice or of human conduct in general, it's possible to use factual evidence only if at some point in the argument or the justification for certain norms certain other norms are taken for granted. In short, I subscribe, certainly, to the very ancient proposition that statements as to what *ought* to be are not deducible from statements of what *is* despite the attempts to confuse the issue by a great number of people who argue that in some way this is possible. On the other hand, I still think that factual matters are relevant to the assessment of statements of what ought to be, but only provided, I repeat this, only insofar as certain norms are in the given context of discussion taken for granted, without, of course, supposing, now, that a norm that is taken for granted in one domain of discussion or justification cannot itself be subjected to evaluation in some other context where some other norms will be taken for granted, and so on.

Let me expand this argument a little. The reason why I take the position that value judgments cannot be derived or deduced from descriptive statements of fact is because of a very simple logical truism that if you have a logically valid argument then a conclusion can contain no term which does not appear in the premises. And, this to me is decisive—that value propositions contain value terms, descriptive propositions don't contain them, and I do not understand by what magic one then thinks that one can derive one from the other. That's the reason why I reject all such attempts.

On the other hand, I don't think that value judgments are merely arbitrary. I think they can be, in some cases at any rate, justified and in principle they could be justified if the available factual information or if the relevant factual information were available. But I think the process of justification itself, and this is the heart of my view, assumes that you can't justify valid judgments by way of introducing factual information, unless you take for granted some other norm that, at least in this context, you accept.

Now, I don't mean, of course, that you then validate the value judgment or justify it as being adequate by deducing it from value judgments. You might do it that way, but in general that's not the way you do it. You show that it's an adequate value judgment or sound one because, in the light of certain norms, the facts indicate that proceeding in accordance with the value judgment that is under adjudication certain norms that are taken for granted would be realized. But this is not a matter of deduction from value judgments, but rather the same kind of argument that is used in order to validate propositions in what is *prima facie* a descriptive or a positive science such as physics or biology or psychology. Or perhaps we could compare it to what happens in courts of law where perhaps the evidence given by any one witness is not conclusive. I'd say, well, if I had to convict a man—or judge a man's behavior—on the basis of what any one individual has to say about it I would have to say I can't make the judgment. Nevertheless, you have a variety of independent pieces of evidence; each one, perhaps, may be insecure; the total effect of this is sometimes overwhelming. So that you say, no reasonable man can turn all of this down even though he might question some individual item of it. And I should say that the same situation applies in respect of ought propositions. None of them is beyond question. It requires perhaps, a fresh domain in which something assumed in one case would be investigated in another.

Yet the difference between such inquiries on factual and value issues must not be overlooked. While there are certainly areas of dispute in the positive sciences, I think in general the situation is that here we simply do not have in a given stage of the dispute enough evidence really to decide. And so, you have fragmentary evidence—some people bank on this and other people bank on that. But then these disagreements, if the science really develops, are eventually eliminated.

I would say it is one of the marks of having a securely established proposition in any of the positive sciences that you have a consensus among those who have acquired an obvious competence in handling that kind of material. And that as long as there are divergences in any area of positive science about some proposition then it seems to me you have to say, well, we have to suspend judgment.

Now, I should say, it seems to me that a comparable thing does not occur with respect to value judgments. That there may be, as far as I know, certain inarbitrable differences and that there be no way of persuading by any appeal to matters of fact an individual who decides to accept certain norms no matter what factual information you may introduce. It seems to me this is one of the things we have to recognize.

Now, I admit there is often, perhaps, more substantive agreement between people who appear to differ than sometimes is represented. That is, perhaps there is much less disagreement on value commitments than sometimes appears. But I am not at all convinced that all such differences can be eliminated simply by advancing a sufficient amount of factual material.

To put it in more general terms: I'm prepared to take the view that human beings have a great deal in common and to the extent they have a great deal in common they will perhaps share a great many norms or commitments. On the other hand, it seems to me it's not irresponsible to say, well there are differences between people and these differences perhaps are inarbitrable and if these differences are of sufficient importance then we say well, you can't reason with them and, I suppose, ultimately, if it's a critical question, you have to use non-rational methods to live. You have to use some kind of force. That is why this kind of dualism is something perhaps I must maintain in conformity with this sort of general outlook.

In short, I have been here, very briefly, and obviously most inadequately, indicating what seem to me to be the logical conditions for warranting norms or value judgments, but it would take, certainly, much more space than is available to spell out the various steps that are involved.

Now let me turn to some of my skeptical doubts about educational theory, insofar as educational theory is an attempt to formulate and justify educational ideals. And I would like to ask, in the first place, can educational aims be derived from any descriptive theory of human nature? And I want to maintain that this is not, in point of fact, possible despite the attempt to supply a foundation for educational goals by a consideration of physical, biological, psychological or, perhaps, even social and anthropological facts.

Let me try to illustrate what I have in mind when I say that it is not possible to use a descriptive theory of human nature as a justification for any particular educational ideal or system of ideals. A number of biologists, in recent years, have attempted to construct what they believe is an objective ethic by arguing somewhat in this fashion. Thus you are obviously familiar with the position of Julian Huxley, who has argued repeatedly that what is ethical in human behavior is something that in some way favors biological evolution, and that any type of society which is conducive to the development of what he believes to be the evolutionary process, is something that is desirable, while anything which obstructs it is undesirable, and that being something that either advances or retards the evolutionary process, then, is a criterion of what is the human good. Similarly, other writers, without being quite explicit about this often use a notion of growth or development as a criterion in terms which one could justify or develop a certain educational ideal.

Now, I think all of these attempts are mistaken. In particular for example, Huxley's attempt to construct an ethics based on evolutionary considerations, seems to me to be a complete *non-sequitur* because one can always, obviously, ask whether despite the fact that the biological evolutionary process has a certain character and that certain things, certain human actions might advance it and other human actions might retard it, it's always pertinent to ask whether one *should* mold one's life or one should mold one's ideals upon these natural processes. It seems to me that on this point Julian Huxley has forgotten what his grandfather so clearly pointed out in his famous essay on evolution and ethics, that it is a first-class mistake to try to ape the evolutionary processes that are going on in various parts of the universe and to construct human life in terms of them. And this would, of course, impart an implicit criticism of so-called social Darwinism, but in part it was a protest, and I think, a rightful protest, against supposing that whenever you are arriving on the way to the future you are thereby arriving at something that is indisputably morally sound. And, similarly, it seems to me, that using categories such as biological growth or biological development does not enable us to determine, certainly under the varying social conditions under which programs can be effected, what educational policies should be adopted or what educational aims should be pursued.

Continuing along the same vein, I would want to maintain that no educational policy can be derived from any biological or psychological theory, either. Sometimes there is an appearance that this can be done, as for example, when people subscribing to various forms of psychoanalytical theory, Freudian or other sorts, use this theory in order to support and to show that certain kinds of educational practices are required if you are not going to develop individuals, who from the point of view of Freudian or other psychoanalytic theory, suffer from various types of frustration. Now, it seems to me, that in all these attempts at deducing educational aims or educational policies from the psychological theory, whether it's the Freudian theory or Spencerian theory or some drive theory, when you do this you are always using this psychological theory in such a fashion that there's already built into it a set of value recommendations, that from the purely descriptive part of the theory nothing follows as to what can be justified as a desirable educational goal or a particular educational policy.

It seems to me that this desire which characterizes even people who regard themselves and have been regarded as in some way unorthodox in their relation to the history of philosophy—the desire somehow to use fundamental philosophical conceptions about the nature of man or the nature of the universe to supply a basis for educational policy—involves a serious *non sequitur*.

Let me, for example, cite one of Dewey's claims. In *Experience and Education*, he says, "a philosophy of education is a plan for conducting education and must be framed with reference to what is to be done and how it is to be done. The more definitely and sincerely it is held that education is a development within, by and for experience, the more important it is that there shall be clear conceptions of what experience is." And, then, in this thesis, which certainly has attracted a great number of people, and I think, undoubtedly Dewey was convinced of this, he said, "Unless experience is so conceived that the result is a plan for deciding upon subject-matter, upon methods of instruction and discipline, and upon material equipment and social organization of the school, it is wholly in the air." So, the thesis here is that we need a general theory of human experience and that when we have this general theory of human experience, we shall be able to deduce from it all these very important propositions as to what should be the subject matter toward methods of instruction, the kind of discipline, material equipment, the organization of the schools and whatnot.

Now, I think this is just a mistaken view. Nothing it seems to me, follows as to what is a desirable educational aim or policy from Dewey's particular theory of knowledge where, according to him, the process of inquiry generates the object of knowledge. This has been a point very much disputed, as many of us know, by professional philosophers, perhaps because they haven't understood what Dewey was saying. It seems to me that one can maintain, as Dewey has done, that the method of inquiry which is illustrated in many of the special scientific disciplines is, perhaps, the most reliable method that men have achieved for acquiring knowledge without subscribing in any way to his particular interpretation of what that method is and a general conception concerning the way in which, in terms of his epistemological conceptions, the objects of knowledge are constituted. So, it seems to me that, in the first place, it is logically impossible to obtain from general considerations of this kind any conclusions as to what is desirable in human affairs, nor, as far as I'm aware, has anybody ever actually done this. And, of course, if I'm right in saying this is logically impossible then nobody could, but nevertheless, I find that so much of the literature of educational fields with which I am familiar is a repeated attempt somehow to argue vehemently for some total philosophical conception on the ground that if you accept this, then, you are in some way committed to a set of educational imperatives.

For example, in a recent book by Mortimer Adler and Milton Mayer, *The Revolution in Education*, they argue exactly the same way in which Dewey does, or perhaps Dewey argues the same way that they do, and in spite of that fact, presumably, their standpoints are so different. Adler and Mayer say that the methods of teaching that are associated with what they call the modernist, the Deweyian educational standpoint, are consequences of the conception of knowing that is essential to Dewey's view, as a process that alters the object known and therefore as essentially productive or practical. Now, it seems to me, in the first place, that any particular technique of teaching that might be adopted has to be tested in terms of its being an adequate means for achieving certain specific ends, and that this recommendation that impedes a subject in one way rather than another, is entirely independent of what particular theory of knowledge you happen to hold. Similarly, take another illustration from Adler and Mayer: they say that the question whether vocational training should be included in a program of liberal education or whether this training should be excluded entirely from liberal education, is a question of principle not of fact, to the extent that it turns on the nature of the mind, and the nature of the processes of learning and knowing. Now, this is again no less or no more balderdash than Dewey's claim that we can generate a theory of educational objectives from a descriptive account of human nature.

In short, I'm extremely skeptical about the usefulness of attempting to supply this sort of generalized sub-structure for a set of educational aims, whether they are very general or whether they are more specific. And, I think, that educational theory must be counted as participating in a blunder when it is construed to say that the acceptance of educational aims and educational policies is made to depend, or in some way to be intimately related to a descriptive theory of human nature, or a descriptive account of democratic society. . . .

Here, I think, as I've indicated, that the philosophy of science has primarily a critical task and that its use in a program of training people for the profession of educational research, is that of generating a sophisticated conception of the nature of the intellectual constructions in educational theory, and in helping to remove many of the misconceptions about the grounds for responsible claims to knowledge. Some of the things, certainly, that a philosophy of science calls attention to are basic distinctions such as that between fact and value and the way in which factual statements require to be supported, the way in which value judgments require to be justified. Philosophy of science contributes a good deal to clarifying the logic of rational belief by indicating the canons of probabilistic reasoning, the meaning of procedures of quantification, the rationale of controlled observation and experiment, the basis for valid extrapolation and, in greater detail, of course, when one deals with specific concepts, a sophisticated conception of the way in which certain key terms are employed in various scientific disciplines.

I find it a very depressing experience to run into, repeatedly, attempts—for example, on the part, not only of physicists, who, perhaps, do not know any better, but of people who have been exposed to, presumably, some kind of a philosophical training and who are concentrating on issues in educational policy—to do the sorts of things, for example, which I found recently in the book by Professor Margenau, a recent book of his called *Open Vistas*, where he tried to show that modern physics, modern quantum physics, in having shown the untenability of a universal mechanistic materialism, thereby has supplied a foundation for democracy. Or when he argues that in a universe in which the determinism of Newtonian mechanics would be true there would be no room for human decision, for human free-will, while, so he argues, current quantum mechanics does allow room for this.

Now, blunders of this elementary kind continue to be made, and they continue to be made not only by persons, of whom we'd say, well, after all, they're entitled to make blunders because they're not professional philosophers. But educational theorists do something no different when they argue from the truth of certain propositions in biology or in psychology to the validity of certain moral educational ideas. And this seems to me to be the main value of developing this skepticism, this refusal to be fooled that is one of the great services that systematic exposure to the critique that philosophers of science have given to particular knowledge can supply.

In short, I would say that knowledge is a very precious, but also a very rare thing and the pursuit of knowledge is a great adventure. The philosophy of science helps to develop, I think, a responsible skeptical approach to claims to have knowledge, so that we can better distinguish between what is the genuine article from what is a specious one. And, I think, when educational theorists, and this is, I suppose, in part, the main tenor of my remarks, recommend certain educational ideals on the supposition that these educational ideals can be established on the basis, simply, of descriptive theories of human nature, then they are offering us, so I think, not knowledge, but something which is only a spurious counterpart of it. And, an attempt to eliminate the repetition of such discussions—and there has been a plethora of them—an attempt to achieve an unpretentious program for educational theorists in a clear articulation of educational ideals, and to justify educational ideals in terms of explicitly stated norms on the basis of credible factual information, is something quite different. To the extent that the philosophy of science enables us to achieve this sort of thing, it seems to me, it has an extremely important role.

10

A Note Against Phantom Entailment

WARD WELDON

A cynical politician once said that he did not care how the people voted as long as his representatives counted the votes. A dean of a school of education once told his philosophy of education professor that he expected the professor to deduce a body of instructions for teachers from philosophical writings and to present those instructions to his students.

To both the politician and the dean, it was the results that mattered. The fact that the process by which those results are achieved inevitably influences and flavors the end-product was ignored. As long as the politician approved of the election outcome and the dean approved of the educational practices recommended by his philosophy of education professor, neither felt any strong desire to investigate or evaluate the process by which those results were achieved.

Election fraud is a serious criminal offense. Phantom entailment, which is the process of giving a seeming respectability to preconceived recommendations by presenting them as if they followed necessarily from the doctrines of respected philosophers, is an intellectual offense with very serious consequences for both teachers and students of educational philosophy. In both types of fraud a spurious appeal is made to a respected process in order to influence the beliefs and/or actions of others in the direction of preselected goals. The *a priori* nature of the goals contrasts sharply with the *a posteriori*

Ward Weldon is Assistant Professor of Education at the University *of Illinois, Chicago Circle Campus.* Especially prepared for this edition.

and presently indeterminate results of the process itself. Both crimes depend for their success on a discontinuity or inferential leap in the process of relating one group of statements to another group of statements.

One example of the nature of this leap is the relation between the cosmology of Alfred North Whitehead and the educational practices that this noted philosopher has recommended. My general conclusion is that no entailment exists between the general philosophy of Whiteheadian organism and Whitehead's views on proper curricula and classroom methods. By this I mean that it is entirely possible for reasonable and intelligent men to accept Whitehead's cosmology in whole or in part but reject his aims and recommended techniques for education. Whitehead's educational views may also be accepted by those who would reject his ideas on the organismic nature of reality. Presenting Whitehead's educational views in a way that allows or encourages students to believe that they are a logical and necessary consequence of certain cosmological views is an example of phantom entailment. There is no compelling force that prevents a student from accepting either while rejecting the other.

This is not to say that there is no relation at all between Whitehead's educational recommendations and his system of philosophy. Philosophy of education would be a farce and a misnomer if the two disciples of philosophy and education could not be related to each other in proper and stimulating ways even when the connection between them can be shown to be less than entailment or *necessary* connection.

The important point to be made here is that when a connection between a philosophic principle and a schooling practice is less than necessary, the individual making the connection must accept at least partial responsibility for the relationship. The decision to see and act upon the relationship is the individual's own; it was not imposed upon him by necessity. Thus, in the final analysis, the student of philosophy of education must bear the burden of his own intellectual freedom. He cannot take over the philosophic thought of another and be relieved of the hard work involved in interpreting the nature of the world and deciding upon one's own stance in that world.

It is easy to smile in condescension at the mental confusion of a dean whose concept of the relation between educational philosophy and educational practice is narrow and dogmatic, resulting in the phantom entailment of preconceived conclusions. A more difficult but more rewarding activity is to state the appropriate or proper relationship that either may or should exist. Such a statement would make it clear that we are not in the business of using any allegedly superior wisdom that we may have gained in the study of philosophy to issue general instructions to future teachers, thereby removing the need for them to wrestle at first-hand with the philosophical questions that teachers face. Our students (and even our deans) have a right to know what we believe our roles to be. A concise statement of either the actual or ideal connection between educational philosophy and educational practice would go a long way toward providing this information.

I propose neither to present such a statement in this article nor to criticize the statements made by others. My contribution is to suggest a semantic continuum that may be useful to educational philosophers as a framework for considering the various relationships that may exist between the two fields conjoined in philosophy of education. The continuum is shown below.

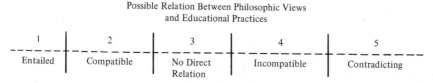

The first item in the continuum represents the necessary and affirmative connection of entailment. The others range from a mild positive form of connection through disconnection and finally to an extreme negative form of connection. Definitions and examples of each of these terms follow.

1. ENTAILMENT

If one statement is entailed by another, it is logically inconsistent, unreasonable, or insane to affirm one statement and deny the other. An extreme but trivial example of entailment is the repetition of identical statements. The principle of identity operates clearly and powerfully in this case; it operates, with reduced effect, in other situations in which statements although not identical are nevertheless considered to be so similar as to be entailed. The syllogistic form of deduction in which the conclusion merely restates proofs that have already been accepted and expressed in the major and minor premises appeals to entailment and the principle of identity. Does this sort of thing happen in educational philosophy? May statements, and particularly statements of a prescriptive or imperative nature, be deduced from the assertions or observations of philosophers?

2. COMPATIBILITY

Three conditions must be met if one statement is to be judged as compatible with another:

(1) Shared terms.
(2) Absence of entailment or contradiction.
(3) Similarity (either emotive or descriptive).

First, the two statements must have shared terms, which are usually expressed or clearly implied. Second, the statements must neither be entailed nor contradictions. That is, there must be no logical necessity, given the first statement, either to affirm or to deny the second. Third, the sender or receiver of the statement must judge that the statements offer support for each other and that the most likely and satisfactory procedure is to affirm both or to deny both together, as a single unit.

We are dealing with a continuum. Therefore, we must expect the categories of entailment and compatibility to shade into each other without a clear and absolute dividing line. An example of compatibility between statements is the assertions:

(1) Masses attract each other.
(2) Unsupported massive objects fall to the earth.

This example falls close to the entailment range of the continuum category of compatibility. If it is possible to think of instances in which it is reasonable to affirm the first statement and deny the second, we are limited to compatibility rather than to the more extreme form of agreement that we have called entailment. No entailment exists here. It is possible to say that masses attract each other; nevertheless, some massive unsupported objects, such as the other planets, will not fall to the earth. In merely approximate and heuristic terms, a compatibility exists when we are of the opinion that in most instances both statements will be affirmed or denied in unison but that neither statement will automatically be rejected if an unusual case can be found causing the other to be labeled false under the specified unusual circumstances. In other words, the two statements are regarded as being closely related but not identical. There is a need to identify and study, rather than sweep under the rug, those admittedly unusual cases in which the expected relationship does not hold true. The category of compatibility begins with an expectation and issues forth into a continuing investigation. The expectation is revisable. It represents a human being's understanding of the way in which the world, including himself, operates. The crime of phantom entailment consists in treating such expectations as if they were handed to us in a fixed form and cannot be changed. Educational philosophy is more similar to an activity of disciplined investigation than to a completed statement of unquestioned dogma.

3. No Direct Relationship

The example of this portion of the continuum may be drawn from any of the multitude of pairs of statements in which an affirmation or denial of the first carries with it no implication for a judgment of the truth or falsity of the second. Such a pair would be:

(1) It is cold today.

(2) The capitol of Egypt is Cairo.

The principle of nonidentity is in operation in this case. Each statement must be judged on its own merits and without regard to any inferences gained from the other statement in the pair. There is an absence of shared terms (either expressed or implied) in the example given. Such an absence is an assurance that we are dealing with statements that fall into the "no direct relationship" midsection of the continuum.

A note of caution: One of the persistent urges in philosophy is the desire to interrelate seemingly disconnected and alien elements. There are many attempts in the history of philosophy to understand the universe as an orderly whole in which all diverse elements find unity in the light of a single principle or assumption. An investigator who would be true to this facet of the nature of philosophy must be open to the possibility that presently unrecognized forms of relationship exist even in pairs of statements that seem to have nothing in common.

4. INCOMPATIBILITY

Statements are incompatible with each other if terms are shared, if the two statements neither entail nor contradict each other, and if the judgment of the sender or receiver is that affirming one of the statements increases the likelihood that the other should be denied.

5. CONTRADICTION

The same sort of logical necessity is involved in contradiction as in entailment. The difference is that it is logically inconsistent to affirm both statements or deny both of them. This continuum is intended to include all of the possible relationships between a pair of statements, one of which is a philosophic generalization and the other of which is a statement about educational practices. The examples given thus far have been general.

Most cases of phantom entailment will turn out to be compatible propositions for which the false claim of a necessary connection has been made. The absence of necessity opens the entire matter for fruitful discussion of the merits of both the philosophy and the educational practice. The third criterion of compatibility asks for an analysis of the perceived similarity. This may frequently demand a reexamination of the philosophic doctrine and a reexamination of the educational practice. Sometimes the student may begin asking fundamental questions about the nature of man and the nature of the universe in order to determine why and how the doctrine and practice are similar or dissimilar. As instructors in philosophy of education, we strive for the level of student interest and scholarship that produces earnest and cogent questions. The use of phantom entailment shuts off questioning by presenting someone else's recommendations buttressed by what may appear to the student as the unassailable authority of some philosopher's argument.

Memorable and effective teachers from Socrates to the present have sought to encourage students to think through, express, and defend their own analysis of the situation. An avoidance of phantom entailment and the frequent, although self-questioning, use of compatible statements can be a rewarding step in the right direction.

The conflict and tension that occurred when the United States acting in its capacity as a victor nation began to impose a democratic educational system upon the Japanese people in 1945 is a general example of an incompatibility between a philosophical position and a set of educational practices. The dominant and habitual modes of thought in Japan were autocratic and absolutistic. Japanese administrators, teachers, and students had good reason to sense and react to this incompatibility. Those Japanese who criticized or questioned the changes made in their educational system during the period of the American occupation were often arrested by the Japanese military or civilian police operating under the authority of the American occupation army led by General Douglas MacArthur. Threatened or actual punishment for educators who had expressed opposition to the new and supposedly more democratic forms of educational practice followed the arrests. The use of police force to stifle criticism and even discussion of new methods and new curricula is an educational practice that is clearly incompatible with the types of educational philosophy held by the American educators and imported into Japan to mold the form of the postwar Japanese educational system. Such a practice was entirely compatible, however, with the then existing Japanese philosophies expressed in emperor worship and the views that all who hold authority in the school system were the direct representatives of a divine head of state. Perhaps the Japanese prewar authoritarian educational practices were also compatible with the values of the American military men who accepted the responsibility of governing Japan during the occupation period.

The use of this cross-cultural example places the equation of the compatibility and incompatibility of educational philosophy with educational practices in a new context. John Dewey, for example, in giving his major work the title, *Democracy and Education,* seems to be expressing the concept that his philosophy of education and his recommended schooling practices were compatible only with those broader social and political philosophies held in democratic countries and in countries aspiring toward democracy.

The question of the compatibility of a political system with an educational one brings this discussion full circle. We began by comparing election fraud with the intellectual fraud of phantom entailment. In those situations where election outcomes are left up to the decisions of voters and where questions about the relevance of a given doctrine to educational practice are left open to students, there is uncertainty about the results. It is this type of uncertainty to which Peirce referred when he wrote:

There must be a real and living doubt, and without this all discussion is idle. . . . When doubt ceases, mental action on the subject comes to an end; and, if it did go on, it would be without a purpose.[1]

Such doubt is essential to active learning; it goes a long way toward making teaching a satisfying and exciting activity.

Of course, doubt is not enough. Doubt is a call to action, not a complete and philosophically satisfying action in itself. The semantic continuum introduced in this article is merely a convenient intellectual tool. It raises and systematizes doubt by asking a series of questions about the relation between philosophical concepts and educational practices. It is to the productive and enlightening resolution of such doubts that philosophers of education properly devote their time and energies. The doubts must be recognized and welcomed if philosophy of education is to be honest. They must eventually be replaced with at least tentative understandings and convictions if philosophy of education is to be rewarding. For us, as for Descartes, doubt is a method but not a destination. Each philosopher of education eventually becomes prescriptive. He accepts the responsibility to say "Here is the way in which I see the world and here is what I am going to do about it as I teach and learn."

---

[1] Charles Sanders Peirce, *The Fixation of Belief*, reprinted in Hartman, ed., *Philosophy of Recent Times, Vol. I* (New York: McGraw-Hill Book Company, Inc., 1967), p. 391.

11

Existential Philosophers
on Education

BRUCE F. BAKER

At the conclusion of his article "Existentialism and Education" Van Cleve Morris states that ". . . we might even conclude that Existentialism would have no traffic with education in any shape or form. Indeed the case might even be developed that Existentialism is the very denial of education as we understand it today."[1] Such a statement is by no means surprising when we consider the approach of Morris and others, such as George Kneller, to the problem of developing an Existentialist philosophy of education. For, although these authors usually mention the views of a number of Existentialists, there is an underlying tendency to identify Existentialism with the ideas of Sartre and attempt to relate his philosophy to education. Thus we find that Sartre's concept of pure freedom for man, his notion of the isolation and solitude of each person that results from the impossibility of authentic human relationships, and his probing descriptions of the basic motivations of human behavior, concluding with the statement that "man is a useless passion," are predominant factors in the attempts of Morris, Kneller, and others to relate Existentialism to education. For example, with regard to the concept of freedom, Kneller says:

[1] Van Cleve Morris, "Existentialism and Education," *Educational Theory*, Vol. 4, No. 4, October, 1954, appearing in Joe Park, ed., *Selected Readings in the Philosophy of Education*, second ed. (New York: Macmillan Publishing Co., Inc., 1963), pp. 551, 552.

Bruce Baker is Associate Professor of Education and Philosophy at the University of Missouri, Kansas City. Bruce F. Baker, "Existential Philosophers on Education," Educational Theory, Vol. XVI, No. 3, July 1966, pp. 216–24. Used by permission of the author and Educational Theory.

Existentialism's third weakness lies in its peculiar understanding of sound values and community relations. . . . Is it fair to grant the existentialist absolute freedom when the consequences of such freedom would by common consent become injurious to the body politic? . . . Small wonder that anxiety, nausea, absurdity, and nothingness become the chief categories of such a system![2]

Morris recognizes the danger of identifying Existentialism with Sartre.

people have begun to think of Sartre and Existentialism almost as synonymous. As a matter of actual fact, Sartre is only a late comer on the Existential stage, and is surprisingly enough, only partially representative of genuine Existentialism today.[3]

But then he goes on to make the following statement:

Now the concept of freedom has always been a subject of much discussion and dispute among philosophers, and all of the older theories wavered between a position of complete determinism on the one hand and some kind of union of freedom within ultimate determinism on the other. Existentialism refuses to walk this tightrope, and flatly and clearly states the case for complete, undiluted, and absolute freedom.[4]

Such statements as these make plain the difficulty of any attempt to inject these notions into American public education as a whole, apart from the question of the desirability of doing so.

However, the point to be made here is that Sartre has written little, if anything, on the educational problems that these authors discuss. And this situation is not unique to Sartre among the Existential philosophers, for most of them have not been concerned with a philosophical examination of educational issues. As a result, Kneller and Morris have decided that the most profitable approach is to infer what Existentialists "would" say about education.[5] Yet, since Existentialists disagree sharply among themselves on so many vital issues, this approach is dangerous at best, especially when the extreme views of Sartre, the most popular figure of the movement, are so often taken as exemplary of the philosophy as a whole.

II

Another approach to the matter might be to examine what has actually been written by Existentialists on education. Even though, as we have noted, the material is for the most part meager, there is some literature by Existential philosophers on the subject. Three of the most significant examples will

---

[2] George F. Kneller, *Existentialism and Education* (New York: Philosophical Library, Inc., 1958), pp. 154, 155.

[3] Morris, "Existentialism and Education," p. 539.

[4] Ibid., p. 542.

[5] See Kneller, pp. viii, ix, 122, and Van Cleve Morris, *Philosophy and the American School* (Boston: Houghton Mifflin Co., 1961), pp. 100, 393.

be briefly discussed in this section: Nietzsche's *On the Future of Our Educational Institutions*, Ortega y Gasset's *Mission of the University*, and Jaspers' *The Idea of the University*.

The first of these works consists of a series of lectures given by Nietzsche at the University of Basle during the first three months of 1872. By this time Nietzsche was a twenty-seven year old professor of classical philology at Basle and, although the seeds of later themes were being sown, especially in *The Birth of Tragedy*, he had not yet formulated his mature thought. As the title of his lectures indicates, Nietzsche is primarily concerned with German educational institutions. In his introduction he indicates two forces which he believes are undermining German schools: "These forces are: a striving to achieve the greatest possible *extension of education* on the one hand, and a tendency *to minimise and to weaken it on the other*."[6] Nietzsche thinks that the attempt to extend education to all reflects merely a concern for economic gain, and, although it is necessary for the masses, it weakens what he considers to be a "true educational institution."[7] This type of institution has as its goal the inculcation of "culture" through awakening in students a concern for classical art and literature, especially that of Hellenic Greece, after a thorough grounding in German language and literature. Nietzsche stresses that this cultural education must take place within a framework of strict discipline: "We recognize the fatal consequences of our present public schools, in that they are unable to inculcate severe and genuine culture, which should consist above all in obedience and habituation."[8] This education would be geared not to the common man but to a select group of persons:

I have long accustomed myself to look with caution upon those who are ardent in the cause of the so-called 'education of the people' in the common meaning of the phrase. . . . The education of the masses cannot, therefore, be our aim; but rather the education of a few picked men for great and lasting works.[9]

Thus, revealing the influence of Schopenhauer, Nietzsche concludes that the product of the "true educational institution" would be a few geniuses whose work is the "pure reflection of the eternal and immutable essence of things."[10]

This brief outline of the main points raised in *On the Future of Our Educational Institutions* represents, in essence, an expression of the type of cultural education Nietzsche thought necessary for German institutions of

---

[6] Friedrich Nietzsche, *On the Future of Our Educational Institutions*, trans. by J. M. Kennedy, *The Complete Works of Friedrich Nietzsche*, ed. by Oscar Levy, v. III (London: Allen and Unwin, 1909), p. 12.

[7] Ibid., p. 95.

[8] Ibid., p. 60.

[9] Ibid., pp. 74, 75.

[10] Ibid., p. 113.

learning as well as a critique of the educational situations he himself had experienced, both as student and teacher. From a certain point of view, these lectures may even be viewed as one instance of the constant battle, still raging, between a "progressive" type of education concerned with utilitarian results and a more conservative standpoint, seeking its roots in classical tradition. In many ways Nietzsche exemplifies an extreme example of the latter position: "I for my own part know of only two exact contraries: *institutions for teaching culture and institutions for teaching how to succeed in life.* All our present institutions belong to the second class; but I am speaking only of the first."[11] His infatuation with Hellenism, the influence of Schopenhauer, and the emphasis on obedience, harsh discipline, and fixed rules—these factors point out the conservative side of Nietzsche. But these views are the result of early influences that, for the most part, either later lose their appeal or are modified by his developing thought. For example, Nietzsche's stress on "obedience and habituation" contrasts with his later concern that each man obey his own conscience in order to become "what he is" (and also, incidentally, contrasts sharply with Morris' statement on "Existentialism's" concept of freedom in education).

As the titles of their works indicate, Ortega and Jaspers direct their attention primarily to the university, whereas Nietzsche speaks in terms of the broad spectrum of educational institutions. Nietzsche recognized that education is primarily geared toward providing a livelihood for the average person, even though he was trying to develop a different notion of education. Ortega agrees with Nietzsche on this point. He conceives of education in terms of an economic principle of supply and demand. All economic activity arises because of some form of scarcity, and this is the case with education:

Man is occupied and preoccupied with education for a reason which is simple, bold, and devoid of glamour: in order to live with assurance and freedom and efficiency, it is necessary to know an enormous number of things, and the child or youth has an extremely limited capacity for learning. . . . Scarcity of the capacity to learn is the cardinal principle of education. It is necessary to provide for teaching precisely in proportion as the learner is unable to learn.[12]

But rather than suppress the importance of this fact, Ortega sees the education of the common man for his role in life as the foundation of the university: "The university, in the strict sense, is to mean that institution which teaches the ordinary student to be a cultured person and a good member of a profession."[13] He maintains that the university has three essential functions, ordered according to importance:

[11] Ibid., p. 98.
[12] José Ortega y Gasset, *Mission of the University*, trans. by Howard Lee Nostrand (Princeton: Princeton University Press, 1944), p. 68.
[13] Ibid., p. 93.

We come to the conclusion therefore that the university's teaching comprises these three functions:

I. The transmission of culture.

II. The teaching of the professions.

III. Scientific research and the training of new scientists.[14]

Like Nietzsche, Ortega considers the transmission of culture to be the fundamental aim, though by culture he means something quite different from Nietzsche's use of the term: "Culture is the system of vital ideas which each age possesses; better yet, it is the system *by* which the age lives."[15] Also, Ortega believes that the first two functions of the university must be set apart from the third; for, with his stress on the ordinary student, his position on the current controversy of "teaching vs. research" is that good teaching and productive research are incompatible:

I have lived close to a good number of the foremost scientists of our time, yet I have not found among them a single good teacher. . . . The selection of professors will depend not on their rank as investigators but on their talent for synthesis and their gift for teaching.[16]

The fact that the university's primary mission is to cultivate and enrich the ordinary man's awareness of the cultural ethos of his time implies, for Ortega, that there is an additional function of the university:

the university must intervene, *as* the university, in current affairs, treating the great themes of the day from its own point of view: cultural, professional, and scientific. . . . the university must assert itself as a major 'spiritual power,' higher than the press, standing for serenity in the midst of frenzy, for seriousness and the grasp of intellect in the face of frivolity and unashamed stupidity.

Then the university, once again, will come to be what it was in its grand hour: an uplifting principle in the history of the western world.[17]

Now for Jaspers, "the university is a community of scholars and students engaged in the task of seeking truth."[18] On this basis he conceives of three essential functions of the university by means of which its basic "idea" may be realized; and these bear striking resemblance to those of Ortega: "Three things are required at a university: professional training, education of the whole man, research. For the university is simultaneously a professional school, a cultural center and a research institute."[19] However, unlike Ortega's three functions of the university, these do not represent a hierarchy of goals:

[14] Ibid., p. 62.

[15] Ibid., p. 81.

[16] Ibid., pp. 92, 93.

[17] Ibid., p. 99.

[18] Karl Jaspers, *The Idea of the University*, ed. by Karl W. Deutsch, trans. by H. A. T. Reiche and H. F. Vanderschmidt (Boston: Beacon Press, 1959), p. 1.

[19] Ibid., p. 40.

In the idea of the university . . . these three are indissolubly united. One cannot be cut off from the others without destroying the intellectual substance of the university, and without at the same time crippling itself. All three are factors of a living whole. By isolating them, the spirit of the university perishes.[20]

And this "spirit of the university" is to be understood in terms of the "intellectual substance" Jaspers mentions. As he says while outlining his mode of approach in the introduction to *The Idea of the University:*

We shall, first, consider the nature of intellectual life in general, one of whose forms is realized in the university. Next, we shall turn to the responsibilities inherent in the corporate realization of intellectual life at the university. Lastly we shall consider the concrete foundations of the university and how these affect its functioning.[21]

Intellectual life is thus the "substance" of the university and is viewed by Jaspers as a life devoted to the relentless pursuit of knowledge: "Within the life of the university teachers and students are driven by a single motive, man's basic quest for knowledge."[22] Through this quest the ultimate goal of "truth" is to be realized. As a result of his understandable concern about the university's involvement in politics, Jaspers emphasizes that this realization must be limited to the theoretical level rather than enter the field of political action. Even so, since the university is the guardian of truth, it represents, for him as for Ortega, a kind of intellectual model: "The university is meant to function as the intellectual conscience of an era."[23]

On the other hand, Jaspers seems to reverse Ortega's ordering of the functions of the university. Instead of aiming primarily toward the cultivation of the common man, the university seeks knowledge and truth, i.e., research. Thus, in a tone somewhat reminiscent of Nietzsche, Jaspers believes that tight restrictions must be placed on the type of student allowed to enter the university:

Equality of intellectual status cannot be decreed. . . . Nor must we be deceived by the dream that all people can achieve the noblest function of humanity. This is a utopian dream which is not realized simply by assuming that it exists already when, in fact, no one knows or is capable of knowing to what extent it can be realized. . . . The university must maintain its aristocratic principles if it is not to fall prey to a universal lowering of standards.[24]

Related to this is the fact that, whereas Ortega maintains that teaching, the primary function of the university, must be separated from research, Jaspers believes that the two must be connected and the functions of the university be seen as a unified whole:

[20] Ibid., p. 41.
[21] Ibid., p. 3.
[22] Ibid., p. 41.
[23] Ibid., p. 121.
[24] Ibid., p. 97.

Moreover, teaching itself is often—even most of the time—stimulating to research. Above all, teaching vitally needs the substance which only research can give it. Hence the combination of research and teaching is the lofty and inalienable basic principle of the university. . . . ideally the best research worker is also the best and only teacher.[25]

If the university is to bear the fruit of genius Jaspers recognizes that the mind must be free of constrictions and declares, in contrast to Nietzsche, that "no authority, no rules and regulations, no supervision of studies such as are found in high schools must be allowed to hamper the university student."[26]

These writings represent an interesting commentary on some important educational issues by three thinkers whose philosophical work has been termed "Existential" in character. There are points of significant agreement among them, but they disagree on so many basic issues that it would be difficult indeed to develop an Existentialist philosophy of education on the basis of these three works.

In addition, these views on education do not seem to be primarily "Existential" in nature. They appear to be written on a different level and for different purposes from their authors' philosophical writing—more from the point of view of the university professor than from that of the Existentialist who is attempting to include education within his particular philosophical position. Thus we find the overriding concern with issues that are of prime importance to the university professor: e.g., academic freedom, teaching vs. research, culture vs. technology, and the impact of the university on society and the state and vice versa. The opinions expressed by these philosophers are significant and vital contributions to this debate; but they do not solve the problem of relating Existentialism to education, for there is really no serious attempt to analyze the notion of education as a whole and to integrate this within the philosopher's own form of Existentialism. Jaspers, for example, mentions the importance of communication, especially Socratic-type discussion, in *The Idea of the University*, and the notion of communication is an important part of his philosophy. Yet in this work he never connects its educational significance to the basic concept of his philosophy, *Existenz*. (In fact, *Existenz* per se is mentioned only in a two-page chapter of the book, the purpose of which is to determine "the foundation of the scientific outlook."[27]) On the other hand, as we have seen, the severe restrictions Nietzsche places upon the student actually contradict the pure individuality of his mature thought.

[25] Ibid., pp. 44, 45.
[26] Ibid., p. 54.
[27] Ibid., p. 29. In the English translation cited, Jaspers' term *Existenz* is misleadingly rendered "human existence" rather than left in the original German; such a translation is more appropriate when Jaspers uses *Dasein*. See Karl Jaspers, *Die Idee der Universität* (Berlin: Springer-Verlag, 1946), pp. 31, 32.

III

Thus it would seem that the views of Nietzsche, Ortega, and Jaspers do not found a concrete basis upon which an Existentialist philosophy of education can be built. However, there has been one noticeable omission from the group of Existentialists who have written on education—Martin Buber. He, more than any other Existentialist, has, in the spirit of Dewey, treated education as a serious topic for philosophical inquiry, one which is an integral part of his I-Thou philosophy.

This is not the place to exposit in depth Buber's philosophy of education; the details of this subject have been well presented elsewhere.[28] What will be noted here are some of the key relationships between his philosophy of education and his philosophy as a whole. Buber's philosophy, as presented in his major work, *I and Thou*, is grounded on the two basic attitudes man may take toward the world, I-It and I-Thou. This delineation of fundamental attitudes is related to the distinction made in his essay "Education" between the two instincts which ground education, the originative or creative and that of communion. Just as he attempts to overcome the subjective-objective dichotomy at the heart of the I-It attitude, Buber is concerned to transcend this same persistent conflict in educational theory. The modern "subjective" emphasis on creativity, like the "objective" stress on the classical tradition, fails to touch the essence of education for Buber.

Education is a form of the fundamental I-Thou relation, the specific embodiment of which in an educational framework is the teacher-student relation. Education is to be understood in terms of the communion between teacher and student because the development of the pupil as a person rests on the impact of one human being upon another: "The relation in education is one of pure dialogue."[29] This does not mean that subject matter is neglected, but that it is seen in proper perspective. Through mutuality the student develops an awareness of the meaning of what the teacher as a person and the author of a book as a Thou present before him. In this way subject matter is brought from the abstract impersonality of objective knowledge to a personally meaningful reality that is alive because it is grounded on that which is "between" man and man.

In order that true dialogue can transpire between teacher and student it is essential that the pupil have confidence in the teacher as a Thou who can be trusted, not a dominating symbol of power:

When the pupil's confidence has been won, his resistance against being educated gives way to a singular happening: he accepts the educator as a person. He feels he

---

[28] See especially Maurice S. Friedman, "Martin Buber's Philosophy of Education," *Educational Theory*, Vol. 6, No. 2, April, 1956, and Maurice S. Friedman, *Martin Buber, The Life of Dialogue* (New York: Harper & Row, Publishers, 1960), Chap. 20.

[29] Martin Buber, *Between Man and Man*, trans. by Ronald Gregor Smith (Boston: Beacon Press, 1955), p. 98.

may trust this man, that this man is not making a business out of him, but is taking part in his life, accepting him before desiring to influence him.[30]

This imposes a heavy responsibility upon the teacher, who is in the position of selecting the "world" of reality and truth of the student. The teacher must attempt to understand the point of view of the student by "experiencing the other side," which Buber calls "inclusion." That is, the teacher must see the student as a Thou to be met in dialogue rather than an It, an object to be manipulated and used to his own advantage. The former alternative makes true education possible; the latter leads inevitably to propaganda. Buber does not believe that teachers can or should maintain a purely objective detachment from the developing attitudes of students, as some have recommended. Teachers, as human beings, cannot divorce themselves of their attitudes and value commitments without destroying themselves as persons. The real issue for Buber is whether the teacher should impose his values upon the student with a view toward domination and exploitation by propaganda or present himself to the student and allow the latter to develop his own self through this meeting with the "other." Thus the teacher must walk a "narrow ridge" between suppression of the student's individuality and the influence required by the nature of the teaching situation, his only guidance being his "attitude"—I-It or I-Thou: "In education, then, there is a lofty asceticism: an asceticism which rejoices in the world, for the sake of the responsibility for a realm of life which is entrusted to us for our influence but not our interference—either by the will to power or by Eros."[31] The basic principle underlying this relation between teacher and student is the education of character—the willingness of the teacher to communicate his whole being or "character" to that of the student in order to help him develop an attitude of responsibility for his own life so that, in his own unique way, he may make an authentic unity of it.

But, to achieve authenticity, this "attitude" must lead the pupil beyond a concern with his own individual development: "He [the teacher] can bring before his pupils the image of a great character who denies no answer to life and the world, but accepts responsibility for everything essential that he meets."[32] By fulfilling his responsibility to the student, the teacher can awaken him to a similar responsibility for his fellow man, society, and the world. Buber's whole I-Thou philosophy can be looked at as a basis for social reconstruction, and his views on education can be seen as the building of the foundation for this reconstruction:

Today the great characters are still 'enemies of the people', they who love their society, yet wish not only to preserve it but to raise it to a higher level. Tomorrow they will be the architects of a new unity of mankind. It is the longing for personal

[30] Ibid., p. 106.
[31] Ibid., p. 95.
[32] Ibid., p. 116.

unity, from which must be born a unity of mankind, which the educator should lay hold of and strengthen in his pupils. Faith in this unity and the will to achieve it is not a 'return' to individualism, but a step beyond all the dividedness of individualism and collectivism. A great and full relation between men and man can only exist between unified and responsible persons. . . . Genuine education of character is genuine education for community.[33]

Buber goes on to extend this idea of the education of character beyond the realm of youth and applies it to his notion of adult education. In the essay "The Demand of the Spirit and Historical Reality" he says:

If the new house that man hopes to erect is not to become his burial chamber, the essence of living together must undergo a change at the same time as the organization of living. . . . He must also *educate* sociologically, he must educate men in living together; he must educate man so he can live with man.[34]

With this goal in mind, Buber has actually implemented his idea of adult education in post-war Israel. The great need of Israel at this time was the unification into one whole of people of diverse backgrounds who were immigrating there. To help alleviate this problem, the Adult Education Centre of the Hebrew University established the School for Adult Education Teachers in 1949 with Buber in charge in order to produce men and women who would go into the immigration camps and attempt to bring the people into the fold of the community. Like the education of youth, this type of adult education is not to be understood merely in terms of an institutionalized activity or a formal transmission of knowledge:

Our aim goes considerably beyond that of imparting knowledge. We are not directly and especially interested in knowledge. We are interested in man. Man must have knowledge, too, but if knowledge becomes the center of the person, it is just the opposite of what we want. We want the wholeness of a person because only whole persons can influence others as we want to influence others. This particular conjunction of situation and person is Adult Education as I understand it.[35]

So both the education of youth and adult education can only be understood in terms of Buber's basic I-Thou philosophy; for the essence of education is the manifestation of the I-Thou relation through the authentic communication of one human being with another.

Thus Buber, in contrast with other major Existentialists, has developed a philosophy of education within his overall philosophy. This is not to say that Buber presents us with the "Existentialist" philosophy of education,

[33] Ibid., p. 116.

[34] Martin Buber, *Pointing the Way*, trans. by Maurice Friedman (New York: Harper & Row, Publishers, 1957), p. 179.

[35] Martin Buber, "Adult Education in Israel," *The Torch*, the official publication of The National Federation of Jewish Men's Clubs, Inc. (Spring, 1952), p. 9.

but only that he has carried out a philosophical examination of education from the standpoint of his own particular brand of Existentialism. By limiting ourselves to this conclusion, we at least avoid, on the one hand, guessing what a variety of thinkers would say regarding this subject and, on the other, attempting to reconcile a number of diverging views on education that are not particularly Existential in nature in order to come up with an Existentialist philosophy of education. And in the end it may well be that Buber's philosophy, which avoids the negative extremes of Sartre and yet which is grounded on a particular conception of Existential authenticity, will prove to be one of the most significant and influential contributions to educational philosophy since Dewey.

12

A Model for Analyzing
a Philosophy of Education

WILLIAM K. FRANKENA

There are two sorts of things that go by the name of philosophy of education today, one traditional and one newish. The newish sort of thing is what is called "analytical philosophy of education." It consists in the analysis of educational concepts, arguments, slogans, and statements. For example, if one tries to define what is meant by teaching, to distinguish teaching from indoctrination, and to relate teaching to learning, or if one tries to determine what is meant by the slogan "Learn by doing!", then one is doing analytical philosophy of education. The analytical philosophy of education. consists entirely of such inquiries. Since I am here seeking to show how to analyze a philosophy of education, this essay is itself an example of analytical philosophy of education. I say that this sort of thing is newish because, although educational philosophers have always included some of it in their works, it is only recently that some of them have come to think that their work should include nothing else.

The other kind of philosophy of education is what educational philosophers have done historically and what some of them still do. I shall call it "normative philosophy of education." It may be eclectic or non-eclectic; idealistic, realistic, or pragmatic; naturalistic or supernaturalistic; traditional or progressive. In all its forms, however, what distinguishes it from

William K. Frankena is Professor of Philosophy at the University of Michigan. William K. Frankena, "A Model for Analyzing a Philosophy of Education," *The High School Journal*, Vol. 50, No. 1 (October 1966), pp. 8–13. Used by permission of the author and *The High School Journal*.

analytical philosophy of education is that it makes normative statements about what education, educators, and the schools should do or not do, about what the aims, content, methods, etc., of education should be or not be.

I

Now consider any such normative philosophy of education, for example, that of Aristotle, Rousseau, Dewey, Whitehead, Russell, Maritain, Brameld, or Phenix. Our problem is to find a scheme for analyzing it, that is, for understanding it and seeing how it is put together, for taking it apart and putting it together again. One cannot evaluate it in any systematic way until one has analyzed it to see just what it says and what its arguments are.

In general, a normative philosophy of education will include statements of three kinds. (a) It must include normative statements about the aims, principles, methods, etc., of education, as Dewey does when he says that the schools should teach reflective thinking. (b) It will probably include—and it should include—some bits of analysis, for example, definitions of education, teaching, and learning. (c) Almost certainly it will contain some statements of empirical fact, hypotheses about their explanation, psychological theories, experimental findings, predictions, and the like, for example, Russell's statement that a child can be made to feel the importance of learning the dull parts of a subject without the use of compulsion. (d) It may also contain statements of a fourth kind—epistemological, metaphysical, or theological ones such as Phenix's assertion that the meaning of a proposition is defined by the method of validating it or Maritain's doctrine that man is a sinful and wounded creature called to divine life. It is not always easy to tell which kind of a statement is being made in a given sentence, and many sentences in works on the philosophy of education are ambiguous and hard to classify.

To analyze a philosophy of education one must find out what statements of these different kinds it contains and how they are related to one another in the author's reasoning. This is relatively easy to do in the case of some authors, for example, Maritain, harder to do in the case of others, for example, Dewey or Whitehead. What follows is an attempt to provide a guide for doing so.[1]

II

Education is primarily a process in which educators and educated interact, and such a process is called education if and only if it issues or is intended to issue in the formation, in the one being educated, of certain desired or desirable abilities, habits, dispositions, skills, character traits, beliefs, or bodies of knowledge (if it is intended to but does not, it is called *bad* education), for example, the habit of reflective thinking, conscien-

---

[1] For similar attempts on my part, see "Toward a Philosophy of the Philosophy of Education," *Harvard Educational Review*, 26, 1956; *Philosophy of Education*, Macmillan, 1965, pp. 1–10; *Three Historical Philosophies of Education*, Scott Foresman, 1965, pp. 6–12.

tiousness, the ability to dance, or a knowledge of astronomy. For convenience, I shall refer to all such states as dispositions. Then education is the process of forming or trying to form such dispositions. Note that what I have just done is a rough analysis of the concept of education.

If this is so, then (1) the *main* task of a normative philosophy of education is to list and define a set of dispositions to be fostered by parents, teachers, and schools (and by the pupil himself). That is, it must say what dispositions are desirable and ought to be cultivated. In saying this it will, of course, be making normative statements, but the definitions of the dispositions listed will be bits of analysis. A complete normative theory of education will, however, do two more things. (2) It will give a line of thought to show that the dispositions listed by it are desirable or should be cultivated. Such a line of reasoning may take various forms, but they must all have the same general pattern. They must bring in some basic premises about the aims or values of life or about the principles to be followed in life—about what is desirable or obligatory. These, again, will be normative judgments, the most fundamental ones. Even Dewey brings in such premises, though he often writes as if he does not. In addition, they must show or at least give reasons for thinking that, if we are to live in the way that is desirable or in the way in which we ought to—if we are to live a good or a moral life—then we must acquire the dispositions listed. It is in this part of a philosophy of education that epistemological, ontological, or theological premises most often appear, but they are not logically required. What *is* logically required is, first, some normative premises stating basic goals or principles, for example, Aristotle's premise that the good life is a happy one consisting of intrinsically excellent activities like contemplation, and second, factual claims stating that certain dispositions are conducive to the achievement of those goals or to the following of those principles, for example, Aristotle's further claim that, if we are to achieve the good life as he sees it, we must cultivate such dispositions as moderation, practical wisdom, and a knowledge of mathematics, physics, and philosophy. If we think of basic normative premises as belonging to Box A, the other premises used here, whether they are religious, philosophical, or empirical, as belonging to Box B, and the conclusions as to the dispositions to be fostered as belonging to Box C, then we can represent this part of a philosophy of education as follows:

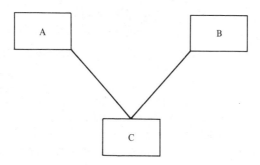

(3) Finally, a complete normative theory of education will tell us what we should do in order to acquire or foster the dispositions recommended by it in Box C, that is, it will make further recommendations about means, methods, curriculum, administration, etc., hopefully accompanying them with its reasons for making them. This means that it will make normative statements of yet a third kind, and that it will support them by giving empirical evidence (discovered by observation and experiment or borrowed from psychology and other disciplines) to show that the methods and measures it advocates are necessary, helpful, or effective in the formation of the dispositions in its Box C (and that other methods are not). The example cited from Russell earlier will do here; in it he argues that compulsion should not be used, since children can be gotten through even the dull parts of a subject without it. This example also shows that premises from Box A may come in even in this part of a philosophy of education, for Russell is assuming the normative principle that compulsion ought not to be used unless it is necessary. Actually, epistemological premises or other premises from Box B may also appear at this stage; for instance, Cardinal Newman uses his epistemological premise that theology is a body of genuine knowledge in an argument to show that theology should belong to the curriculum of a university. Neglecting such important points, however, we may represent this part of a philosophy of education as follows, taking Box C as giving the dispositions to be fostered, Box D as containing factual statements of the form " Method X is necessary, effective, or at least helpful in the formation of one or more of these dispositions (or the opposite)," and Box E as including recommendations of the form " Method X should (or should not) be used ":

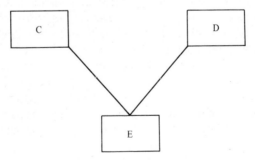

It should be added that bits of analysis may also show up in this part of a theory, for example, in a distinction between indoctrination and teaching or in a definition of compulsion.

III

It will now be clear that a full-fledged normative philosophy of education will have two parts, each probably including some bits of analysis; one part falling into the ABC pattern given above and the other into the CDE pattern. In its actual presentation, however, the two parts are often mingled and the patterns are often left unclear, for instance, in Whitehead's essays on education. Of the two parts, the first is the more properly philosophical, and the second is the more practical. Combining the two parts, we may represent a complete normative philosophy of education as follows:

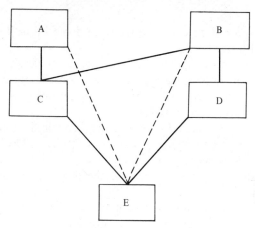

Here the dotted lines are intended to take care of the fact, noted earlier, that premises from Boxes A and B may be used in arriving at the recommendations made in Box E.

It will also be clear that there may be three kinds of normative philosophy of education: (a) one that is complete in the way just indicated; (b) one that does only what was described as the first part of the complete task, giving us only what falls into the ABC pattern, that is, one that provides us only with a list of dispositions to be fostered together with a rationale showing us that they should be fostered and why, leaving the task of implementation to educational scientists, administrators, and teachers; and (c) one that simply begins with a list of dispositions to be cultivated and goes on to give us what falls into the CDE pattern or into what was referred to as the second part of the complete task, telling us what we should do to foster the dispositions listed most effectively and giving us the evidence and arguments to show why we should adopt those methods and procedures. A writer who does the third kind of thing might take his list of dispositions from some more philosophical work, or he might be eclectic, picking up the dispositions on his list from various sources, or he might simply take them to be the dispositions regarded as desirable by society, parents, the state, the church, school boards, or even the pupils themselves—remember how Bianca complains to her would-be educators in *The Taming of a Shrew*:

> Why, gentlemen, you do me double wrong,
> To strive for that which resteth in my choice:
> I am no breeching scholar in the schools;
> I'll not be tied to hours nor 'pointed times,
> But learn my lessons as I please myself.

We can also now see just what one must do in order to understand any complete normative philosophy of education that is placed before one (an analytical philosophy of education is another matter). If one knows this, one will also be able to analyze any less complete normative philosophy of education.

(1) (1) One must first look to see what dispositions it says education should foster (Box C).

(2) Next, one must try to determine the rationale given to show that education should foster those dispositions. To do this one must:

(a) See what its basic normative premises are—its basic values, principles, or ends (Box A).

(b) See what factual premises are brought in (implicitly or explicitly), empirical, theological, or philosophical (Box B).

(c) See how these go together to make a line of argument of the ABC pattern to show that the dispositions listed should be cultivated.

(3) Then one should look for recommendations about ways and means of teaching, administering, etc. (Box E).

(4) Fourthly, one must seek to discover the rationales for these recommendations. To do this one must:

(a) See what factual statements based on observation and experience are brought in (possibly borrowed from psychology, etc.) (Box D).

(b) See if any premises from Boxes A or B are used here.

(c) See how these go together to make a line of argument (or a battery of separate arguments) to show that the ways and means recommended should be used in the cultivation of the dispositions listed (Pattern CDE).

(5) All along, of course, one should notice any definitions or bits of analysis that occur and see how they fit into the discussion.

Finally, it can also be seen from the above analysis of a normative philosophy of education what is involved in "building" one of one's own. However, this should now be so obvious that it need not be spelled out.

13

The Aims of Education

ALFRED NORTH WHITEHEAD

Culture is activity of thought, and receptiveness to beauty and humane feeling. Scraps of information have nothing to do with it. A merely well-informed man is the most useless bore on God's earth. What we should aim at producing is men who possess both culture and expert knowledge in some special direction. Their expert knowledge will give them the ground to start from, and their culture will lead them as deep as philosophy and as high as art. We have to remember that the valuable intellectual development is self-development, and that it mostly takes place between the ages of sixteen and thirty. As to training, the most important part is given by mothers before the age of twelve. A saying due to Archbishop Temple illustrates my meaning. Surprise was expressed at the success in after-life of a man, who as a boy at Rugby had been somewhat undistinguished. He answered, "It is not what they are at eighteen, it is what they become afterwards that matters."

In training a child to activity of thought, above all things we must beware of what I will call "inert ideas"—that is to say, ideas that are merely received into the mind without being utilised, or tested, or thrown into fresh combinations.

In the history of education, the most striking phenomenon is that schools of learning, which at one epoch are alive with a ferment of genius, in a succeeding generation exhibit merely pedantry and routine. The reason is,

Alfred North Whitehead (February 15, 1861–December 30, 1947) was a mathematician, philosopher, and educator. Alfred N. Whitehead, *The Aims of Education and Other Essays.* New York: New American Library, 1949, pp. 13–26. Copyright 1929 by Macmillan Publishing Co., Inc. Used by permission of Macmillan Publishing Co., Inc.

that they are overladen with inert ideas. Education with inert ideas is not only useless: it is, above all things, harmful—*Corruptio optimi, pessima.* Except at rare intervals of intellectual ferment, education in the past has been radically infected with inert ideas. That is the reason why uneducated clever women, who have seen much of the world, are in middle life so much the most cultured part of the community. They have been saved from this horrible burden of inert ideas. Every intellectual revolution which has ever stirred humanity into greatness has been a passionate protest against inert ideas. Then, alas, with pathetic ignorance of human psychology, it has proceeded by some educational scheme to bind humanity afresh with inert ideas of its own fashioning.

Let us now ask how in our system of education we are to guard against this mental dryrot. We enunciate two educational commandments, " Do not teach too many subjects," and again, "What you teach, teach thoroughly."

The result of teaching small parts of a large number of subjects is the passive reception of disconnected ideas, not illumined with any spark of vitality. Let the main ideas which are introduced into a child's education be few and important, and let them be thrown into every combination possible. The child should make them his own, and should understand their application here and now in the circumstances of his actual life. From the very beginning of his education, the child should experience the joy of discovery. The discovery which he has to make, is that general ideas give an understanding of that stream of events which pours through his life, which is his life. By understanding I mean more than a mere logical analysis, though that is included. I mean "understanding" in the sense in which it is used in the French proverb, "To understand all, is to forgive all." Pedants sneer at an education which is useful. But if education is not useful, what is it? Is it a talent, to be hidden away in a napkin? Of course, education should be useful, whatever your aim in life. It was useful to Saint Augustine and it was useful to Napoleon. It is useful, because understanding is useful.

I pass lightly over that understanding which should be given by the literary side of education. Nor do I wish to be supposed to pronounce on the relative merits of a classical or a modern curriculum. I would only remark that the understanding which we want is an understanding of an insistent present. The only use of a knowledge of the past is to equip us for the present. No more deadly harm can be done to young minds than by depreciation of the present. The present contains all that there is. It is holy ground; for it is the past, and it is the future. At the same time it must be observed that an age is no less past if it existed two hundred years ago than if it existed two thousand years ago. Do not be deceived by the pedantry of dates. The ages of Shakespeare and of Molière are no less past than are the ages of Sophocles and of Virgil. The communion of saints is a great and inspiring assemblage, but it has only one possible hall of meeting, and that is, the present; and the mere lapse of time through which any particular group of saints must travel to reach that meeting-place, makes very little difference.

Passing now to the scientific and logical side of education, we remember that here also ideas which are not utilised are positively harmful. By utilising an idea, I mean relating it to that stream, compounded of sense perceptions, feelings, hopes, desires, and of mental activities adjusting thought to thought, which forms our life. I can imagine a set of beings which might fortify their souls by passively reviewing disconnected ideas. Humanity is not built that way—except perhaps some editors of newspapers.

In scientific training, the first thing to do with an idea is to prove it. But allow me for one moment to extend the meaning of "prove"; I mean—to prove its worth. Now an idea is not worth much unless the propositions in which it is embodied are true. Accordingly an essential part of the proof of an idea is the proof, either by experiment or by logic, of the truth of the propositions. But it is not essential that this proof of the truth should constitute the first introduction to the idea. After all, its assertion by the authority of respectable teachers is sufficient evidence to begin with. In our first contact with a set of propositions, we commence by appreciating their importance. That is what we all do in after-life. We do not attempt, in the strict sense, to prove or to disprove anything, unless its importance makes it worthy of that honour. These two processes of proof, in the narrow sense, and of appreciation, do not require a rigid separation in time. Both can be proceeded with nearly concurrently. But in so far as either process must have the priority, it should be that of appreciation by use.

Furthermore, we should not endeavour to use propositions in isolation. Emphatically I do not mean, a neat little set of experiments to illustrate Proposition I and then the proof of Proposition I, a neat little set of experiments to illustrate Proposition II and then the proof of Proposition II, and so on to the end of the book. Nothing could be more boring. Inter-related truths are utilised *en bloc*, and the various propositions are employed in any order, and with any reiteration. Choose some important applications of your theoretical subject; and study them concurrently with the systematic theoretical exposition. Keep the theoretical exposition short and simple, but let it be strict and rigid so far as it goes. It should not be too long for it to be easily known with thoroughness and accuracy. The consequences of a plethora of half-digested theoretical knowledge are deplorable. Also the theory should not be muddled up with the practice. The child should have no doubt when it is proving and when it is utilising. My point is that what is proved should be utilised, and that what is utilised should—so far as is practicable—be proved. I am far from asserting that proof and utilisation are the same thing.

At this point of my discourse, I can most directly carry forward my argument in the outward form of a digression. We are only just realising that the art and science of education require a genius and a study of their own; and that this genius and this science are more than a bare knowledge of some branch of science or of literature. This truth was partially perceived in the past generation; and headmasters, somewhat crudely, were apt to supersede learning in their colleagues by requiring left-hand bowling and a taste for football. But culture is more than cricket, and more than football, and more than extent of knowledge.

Education is the acquisition of the art of the utilisation of knowledge. This is an art very difficult to impart. Whenever a text-book is written of real educational worth, you may be quite certain that some reviewer will say that it will be difficult to teach from it. Of course it will be difficult to teach from it. If it were easy, the book ought to be burned; for it cannot be educational. In education, as elsewhere, the broad primrose path leads to a nasty place. This evil path is represented by a book or a set of lectures which will practically enable the student to learn by heart all the questions likely to be asked at the next external examination. And I may say in passing that no educational system is possible unless every question directly asked of a pupil at any examination is either framed or modified by the actual teacher of that pupil in that subject. The external assessor may report on the curriculum or on the performance of the pupils, but never should be allowed to ask the pupil a question which has not been strictly supervised by the actual teacher, or at least inspired by a long conference with him. There are a few exceptions to this rule, but they are exceptions, and could easily be allowed for under the general rule.

We now return to my previous point, that theoretical ideas should always find important applications within the pupil's curriculum. This is not an easy doctrine to apply, but a very hard one. It contains within itself the problem of keeping knowledge alive, of preventing it from becoming inert, which is the central problem of all education.

The best procedure will depend on several factors, none of which can be neglected, namely, the genius of the teacher, the intellectual type of the pupils, their prospects in life, the opportunities offered by the immediate surroundings of the school, and allied factors of this sort. It is for this reason that the uniform external examination is so deadly. We do not denounce it because we are cranks, and like denouncing established things. We are not so childish. Also, of course, such examinations have their use in testing slackness. Our reason of dislike is very definite and very practical. It kills the best part of culture. When you analyse in the light of experience the central task of education, you find that its successful accomplishment depends on a delicate adjustment of many variable factors. The reason is that we are dealing with human minds, and not with dead matter. The evocation of curiosity, of judgment, of the power of mastering a complicated tangle of circumstances, the use of theory in giving foresight in special cases—all these powers are not to be imparted by a set rule embodied in one schedule of examination subjects.

I appeal to you, as practical teachers. With good discipline, it is always possible to pump into the minds of a class a certain quantity of inert knowledge. You take a text-book and make them learn it. So far, so good. The child then knows how to solve a quadratic equation. But what is the point of teaching a child to solve a quadratic equation? There is a traditional answer to this question. It runs thus: The mind is an instrument, you first sharpen it, and then use it; the acquisition of the power of solving a quadratic equation is part of the process of sharpening the mind. Now there is just enough truth in this answer to have made it live through the ages. But for all its half-truth, it embodies a radical error which bids fair to stifle the genius of the modern world. I do not know who was first responsible for this analogy of the mind to a dead instrument. For aught I know, it may have been one of the seven wise men of Greece, or a committee of the whole lot of them. Whoever was the originator, there can be no doubt of the authority which it has acquired by the continuous approval bestowed upon it by eminent persons. But whatever its weight of authority, whatever the high approval which it can quote, I have no hesitation in denouncing it as one of the most fatal, erroneous, and dangerous conceptions ever introduced into the theory of education. The mind is never passive; it is a perpetual activity, delicate, receptive, responsive to stimulus. You cannot postpone its life until you have sharpened it. Whatever interest attaches to your subject-matter must be evoked here and now; whatever powers you are strengthening in the pupil, must be exercised here and now; whatever possibilities of mental life your teaching should impart, must be exhibited here and now. That is the golden rule of education, and a very difficult rule to follow.

The difficulty is just this: the apprehension of general ideas, intellectual habits of mind, and pleasurable interest in mental achievement can be evoked by no form of words, however accurately adjusted. All practical teachers know that education is a patient process of the mastery of details, minute by minute, hour by hour, day by day. There is no royal road to learning through an airy path of brilliant generalisations. There is a proverb about the difficulty of seeing the wood because of the trees. That difficulty is exactly the point which I am enforcing. The problem of education is to make the pupil see the wood by means of the trees.

The solution which I am urging, is to eradicate the fatal disconnection of subjects which kills the vitality of our modern curriculum. There is only one subject-matter for education, and that is Life in all its manifestations. Instead of this single unity, we offer children—Algebra, from which nothing follows; Geometry, from which nothing follows; Science, from which nothing follows; History, from which nothing follows; a Couple of Languages, never mastered; and lastly, most dreary of all, Literature, represented by plays of Shakespeare, with philological notes and short analyses of plot and character to be in substance committed to memory. Can such a list be said to represent Life, as it is known in the midst of the living of it? The best that can be said of it is, that it is a rapid table of contents which a deity might run over in his mind while he was thinking of creating a world, and had not yet determined how to put it together.

Let us now return to quadratic equations. We still have on hand the unanswered question. Why should children be taught their solution? Unless quadratic equations fit into a connected curriculum, of course there is no reason to teach anything about them. Furthermore, extensive as should be the place of mathematics in a complete culture, I am a little doubtful whether for many types of boys algebraic solutions of quadratic equations do not lie on the specialist side of mathematics. I may here remind you that as yet I have not said anything of the psychology or the content of the specialism, which is so necessary a part of an ideal education. But all that is an evasion of our real question, I merely state it in order to avoid being misunderstood in my answer.

Quadratic equations are part of algebra, and algebra is the intellectual instrument which has been created for rendering clear the quantitative aspects of the world. There is no getting out of it. Through and through the world is infected with quantity. To talk sense, is to talk in quantities. It is no use saying that the nation is large—How large? It is no use saying that radium is scarce—How scarce? You cannot evade quantity. You may fly to poetry and to music, and quantity and number will face you in your rhythms and your octaves. Elegant intellects which despise the theory of quantity, are but half developed. They are more to be pitied than blamed. The scraps of gibberish, which in their school-days were taught to them in the name of algebra, deserve some contempt.

This question of the degeneration of algebra into gibberish, both in word and in fact, affords a pathetic instance of the uselessness of reforming educational schedules without a clear conception of the attributes which you wish to evoke in the living minds of the children. A few years ago there was an outcry that school algebra was in need of reform, but there was a general agreement that graphs would put everything right. So all sorts of things were extruded, and graphs were introduced. So far as I can see, with no sort of idea behind them, but just graphs. Now every examination paper has one or two questions on graphs. Personally, I am an enthusiastic adherent of graphs. But I wonder whether as yet we have gained very much. You cannot put life into any schedule of general education unless you succeed in exhibiting its relation to some essential characteristic of all intelligent or emotional perception. It is a hard saying, but it is true; and I do not see how to make it any easier. In making these little formal alterations you are beaten by the very nature of things. You are pitted against too skilful an adversary, who will see to it that the pea is always under the other thimble.

Reformation must begin at the other end. First, you must make up your mind as to those quantitative aspects of the world which are simple enough to be introduced into general education; then a schedule of algebra should be framed which will about find its exemplification in these applications. We need not fear for our pet graphs, they will be there in plenty when we once begin to treat algebra as a serious means of studying the world. Some of the simplest applications will be found in the quantities which occur in the simplest study of society. The curves of history are more vivid and more informing than the dry catalogues of names and dates which comprise the greater part of that arid school study. What purpose is effected by a catalogue of undistinguished kings and queens? Tom, Dick, or Harry, they are all dead. General resurrections are failures, and are better postponed. The quantitative flux of the forces of modern society is capable of very simple exhibition. Meanwhile, the ideas of the variable, of the function, of rate of change, of equations and their solution, of elimination, are being studied as an abstract science for their own sake. Not, of course, in the pompous phrases with which I am alluding to them, here, but with that iteration of simple special cases proper to teaching.

If this course be followed, the route from Chaucer to the Black Death, from the Black Death to modern Labour troubles, will connect the tales of the mediæval pilgrims with the abstract science of algebra, both yielding diverse aspects of that single theme, Life. I know what most of you are thinking at this point. It is that the exact course which I have sketched out is not the particular one which you would have chosen, or even see how to work. I quite agree. I am not claiming that I could do it myself. But your objection is the precise reason why a common external examination system is fatal to education. The process of exhibiting the applications of knowledge must, for its success, essentially depend on the character of the pupils and the genius of the teacher. Of course I have left out the easiest applications with which most of us are more at home. I mean the quantitative sides of sciences, such as mechanics and physics.

Again, in the same connection we plot the statistics of social phenomena against the time. We then eliminate the time between suitable pairs. We can speculate how far we have exhibited a real causal connection, or how far a mere temporal coincidence. We notice that we might have plotted against the time one set of statistics for one country and another set for another country, and thus, with suitable choice of subjects, have obtained graphs which certainly exhibited mere coincidence. Also other graphs exhibit obvious causal connections. We wonder how to discriminate. And so are drawn on as far as we will.

But in considering this description, I must beg you to remember what I have been insisting on above. In the first place, one train of thought will not suit all groups of children. For example, I should expect that artisan children will want something more concrete and, in a sense, swifter than I have set down here. Perhaps I am wrong, but that is what I should guess. In the second place, I am not contemplating one beautiful lecture stimulating, once and for all, an admiring class. That is not the way in which education proceeds. No; all the time the pupils are hard at work solving examples, drawing graphs, and making experiments, until they have a thorough hold on the whole subject. I am describing the interspersed explanations, the directions which should be given to their thoughts. The pupils have got to be made to feel that they are studying something, and are not merely executing intellectual minuets.

Finally, if you are teaching pupils for some general examination, the problem of sound teaching is greatly complicated. Have you ever noticed the zig-zag moulding round a Norman arch? The ancient work is beautiful, the modern work is hideous. The reason is, that the modern work is done to exact measure, the ancient work is varied according to the idiosyncrasy of the workman. Here it is crowded, and there it is expanded. Now the essence of getting pupils through examinations is to give equal weight to all parts of the schedule. But mankind is naturally specialist. One man sees a whole subject, where another can find only a few detached examples. I know that it seems contradictory to allow for specialism in a curriculum especially designed for a broad culture. Without contradictions the world would be simpler, and perhaps duller. But I am certain that in education wherever you exclude specialism you destroy life.

We now come to the other great branch of a general mathematical education, namely Geometry. The same principles apply. The theoretical part should be clear-cut, rigid, short, and important. Every proposition not absolutely necessary to exhibit the main connection of ideas should be cut out, but the great fundamental ideas should be all there. No omission of concepts, such as those of Similarity and Proportion. We must remember that, owing to the aid rendered by the visual presence of a figure, Geometry is a field of unequalled excellence for the exercise of the deductive faculties of reasoning. Then, of course, there follows Geometrical Drawing, with its training for the hand and eye.

But, like Algebra, Geometry and Geometrical Drawing must be extended beyond the mere circle of geometrical ideas. In an industrial neighbourhood, machinery and workshop practice form the appropriate extension. For example, in the London Polytechnics this has been achieved with conspicuous success. For many secondary schools I suggest that surveying and maps are the natural applications. In particular, plane-table surveying should lead pupils to a vivid apprehension of the immediate application of geometric truths. Simple drawing apparatus, a surveyor's chain, and a surveyor's compass, should enable the pupils to rise from the survey and mensuration of a field to the construction of the map of a small district. The best education is to be found in gaining the utmost information from the simplest apparatus. The provision of elaborate instruments is greatly to be deprecated. To have constructed the map of a small district, to have considered its roads, its contours, its geology, its climate, its relation to other districts, the effects on the status of its inhabitants, will teach more history and geography than any knowledge of Perkin Warbeck or of

Behren's Straits. I mean not a nebulous lecture on the subject, but a serious investigation in which the real facts are definitely ascertained by the aid of accurate theoretical knowledge. A typical mathematical problem should be: Survey such and such a field, draw a plan of it to such and such a scale, and find the area. It would be quite a good procedure to impart the necessary geometrical propositions without their proofs. Then, concurrently in the same term, the proofs of the propositions would be learnt while the survey was being made.

Fortunately, the specialist side of education presents an easier problem than does the provision of a general culture. For this there are many reasons. One is that many of the principles of procedure to be observed are the same in both cases, and it is unnecessary to recapitulate. Another reason is that specialist training takes place—or should take place—at a more advanced stage of the pupil's course, and thus there is easier material to work upon. But undoubtedly the chief reason is that the specialist study is normally a study of peculiar interest to the student. He is studying it because, for some reason, he wants to know it. This makes all the difference. The general culture is designed to foster an activity of mind; the specialist course utilises this activity. But it does not do to lay too much stress on these neat antitheses. As we have already seen, in the general course foci of special interest will arise; and similarly in the special study, the external connections of the subject drag thought outwards.

Again, there is not one course of study which merely gives general culture, and another which gives special knowledge. The subjects pursued for the sake of a general education are special subjects specially studied; and, on the other hand, one of the ways of encouraging general mental activity is to foster a special devotion. You may not divide the seamless coat of learning. What education has to impart is an intimate sense for the power of ideas, for the beauty of ideas, and for the structure of ideas, together with a particular body of knowledge which has peculiar reference to the life of the being possessing it.

The appreciation of the structure of ideas is that side of a cultured mind which can only grow under the influence of a special study. I mean that eye for the whole chessboard, for the bearing of one set of ideas on another. Nothing but a special study can give any appreciation for the exact formulation of general ideas, for their relations when formulated, for their service in the comprehension of life. A mind so disciplined should be both more abstract and more concrete. It has been trained in the comprehension of abstract thought and in the analysis of facts.

Finally, there should grow the most austere of all mental qualities; I mean the sense for style. It is an æsthetic sense, based on admiration for the direct attainment of a foreseen end, simply and without waste. Style in art, style in literature, style in science, style in logic, style in practical execution have fundamentally the same æsthetic qualities, namely, attainment and restraint. The love of a subject in itself and for itself, where it is not the sleepy pleasure of pacing a mental quarterdeck, is the love of style as manifested in that study.

Here we are brought back to the position from which we started, the utility of education. Style, in its finest sense, is the last acquirement of the educated mind; it is also the most useful. It pervades the whole being. The administrator with a sense for style hates waste; the engineer with a sense for style economises his material; the artisan with a sense for style prefers good work. Style is the ultimate morality of mind.

But above style, and above knowledge, there is something, a vague shape like fate above the Greek gods. That something is Power. Style is the fashioning of power, the restraining of power. But, after all, the power of attainment of the desired end is fundamental. The first thing is to get there. Do not bother about your style, but solve your problem, justify the ways of God to man, administer your province, or do whatever else is set before you.

Where, then, does style help? In this, with style the end is attained without side issues, without raising undesirable inflammations. With style you attain your end and nothing but your end. With style the effect of your activity is calculable, and foresight is the last gift of gods to men. With style your power is increased, for your mind is not distracted with irrelevancies, and you are more likely to attain your object. Now style is the exclusive privilege of the expert. Whoever heard of the style of an amateur painter, of the style of an amateur poet? Style is always the product of specialist study, the peculiar contribution of specialism to culture.

English education in its present phase suffers from a lack of definite aim, and from an external machinery which kills its vitality. Hitherto in this address I have been considering the aims which should govern education. In this respect England halts between two opinions. It has not decided whether to produce amateurs or experts. The profound change in the world which the nineteenth century has produced is that the growth of knowledge has given foresight. The amateur is essentially a man with appreciation and with immense versatility in mastering a given routine. But he lacks the foresight which comes from special knowledge. The object of this address is to suggest how to produce the expert without loss of the essential virtues of the amateur. The machinery of our secondary education is rigid where it should be yielding, and lax where it should be rigid. Every school is bound on pain of extinction to train its boys for a small set of definite examinations. No headmaster has a free hand to develop his general education or his specialist studies in accordance with the opportunities of his school, which are created by its staff, its environment, its class of boys, and its endowments. I suggest that no system of external tests which aims primarily at examining individual scholars can result in anything but educational waste.

Primarily it is the schools and not the scholars which should be inspected. Each school should grant its own leaving certificates, based on its own curriculum. The standards of these schools should be sampled and corrected. But the first requisite for educational reform is the school as a unit, with its approved curriculum based on its own needs, and evolved by its own staff. If we fail to secure that, we simply fall from one formalism into another, from one dung-hill of inert ideas into another.

In stating that the school is the true educational unit in any national system for the safeguarding of efficiency, I have conceived the alternative system as being the external examination of the individual scholar. But every Scylla is faced by its Charybdis—or, in more homely language, there is a ditch on both sides of the road. It will be equally fatal to education if we fall into the hands of a supervising department which is under the impression that it can divide all schools into two or three rigid categories, each type being forced to adopt a rigid curriculum. When I say that the school is the educational unit, I mean exactly what I say, no larger unit, no smaller unit. Each school must have the claim to be considered in relation to its special circumstances. The classifying of schools for some purposes is necessary. But no absolutely rigid curriculum, not modified by its own staff, should be permissible. Exactly the same principles apply, with the proper modifications, to universities and to technical colleges.

When one considers in its length and in its breadth the importance of this question of the education of a nation's young, the broken lives, the defeated hopes, the national failures, which result from the frivolous inertia with which it is treated, it is difficult to restrain within oneself a savage rage. In the conditions of modern life the rule is absolute, the race which does not value trained intelligence is doomed. Not all your heroism, not all your social charm, not all your wit, not all your victories on land or at sea, can move back the finger of fate. To-day we maintain ourselves. To-morrow science will have moved forward yet one more step, and there will be no appeal from the judgment which will then be pronounced on the uneducated.

We can be content with no less than the old summary of educational ideal which has been current at any time from the dawn of our civilization. The essence of education is that it be religious.

Pray, what is religious education?

A religious education is an education which inculcates duty and reverence. Duty arises from our potential control over the course of events. Where attainable knowledge could have changed the issue, ignorance has the guilt of vice. And the foundation of reverence is this perception, that the present holds within itself the complete sum of existence, backwards and forwards, that whole amplitude of time, which is eternity.

—Presidential address to the Mathematical Association of England, 1916.

14

The Rhythm of Education

Alfred North Whitehead

By the Rhythm of Education I denote a certain principle which in its practical application is well known to everyone with educational experience. Accordingly, when I remember that I am speaking to an audience of some of the leading educationalists in England, I have no expectation that I shall be saying anything that is new to you. I do think, however, that the principle has not been subjected to an adequate discussion taking account of all the factors which should guide its application.

I first seek for the baldest statement of what I mean by the Rhythm of Education, a statement so bald as to exhibit the point of this address in its utter obviousness. The principle is merely this—that different subjects and modes of study should be undertaken by pupils at fitting times when they have reached the proper stage of mental development. You will agree with me that this is a truism, never doubted and known to all. I am really anxious to emphasize the obvious character of the foundational idea of my address; for one reason, because this audience will certainly find it out for itself. But the other reason, the reason why I choose this subject for discourse, is that I do not think that this obvious truth has been handled in educational practice with due attention to the psychology of the pupils.

Alfred North Whitehead (February 15, 1861–December 30, 1947) was a mathematician, philosopher, and educator. Alfred N. Whitehead, *The Aims of Education and Other Essays.* New York: New American Library, 1949, pp. 27–40. Copyright 1929 by Macmillan Publishing Co., Inc. Used by permission of Macmillan Publishing Co., Inc.

THE TASKS OF INFANCY

I commence by challenging the adequacy of some principles by which the subjects for study are often classified in order. By this I mean that these principles can only be accepted as correct if they are so explained as to be explained away. Consider first the criterion of difficulty. It is not true that the easier subjects should precede the harder. On the contrary, some of the hardest must come first because nature so dictates, and because they are essential to life. The first intellectual task which confronts an infant is the acquirement of spoken language. What an appalling task, the correlation of meanings with sounds! It requires an analysis of ideas and an analysis of sounds. We all know that the infant does it, and that the miracle of his achievement is explicable. But so are all miracles, and yet to the wise they remain miracles. All I ask is that with this example staring us in the face we should cease talking nonsense about postponing the harder subjects.

What is the next subject in the education of the infant minds? The acquirement of written language; that is to say, the correlation of sounds with shapes. Great heavens! Have our educationists gone mad? They are setting babbling mites of six years old to tasks which might daunt a sage after life-long toil. Again, the hardest task in mathematics is the study of the elements of algebra, and yet this stage must precede the comparative simplicity of the differential calculus.

I will not elaborate my point further; I merely restate it in the form, that the postponement of difficulty is no safe clue for the maze of educational practice.

The alternative principle of order among subjects is that of necessary antecedence. There we are obviously on firmer ground. It is impossible to read *Hamlet* until you can read; and the study of integers must precede the study of fractions. And yet even this firm principle dissolves under scrutiny. It is certainly true, but it is only true if you give an artificial limitation to the concept of a subject for study. The danger of the principle is that it is accepted in one sense, for which it is almost a necessary truth, and that it is applied in another sense for which it is false. You cannot read Homer before you can read; but many a child, and in ages past many a man, has sailed with Odysseus over the seas of Romance by the help of the spoken word of a mother, or of some wandering bard. The uncritical application of the principle of the necessary antecedence of some subjects to others has, in the hands of dull people with a turn for organisation, produced in education the dryness of the Sahara.

STAGES OF MENTAL GROWTH

The reason for the title which I have chosen for this address, the Rhythm of Education, is derived from yet another criticism of current ideas.

The pupil's progress is often conceived as a uniform steady advance undifferentiated by change of type or alteration in pace; for example, a boy may be conceived as starting Latin at ten years of age and by a uniform progression steadily developing into a classical scholar at the age of eighteen or twenty. I hold that this conception of education is based upon a false psychology of the process of mental development which has gravely hindered the effectiveness of our methods. Life is essentially periodic. It comprises daily periods, with their alternations of work and play, of activity and of sleep, and seasonal periods, which dictate our terms and our holidays; and also it is composed to well-marked yearly periods. These are the gross obvious periods which no one can overlook. There are also subtler periods of mental growth, with their cyclic recurrences, yet always different as we pass from cycle to cycle, though the subordinate stages are reproduced in each cycle. That is why I have chosen the term "rhythmic," as meaning essentially the conveyance of difference within a framework of repetition. Lack of attention to the rhythm and character of mental growth is a main source of wooden futility in education. I think that Hegel was right when he analysed progress into three stages, which he called Thesis, Antithesis, and Synthesis; though for the purpose of the application of his idea to educational theory I do not think that the names he gave are very happily suggestive. In relation to intellectual progress I would term them, the stage of romance, the stage of precision, and th stage of generalisation.

THE STAGE OF ROMANCE

The stage of romance is the stage of first apprehension. The subject-matter has the vividness of novelty; it holds within itself unexplored connexions with possibilities half-disclosed by glimpses and half-concealed by the wealth of material. In this stage knowledge is not dominated by systematic procedure. Such system as there must be is created piecemeal *ad hoc*. We are in the presence of immediate cognisance of fact, only intermittently subjecting fact to systematic dissection. Romantic emotion is essentially the excitement consequent on the transition from the bare facts to the first realisations of the import of their unexplored relationships. For example, Crusoe was a mere man, the sand was mere sand, the footprint was a mere footprint, and the island a mere island, and Europe was the busy world of men. But the sudden perception of the half-disclosed and half-hidden possibilities relating Crusoe and the sand and the footprint and the lonely island secluded from Europe constitutes romance. I have had to take an extreme case for illustration in order to make my meaning perfectly plain. But construe it as an allegory representing the first stage in a cycle of progress. Education must essentially be a setting in order of a ferment already stirring in the mind: you cannot educate mind *in vacuo*. In our conception of education we tend to confine it to the second stage of the cycle; namely, to the stage of precision.

But we cannot so limit our task without misconceiving the whole problem. We are concerned alike with the ferment, with the acquirement of precision, and with the subsequent fruition.

THE STAGE OF PRECISION

The stage of precision also represents an addition to knowledge. In this stage, width of relationship is subordinated to exactness of formulation. It is the stage of grammar, the grammar of language and the grammar of science. It proceeds by forcing on the students' acceptance a given way of analysing the facts, bit by bit. New facts are added, but they are the facts which fit into the analysis.

It is evident that a stage of precision is barren without a previous stage of romance: unless there are facts which have already been vaguely apprehended in their broad generality, the previous analysis is an analysis of nothing. It is simply a series of meaningless statements about bare facts, produced artificially and without any further relevance. I repeat that in this stage we do not merely remain within the circle of the facts elicited in the romantic epoch. The facts of romance have disclosed ideas with possibilities of wide significance, and in the stage of precise progress we acquire other facts in a systematic order, which thereby form both a disclosure and an analysis of the general subject-matter of the romance.

THE STAGE OF GENERALISATION

The final stage of generalisation is Hegel's synthesis. It is a return to romanticism with added advantage of classified ideas and relevant technique. It is the fruition which has been the goal of the precise training. It is the final success. I am afraid that I have had to give a dry analysis of somewhat obvious ideas. It has been necessary to do so because my subsequent remarks presuppose that we have clearly in our minds the essential character of this three-fold cycle.

THE CYCLIC PROCESSES

Education should consist in a continual repetition of such cycles. Each lesson in its minor way should form an eddy cycle issuing in its own subordinate process. Longer periods should issue in definite attainments, which then form the starting-grounds for fresh cycles. We should banish the idea of a mythical, far-off end of education. The pupils must be continually enjoying some fruition and starting afresh—if the teacher is stimulating in exact proportion to his success in satisfying the rhythmic cravings of his pupils.

An infant's first romance is its awakening to the apprehension of objects and to the appreciation of their connexions. Its growth in mentality takes the exterior form of occupying itself in the co-ordination of its perceptions with its bodily activities. Its first stage of precision is mastering spoken language as an instrument for classifying its contemplation of objects and for strengthening its apprehension of emotional relations with other beings. Its first stage of generalisation is the use of language for a classified and enlarged enjoyment of objects.

This first cycle of intellectual progress from the achievement of perception to the acquirement of language, and from the acquirement of language to classified thought and keener perception, will bear more careful study. It is the only cycle of progress which we can observe in its purely natural state. The later cycles are necessarily tinged by the procedure of the current mode of education. There is a characteristic of it which is often sadly lacking in subsequent education; I mean, that it achieves complete success. At the end of it the child *can* speak, its ideas *are* classified, and its perceptions *are* sharpened. The cycle achieves its object. This is a great deal more than can be said for most systems of education as applied to most pupils. But why should this be so? Certainly, a new-born baby looks a most unpromising subject for intellectual progress when we remember the difficulty of the task before it. I suppose it is because nature, in the form of surrounding circumstances, sets it a task for which the normal development of its brain is exactly fitted. I do not think that there is any particular mystery about the fact of a child learning to speak and in consequence thinking all the better; but it does offer food for reflection.

In the subsequent education we have not sought for cyclic processes which in a finite time run their course and within their own limited sphere achieve a complete success. This completion is one outstanding character in the natural cycle for infants. Later on we start a child on some subject, say Latin, at the age of ten, and hope by a uniform system of formal training to achieve success at the age of twenty. The natural result is failure, both in interest and in acquirement. When I speak of failure, I am comparing our results with the brilliant success of the first natural cycle. I do not think that it is because our tasks are intrinsically too hard, when I remember that the infant's cycle is the hardest of all. It is because our tasks are set in an unnatural way, without rhythm and without the stimulus of intermediate successes and without concentration.

I have not yet spoken of this character of concentration which so conspicuously attaches to the infant's progress. The whole being of the infant is absorbed in the practice of its cycle. It has nothing else to divert its mental development. In this respect there is a striking difference between this natural cycle and the subsequent history of the student's development. It is perfectly obvious that life is very various and that the mind and brain naturally develop so as to adapt themselves to the many-hued world in which their lot is cast. Still, after making allowance for this consideration, we will be wise to preserve some measure of concentration for each of the subsequent cycles. In particular, we should avoid a competition of diverse subjects in the same stage of their cycles. The fault of the older education was unrhythmic concentration on a single undifferentiated subject. Our modern system, with its insistence on a preliminary general education, and with its easy toleration of the analysis of knowledge into distinct subjects, is an equally unrhythmic collection of distracting scraps. I am pleading that we shall endeavour to weave in the learner's mind a harmony of patterns, by co-ordinating the various elements of instruction into subordinate cycles each of intrinsic worth for the immediate apprehension of the pupil. We must garner our crops each in its due season.

The Romance of Adolescence

We will now pass to some concrete applications of the ideas which have been devloped in the former part of my address.

The first cycle of infancy is succeeded by the cycle of adolescence, which opens with by far the greatest stage of romance which we ever experience. It is in this stage that the lines of character are graven. How the child emerges from the romantic stage of adolescence is how the subsequent life will be moulded by ideals and coloured by imagination. It rapidly follows on the generalisation of capacity produced by the acquirement of spoken language and of reading. The stage of generalisation belonging to the infantile cycle is comparatively short because the romantic material of infancy is so scanty. The initial knowledge of the world in any developed sense of the word "knowledge" really commences after the achievement of the first cycle, and thus issues in the tremendous age of romance. Ideas, facts, relationships, stories, histories, possibilities, artistry in words, in sounds, in form and in colour, crowd into the child's life, stir his feelings, excite his appreciation, and incite his impulses to kindred activities. It is a saddening thought that on this golden age there falls so often the shadow of the crammer. I am thinking of a period of about four years of the child's life, roughly, in ordinary cases, falling between the age of eight and twelve or thirteen. It is the first great period of the utilisation of the native language, and of developed powers of observation and of manipulation. The infant cannot manipulate, the child can; the infant cannot observe, the child can; the infant cannot retain thoughts by the recollection of words, the child can. The child thus enters upon a new world.

Of course, the stage of precision prolongs itself as recurring in minor cycles which form eddies in the great romance. The perfecting of writing, of spelling, of the elements of arithmetic, and of lists of simple facts, such as the Kings of England, are all elements of precision, very necessary both as training in concentration and as useful acquirements. However, these are essentially fragmentary in character, whereas the great romance is the flood which bears on the child towards the life of the spirit.

The success of the Montessori system is due to its recognition of the dominance of romance at this period of growth. If this be the explanation, it also points to the limitations in the usefulness of that method. It is the system which in some measure is essential for every romantic stage. Its essence is browsing and the encouragement of vivid freshness. But it lacks the restraint which is necessary for the great stages of precision.

THE MASTERY OF LANGUAGE

As he nears the end of the great romance the cyclic course of growth is swinging the child over towards an aptitude for exact knowledge. Language is now the natural subject-matter for concentrated attack. It is the mode of expression with which he is thoroughly familiar. He is acquainted with stories, histories, and poems illustrating the lives of other people and of other civilisations. Accordingly, from the age of eleven onwards there is wanted a gradually increasing concentration towards precise knowledge of language. Finally, the three years from twelve to fifteen should be dominated by a mass attack upon language, so planned that a definite result, in itself worth having, is thereby achieved. I should guess that within these limits of time, and given adequate concentration, we might ask that at the end of that period the children should have command of English, should be able to read fluently fairly simple French, and should have completed the elementary stage of Latin; I mean, a precise knowledge of the more straightforward parts of Latin grammar, the knowledge of the construction of Latin sentences, and the reading of some parts of appropriate Latin authors, perhaps simplified and largely supplemented by the aid of the best literary translations so that their reading of the original, plus translation, gives them a grip of the book as a literary whole. I conceive that such a measure of attainment in these three languages is well within the reach of the ordinary child, provided that he has not been distracted by the effort at precision in a multiplicity of other subjects. Also some more gifted children could go further. The Latin would come to them easily, so that it would be possible to start Greek before the end of the period, always provided their bent is literary and that they mean later to pursue that study at least for some years. Other subjects will occupy a subordinate place in the time-table and will be undertaken in a different spirit. In the first place, it must be remembered that the semi-literary subjects, such as history, will largely have been provided in the study of the languages. It will be hardly possible to read some English, French, and Latin literature without imparting some knowledge of European history. I do not mean that all special history teaching should be abandoned. I do, however, suggest that the subject should be exhibited in what I have termed the romantic spirit, and that the pupils should not be subjected to the test of precise recollection of details on any large systematic scale.

At this period of growth science should be in its stage of romance. The pupils should see for themselves, and experiment for themselves, with only fragmentary precision of thought. The essence of the importance of science, both for interest in theory or for technological purposes, lies in its application to concrete detail, and every such application evokes a novel problem for research. Accordingly, all training in science should begin as well as end in research, and in getting hold of the subject-matter as it occurs in nature. The exact form of guidance suitable to this age and the exact limitations of experiment are matters depending on experiments. But I plead that this period is the true age for the romance of science.

Concentration on Science

Towards the age of fifteen the age of precision in language and of romance in science draws to its close, to be succeeded by a period of generalisation in language and of precision in science. This should be a short period, but one of vital importance. I am thinking of about one year's work, and I suggest that it would be well decisively to alter the balance of the preceding curriculum. There should be a concentration on science and a decided diminution of the linguistic work. A year's work on science, coming on the top of the previous romantic study, should make everyone understand the main principles, which govern the development of mechanics, physics, chemistry, algebra and geometry. Understand that they are not beginning these subjects, but they are putting together a previous discursive study by an exact formulation of their main ideas. For example, take algebra and geometry, which I single out as being subjects with which I have some slight familiarity. In the previous three years there has been work on the applications of the simplest algebraic formulæ and geometrical propositions to problems of surveying, or of some other scientific work involving calculations. In this way arithmetic has been carefully strengthened by the insistence on definite numerical results, and familiarity with the ideas of literal formulæ and of geometrical properties has been gained; also some minor methods of manipulation have been inculcated. There is thus no long time to be wasted in getting used to the ideas of the sciences. The pupils are ready for the small body of algebraic and geometrical truths which they ought to know thoroughly. Furthermore, in the previous period some boys will have shown an aptitude for mathematics and will have pushed on a little more, besides in the final year somewhat emphasising their mathematics at the expense of some of the other subjects. I am simply taking mathematics as an illustration.

Meanwhile, the cycle of language is in its stage of generalisation. In this stage the precise study of grammar and composition is discontinued, and the language study is confined to reading the literature with emphasised attention to its ideas and to the general history in which it is embedded; also the time allotted to history will pass into the precise study of a short definite period, chosen to illustrate exactly what does happen at an important epoch and also to show how to pass the simpler types of judgments on men and policies.

I have now sketched in outline the course of education from babyhood to about sixteen and a half, arranged with some attention to the rhythmic pulses of life. In some such way a general education is possible in which the pupil throughout has the advantage of concentration and of freshness. Thus precision will always illustrate subject-matter already apprehended and crying out for drastic treatment. Every pupil will have concentrated in turn on a variety of different subjects, and will know where his strong points lie. Finally—and this of all the objects to be attained is the most dear to my heart—the science students will have obtained both an invaluable literary education and also at the most impressionable age an early initiation into habits of thinking for themselves in the region of science.

After the age of sixteen new problems arise. For literary students science passes into the stage of generalisation, largely in the form of lectures on its main results and general ideas. New cycles of linguistic, literary, and historical study commence. But further detail is now unnecessary. For the scientists the preceding stage of precision maintains itself to the close of the school period with an increasing apprehension of wider general ideas.

However, at this period of education the problem is too individual, or at least breaks up into too many cases, to be susceptible of broad general treatment. I do suggest, nevertheless, that all scientists should now keep up their French, and initiate the study of German if they have not already acquired it.

UNIVERSITY EDUCATION

I should now like, if you will bear with me, to make some remarks respecting the import of these ideas for a University education.

The whole period of growth from infancy to manhood forms one grand cycle. Its stage of romance stretches across the first dozen years of its life, its stage of precision comprises the whole school period of secondary education, and its stage of generalisation is the period of entrance into manhood. For those whose formal education is prolonged beyond the school age, the University course or its equivalent is the great period of generalisation. The spirit of generalisation should dominate a University. The lectures should be addressed to those to whom details and procedure are familiar; that is to say, familiar at least in the sense of being so congruous to pre-existing training as to be easily acquirable. During the school period the student has been mentally bending over his desk; at the University he should stand up and look around. For this reason it is fatal if the first year at the University be frittered away in going over the old work in the old spirit. At school the boy painfully rises from the particular towards glimpses at general ideas; at the University he should start from general ideas and study their applications to concrete cases. A well-planned University course is a study of the wide sweep of generality. I do not mean that it should be abstract in the sense of divorce from concrete fact, but that concrete fact should be studied as illustrating the scope of general ideas.

Cultivation of Mental Power

This is the aspect of University training in which theoretical interest and practical utility coincide. Whatever be the detail with which you cram your student, the chance of his meeting in after-life exactly that detail is almost infinitesimal; and if he does meet it, he will probably have forgotten what you taught him about it. The really useful training yields a comprehension of a few general principles with a thorough grounding in the way they apply to a variety of concrete details. In subsequent practice the men will have forgotten your particular details; but they will remember by an unconscious common sense how to apply principles to immediate circumstances. Your learning is useless to you till you have lost your textbooks, burnt your lecture notes, and forgotten the minutiæ which you learnt by heart for the examination. What, in the way of detail, you continually require will stick in your memory as obvious facts like the sun and moon; and what you casually require can be looked up in any work of reference. The function of a University is to enable you to shed details in favour of principles. When I speak of principles I am hardly even thinking of verbal formulations. A principle which has thoroughly soaked into you is rather a mental habit than a formal statement. It becomes the way the mind reacts to the appropriate stimulus in the form of illustrative circumstances. Nobody goes about with his knowledge clearly and consciously before him. Mental cultivation is nothing else than the satisfactory way in which the mind will function when it is poked up into activity. Learning is often spoken of as if we are watching the open pages of all the books which we have ever read, and then, when occasion arises, we select the right page to read aloud to the universe.

Luckily, the truth is far otherwise from this crude idea; and for this reason the antagonism between the claims of pure knowledge and professional acquirement should be much less acute than a faulty view of education would lead us to anticipate. I can put my point otherwise by saying that the ideal of a University is not so much knowledge, as power. Its business is to convert the knowledge of a boy into the power of man.

THE RHYTHMIC CHARACTER OF GROWTH

I will conclude with two remarks which I wish to make by way of caution in the interpretation of my meaning. The point of this address is the rhythmic character of growth. The interior spiritual life of man is a web of many strands. They do not all grow together by uniform extension. I have tried to illustrate this truth by considering the normal unfolding of the capacities of a child in somewhat favourable circumstances but otherwise with fair average capacities. Perhaps I have misconstrued the usual phenomena. It is very likely that I have so failed, for the evidence is complex and difficult. But do not let any failure in this respect prejudice the main point which I am here to enforce. It is that the development of mentality exhibits itself as a rhythm involving an interweaving of cycles, the whole process being dominated by a greater cycle of the same general character as its minor eddies. Furthermore, this rhythm exhibits certain ascertainable general laws which are valid for most pupils, and the quality of our teaching should be so adapted as to suit the stage in the rhythm to which our pupils have advanced. The problem of a curriculum is not so much the succession of subjects; for all subjects should in essence be begun with the dawn of mentality. The truly important order is the order of quality which the educational procedure should assume.

My second caution is to ask you not to exaggerate into sharpness the distinction between the three stages of a cycle. I strongly suspect that many of you when you heard me detail the three stages in each cycle, said to yourselves—How like a mathematician to make such formal divisions! I assure you that it is not mathematics but literary incompetence that may have led me into the error against which I am warning you. Of course, I mean throughout a distinction of emphasis, of pervasive quality—romance, precision, generalisation, are all present throughout. But there is an alternation of dominance, and it is this alternation which constitutes the cycles.

—Address to the Training College Association of London, 1922.

15

Democracy and Education

JOHN DEWEY

THE SCHOOL AS A SPECIAL ENVIRONMENT

Hence a special mode of social intercourse is instituted, the school, to care for such matters.

This mode of association has three functions sufficiently specific, as compared with ordinary associations of life, to be noted. First, a complex civilization is too complex to be assimilated *in toto*. It has to be broken up into portions, as it were, and assimilated piecemeal, in a gradual and graded way. The relationships of our present social life are so numerous and so interwoven that a child placed in the most favorable position could not readily share in many of the most important of them. Not sharing in them, their meaning would not be communicated to him, would not become a part of his own mental disposition. There would be no seeing the trees because of the forest. Business, politics, art, science, religion, would make all at once a clamor for attention; confusion would be the outcome. The first office of the social organ we call the school is to provide a *simplified* environment. It selects the features which are fairly fundamental and capable of being responded to by the young. Then it establishes a progressive order, using the factors first acquired as means of gaining insight into what is more complicated.

John Dewey (October 20, 1859–June 1, 1952) was a philosopher and educator. John Dewey, *Democracy and Education.* New York: Macmillan Publishing Co., Inc., 1916, pp. 23–25, 32, 33–34, 49–53, 54–56, 59–61, 89–92, 100–102, 117, 148–150, 151–152, 163–164, 176–177, 180, 183–184, 193–194, 197–200, 210, 212, 214–217, 397, 398, 414–415. Copyright 1916 by Macmillan Publishing Co., Inc. Used by permission.

In the second place, it is the business of the school environment to eliminate, so far as possible, the unworthy features of the existing environment from influence upon mental habitudes. It establishes a purified medium of action. Selection aims not only at simplifying but at weeding out what is undesirable. Every society gets encumbered with what is trivial, with dead wood from the past, and with what is positively perverse. The school has the duty of omitting such things from the environment which it supplies, and thereby doing what it can to counteract their influence in the ordinary social environment. By selecting the best for its exclusive use, it strives to reënforce the power of this best. As a society becomes more enlightened, it realizes that it is responsible *not* to transmit and conserve the whole of its existing achievements, but only such as make for a better future society. The school is its chief agency for the accomplishment of this end.

In the third place, it is the office of the school environment to balance the various elements in the social environment, and to see to it that each individual gets an opportunity to escape from the limitations of the social group in which he was born, and to come into living contact with a broader environment. Such words as 'society' and 'community' are likely to be misleading, for they have a tendency to make us think there is a single thing corresponding to the single word. As a matter of fact, a modern society is many societies more or less loosely connected. Each household with its immediate extension of friends makes a society; the village or street group of playmates is a community; each business group, each club, is another. Passing beyond these more intimate groups, there is in a country like our own a variety of races, religious affiliations, economic divisions. Inside the modern city, in spite of its nominal political unity, there are probably more communities, more differing customs, traditions, aspirations, and forms of government or control, than existed in an entire continent at an earlier epoch.

Each such group exercises a formative influence on the active dispositions of its members. A clique, a club, a gang, a Fagin's household of thieves, the prisoners in a jail, provide educative environments for those who enter into their collective or conjoint activities, as truly as a church, a labor union, a business partnership, or a political party. Each of them is a mode of associated or community life, quite as much as is a family, a town, or a state. There are also communities whose members have little or no direct contact with one another, like the guild of artists, the republic of letters, the members of the professional learned class scattered over the face of the earth. For they have aims in common, and the activity of each member is directly modified by knowledge of what others are doing.

MODES OF SOCIAL DIRECTION

1. When others are not doing what we would like them to or are threatening disobedience, we are most conscious of the need of controlling

them and of the influences by which they are controlled. In such cases, our control becomes most direct, and at this point we are most likely to make the mistakes just spoken of. We are even likely to take the influence of superior force for control, forgetting that while we may lead a horse to water we cannot make him drink; and that while we can shut a man up in a penitentiary we cannot make him penitent. In all such cases of immediate action upon others, we need to discriminate between physical results and moral results. A person may be in such a condition that forcible feeding or enforced confinement is necessary for his own good. A child may have to be snatched with roughness away from a fire so that he shall not be burnt. But no improvement of disposition, no educative effect, need follow. A harsh and commanding tone may be effectual in keeping a child away from the fire, and the same desirable physical effect will follow as if he had been snatched away. But there may be no more obedience of a moral sort in one case than in the other. A man can be prevented from breaking into other persons' houses by shutting him up, but shutting him up may not alter his disposition to commit burglary. When we confuse a physical with an educative result, we always lose the chance of enlisting the person's own participating disposition in getting the result desired, and thereby of developing within him an intrinsic and persisting direction in the right way.

2. These methods of control are so obvious (because so intentionally employed) that it would hardly be worth while to mention them if it were not that notice may now be taken, by way of contrast, of the other more important and permanent mode of control. This other method resides in the ways in which persons, with whom the immature being is associated, *use things*; the instrumentalities with which they accomplish their own ends. The very existence of the social medium in which an individual lives, moves, and has his being is the standing effective agency of directing his activity.

This fact makes it necessary for us to examine in greater detail what is meant by the social environment. We are given to separating from each other the physical and social environments in which we live. The separation is responsible on one hand for an exaggeration of the moral importance of the more direct or personal modes of control of which we have been speaking; and on the other hand for an exaggeration, in current psychology and philosophy, of the *intellectual* possibilities of contact with a purely physical environment. There is not, in fact, any such thing as the direct influence of one human being on another apart from use of the physical environment as an intermediary. A smile, a frown, a rebuke, a word of warning or encouragement, all involve some physical change. Otherwise, the attitude of one would not get over to alter the attitude of another. Comparatively speaking, such modes of influence may be regarded as personal. The physical medium is reduced to a mere means of personal contact. In contrast with such direct modes of mutual influence stand associations in common pursuits involving the use of things as means and as measures of results. Even if the mother never told her daughter to help her, or never rebuked her for not helping, the child would be subjected to direction in her activities by the mere fact that she was engaged, along with the parent, in the household life. Imitation, emulation, the need of working together, enforce control.

THE CONDITIONS OF GROWTH

In directing the activities of the young, society determines its own future in determining that of the young. Since the young at a given time will at some later date compose the society of that period, the latter's nature will largely turn upon the direction children's activities were given at an earlier period. This cumulative movement of action toward a later result is what is meant by growth.

The primary condition of growth is immaturity. This may seem to be a mere truism—saying that a being can develop only in some point in which he is undeveloped. But the prefix 'im' of the word immaturity means something positive, not a mere void or lack. It is noteworthy that the terms 'capacity' and 'potentiality' have a double meaning, one sense being negative, the other positive. Capacity may denote mere receptivity, like the capacity of a quart measure. We may mean by potentiality a merely dormant or quiescent state—a capacity to become something different under external influences. But we also mean by capacity an ability, a power; and by potentiality potency, force. Now when we say that immaturity means the possibility of growth, we are not referring to absence of powers which may exist at a later time; we express a force positively present—the *ability* to develop.

Our tendency to take immaturity as mere lack, and growth as something which fills up the gap between the immature and the mature is due to regarding childhood *comparatively*, instead of intrinsically. We treat it simply as a privation because we are measuring it by adulthood as a fixed standard. This fixes attention upon what the child has not, and will not have till he becomes a man. This comparative standpoint is legitimate enough for some purposes, but if we make it final, the question arises whether we are not guilty of an overweening presumption. Children, if they could express themselves articulately and sincerely, would tell a different tale; and there is excellent adult authority for the conviction that for certain moral and intellectual purposes adults must become as little children.

The seriousness of the assumption of the negative quality of the possibilities of immaturity is apparent when we reflect that it sets up as an ideal and standard a static end. The fulfillment of growing is taken to mean an *accomplished* growth: that is to say, an Ungrowth, something which is no longer growing. The futility of the assumption is seen in the fact that every adult resents the imputation of having no further possibilities of growth; and so far as he finds that they are closed to him mourns the fact as evidence of loss, instead of falling back on the achieved as adequate manifestation of power. Why an unequal measure for child and man?

Taken absolutely, instead of comparatively, immaturity designates a positive force or ability—the *power* to grow. We do not have to draw out or educe positive activities from a child, as some educational doctrines would have it. Where there is life, there are already eager and impassioned activities. Growth is not something done to them; it is something they do. The positive and constructive aspect of possibility gives the key to understanding the two chief traits of immaturity, dependence and plasticity. (1) It sounds absurd to hear dependence spoken of as something positive, still more absurd as a power. Yet if helplessness were all there were in dependence, no development could ever take place. A merely impotent being has to be carried, forever, by others. The fact that dependence is accompanied by growth in ability, not by an ever increasing lapse into parasitism, suggests that it is already something constructive. Being merely sheltered by others would not promote growth. For (2) it would only build a wall around impotence. With reference to the physical world, the child is helpless. He lacks at birth and for a long time thereafter power to make his way physically, to make his own living. If he had to do that by himself, he would hardly survive an hour. On this side his helplessness is almost complete. The young of the brutes are immeasurably his superiors. He is physically weak and not able to turn the strength which he possesses to coping with the physical environment.

1. The thoroughgoing character of this helplessness suggests, however, some compensating power. The relative ability of the young of brute animals to adapt themselves fairly well to physical conditions from an early period suggests the fact that their life is not intimately bound up with the life of those about them. They are compelled, so to speak, to have physical gifts because they are lacking in social gifts. Human infants, on the other hand, can get along with physical incapacity just because of their social capacity. We sometimes talk and think as if they simply happened to be *physically* in a social environment; as if social forces exclusively existed in the adults who take care of them, they being passive recipients. If it were said that children are themselves marvelously endowed with *power* to enlist the coöperative attention of others, this would be thought to be a backhanded way of saying that others are marvelously attentive to the needs of children. But observation shows that children are gifted with an equipment of the first order for social intercourse. Few grown-up persons retain all of the flexible and sensitive ability of children to vibrate sympathetically with the attitudes and doings of those about them. Inattention to physical things (going with incapacity to control them) is accompanied by a corresponding intensification of interest and attention as to the doings of people. The native mechanism of the child and his impulses all tend to facile social responsiveness. The statement that children, before adolescence, are egotistically

self-centered, even if it were true, would not contradict the truth of this statement. It would simply indicate that their social responsiveness is employed on their own behalf, not that it does not exist. But the statement is not true as matter of fact. The facts which are cited in support of the alleged pure egoism of children really show the intensity and directness with which they go to their mark. If the ends which form the mark seem narrow and selfish to adults, it is only because adults (by means of a similar engrossment in their day) have mastered these ends, which have consequently ceased to interest them. Most of the remainder of children's alleged native egoism is simply an egoism which runs counter to an adult's egoism. To a grown-up person who is too absorbed in his own affairs to take an interest in children's affairs, children doubtless seem unreasonably engrossed in *their* own affairs.

From a social standpoint, dependence denotes a power rather than a weakness; it involves interdependence. There is always a danger that increased personal independence will decrease the social capcity of an individual. In making him more self-reliant, it may make him more self-sufficient; it may lead to aloofness and indifference. It often makes an individual so insensitive in his relations to others as to develop an illusion of being really able to stand and act alone—an unnamed form of insanity which is responsible for a large part of the remediable suffering of the world.

2. The specific adaptability of an immature creature for growth constitutes his *plasticity*. This is something quite different from the plasticity of putty or wax. It is not a capacity to take on change of form in accord with external pressure. It lies near the pliable elasticity by which some persons take on the color of their surroundings while retaining their own bent. But it is something deeper than this. It is essentially the ability to learn from experience; the power to retain from one experience something which is of avail in coping with the difficulties of a later situation. This means power to modify actions on the basis of the results of prior experiences, the power to *develop dispositions*. Without it, the acquisition of habits is impossible.

Habits as Expressions of Growth

We have already noted that plasticity is the capacity to retain and carry over from prior experience factors which modify subsequent activities. This signifies the capacity to acquire habits, or develop definite dispositions. We have now to consider the salient features of habits. In the first place, a habit is a form of executive skill, of efficiency in doing. A habit means an ability to use natural conditions as means to ends. It is an active control of the environment through control of the organs of action. We are perhaps apt to emphasize the control of the body at the expense of control of the environment. We think of walking, talking, playing the piano, the specialized skills characteristic of the etcher, the surgeon, the bridge-builder, as if they were simply ease, deftness, and accuracy on the part of the organism. They are that, of course; but the measure of the value of these qualities lies in the economical and effective control of the environment which they secure. To be able to walk is to have certain properties of nature at our disposal—and so with all other habits.

Education is not infrequently defined as consisting in the acquisition of those habits that effect an adjustment of an individual and his environment. The definition expresses an essential phase of growth. But it is essential that adjustment be understood in its active sense of *control* of means for achieving ends. If we think of a habit simply as a change wrought in the organism, ignoring the fact that this change consists in ability to effect subsequent changes in the environment, we shall be led to think of 'adjustment' as a conformity to environment as wax conforms to the seal which impresses it. The environment is thought of as something fixed, providing in its fixity the end and standard of changes taking place in the organism; adjustment is just fitting ourselves to this fixity of external conditions.[1] Habit as *habituation* is indeed something *relatively* passive; we get used to our surroundings—to our clothing, our shoes, and gloves; to the atmosphere as long as it is fairly equable; to our daily associates, etc. Conformity to the environment, a change wrought in the organism without reference to ability to modify surroundings, is a marked trait of such habituations. Aside from the fact that we are not entitled to carry over the traits of such adjustments (which might well be called *accommodations*, to mark them off from active adjustments) into habits of active use of our surroundings, two features of habituations are worth notice. In the first place, we get used to things by *first* using them.

Consider getting used to a strange city. At first, there is excessive stimulation and excessive and ill-adapted response. Gradually certain stimuli are selected because of their relevancy, and others are degraded. We can say either that we do not respond to them any longer, or more truly that we have effected a persistent response to them—an equilibrium of adjustment. This means, in the second place, that this enduring adjustment supplies the background upon which are made specific adjustments, as occasion arises. We are never interested in changing the *whole* environment; there is much that we take for granted and accept just as it already is. Upon this background our activities focus at certain points in an endeavor to introduce needed changes. Habituation is thus our adjustment to an environment which at the time we are not concerned with modifying, and which supplies a leverage to our active habits.

---

[1] This conception is, of course, a logical correlate of the conceptions of the external relation of stimulus and response, considered in the last chapter [*Democracy and Education*], and of the negative conceptions of immaturity and plasticity noted in this chapter.

THE EDUCATIONAL BEARINGS OF THE CONCEPTION OF DEVELOPMENT

We have had so far but little to say in this chapter about education. We have been occupied with the conditions and implications of growth. If our conclusions are justified, they carry with them, however, definite educational consequences. When it is said that education is development, everything depends upon *how* development is conceived. Our net conclusion is that life is development, and that developing, growing, is life. Translated into its educational equivalents, this means (*i*) that the educational process has no end beyond itself; it is its own end; and that (*ii*) the educational process is one of continual reorganizing, reconstructing, transforming.

1. Development when it is interpreted in *comparative* terms, that is, with respect to the special traits of child and adult life, means the direction of power into special channels: the formation of habits involving executive skill, definiteness of interest, and specific objects of observation and thought. But the comparative view is not final. The child has specific powers; to ignore that fact is to stunt or distort the organs upon which his growth depends. The adult uses his powers to transform his environment, thereby occasioning new stimuli which redirect his powers and keep them developing. Ignoring this fact means arrested development, a passive accommodation. Normal child and normal adult alike, in other words, are engaged in growing. The difference between them is not the difference between growth and no growth, but between the modes of growth appropriate to different conditions. With respect to the development of powers devoted to coping with specific scientific and economic problems, we may say the child should be growing in manhood. With respect to sympathetic curiosity, unbiased responsiveness, and openness of mind, we may say that the adult should be growing in childlikeness. One statement is as true as the other.

Three ideas which have been criticized, namely, the merely privative nature of immaturity, static adjustment to a fixed environment, and rigidity of habit, are all connected with a false idea of growth or development—that it is a movement toward a fixed goal. Growth is regarded as *having* an end, instead of *being* an end. The educational counterparts of the three fallacious ideas are first, failure to take account of the instinctive or native powers of the young; secondly, failure to develop initiative in coping with novel situations; thirdly, an undue emphasis upon drill and other devices which secure automatic skill at the expense of personal perception. In all cases, the adult environment is accepted as a standard for the child. He is to be brought up *to* it.

Natural instincts are either disregarded or treated as nuisances—as obnoxious traits to be suppressed, or at all events to be brought into conformity with external standards. Since conformity is the aim, what is distinctively individual in a young person is brushed aside, or regarded as a source of mischief or anarchy. Conformity is made equivalent to uniformity. Consequently, there are induced lack of interest in the novel, aversion to progress, and dread of the uncertain and the unknown. Since the end of growth is outside of and beyond the process of growing, external agents have to be resorted to to induce movement toward it. Whenever a method of education is stigmatized as mechanical, we may be sure that external pressure is brought to bear to reach an external end.

2. Since in reality there is nothing to which growth is relative save more growth, there is nothing to which education is subordinate save more education. It is a commonplace to say that education should not cease when one leaves school. The point of this commonplace is that the purpose of school education is to insure the continuance of education by organizing the powers that insure growth. The inclination to learn from life itself and to make the conditions of life such that all will learn in the process of living is the finest product of schooling.

When we abandon the attempt to define immaturity by means of fixed comparison with adult accomplishments, we are compelled to give up thinking of it as denoting lack of desired traits. Abandoning this notion, we are also forced to surrender our habit of thinking of instruction as a method of supplying this lack by pouring knowledge into a mental and moral hole which awaits filling. Since life means growth, a living creature lives as truly and positively at one stage as at another, with the same intrinsic fullness and the same absolute claims. Hence education means the enterprise of supplying the conditions which insure growth, or adequacy of life, irrespective of age. We first look with impatience upon immaturity, regarding it as something to be got over as rapidly as possible. Then the adult formed by such educative methods looks back with impatient regret upon childhood and youth as a scene of lost opportunities and wasted powers. This ironical situation will endure till it is recognized that living has its own intrinsic quality and that the business of education is with that quality.

Realization that life is growth protects us from that so-called idealizing of childhood which in effect is nothing but lazy indulgence. Life is not to be identified with every superficial act and interest. Even though it is not always easy to tell whether what appears to be mere surface fooling is a sign of some nascent as yet untrained power, we must remember that manifestations are not to be accepted as ends in themselves. They are signs of possible growth. They are to be turned into means of development, of carrying power forward, not indulged or cultivated for their own sake. Excessive attention to surface phenomena (even in the way of rebuke as well as of encouragement) may lead to their fixation and thus to arrested development. What impulses are moving toward, not what they have been, is the important thing for parent and teacher.

EDUCATION AS RECONSTRUCTION

In its contrast with the ideas both of unfolding of latent powers from within, and of formation from without, whether by physical nature or by the cultural products of the past, the ideal of growth results in the conception that education is a constant reorganizing or reconstructing of experience. It has all the time an immediate end, and so far as activity is educative, it reaches that end—the direct transformation of the quality of experience. Infancy, youth, adult life—all stand on the same educative level in the sense that what is really *learned* at any and every stage of experience constitutes the value of that experience, and in the sense that it is the chief business of life at every point to make living thus contribute to an enrichment of its own perceptible meaning.

We thus reach a technical definition of education: It is that reconstruction or reorganization of experience which adds to the meaning of experience, and which increases ability to direct the course of subsequent experience. (1) The increment of meaning corresponds to the increased perception of the connections and continuities of the activities in which we are engaged. The activity begins in an impulsive form; that is, it is blind. It does not know what it is about; that is to say, what are its interactions with other activities. An activity which brings education or instruction with it makes one aware of some of the connections which had been imperceptible. To recur to our example, a child who reaches for a bright light gets burned. Henceforth he *knows* that a certain act of touching in connection with a certain act of vision (and *vice versa*) means heat and pain; or, a certain light means a source of heat. The acts by which a scientific man in his laboratory learns more about flame differ no whit in principle. By doing certain things, he makes perceptible certain connections of heat with other things, which had been previously ignored. Thus his acts in relation to these things get more meaning; he knows better what he is doing or 'is about' when he has to do with them; he can *intend* consequences instead of just letting them happen— all synonymous ways of saying the same thing. At the same stroke, the flame has gained in meaning; all that is known about combustion, oxidation, about light and temperature, may become an intrinsic part of its intellectual content.

(2) The other side of an educative experience is an added power of subsequent direction or control. To say that one knows what he is about, or can intend certain consequences, is to say, of course, that he can better anticipate what is going to happen; that he can, therefore, get ready or prepare in advance so as to secure beneficial consequences and avert undesirable ones. A genuinely educative experience, then, one in which instruction is conveyed and ability increased, is contradistinguished from a routine activity on one hand, and a capricious activity on the other. (*a*) In the latter one 'does not care what happens'; one just lets himself go and

avoids connecting the consequences of one's act (the evidences of its connections with other things) with the act. It is customary to frown upon such aimless random activity, treating it as willful mischief or carelessness or lawlessness. But there is a tendency to seek the cause of such aimless activities in the youth's own disposition, isolated from everything else. But in fact such activity is explosive, and due to maladjustment with surroundings. Individuals act capriciously whenever they act under external dictation, or from being told, without having a purpose of their own or perceiving the bearing of the deed upon other acts. One may learn by doing something which he does not understand; even in the most intelligent action, we do much which we do not mean, because the largest portion of the connections of the act we consciously intend are not perceived or anticipated. But we learn only because after the act is performed we note results which we had not noted before. But much work in school consists in setting up rules by which pupils are to act of such a sort that even after pupils have acted, they are not led to see the connection between the result—say the answer—and the method pursued. So far as they are concerned, the whole thing is a trick and a kind of miracle. Such action is essentially capricious, and leads to capricious habits. (*b*) Routine action, action which is automatic, may increase skill to do a *particular* thing. In so far, it might be said to have an educative effect. But it does not lead to new perceptions of bearings and connections; it limits rather than widens the meaning-horizon. And since the environment changes and our way of acting has to be modified in order successfully to keep a balanced connection with things, an isolated uniform way of acting becomes disastrous at some critical moment. The vaunted 'skill' turns out gross ineptitude.

The essential contrast of the idea of education as continuous reconstruction with the other one-sided conceptions which have been criticized in this and the previous chapter is that it identifies the end (the result) and the process. This is verbally self-contradictory, but only verbally. It means that experience as an active process occupies time and that its later period completes its earlier portion; it brings to light connections involved but hitherto unperceived. The later outcome thus reveals the meaning of the earlier, while the experience as a whole establishes a bent or disposition toward the things possessing this meaning. Every such continuous experience or activity is educative, and all education resides in having such experiences.

It remains only to point out (what will receive more ample attention later) that the reconstruction of experience may be social as well as personal. For purposes of simplification we have spoken in the earlier chapters somewhat as if the education of the immature which fills them with the spirit of the social group to which they belong, were a sort of catching up of the child with the aptitudes and resources of the adult group. In static societies, societies which make the maintenance of established custom their measure of value, this conception applies in the main. But not in progressive communities. They endeavor to shape the experiences of the young so that instead of reproducing current habits, better habits shall be formed, and thus the future adult society be an improvement on their own. Men have long had some intimation of the extent to which education may be consciously used to eliminate obvious social evils through starting the young on paths which shall not produce these ills, and some idea of the extent in which education may be made an instrument of realizing the better hopes of men. But we are doubtless far from realizing the potential efficacy of education as a constructive agency of improving society, from realizing that it represents not only a development of children and youth but also of the future society of which they will be the constituents.

THE DEMOCRATIC IDEAL

The two elements in our criterion both point to democracy. The first signifies not only more numerous and more varied points of shared common interest, but greater reliance upon the recognition of mutual interests as a factor in social control. The second means not only freer interaction between social groups (once isolated so far as intention could keep up a separation) but change in social habit—its continuous readjustment through meeting the new situations produced by varied intercourse. And these two traits are precisely what characterize the democratically constituted society.

Upon the educational side, we note first that the realization of a form of social life in which interests are mutually interpenetrating, and where progress, or readjustment, is an important consideration, makes a democratic community more interested than other communities have cause to be in deliberate and systematic education. The devotion of democracy to education is a familiar fact. The superficial explanation is that a government resting upon popular suffrage cannot be successful unless those who elect and who obey their governors are educated. Since a democratic society repudiates the principle of external authority, it must find a substitute in voluntary disposition and interest; these can be created only by education. But there is a deeper explanation. A democracy is more than a form of government; it is primarily a mode of associated living, of conjoint communicated experience. The extension in space of the number of individuals who participate in an interest so that each has to refer his own action to that of others, and to consider the action of others to give point and direction to his own, is equivalent to the breaking down of those barriers of class, race, and national territory which kept men from perceiving the full import of their activity. These more numerous and more varied points of contact denote a greater diversity of stimuli to which an individual has to respond; they consequently put a premium on variation in his action. They secure a liberation of powers which remain suppressed as long as the incitations to action are partial, as they must be in a group which in its exclusiveness shuts out many interests.

The widening of the area of shared concerns, and the liberation of a greater diversity of personal capacities which characterize a democracy, are not of course the product of deliberation and conscious effort. On the contrary, they were caused by the development of modes of manufacture and commerce, travel, migration, and intercommunication which flowed from the command of science over natural energy. But after greater individualization on one hand, and a broader community of interest on the other have come into existence, it is a matter of deliberate effort to sustain and extend them. Obviously a society to which stratification into separate classes would be fatal, must see to it that intellectual opportunities are accessible to all on equable and easy terms. A society marked off into classes need be specially attentive only to the education of its ruling elements. A society which is mobile, which is full of channels for the distribution of a change occurring anywhere, must see to it that its members are educated to personal initiative and adaptability. Otherwise, they will be overwhelmed by the changes in which they are caught and whose significance or connections they do not perceive. The result will be a confusion in which a few will appropriate to themselves the results of the blind and externally directed activities of others.

The Nature of an Aim

The account of education given in our earlier chapters virtually anticipated the results reached in a discussion of the purport of education in a democratic community. For it assumed that the aim of education is to enable individuals to continue their education—or that the object and reward of learning is continued capacity for growth. Now this idea cannot be applied to *all* the members of a society except where intercourse of man with man is mutual, and except where there is adequate provision for the reconstruction of social habits and institutions by means of wide stimulation arising from equitably distributed interests. And this means a democratic society. In our search for aims in education, we are not concerned, therefore, with finding an end outside of the educative process to which education is subordinate. Our whole conception forbids. We are rather concerned with the contrast which exists when aims belong within the process in which they operate and when they are set up from without. And the latter state of affairs must obtain when social relationships are not equitably balanced. For in that case, some portions of the whole social group will find their aims determined by an external dictation; their aims will not arise from the free growth of their own experience, and their nominal aims will be means to more ulterior ends of others rather than truly their own.

INTEREST

Interest, concern, mean that self and world are engaged with each other in a developing situation.

The word interest, in its ordinary usage, expresses (*i*) the whole state of active development, (*ii*) the objective results that are foreseen and wanted, and (*iii*) the personal emotional inclination. (*i*) An occupation, employment, pursuit, business is often referred to as an interest. Thus we say that a man's interest is politics, or journalism, or philanthropy, or archæology, or collecting Japanese prints, or banking. (*ii*) By an interest we also mean the point at which an object touches or engages a man; the point where it influences him. In some legal transactions a man has to prove " interest " in order to have a standing at court. He has to show that some proposed step concerns his affairs. A silent partner has an interest in a business, although he takes no active part in its conduct, because its prosperity or decline affects his profits and liabilities. (*iii*) When we speak of a man as interested in this or that the emphasis falls directly upon his personal attitude. To be interested is to be absorbed in, wrapped up in, carried away by, some object. To take an interest is to be on the alert, to care about, to be attentive. We say of an interested person both that he has lost himself in some affair and that he has found himself in it. Both terms express the engrossment of the self in an object.

When the place of interest in education is spoken of in a depreciatory way, it will be found that the second of the meanings mentioned is first exaggerated and then isolated. Interest is taken to mean merely the effect of an object upon personal advantage or disadvantage, success or failure. Separated from any objective development of affairs, these are reduced to mere personal states of pleasure or pain. Educationally, it then follows that to attach importance to interest means to attach some feature of seductiveness to material otherwise indifferent; to secure attention and effort by offering a bribe of pleasure. This procedure is properly stigmatized as " soft " pedagogy; as a " soup-kitchen " theory of education.

But the objection is based upon the fact—or assumption—that the forms of skill to be acquired and the subject matter to be appropriated have no interest on their own account: in other words, they are supposed to be irrelevant to the normal activities of the pupils. The remedy is not in finding fault with the doctrine of interest, any more than it is to search for some pleasant bait that may be hitched to the alien material. It is to discover objects and modes of action, which are connected with present powers. The function of this material in engaging activity and carrying it on consistently and continuously *is* its interest. If the material operates in this way there is no call either to hunt for devices which will make it interesting or to appeal to arbitrary, semi-coerced effort.

The word interest suggests, etymologically, what is *between*—that which connects two things otherwise distant. In education, the distance covered may be looked at as temporary. The fact that a process takes time to mature is so obvious a fact that we rarely make it explicit. We overlook the fact that in growth there is ground to be covered between an initial stage of process and the completing period; that there is something intervening. In learning, the present powers of the pupil are the initial stage; the aim of the teacher represents the remote limit. Between the two lie *means*—that is, middle conditions:—acts to be performed; difficulties to be overcome; appliances to be used. Only *through* them, in the literal time sense, will the initial activities reach a satisfactory consummation.

These intermediate conditions are of interest precisely because the development of existing activities into the foreseen and desired end depends upon them. To be means for the achieving of present tendencies to be "between" the agent and his end, to be of interest, are different names for the same thing. When material has to be made interesting, it signifies that as presented, it lacks connection with purposes and present power: or that if the connection be there, it is not perceived. To make it interesting by leading one to realize the connection that exists is simply good sense; to make it interesting by extraneous and artificial inducements deserves all the bad names which have been applied to the doctrine of interest in education.

So much for the meaning of the term interest. Now for that of discipline. Where an activity takes time, where many means and obstacles lie between its initiation and completion, deliberation and persistence are required. It is obvious that a very large part of the everyday meaning of will is precisely the deliberate or conscious disposition to persist and endure in a planned course of action in spite of difficulties and contrary solicitations. A man of strong will, in the popular usage of the words, is a man who is neither fickle nor halfhearted in achieving chosen ends. His ability is executive; that is, he persistently and energetically strives to execute or carry out his aims. A weak will is unstable as water.

DISCIPLINE

A person who is trained to consider his actions, to undertake them deliberately, is in so far forth disciplined. Add to this ability a power to endure in an intelligently chosen course in face of distraction, confusion, and difficulty, and you have the essence of discipline. Discipline means power at command; mastery of the resources available for carrying through the action undertaken. To know what one is to do and to move to do it promptly and by use of the requisite means is to be disciplined, whether we are thinking of an army or a mind. Discipline is positive. To cow the spirit, to subdue inclination, to compel obedience, to mortify the flesh, to make a subordinate perform an uncongenial task—these things are or are not disciplinary according as they do or do not tend to the development of power to recognize what one is about and to persistence in accomplishment.

It is hardly necessary to press the point that interest and discipline are connected, not opposed. (*i*) Even the more purely intellectual phase of trained power—apprehension of what one is doing as exhibited in consequences—is not possible without interest. Deliberation will be perfunctory and superficial where there is no interest. Parents and teachers often complain—and correctly—that children "do not want to hear, or want to understand." Their minds are not upon the subject precisely because it does not touch them; it does not enter into their concerns. This is a state of things that needs to be remedied, but the remedy is not in the use of methods which increase indifference and aversion. Even punishing a child for inattention is one way of trying to make him realize that the matter is *not* a thing of complete unconcern; it is one way of arousing "interest," or bringing about a sense of connection. In the long run, its value is measured by whether it supplies a mere physical excitation to act in the way desired by the adult or whether it leads the child "to think"—that is, to reflect upon his acts and impregnate them with aims. (*ii*) That interest is requisite for executive persistence is even more obvious. Employers do not advertise for workmen who are not interested in what they are doing. If one were engaging a lawyer or a doctor, it would never occur to one to reason that the person engaged would stick to his work more conscientiously if it was so uncongenial to him that he did it merely from a sense of obligation. Interest measures—or rather *is*—the depth of the grip which the foreseen end has upon one in moving one to act for its realization.

THE NATURE OF EXPERIENCE

The nature of experience can be understood only by noting that it includes an active and a passive element peculiarly combined. On the active hand, experience is *trying*—a meaning which is made explicit in the connected term experiment. On the passive, it is *undergoing*. When we experience something we act upon it, we do something with it; then we suffer or undergo the consequences. We do something to the thing and then it does something to us in return: such is the peculiar combination. The connection of these two phases of experience measures the fruitfulness or value of the experience. Mere activity does not constitute experience. It is dispersive, centrifugal, dissipating. Experience as trying involves change, but change is meaningless transition unless it is consciously connected with the return wave of consequences which flow from it. When an activity is continued *into* the undergoing of consequences, when the change made by action is reflected back into a change made in us, the mere flux is loaded with significance. We learn something. It is not experience when a child merely sticks his finger into a flame; it is experience when the movement is connected with the pain which he undergoes in consequence. Henceforth the sticking of the finger into flame *means* a burn. Being burned is a mere physical change, like the burning of a stick of wood, if it is not perceived as a consequence of some other action.

Blind and capricious impulses hurry us on heedlessly from one thing to another. So far as this happens, everything is writ in water. There is none of that cumulative growth which makes an experience in any vital sense of that term. On the other hand, many things happen to us in the way of pleasure and pain which we do not connect with any prior activity of our own. They are mere accidents so far as we are concerned. There is no before or after to such experience; no retrospect nor outlook, and consequently no meaning. We get nothing which may be carried over to foresee what is likely to happen next, and no gain in ability to adjust ourselves to what is coming— no added control. Only by courtesy can such an experience be called experience. To "learn from experience" is to make a backward and forward connection between what we do to things and what we enjoy or suffer from things in consequence. Under such conditions, doing becomes a trying; an experiment with the world to find out what it is like; the undergoing becomes instruction—discovery of the connection of things.

EXPERIENCE AND THINKING

So much for the general features of a reflective experience. They are (*i*) perplexity, confusion, doubt, due to the fact that one is implicated in an incomplete situation whose full character is not yet determined; (*ii*) a conjectural anticipation—a tentative interpretation of the given elements, attributing to them a tendency to effect certain consequences; (*iii*) a careful survey (examination, inspection, exploration, analysis) of all attainable consideration which will define and clarify the problem in hand; (*iv*) a consequent elaboration of the tentative hypothesis to make it more precise and more consistent, because squaring with a wider range of facts; (*v*) taking one stand upon the projected hypothesis as a plan of action which is applied to the existing state of affairs: doing something overtly to bring about the anticipated result, and thereby testing the hypothesis. It is the extent and accuracy of steps three and four which mark off a distinctive reflective experience from one on the trial and error plane. They make *thinking* itself into an experience. Nevertheless, we never get wholly beyond the trial and error situation. Our most elaborate and rationally consistent thought has to be tried in the world and thereby tried out. And since it can never take into account all the connections, it can never cover with perfect accuracy all the consequences. Yet a thoughtful survey of conditions is so careful, and the guessing at results so controlled, that we have a right to mark off the reflective experience from the grosser trial and error forms of action.

Thinking in Education

The initial stage of that developing experience which is called thinking is *experience*. This remark may sound like a silly truism. It ought to be one; but unfortunately it is not. On the contrary, thinking is often regarded both in philosophic theory and in educational practice as something cut off from experience, and capable of being cultivated in isolation. In fact, the inherent limitations of experience are often urged as the sufficient ground for attention to thinking. Experience is then thought to be confined to the senses and appetites; to a mere material world, while thinking proceeds from a higher faculty (of reason), and is occupied with spiritual or at least literary things. So oftentimes, a sharp distinction is made between pure mathematics as a peculiarly fit subject matter of thought (since it has nothing to do with physical existences) and applied mathematics, which has utilitarian but not mental value.

Speaking generally, the fundamental fallacy in methods of instruction lies in supposing that experience on the part of pupils may be assumed. What is here insisted upon is the necessity of an actual empirical situation as the initiating phase of thought. Experience is here taken as previously defined: trying to do something and having the thing perceptibly do something to one in return. The fallacy consists in supposing that we can begin with ready-made subject matter of arithmetic, or geography, or whatever, irrespective of some direct personal experience of a situation.

No one has ever explained why children are so full of questions outside of the school (so that they pester grown-up persons if they get any encouragement), and the conspicuous absence of display of curiosity about the subject matter of school lessons. Reflection on this striking contrast will throw light upon the question of how far customary school conditions supply a context of experience in which problems naturally suggest themselves. No amount of improvement in the personal technique of the instructor will wholly remedy this state of things. There must be more actual material, more *stuff*, more appliances, and more opportunities for doing things, before the gap can be overcome. And where children are engaged in doing things and in discussing what arises in the course of their doing, it is found, even with comparatively indifferent modes of instruction, that children's inquiries are spontaneous and numerous, and the proposals of solution advanced, varied, and ingenious.

As a consequence of the absence of the materials and occupations which generate real problems, the pupil's problems are not his; or, rather, they are his *only as* a pupil, not as a human being. Hence the lamentable waste in carrying over such expertness as is achieved in dealing with them to the affairs of life beyond the schoolroom. A pupil has a problem, but it is the problem of meeting the peculiar requirements set by the teacher. His problem becomes that of finding out what the teacher wants, what will satisfy the teacher in recitation and examination and outward deportment. Relationship to subject matter is no longer direct. The occasions and material of thought are not found in the arithmetic or the history or geography itself, but in skillfully adapting that material to the teacher's requirements. The pupil studies, but unconsciously to himself the objects of his study are the conventions and standards of the school system and school authority, not the nominal "studies." The thinking thus evoked is artificially one-sided at the best. At its worst, the problem of the pupil is not how to meet the requirements of school life, but how to *seem* to meet them—or, how to come near enough to meeting them to slide along without an undue amount of friction. The type of judgment formed by these devices is not a desirable addition to character. If these statements give too highly colored a picture of usual school methods, the exaggeration may at least serve to illustrate the point: the need of active pursuits, involving the use of material to accomplish purposes, if there are to be situations which normally generate problems occasioning thoughtful inquiry.

The Unity of Subject Matter and Method

The trinity of school topics is subject matter, methods, and administration or government. . . . Before taking it up, it may be well, however, to call express attention to one implication of our theory; the connection of subject matter and method with each other. The idea that mind and world of things and persons are two separate and independent realms—a theory which philosophically is known as dualism—carries with it the conclusion that method and subject matter of instruction are separate affairs. Subject matter then becomes a ready-made systematized classification of the facts and principles of the world of nature and man. Method then has for its province a consideration of the ways in which this antecedent subject matter may be best presented to and impressed upon the mind; or, a consideration of the ways in which the mind may be externally brought to bear upon the matter so as to facilitate its acquisition and possession. In theory, at least, one might deduce from a science of mind as something existing by itself a complete theory of methods of learning, with no knowledge of the subjects to which the methods are to be applied. Since many who are actually most proficient in various branches of subject matter are wholly innocent of these methods, this state of affairs gives opportunity for the retort that pedagogy, as an alleged science of methods of the mind in learning, is futile—a mere screen for concealing the necessity a teacher is under of profound and accurate acquaintance with the subject in hand.

But since thinking is a directed movement of subject matter to a completing issue, and since mind is the deliberate and intentional phase of the process, the notion of any such split is radically false. The fact that the material of a science is organized is evidence that it has already been subjected to intelligence; it has been methodized, so to say. Zoölogy as a systematic branch of knowledge represents crude, scattered facts of our ordinary acquaintance with animals after they have been subjected to careful examination, to deliberate supplementation, and to arrangement to bring out connections which assist observation, memory, and further inquiry. Instead of furnishing a starting point for learning, they mark out a consummation. Method means that arrangement *of* subject matter which makes it most effective in use. Never is method something outside of the material.

How about method from the standpoint of an individual who is dealing with subject matter? Again, it is not something external. It is simply an effective treatment *of* material—efficiency meaning such treatment as utilizes the material (puts it to a purpose) with a minimum of waste of time and energy. We can distinguish a *way* of acting, and discuss it by itself; but the way *exists* only as a way-of-dealing-with-material. Method is not antithetical to subject matter; it is the effective direction of subject matter to desired results. It is antithetical to random and ill-considered action—ill-considered signifying ill-adapted.

THE NATURE OF METHOD

A consideration of some evils in education that flow from the isolation of method from subject matter will make the point more definite. (*i*) In the first place, there is the neglect (of which we have spoken) of concrete situations of experience. There can be no discovery of a method without cases to be studied. The method is derived from observation of what actually happens, with a view to seeing that it happen better next time. But in instruction and discipline, there is rarely sufficient opportunity for children and youth to have the direct normal experiences from which educators might derive an idea of method or order of best development. Experiences are had under conditions of such constraint that they throw little or no light upon the normal course of an experience to its fruition. "Methods" have then to be authoritatively recommended to teachers, instead of being an expression of their own intelligent observations. Under such circumstances, they have a mechanical uniformity, assumed to be alike for all minds. Where flexible personal experiences are promoted by providing an environment which calls out directed occupations in work and play, the methods ascertained will vary with individuals—for it is certain that each individual has something characteristic in his way of going at things.

(*ii*) In the second place, the notion of methods isolated from subject matter is responsible for the false conceptions of discipline and interest already noted. When the effective way of managing material is treated as something ready-made apart from material, there are just three possible ways in which to establish a relationship lacking by assumption. One is to utilize excitement, shock of pleasure, tickling the palate. Another is to make the consequences of not attending painful; we may use the menace of harm to motivate concern with the alien subject matter. Or a direct appeal may be made to the person to put forth effort without any reason. We may rely upon immediate strain of "will." In practice, however, the latter method is effectual only when instigated by fear of unpleasant results.

(*iii*) In the third place, the act of learning is made a direct and conscious end in itself. Under normal conditions, learning is a product and reward of occupation with subject matter. Children do not set out, consciously, to learn walking or talking. One sets out to give his impulses for communication and for fuller intercourse with others a show. He learns in consequence of his direct activities. The better methods of teaching a child, say, to read, follow the same road. They do not fix his attention upon the fact that he has to learn something and so make his attitude self-conscious and constrained. They engage his activities, and in the process of engagement he learns: the same is true of the more successful methods in dealing with number or whatever. But when the subject matter is not used in carrying forward impulses and habits to significant results, it is just something to be learned. The pupil's attitude to it is just that of having to learn it. Conditions more unfavorable to an alert and concentrated response would be hard to devise. Frontal attacks are even more wasteful in learning than in war. This does not mean, however, that students are to be seduced unaware into preoccupation with lessons. It means that they shall be occupied with them for real reasons or ends, and not just as something to be learned. This is accomplished whenever the pupil perceives the place occupied by the subject matter in the fulfilling of some experience.

(*iv*) In the fourth place, under the influence of the conception of the separation of mind and material, method tends to be reduced to a cut and dried routine, to following mechanically prescribed steps. No one can tell in how many schoolrooms children reciting in arithmetic or grammar are compelled to go through, under the alleged sanction of method, certain preordained verbal formulæ. Instead of being encouraged to attack their topics directly, experimenting with methods that seem promising and learning to discriminate by the consequences that accrue, it is assumed that there is one fixed method to be followed. It is also naïvely assumed that if the pupils make their statements and explanations in a certain form of "analysis," their mental habits will in time conform. Nothing has brought pedagogical theory into greater disrepute than the belief that it is identified with handing out to teachers recipes and models to be followed in teaching. Flexibility and initiative in dealing with problems are characteristic of any conception to which method is a way of managing material to develop a conclusion. Mechanical rigid woodenness is an inevitable corollary of any theory which separates mind from activity motivated by a purpose.

It would be much better to have fewer facts and truths in instruction—that is, fewer things supposedly accepted—if a smaller number of situations could be intellectually worked out to the point where conviction meant something real—some identification of the self with the type of conduct demanded by facts and foresight of results. The most permanent bad results of undue complication of school subjects and congestion of school studies and lessons are not the worry, nervous strain, and superficial acquaintance that follow (serious as these are), but the failure to make clear what is involved in really knowing and believing a thing. Intellectual responsibility means severe standards in this regard. These standards can be built up only through practice in following up and acting upon the meaning of what is acquired.

Intellectual *thoroughness* is thus another name for the attitude we are considering. There is a kind of thoroughness which is almost purely physical: the kind that signifies mechanical and exhausting drill upon all the details of a subject. Intellectual thoroughness is *seeing a thing through*. It depends upon a unity of purpose to which details are subordinated, not upon presenting a multitude of disconnected details. It is manifested in the firmness with which the full meaning of the purpose is developed, not in attention, however "conscientious" it may be, to the steps of action externally imposed and directed.

SUBJECT MATTER OF EDUCATOR AND OF LEARNER

So far as the nature of subject matter in principle is concerned, there is nothing to add to what has been said (see *ante*, p. 158 [*Democracy and Education*]). It consists of the facts observed, recalled, read, and talked about, and the ideas suggested, in course of a development of a situation having a purpose. This statement needs to be rendered more specific by connecting it with the materials of school instruction, the studies which make up the curriculum. What is the significance of our definition in application to reading, writing, mathematics, history, nature study, drawing, singing, physics, chemistry, modern and foreign languages and so on?

Let us recur to two of the points made earlier in our discussion. The educator's part in the enterprise of education is to furnish the environment which stimulates responses and directs the learner's course. In last analysis, *all* that the educator can do is modify stimuli so that response will as surely as is possible result in the formation of desirable intellectual and emotional dispositions. Obviously studies or the subject matter of the curriculum have intimately to do with this business of supplying an environment. The other point is the necessity of a social environment to give meaning to habits formed. In what we have termed informal education, subject matter is carried directly in the matrix of social intercourse.

The Nature of Subject Matter

The points need to be considered from the standpoint of instructor and of student. To the former, the significance of a knowledge of subject matter, going far beyond the present knowledge of pupils, is to supply definite standards and to reveal to him the possibilities of the crude activities of the immature. (*i*) The material of school studies translates into concrete and detailed terms the meanings of current social life which it is desirable to transmit. It puts clearly before the instructor the essential ingredients of the culture to be perpetuated, in such an organized form as to protect him from the haphazard efforts he would be likely to indulge in if the meanings had not been standardized. (*ii*) A knowledge of the ideas which have been achieved in the past as the outcome of activity places the educator in a position to perceive the meaning of the seeming impulsive and aimless reactions of the young, and to provide the stimuli needed to direct them so that they will amount to something. The more the educator knows of music the more he can perceive the possibilities of the inchoate musical impulses of a child. Organized subject matter represents the ripe fruitage of experiences like theirs, experiences involving the same world, and powers and needs similar to theirs. It does not represent perfection or infallible wisdom; but it is the best at command to further new experiences which may, in some respects at least, surpass the achievements embodied in existing knowledge and works of art.

From the standpoint of the educator, in other words, the various studies represent working resources, available capital. Their remoteness from the experience of the young is not, however, seeming; it is real. The subject matter of the learner is not, therefore, it cannot be, identical with the formulated, the crystallized, and systematized subject matter of the adult; the material as found in books and in works of art, etc. The latter represents the *possibilities* of the former; not its existing state. It enters directly into the activities of the expert and the educator, not into that of the beginner, the learner. Failure to bear in mind the difference in subject matter from the respective standpoints of teacher and student is responsible for most of the mistakes made in the use of texts and other expressions of preëxistent knowledge.

The need for a knowledge of the constitution and functions, in the concrete, of human nature is great just because the teacher's attitude to subject matter is so different from that of the pupil. The teacher presents in actuality what the pupil represents only in *posse*. That is, the teacher already knows the things which the student is only learning. Hence the problem of the two is radically unlike. When engaged in the direct act of teaching, the instructor needs to have subject matter at his fingers' ends; his attention should be upon the attitude and response of the pupil. To understand the latter in its interplay with subject matter is his task, while the pupil's mind, naturally, should be not on itself but on the topic in hand. Or to state the same point in a somewhat different manner: the teacher should be occupied not with subject matter in itself but in its interaction with the pupil's present needs and capacities. Hence simple scholarship is not enough. In fact, there are certain features of scholarship or mastered subject matter—taken by itself—which get in the way of effective teaching *unless* the instructor's habitual attitude is one of concern with its interplay in the pupil's own experience. In the first place, his knowledge extends indefinitely beyond the range of the pupil's acquaintance. It involves principles which are beyond the immature pupil's understanding and interest. In and of itself, it may no more represent the living world of the pupil's experience than the astronomer's knowledge of Mars represents a baby's acquaintance with the room in which he stays. In the second place, the method of organization of the material of achieved scholarship differs from that of the beginner. It is not true that the experience of the young is unorganized—that it consists of isolated scraps. But it is organized in connection with direct practical centers of interest. The child's home is, for example, the organizing center of his geographical knowledge. His own movements about the locality, his journeys abroad, the tales of his friends, give the ties which hold his items of information together. But the geography of the geographer, of the one who has already developed the implications of these smaller experiences, is organized on the basis of the relationship which the various facts bear to one another—not the relations which they bear to his house, bodily movements, and friends. To the one who is learned, subject matter is extensive, accurately defined, and logically interrelated. To the one who is learning, it is fluid, partial, and connected through his personal occupations.[2] The problem of teaching is to keep the experience of the student moving in the direction of what the expert already knows. Hence the need that the teacher know both subject matter and the characteristic needs and capacities of the student.

The Development of Subject Matter in the Learner

It is possible, without doing violence to the facts, to mark off three fairly typical stages in the growth of subject matter in the experience of the learner. In its first estate, knowledge exists as the content of intelligent ability—power to do. This kind of subject matter, or known material, is expressed in familiarity or acquaintance with things. Then this material gradually is surcharged and deepened through communicated knowledge or information. Finally, it is enlarged and worked over into rationally or logically organized material—that of the one who, relatively speaking, is expert in the subject.

[2] Since the learned man should also still be a learner, it will be understood that these contrasts are relative, not absolute. But in the earlier stages of learning at least they are practically all-important.

Theories of Knowledge

While the content of knowledge is what *has* happened, what is taken as finished and hence settled and sure, the *reference* of knowledge is future or prospective. For knowledge furnishes the means of understanding or giving meaning to what is still going on and what is to be done. The knowledge of a physician is what he has found out by personal acquaintance and by study of what others have ascertained and recorded. But it is knowledge to him because it supplies the resources by which he interprets the unknown things which confront him, fills out the partial obvious facts with connected suggested phenomena, foresees their probable future, and makes plans accordingly. When knowledge is cut off from use in giving meaning to what is blind and baffling, it drops out of consciousness entirely or else becomes an object of æsthetic contemplation.

Yet many of the philosophic schools of method which have been mentioned transform the ignoring into a virtual denial. They regard knowledge as something complete in itself irrespective of its availability in dealing with what is yet to be. And it is this omission which vitiates them and which makes them stand as sponsors for educational methods which an adequate conception of knowledge condemns. For one has only to call to him what is sometimes treated in schools as acquisition of knowledge to realize how lacking it is in any fruitful connection with the ongoing experience of the students—how largely it seems to be believed that the mere appropriation of subject matter which happens to be stored in books constitutes knowledge. No matter how true what is learned to those who found it out and in whose experience it functioned, there is nothing which makes it knowledge to the pupils. It might as well be something about Mars or about some fanciful country unless it fructifies in the individual's own life.

The Social and the Moral

All of the separations which we have been criticizing—and which the idea of education set forth in the previous chapters is designed to avoid—spring from taking morals too narrowly—giving them, on one side, a sentimental goody-goody turn without reference to effective ability to do what is socially needed, and, on the other side, overemphasizing convention and tradition so as to limit morals to a list of definitely stated acts. As a matter of fact, morals are as broad as acts which concern our relationships with others. And potentially this includes all our acts, even though their social bearing may not be thought of at the time of performance. For every act, by the principle of habit, modifies disposition—it sets up a certain kind of inclination and desire. And it is impossible to tell when the habit thus strengthened may have a direct and perceptible influence on our association with others. Certain traits of character have such an obvious connection with our social relationships that we call them "moral" in an emphatic sense—truthfulness, honesty, chastity, amiability, etc. But this only means that they are, as compared with some other attitudes, central:—that they carry other attitudes with them. They are moral in an emphatic sense not because they are isolated and exclusive, but because they are so intimately connected with thousands of other attitudes which we do not explicitly recognize—which perhaps we have not even names for. To call them virtues in their isolation is like taking the skeleton for the living body. The bones are certainly important, but their importance lies in the fact that they support other organs of the body in such a way as to make them capable of integrated effective activity. And the same is true of the qualities of character which we specifically designate virtues. Morals concern nothing less than the whole character, and the whole character is identical with the man in all his concrete make-up and manifestations. To possess virtue does not signify to have cultivated a few nameable and exclusive traits; it means to be fully and adequately what one is capable of becoming through association with others in all the offices of life.

16

Experience and Education

JOHN DEWEY

TRADITIONAL VS. PROGRESSIVE EDUCATION

The Traditional scheme is, in essence, one of imposition from above and from outside. It imposes adult standards, subject-matter, and methods upon those who are only growing slowly toward maturity. The gap is so great that the required subject-matter, the methods of learning and of behaving are foreign to the existing capacities of the young. They are beyond the reach of the experience the young learners already possess. Consequently, they must be imposed; even though good teachers will use devices of art to cover up the imposition so as to relieve it of obviously brutal features.

If one attempts to formulate the philosophy of education implicit in the practices of the newer education, we may, I think, discover certain common principles amid the variety of progressive schools now existing. To imposition from above is opposed expression and cultivation of individuality; to external discipline is opposed free activity; to learning from texts and teachers, learning through experience; to acquisition of isolated skills and techniques by drill, is opposed acquisition of them as means of attaining ends which make direct vital appeal; to preparation for a more or less remote future is opposed making the most of the opportunities of present life; to static aims and materials is opposed acquaintance with a changing world.

John Dewey (October 20, 1859–June 1, 1952) was a philosopher and educator. John Dewey, *Experience and Education.* Tiffin, Ohio (238 East Perry Street): Kappa Delta Pi, pp. 4, 5–6, 9–10, 13–14, 16, 29–32, 34–35, 38–42, 60–63, 65–66, 69–71, 72, 88–89, 95, 96–97, 114–115. Copyright 1938 by Kappa Delta Pi. Used by permission.

What is indicated in the foregoing remarks is that the general principles of the new education do not of themselves solve any of the problems of the actual or practical conduct and management of progressive schools. Rather, they set new problems which have to be worked out on the basis of a new philosophy of experience. The problems are not even recognized, to say nothing of being solved, when it is assumed that it suffices to reject the ideas and practices of the old education and then go to the opposite extreme. Yet I am sure that you will appreciate what is meant when I say that many of the newer schools tend to make little or nothing of organized subject-matter of study; to proceed as if any form of direction and guidance by adults were an invasion of individual freedom, and as if the idea that education should be concerned with the present and future meant that acquaintance with the past has little or no role to play in education. Without pressing these defects to the point of exaggeration, they at least illustrate what is meant by a theory and practice of education which proceeds negatively or by reaction against what has been current in education rather than by a positive and constructive development of purposes, methods, and subject-matter on the foundation of a theory of experience and its educational potentialities.

It is not too much to say that an educational philosophy which professes to be based on the idea of freedom may become as dogmatic as ever was the traditional education which is reacted against. For any theory and set of practices is dogmatic which is not based upon critical examination of its own underlying principles.

THE NEED FOR A THEORY OF EXPERIENCE

. . . Any experience is mis-educative that has the effect of arresting or distorting the growth of further experience. An experience may be such as to engender callousness; it may produce lack of sensitivity and of responsiveness. Then the possibilities of having richer experience in the future are restricted. Again, a given experience may increase a person's automatic skill in a particular direction and yet tend to land him in a groove or rut; the effect again is to narrow the field of further experience. An experience may be immediately enjoyable and yet promote the formation of a slack and careless attitude; this attitude then operates to modify the quality of subsequent experiences so as to prevent a person from getting out of them what they have to give. Again, experiences may be so disconnected from one another that, while each is agreeable or even exciting in itself, they are not linked cumulatively to one another. Energy is then dissipated and a person becomes scatterbrained. Each experience may be lively, vivid, and "interesting," and yet their disconnectedness may artificially generate dispersive, disintegrated, centrifugal habits.

Everything depends upon the *quality* of the experience which is had. The quality of any experience has two aspects. There is an immediate aspect of agreeableness or disagreeableness, and there is its influence upon later experiences. The first is obvious and easy to judge. The *effect* of an experience is not borne on its face. It sets a problem to the educator. It is his business to arrange for the kind of experiences which, while they do not repel the student, but rather engage his activities are, nevertheless, more than immediately enjoyable since they promote having desirable future experiences.

CRITERIA OF EXPERIENCE

I return now to the question of continuity as a criterion by which to discriminate between experiences which are educative and those which are mis-educative. As we have seen, there is some kind of continuity in any case since every experience affects for better or worse the attitudes which help decide the quality of further experiences, by setting up certain preference and aversion, and making it easier or harder to act for this or that end. Moreover, every experience influences in some degree the objective conditions under which further experiences are had. For example, a child who learns to speak has a new facility and new desire. But he has also widened the external conditions of subsequent learning. When he learns to read, he similarly opens up a new environment. If a person decides to become a teacher, lawyer, physician, or stockbroker, when he executes his intention he thereby necessarily determines to some extent the environment in which he will act in the future. He has rendered himself more sensitive and responsive to certain conditions, and relatively immune to those things about him that would have been stimuli if he had made another choice.

But, while the principle of continuity applies in some way in every case, the quality of the present experience influences the *way* in which the principle applies. We speak of spoiling a child and of the spoilt child. The effect of overindulging a child is a continuing one. It sets up an attitude which operates as an automatic demand that persons and objects cater to his desires and caprices in the future. It makes him seek the kind of situation that will enable him to do what he feels like doing at the time. It renders him averse to and comparatively incompetent in situations which require effort and perseverance in overcoming obstacles. There is no paradox in the fact that the principle of the continuity of experience may operate so as to leave a person arrested on a low plane of development, in a way which limits later capacity for growth.

On the other hand, if an experience arouses curiosity, strengthens initiative, and sets up desires and purposes that are sufficiently intense to carry a person over dead places in the future, continuity works in a very different way. Every experience is a moving force. Its value can be judged only on the ground of what it moves toward and into. The greater maturity of experience which should belong to the adult as educator puts him in a position to evaluate each experience of the young in a way in which the one having the less mature experience cannot do. It is then the business of the educator to see in what direction an experience is heading. There is no point in his being more mature if, instead of using his greater insight to help organize the conditions of the experience of the immature, he throws away his insight. Failure to take the moving force of an experience into account so as to judge and direct it on the ground of what it is moving into means disloyalty to the principle of experience itself.

In a word, we live from birth to death in a world of persons and things which in large measure is what it is because of what has been done and transmitted from previous human activities. When this fact is ignored, experience is treated as if it were something which goes on exclusively inside an individual's body and mind. It ought not to be necessary to say that experience does not occur in a vacuum. There are sources outside an individual which give rise to experience. It is constantly fed from these springs. No one would question that a child in a slum tenement has a different experience from that of a child in a cultured home; that the country lad has a different kind of experience from the city boy, or a boy on the seashore one different from the lad who is brought up on inland prairies. Ordinarily we take such facts for granted as too commonplace to record. But when their educational import is recognized, they indicate the second way in which the educator can direct the experience of the young without engaging in imposition. A primary responsibility of educators is that they not only be aware of the general principle of the shaping of actual experience by environing conditions, but that they also recognize in the concrete what surroundings are conducive to having experiences that lead to growth.

The word "interaction," which has just been used, expresses the second chief principle for interpreting an experience in its educational function and force. It assigns equal rights to both factors in experience—objective and internal conditions. Any normal experience is an interplay of these two sets of conditions. Taken together, or in their interaction, they form what we call a *situation*. The trouble with traditional education was not that it emphasized the external conditions that enter into the control of the experiences but that it paid so little attention to the internal factors which also decide what kind of experience is had. It violated the principle of interaction from one side. But this violation is no reason why the new education should violate the principle from the other side—except upon the basis of the extreme *Either-Or* educational philosophy which has been mentioned.

The illustration drawn from the need for regulation of the objective conditions of a baby's development indicates, first, that the parent has responsibility for arranging the conditions under which an infant's experience of food, sleep, etc., occurs, and, secondly, that the responsibility is fulfilled by utilizing the funded experience of the past, as this is represented, say, by the advice of competent physicians and others who have made a special study of normal physical growth. Does it limit the freedom of the mother when she uses the body of knowledge thus provided to regulate the objective conditions of nourishment and sleep? Or does the enlargement of her intelligence in fulfilling her parental function widen her freedom? Doubtless if a fetish were made of the advice and directions so that they came to be inflexible dictates to be followed under every possible condition, then restriction of freedom of both parent and child would occur. But this restriction would also be a limitation of the intelligence that is exercised in personal judgment.

In what respect does regulation of objective conditions limit the freedom of the baby? Some limitation is certainly placed upon its immediate movements and inclinations when it is put in its crib, at a time when it wants to continue playing, or does not get food at the moment it would like it, or when it isn't picked up and dandled when it cries for attention. Restriction also occurs when mother or nurse snatches a child away from an open fire into which it is about to fall. I shall have more to say later about freedom. Here it is enough to ask whether freedom is to be thought of and adjudged on the basis of relatively momentary incidents or whether its meaning is found in the continuity of developing experience.

The statement that individuals live in a world means, in the concrete, that they live in a series of situations. And when it is said that they live *in* these situations, the meaning of the word " in " is different from its meaning when it is said that pennies are " in " a pocket or paint is " in " a can. It means, once more, that interaction is going on between an individual and objects and other persons. The conceptions of *situation* and of *interaction* are inseparable from each other. An experience is always what it is because of a transaction taking place between an individual and what, at the time, constitutes his environment, whether the latter consists of persons with whom he is talking about some topic or event, the subject talked about being also a part of the situation; or the toys with which he is playing; the book he is reading (in which his environing conditions at the time may be England or ancient Greece or an imaginary region); or the materials of an experiment he is performing. The environment, in other words, is whatever conditions interact with personal needs, desires, purposes, and capacities to create the experience which is had. Even when a person builds a castle in the air he is interacting with the objects which he constructs in fancy.

SOCIAL CONTROL

. . . The school was not a group or community held together by participation in common activities. Consequently, the normal, proper conditions of control were lacking. Their absence was made up for, and to a considerable extent had to be made up for, by the direct intervention of the teacher, who, as the saying went, "*kept* order." He kept it because order was in the teacher's keeping, instead of residing in the shared work being done.

The conclusion is that in what are called the new schools, the primary source of social control resides in the very nature of the work done as a social enterprise in which all individuals have an opportunity to contribute and to which all feel a responsibility. Most children are naturally "sociable." Isolation is even more irksome to them than to adults. A genuine community life has its ground in this natural sociability. But community life does not organize itself in an enduring way purely spontaneously. It requires thought and planning ahead. The educator is responsible for a knowledge of individuals and for a knowledge of subject-matter that will enable activities to be selected which lend themselves to social organization, an organization in which all individuals have an opportunity to contribute something, and in which the activities in which all participate are the chief carrier of control.

I am not romantic enough about the young to suppose that every pupil will respond or that any child of normally strong impulses will respond on every occasion. There are likely to be some who, when they come to school, are already victims of injurious conditions outside of the school and who have become so passive and unduly docile that they fail to contribute. There will be others who, because of previous experience, are bumptious and unruly and perhaps downright rebellious. But it is certain that the general principle of social control cannot be predicated upon such cases. It is also true that no general rule can be laid down for dealing with such cases. The teacher has to deal with them individually. They fall into general classes, but no two are exactly alike. The educator has to discover as best he or she can the causes for the recalcitrant attitudes. He or she cannot, if the educational process is to go on, make it a question of pitting one will against another in order to see which is strongest, nor yet allow the unruly and non-participating pupils to stand permanently in the way of the educative activities of others. Exclusion perhaps is the only available measure at a given juncture, but it is no solution. For it may strengthen the very causes which have brought about the undesirable anti-social attitude, such as desire for attention or to show off.

It is absurd to exclude the teacher from membership in the group. As the most mature member of the group he has a peculiar responsibility for the conduct of the interactions and intercommunications which are the very life of the group as a community. That children are individuals whose freedom should be respected while the more mature person should have no freedom as an individual is an idea to absurd to require refutation. The tendency to exclude the teacher from a positive and leading share in the direction of the activities of the community of which he is a member is another instance of reaction from one extreme to another. When pupils were a class rather than a social group, the teacher necessarily acted largely from the outside, not as a director of processes of exchange in which all had a share. When education is based upon experience and educative experience is seen to be a social process, the situation changes radically. The teacher loses the position of external boss or dictator but takes on that of leader of group activities.

THE NATURE OF FREEDOM

At the risk of repeating what has been often said by me I want to say something about the other side of the problem of social control, namely, the nature of freedom. The only freedom that is of enduring importance is freedom of intelligence, that is to say, freedom of observation and of judgment exercised in behalf of purposes that are intrinsically worth while. The commonest mistake made about freedom is, I think, to identify it with freedom of movement, or with the external or physical side of activity. Now, this external and physical side of activity cannot be separated from the internal side of activity; from freedom of thought, desire, and purpose. The limitation that was put upon outward action by the fixed arrangements of the typical traditional schoolroom, with its fixed rows of desks and its military regimen of pupils who were permitted to move only at certain fixed signals, put a great restriction upon intellectual and moral freedom. Straitjacket and chain-gang procedures had to be done away with if there was to be a chance for growth of individuals in the intellectual springs of freedom without which there is no assurance of genuine and continued normal growth.

But the fact still remains that an increased measure of freedom of outer movement is a *means*, not an end. The educational problem is not solved when this aspect of freedom is obtained. Everything then depends, so far as education is concerned, upon what is done with this added liberty. What end does it serve? What consequences flow from it? Let me speak first of the advantages which reside potentially in increase of outward freedom. In the first place, without its existence it is practically impossible for a teacher to gain knowledge of the individuals with whom he is concerned. Enforced quiet and acquiescence prevent pupils from disclosing their real natures. They enforce artificial uniformity.

The other important advantage of increased outward freedom is found in the very nature of the learning process. That the older methods set a premium upon passivity and receptivity has been pointed out. Physical quiescence puts a tremendous premium upon these traits. The only escape from them in the standardized school is an activity which is irregular and perhaps disobedient. There cannot be complete quietude in a laboratory or workshop. The non-social character of the traditional school is seen in the fact that it erected silence into one of its prime virtues.

PROGRESSIVE ORGANIZATION OF SUBJECT-MATTER

... It is a cardinal precept of the newer school of education that the beginning of instruction shall be made with the experience learners already have; that this experience and the capacities that have been developed during its course provide the starting point for all further learning. I am not so sure that the other condition, that of orderly development toward expansion and organization of subject-matter through growth of experience, receives as much attention. Yet the principle of continuity of educative experience requires that equal thought and attention be given to solution of this aspect of the educational problem. Undoubtedly this phase of the problem is more difficult than the other. Those who deal with the pre-school child, with the kindergarten child, and with the boy and girl of the early primary years do not have much difficulty in determining the range of past experience or in finding activities that connect in vital ways with it. With older children both factors of the problem offer increased difficulties to the educator. It is harder to find out the background of the experience of individuals and harder to find out just how the subject-matters already contained in that experience shall be directed so as to lead out to larger and better organized fields.

That up to the present time the weakest point in progressive schools is in the matter of selection and organization of intellectual subject-matter is, I think, inevitable under the circumstances. It is as inevitable as it is right and proper that they should break loose from the cut and dried material which formed the staple of the old education. In addition, the field of experience is very wide and it varies in its contents from place to place and from time to time.

Once more, it is part of the educator's responsibility to see equally to two things: First, that the problem grows out of the conditions of the experience being had in the present, and that it is within the range of the capacity of students; and, secondly, that it is such that it arouses in the learner an active quest for information and for production of new ideas.

EXPERIENCE—THE MEANS AND GOAL OF EDUCATION

For I am so confident of the potentialities of education when it is treated as intelligently directed development of the possibilities inherent in ordinary experience that I do not feel it necessary to criticize here the other route nor to advance arguments in favor of taking the route of experience. The only ground for anticipating failure in taking this path resides to my mind in the danger that experience and the experimental method will not be adequately conceived. There is no discipline in the world so severe as the discipline of experience subjected to the tests of intelligent development and direction. Hence the only ground I can see for even a temporary reaction against the standards, aims, and methods of the newer education is the failure of educators who professedly adopt them to be faithful to them in practice. As I have emphasized more than once, the road of the new education is not an easier one to follow than the old road but a more strenuous and difficult one. It will remain so until it has attained its majority and that attainment will require many years of serious co-operative work on the part of its adherents. The greatest danger that attends its future is, I believe, the idea that it is an easy way to follow, so easy that its course may be improvised, if not in an impromptu fashion, at least almost from day to day or from week to week. It is for this reason that instead of extolling its principles, I have confined myself to showing certain conditions which must be fulfilled if it is to have the successful career which by right belongs to it.

Four

Some Normative Issues in Education

Introduction to Part Four

In the previous parts of this book we inquired into what philosophers do, we learned to use some of their methods and tools, and we perused some of their views. As a result of this inquiry, the student may have been led to conclude that philosophers of education either make concept analyses or spend their time working out general philosophies of education. But this would be a mistake. Some philosophers would claim that they did neither of these things, at least not regularly or primarily. Instead, they see themselves as engaged in a kind of normative philosophy in which some issue that is pertinent to education is identified, relevant philosophical matters are examined, scientific evidence is weighed, and conclusions are reached about what would be the soundest and wisest thing to do. Such a philosopher may eschew all synoptic philosophies or he may operate with at least one foot comfortably and firmly planted in some conventional philosophical stronghold such as realism or pragmatism. He may or may not be an analyst, although he may elect some of the analyst's methods as he deals with his normative issues.

The student of philosophy of education must become acquainted with this approach to philosophy of education. In order to do this he will have use for a set of criteria for identifying normative issues.

Fortunately, several years ago C. J. Ducasse undertook to discuss the function and nature of the philosophy of education.[1] In the course of his discussion he identified the nature of questions that give rise to the need for a philosophy of education. Drawing heavily upon Ducasse, and taking certain liberties with his ideas, the following are presented as a set of criteria for identifying normative issues in education:

(1) Does the question *concern education*?

(2) Is it a *practical question;* that is, does it concern a *choice to be made* between two or more alternatives?

(3) Is the choice either between *alternative means* available to a given

---

[1] C. J. Ducasse, "On the Function and Nature of the Philosophy of Education," Christopher J. Lucas (ed.), *What Is Philosophy of Education?* (New York: Macmillan Publishing Co., Inc., 1969), pp. 167–75.

      end; or/and between *alternative ends* attainable with the means possessed?

(4) Is it a question of which alternative would be *wisest* to choose?

(5) Is it a question that common judgment finds itself unable to answer responsibly with confidence; i.e., is it a question in whose case *doubt* or *dispute* actually exists, and where a responsible, not an arbitrary, answer is desired?

The last part of this book deals with normative issues. The first four chapters in this part are essentially concerned with the means of education. Should teachers teach, and if so, how? The three chapters that follow are devoted to the place of religion in education—a long-standing question that refuses to disappear. The final three chapters attempt to describe the nature and probable influence of the educated person on society and are, therefore, most closely related to the goals of education.

By using the listed criteria and studying how others have dealt with such problems (as discussed in the next few chapters), the student can generate his own answers to the pertinent normative issues that he identifies.

A. Means

One of the recurring normative issues in education is what means should be used to achieve certain goals or ends? The scientist in education is especially concerned with this issue. Much of his effort may be devoted to attempts at discovering experimentally what teaching procedure will most economically and efficiently achieve a certain agreed-upon aim or goal.

The philosopher *qua* philosopher does not experiment. Nevertheless, philosophers deal with means in a number of important and interesting ways. B. Paul Komisar, for example, questions the conventional role of the teacher as one who "gives" an education, and Waltraut J. Stein describes how she develops classroom teaching procedures within the context of European phenomenology and existentialism and her own teaching experience. Frederick C. Neff, on the other hand, assays performance-based teaching, a much discussed means in contemporary education. Finally, Joe Park points out that schooling is but one means to acquire an education and hypothesizes that much of what is learned throughout life is probably learned outside the classroom. Furthermore, what is learned outside of school is often not closely related to what is learned in school. Several options for establishing a better accommodation between schooling and learning outside the classroom are examined.

17

Is Teaching Phoney?

B. Paul Komisar

To a less than happy degree, a distinct tone of carping has characterized one region of discussion in education. The region I refer to is the debate accompanying the introduction and limited encroachment of machinery and new forms of organization into the classroom, traditionally the precinct of the single, human-type teacher.

It is easy to be displeased by this, but more disheartening yet is the futile way the debate is joined. Controversy seems to have arisen in answer to such a question as "Is programmed instruction better than lecturing?", a question which puts the onus of proof on the innovation. Then demonstrations of greater or, what is more likely, equal effectiveness in the new techniques are countered with claims of further sacrosanct, often indiscernable features in the traditional ways. And so it goes on, jejunely.

In what follows, I want to do two things: (1) suggest what is wrong with the debate as presently conducted; and (2) even more suggestively do an analysis of teaching which might recast our conception of it. The " it " in the preceding sentence is ambiguous by intent. For it is the hope here that the analysis will contribute something to the rationality of the debate as well as give us a glimpse of the terror that is in teaching, debate or no debate.

The new forms of "teaching" alluded to above include teaching machines, computer-based instruction, and other offsprings of technology, as well as any conception of the teacher as a guide, stage-manager, or resource

B. Paul Komisar is Professor of Education at Temple University. B. Paul Komisar, "Is Teaching Phoney?" *Teachers College Record*, Vol. 70, No. 5 (February 1969), pp. 407–11. Used by permission of the author and *Teachers College Record*.

rather than a director of learning. So the first suggestion is that those in education who advocate these forms are radicals and not merely revisionists. They are radicals because teaching machines *et al.* are *not* new methods of teaching; rather they represent a different kind of social encounter to replace the kind we call *teaching*. The case for claiming radical innovation is as follows:

1. *Offerings*. In all human encounters it can be said a person makes something available to another: our paths intersect, we perceive one another and offer our discourse, demeanor and movements. When the elements are combined in intelligible ways, we get the minimum to be expected in any social encounter, what I will call an offering. An offering, on the view adopted here, is a social object adequately describable on its *own* terms, supplemented perhaps by reference to the offerer. So I may whine, wail, bleat, or blubber in your presence, but that *that* is what I do can be correctly reported *without reference to you*. My act, so to speak, though done in your presence is describable as done by me (of course I may have annoyed *you*, but that is another matter, or act). Indeed I can be said to have done that act in your company without your having noted it or noted it as such, and certainly it is not necessary that you acknowledge it. The point to be made in calling this an *offering* is that the act is made available to you; you *might* be of a mind to notice or even make something of it. But you need not; as an act it remains what it is whether or not it has this effect.

2. *Gifts and Services*. When what we make available to another requires for its completeness participation by the second party (perhaps some *change* in the other), then we have not offerings but gifts and services. Gifts and services, then, are offerings marked by being obtrusive. They have a "built-in" effect and require a recipient in order to achieve their alleged being. Hence an adequate description of either will mention a recipient. We give friendship, sympathy, and advice *to someone*; we don't just do them of ourselves. So these are gifts or services, not offerings; and we cannot describe what they are without mention of the other to which they are directed.

But what in turn sets off gifts from services is whether solicitation is a precondition for esteem. If I am a therapist and you invite my ministrations, then what I give is (genuine) therapy. But foisted "therapy" is not that at all but rather meddling or impertinence: it gives offense not aid. The same applies to training; to direct it at me without my leave is to be arrogant not helpful, obtruse not obliging. I am not sure, but the same may be true of comedy. If your antics are not invited or, at minimum, welcome, then you are being more vexing than entertaining. Ergo these are all *services*, by which is meant that without solicitation or acceptance they lose the right to be called (simply) by their initial names.

Gifts are the antithesis. My failure to request or accede to your act does not make it lose face or strip it of being; it remains what it is. Like services, gifts essentially intrude on the other, but it is an intrusion lacking power to modify the nature of the act. Thus we *give* friendship, love, joy, loyalty, and, not to side with the angels, subservience, enmity, and hurt. These need not be wanted to be honorably what they allege to be. Whether it sits easily or not with the recipient, friendship given remains friendship. (Indeed to woo or welcome the pain that is given transmutes the gift. It becomes significantly something else.)

On the whole, services are more mundane than gifts, though one can give services to the state, I suppose, or sing for kings. Yet services restrict the other's freedom less than gifts (and offerings seem to restrict it not at all). There isn't much one can do to choose or control a gift except to avoid the likely circumstances or make oneself an unlikely receiver. To lose a little love may be to gain a little freedom. But if you are given loyalty, then you are one who commands loyalty (that much anyway), and not much is to be done about it *post eventum*. The gift has obliterated the freedom to choose. Not surprisingly this lack of choice tends to characterize the giver too. Gifts tend to be spontaneous; it detracts from the gift, often, to plot the giving. A *contrived* insult is a mark of respect, and that much easier to bear.

Teaching as Intrusion

To return to our topic. Teaching, I would contend, is obtrusive in two ways. What we call effective teaching is an activity which makes substantial changes in the students' non-substantial self, his mind-stuff. (Effective whining can be just whining that makes the whiner less wrought.) More than this, the many expressions we use to label sundry phases of teaching all seem to imply a piercing of the student's perceptual line of defense. Thus we say we reassure the student, give him praise, clear up his muddled ideas, and so on. All this suggests a necessary intrusion of teacher on student.

So the obvious is true, to teach and to leave the learner unaffected is not to have been teaching at all. To reassure or prove something to a student is *to do something to him*. And one cannot prove the thing so the student can decide whether he wants it proved to him!

But for those who would view reassurance and reports, proofs and praise as trivial intrusions, not to be taken weightily, another point is waiting. If it is not teaching itself which is essentially intrusive (though I would argue that it is), then no one can dispute that the way we conduct it makes it significantly so. A good part of our institution of education is hedged about with rule and law the upshot of which, it must appear to student and observer alike, is to make the teacher's intrusion on the student massive and mandatory.

The above remarks are all in aid of showing that teaching either by its conception or circumstances is *not* an offering simpliciter. And, consequently, my contention that the advocates of the new methods and machines, in which teachers are supposed not to intrude, are not urging new forms of teaching but urging a substitute for teaching or a radical change in its institutional conditions. But to make teaching an offering by such radical surgery is just one more case of a cure that kills.

It might be objected, however, that the original choice abides; should we or should we not adopt these new forms? To label the innovators radicals would seem to merely reword but not resolve the issue. But I suggest that a smidgin of strictness is just the ticket here. New phraseology inspires new focus. Posed as a radical dichotomy between teaching and some total replacement, we are encouraged to ask: "Is teaching itself obsolete?" And "Is teaching obsolete?" asks not for repeated matching of features in the new with ever more arcane qualities in the old, rather it directs us to seek for some quality in teaching which debilitates it absolutely. I suggest that there is such a quality.

A ROOT PHONINESS

Due to its nature or circumstances, teaching is an inauthentic human encounter. In terms of a distinction made earlier, teaching is service masquerading as gift. Though we present it as a gift, it lacks gift features: teaching has not the immediate and intrinsic worth possessed by joy or splendor (though we try to so ornament it); nor does the activity arise spontaneously, on impulse, without forethought, things which render the meanest gifts as at least honest. No, teaching is a contrivance in two ways: its value is the value of invention and appliance, and its performance arises by craft and emerges in plot. The very model of rational action urged on teachers in conventional educational wisdom is the model of adapting means to ends, the model for planned intervention.

Yet despite these deviations from gift traits, teaching does not wait upon client demand or acquiescence; it is thrust upon minds not fit out to welcome, avoid, or even appraise it. Imagine, as was noted above, trying to make a mind aware so it can choose whether to become so; or imagine a school denied the privilege of instructing unless conducted under the auspices of a contract made with students.

So there is a root phoniness in teaching. It ought to be a simple service like radio repair but we treat it as a gratuity. And this explains much that was heretofore inexplicable. It accounts for our odd fascination with recurrent proposals to conduct teaching by indirection (Education According to Nature; the Project Method), and it explains the dream of teacher as Itinerant Pedagogue. These myths of *Teaching as Offering* are just that, yet the more sensitive among us cleave to them even as the more creative are propounding new instances. Still, worse forms of expiation have been tried.

Atonement for what? Why, for the destruction which comes from viewing teaching as a boon. There is space for but one example. Teaching requires mutual confidence between student and teacher; for the activity to get anywhere, each must have trust in the general credibility and veracity of the other. I suppose each teacher has had moments of terror when this trust dies or even fails to appear. (Some teachers live with this terror.) In any honest service, both parties have an obvious and immediate recourse— termination. We need not brook the tasteless bard or baker. Since teaching cannot prosper without respect, then let it not be tried at all. But in what presently passes for education, we are denied this obliging expedient. The logistics of institutional education seem not to abide the simple graces, and corruption of teaching is seen as a price worth paying.

Furthermore, we have, not unnaturally, fostered a rhetoric that undercuts this essential trust. For the ideology of education holds that teacher authority should not be the main source of student belief; rather the source should be some "objective," impersonal authority. The idea that students can learn only or even mainly from actual experiments, original sources, and hard data is wild doctrine, but one we *need* if we are to pretend that teaching lives after trust in the teacher dies.

Finally, and not the least trivially, it is not now a mystery why there is more strain and fatigue in teaching than any time and motion study would lead one to predict. It is exquisite agony to make condescension a practice, but to make it the practice of a profession is unbearable.

18

Exploiting Existential Tensions in the Classroom

WALTRAUT J. STEIN

As a philosopher thrust into a college classroom, I find myself forced to reflect on the educational process—its methods and goals. I would like to ask you to reflect with me on some aspects of being human that I have been attempting to enunciate in the context of European phenomenology and existentialism[1] and what these ideas can mean for educational theory and practice.

It seems to me that the human position is basically paradoxical. By "human position" I mean man's relation to the world or the situation, including his relation to his fellow men. One dimension of this paradox, which I would like to call "cosmopathy," appears as one realizes that a person always finds himself in some mood or other in relation to the world he perceives, which relation places him in immediate contact with the world. I conceive of a mood as an "attunement" between the feeling tone in oneself and the tone of the world to which one is sensitive. For instance, when one feels "low," the tone of the world is also "low." Since the tone in oneself is seldom in perfect harmony with the tone of the world, human expression can be viewed as the attempt to increase this harmony. The central argument

Waltraut J. Stein is Associate Professor of Psychology, West Georgia College, Carrollton, Georgia. Waltraut J. Stein, "Exploiting Existential Tensions in the Classroom," Teachers College Record, Vol. 70, No. 8 (May 1969), pp. 747–753. Used by permission of the author and Teachers College Record.

[1] "Cosmopathy and Interpersonal Relations," to be published in Joseph Smith, Ed., Phenomenology in Perspective. Publisher to be announced.

here is that feeling, understood as mood, and perceiving, in which the model is seeing, are *co-primordial* in conceiving of man's relation to the world. This contention is in contrast with the view of Edmund Husserl, whom I interpret as taking perceiving to be primary. It is also in contrast with the view of Martin Heidegger who takes feeling or *Befindlichkeit* as primary. My view is that if one did not see or perceive, the world would not appear, and, if one did not feel at least alive, he himself would not appear as the subject of experience. Thus both kinds of experiencing are required for us to speak meaningfully of man's immediate relation to the world, of his cosmopathic position.

READING THE WORLD

However, as I continue to reflect on the human position, I find myself compelled to acknowledge another dimension, which I would like to call "extra-cosmopathy." It appears that there is a great deal of dis-harmony, not only between man and man, but also between man's grasp of his total situation and what this situation actually is. For instance, I frequently find my best-laid plans going awry simply because I did not "read" the world correctly. At the same time, the very fact that I am in a position to "read" the world at all, to reflect on my situation and to plan to affect it, indicates that I am outside of or beyond this situation and that the human position is not entirely one of immediate involvement. My conclusion, thus, is that man is not only subject to his situation and determined by his immediate, unreflective involvement in it, but that he is also simultaneously beyond this situation in a position to reflect on it and to control it or at least to affect it.

You will recall that Archimedes believed that if there were a place for him to stand *outside* of the earth, he could move it. To do so, I think that he also realized that he would have to make contact with the earth from this position outside of it, to place himself in touch with it at the same time as he assumed a distance from it. My contention is that the human position is metaphysically actually much like the physical position Archimedes envisioned. Man is both in the world in cosmopathic contact with it at the same time as he is outside of or beyond the world in a position of extra-cosmopathy.

This paradoxical position becomes particularly clear in the case of interpersonal relations. People are together, grasp one another as persons, sympathize and empathize with one another, in spite of some philosophers' endless disputes over the existence of other minds. At the same time, however, people do not understand one another completely and often feel frustrated in their attempts to communicate with one another. This indicates, it seems to me, that each man is both inescapably bound to his fellow men in a social milieu and at the same time isolated from them: in some respects he stands uniquely beyond all human contact in metaphysical isolation.

In summary, then, I would like to suggest that the human position is the paradoxical one of being simultaneously in the world and beyond it in the modalities of being absorbed in a situation and reflective, bound and free, with others and alone. The recognition of the full phenomenon of being human involves the recognition of this paradoxical position.

EXISTENTIAL TENSION

Now, if the above view has any merit in it, one can see that there is a tension involved in being human as man struggles to come to terms with his paradoxical position. I would like to call this "existential tension." Further, if this paradoxical position is inherent to being human, it is also clear that existential tension cannot be eliminated. However, it can doubtless be denied or deadened so that to all intents and purposes the person is asleep, leading the zombie existence of a sleep walker. I am thinking of the person who passively does as he is told, absorbs all facts indiscriminately like a blotter, and never permits himself to be alone so that he could become aware of his isolation. Yet, once one recognizes the tension of existence, I believe that there is also a way of affirming this tension or of exploiting it that can facilitate the active setting and realization of human goals, including educational ones. It is this attitude toward the human position that I would like to explore with you a little further.

Why do I talk of "exploiting" existential tension? Because in the case of education at least, I agree with John Dewey that learning really takes place when there is a problem to be solved or a tension that demands relief. Thus he who can create an environment that involves tension but not paralyzing anxiety or fear can use the human position itself to advance the educational process.

What could be the goal of such a process? The answer to this, of course, involves a value commitment. At this point in my career and in the light of the conception of the human position I have been developing, I would suggest the following: the goal of any educational process is to equip the educated person with the means of realizing his own goals in the context of his cultural heritage in a way that at the same time creatively advances this heritage. The educated person, while often willing and able to adapt himself to the situation within which he finds himself, is also in a position to adapt the situation to himself when he deems it necessary, to revise his culture, and so to advance it. More specifically, the teacher's task is to confront the student with his heritage, give him the tools for grasping it, and, finally, give him the tools for advancing it creatively. And, as the teacher is aware of her student's extra-cosmopathic position, she recognizes that her duty is also to lead him into awareness of his own uniqueness so that he may set his own peculiar goals in the light of his needs, abilities, and particular situation. She must let him find a way to "move the world" at the same time as he enhances, rather than loses, himself. When the teacher is successful, the student becomes aware of the world into which he has been born and of his own paradoxical position in relation to it, finding that he can use the energy of this existential tension to create a style of life that is meaningful and satisfactory to himself and others.

CREATING CLASSROOM CLIMATES

To conclude this paper, I would like to elaborate somewhat on the general statements just made and to suggest how a teacher can create a climate of useful existential tension in her classroom. These are intended as general suggestions in regard to attitude and not as specific techniques.

1. The first tension to be maintained, particularly in the student, is the tension of receptivity and activity in relation to the teacher and the subject matter. The student must be receptive to the teacher's presentation of the subject matter and be willing to learn from her. At the same time, he must engage in an active, critical dialogue with the textbook, the teacher, and with his fellow students. This means that the student must trust his teacher to present him with his heritage and yet be ready to challenge both the presentation and the heritage. Borrowing a term from Gabriel Marcel, this climate may be called one of "active receptivity" on the part of the student. It requires that the teacher present herself an authority who is usually reliable, and yet as an authority who is fallible and not final. The textbook should be taken in the same way so that at the end of the course the student feels that he has learned something at the same time as he realizes that there is still much that he himself either does not know or that has not yet been said about the subject.

2. This leads to the second attitude that the teacher can foster both in herself and in her students, which may be called an attitude of insecure openness. Both teacher and student should try to remember that no one has "all the answers" and yet recognize that there are some provisional answers that can be understood and that can provide a basis for action. He who is dogmatically sure that he knows closes the door to further inquiry. The door of inquiry is similarly closed to him who is skeptically certain that there is nothing that can really be known. These are both secure and comfortable positions that continually tempt the teacher and her students. To forge a path between these positions can provide the teacher with a real challenge. On such a path one both believes that one does not yet have the knowledge one desires and also that such knowledge is attainable. For he who lacks the security either of being sure he knows or of being sure that knowledge is

impossible is in an insecure position in which learning relevant to his life can take place. The teacher should permit some closure, provide the student with the provisional answers she herself has found, and at the same time she should make him yearn for better answers as he remains awake to carry on his heritage of the love of wisdom or truth with its accompanying belief that truth is attainable. Nietzsche may have had a college classroom in mind when he said, "Blessed are the sleepy ones, for they shall soon drop off." The teacher's task is to stay awake herself along with her students and to remain genuinely alive with them to the challenges presented by their respective human positions.

3. The teacher should try to earn the trust of her students at the same time as she presents herself as a fallible person who has some "knowledge of the way" but would like to have more. At times a teacher may find it useful to foster awe toward herself or a certain charisma, but when this is done, there is always the danger that students will become dependent on her and cease to learn when separated from her. Fear of failing grades, of displeasing the teacher, of being ridiculed by one's fellow students probably do more to hinder learning by distracting from the value of the subject matter and by emotionally paralyzing the student. Just as a deer caught in the headlights of a car is paralyzed with fear and cannot act rationally or think straight, so a student imbued with fear of the classroom situation may panic and find that his mind "goes blank." Of course, this only occurs in extreme cases. Usually a student caught in such a situation simply mimics his teacher, presenting her with an inferior image of herself. Though I do not want to deny that memory work is at times necessary, even if at the time the student does not completely understand what he is memorizing, this should not be the central educational vehicle. The student is different from the teacher, I have been maintaining, standing in an extra-cosmopathic position in negative relation to her, so that an attempt to become her must always produce an inferior product. If one had a standard mold and standard materials in a classroom, as one does in a factory, one could produce a line of standard products. But precisely the exciting thing about being human and of dealing with human beings, is that one has no such final standard and that one's material varies infinitely. There are many possible good products, none of which is or can be a duplicate of any other.

This means, once more, that the teacher must respect her students as unique beings with interests and needs that are not hers. Such respect requires not only respect for their intelligence and for their view of the world, but also an honesty with them in the belief that they are willing to collaborate in the educational process, once they understand it. Of course, the teacher must attempt to assess the state of knowledge or ignorance of her students when they enter her class. But she must do more than this: at the same time as she wants them to trust her for guidance, she wants them to guide themselves, for each person to really find *his own* unique position in the world. This, it seems to me, is the central existential tension that a teacher must exploit if the cultural heritage is both to be assimilated and advanced. When Nietzsche's followers asked him, "How can we become your disciples?" he replied, "Follow you, not me." At the proper moment the teacher must be willing to let her students go. I would like to indicate a more specific technique for doing this very briefly here. In my introductory ethics class, I ask the students to review their written work periodically in an attempt to make explicit who they are in response to the subject matter as well as to determine the direction of their thinking and their lives. It is hoped that this periodic "recollection," to use another of Marcel's terms, will permit them to recognize their own extra-cosmopathic position and to distinguish themselves from the teacher and the text. The response of the students to this technique was at first mixed, partly, I believe, because this kind of recollection is most difficult and strange to many of them, so that they do not clearly understand what is expected; and possibly it is somewhat of an invasion of their privacy. However, by the end of the course almost all the students acknowledged that these attempts had proved valuable to them.

4. I would like to suggest one final way in which a teacher can exploit existential tension in her classroom when she is particularly interested in developing her students' creativity. On the one hand, she can foster an atmosphere of freedom to explore varied possibilities, to let oneself go, to give free reign to preconscious processes, to use one's imagination. She can accept all of her exploring students' more or less random products. On the other hand, she can demand discipline and guide her students into gaining control over the products of their unstructured explorations. By discipline, I mean that the teacher can provide her students with tools for putting their imaginative products into a form that is coherent and beautiful. These tools may be linguistic or mathematical, as well as the tools of the traditional arts. Part of this attempt at discipline also involves communicating to students that learning is not always fun and games, that it is often hard work that one must force oneself to undertake, and that things worthwhile are sometimes as difficult as they are rare. To be genuinely creative, one must, first of all, have a sensitive grasp of the total human situation in which one finds oneself and be able to see some of the possibilities in it. It is from this that one selects the subject matter of creation. Secondly, one must have a vision of an ideal that appears to be realizable. Finally, one requires the tools and the training for molding the selected subject matter to conform to one's ideal. Thus it is clear that mastering subject matter is necessary for having something to mold, that free exploration is necessary for determining possibilities and for establishing the ideal, and that discipline is necessary for molding the subject matter. A tension arises because these steps can seldom be undertaken consecutively or alternatively; rather, one must keep them all in mind in every teaching situation, though one phase or the other usually predominates. It is, of course, quite clear to me that every student does not have the

intelligence, inspiration, or skill to be a great creator; yet it is equally clear to me that any person can increase his mastery over his own life and mold it into something more satisfactory when the potentialities he has for doing so are nurtured rather than suppressed.

Towards Collaboration

When the attempt is made to foster the emotional climate suggested here, I think that the student and teacher can begin to define their respective roles in the educational process, about which definition there presently seems to be some confusion, particularly on college campuses. The classroom situation that I have been prescribing is neither an authoritarian nor a democratic one. Rather, it is one in which students and teacher are attempting to collaborate in a task in which both must be willing to change, though the explicit goal of the task is change in the student. The tension involved is not the tension of a power struggle in which the contest is to see whether the student or the teacher wins. Rather, it is the tension of becoming oneself in a world that is sometimes recalcitrant to one's efforts. Yet even more than this, it is the tension involved in exploring the world, understanding it as thoroughly as one can, and then of finding one's proper position in relation to it. Finally, it is the tension of staying constantly awake and of refusing to close the doors entirely to further exploration and discovery. When a teacher and her students become aware of what they are struggling about, they can enter into a genuine collaborative effort to attain these goals, and, like Socrates, direct their efforts at finding the truth.

19

Performance-Based Teaching—
A New Orthodoxy?

FREDERICK C. NEFF

I

It has been remarked that one of the reasons that John Dewey's educational views caught on and were so widely adopted was that he was so little understood. It might be added that one of the reasons that Progressive Education came under attack and eventually faltered was that its practitioners tended to identify it almost exclusively with method and either ignored or failed to understand its theoretical underpinnings and philosophic goals. We are now offered a method of teaching that singles out "performance" as the test of a learner's knowledge, skills, and attitudes, the assumption apparently being that whatever is learned has its behavioral counterpart. Whether the method called "performance-based teaching" will survive as a viable movement or whether, like Progressive Education, it founders for lack of purpose, will ultimately depend, not upon the efficiency of its methodology, but upon the extent to which it can be directed toward defensible ends. This is to say that classroom procedures and teaching devices have no inherent value. They can be assessed only in terms of the beliefs, attitudes, and habits of thought they are designed to foster.

Frederick C. Neff is Professor of Education and chairman of the department of History and Philosophy of Education at Wayne State University. Paper read before the Midwest Region Philosophy of Education Society, November, 1972.

Thomas Huxley once observed that it is the fate of every new truth to begin as a heresy and to end as a superstition. What sets this evolutionary process in motion is the unresisted temptation to capture new ideas and to contain them within the confines of a method—to formalize, ritualize, and institutionalize them. As a result, method is initially enlisted in the realization of an idea, then is joined with the idea, then becomes indistinguishable from the idea, and, finally, replaces the idea. Reductionism in this sense represents the tendency to confound means with the ends they were originally designed to serve, culminating in some instances in an actual substitution of means for ends.

Aristotle, for example, was himself an empiricist and a champion of observation and testing, but it was not long before his outlook became reduced to and identified with the fruits of his own necessarily limited observations; "Aristotelianism" thus came to represent a circumscribed methodology that Aristotle himself would have disavowed. Jesus was a moral and humane teacher who preached tolerance and compassion, but eventually tolerance and compassion became ritualized and reduced to the performance of specified acts at appointed times and places. The thrust of ideas represented in the thought of Hegel became, in both Marxism and fascism, reduced to politics and ideology. Among his interpreters, the imaginative and figurative creations of Freud often became reduced to ghostly demons and ancestral entities that were thought to enslave our feelings and proscribe our behavior. In the thought of John Dewey, the emphasis upon practicality was assumed by many to mean an exclusive attention to method and overt acts of performance, whereas it was Dewey who reminded us that "theory is . . . in the end the most practical of all things." The point is that when ends become reduced to means, when the performance of acts becomes a substitute for a thoughtful appraisal of purpose, performance behavior becomes an end in itself, and purpose and meaning become obscured. This is what has happened wherever science has been reduced to scientism, wherever religion has been reduced to ritual, and wherever education has been reduced to method. To the thoughtful educator, the attempt to reduce all education to acts of performance thus becomes a matter of serious concern.

II

To say that because teaching is an activity it is therefore reducible to a kind of performance behavior is a grossly deceptive statement. The notion that, because man is an animal, he is therefore nothing but an animal, the late evolutionary naturalist Sir Julian Huxley called the "nothing-but fallacy." A similar sort of fallacy appears when it is argued that because teaching and learning occasionally involve, make use of, and are manifested in performance, education is therefore nothing but performance. When it is applied to areas of learning that are by nature or by definition nontheoretical—where specific knowledge or simple skills are involved—the performance argument is fairly adequate. The best way to evince the fact that one has learned how to swim is to demonstrate swimming ability through performance. If typing or shorthand skills are in question, performance is called for by way of demonstrating that one can typewrite or take dictation in shorthand. Reading and computation skills are likewise subject to measurement in terms of performance. Has one learned how to operate a lathe? Again, the test is performance.

When, however, we begin to move into historical, moral, and humanistic areas of learning—where attitudes, perspective, and judgment are called for—we begin to sense the inappropriateness of attempting to apply the criterion of "performance." Mastery of a knowledge of history—if we mean something vastly more than a mere ability to recite facts—is not reducible to a "performance"; rather, its significance resides in the extent to which judgments about and perspectives on the past, present, and future are modified by virtue of historical knowledge. What is meant by integrity or character is not mastery of a series of discrete acts, each of which is to be identified, categorized, and labeled a "performance of character." On the contrary, character represents an attitude whereby a high degree of moral consistency obtains in human conduct. Otherwise, we should be compelled to say that during the intervals between the performance of specific moral acts, a man had no character. It is the perdurable idea, moral principle, or attitude—not the performance of separate acts—that constitutes what is meant by character. This is to say that, although acts of behavior may from time to time be representative of character, character itself is neither reducible to nor confined within such acts. Historical knowledge or moral integrity is thus not itself a form of behavior; rather, it is knowledge and integrity that shape and give meaning to behavior.

The ability to distinguish between the gross and the subtle, between immediate objectives and long-range purposes, and between the appropriate and the inappropriate is what demarcates the classroom hack from the master educator. Whereas the hack conceives teaching as limited to ritual and performance, the educator views it as a means for the liberation of intelligence. Although both may engage in activities that may loosely be termed "performance behavior," the hack is a captive of his method, while the educator utilizes methods only as they are consonant with his goals. The former conceives "performance" in terms of drug-store prescriptions and cookbook recipes, the latter in light of the ends he seeks to accomplish. The hack resorts to coercive manipulation through rewards and punishments; the educator employs discussion, mutual understanding, and inquiry. The former uses the method of imposition; the latter is concerned with the refinement of choice-making abilities in the context of alternatives.

III

It serves little purpose to argue that, because everything man does involves some sort of behavior, therefore behavior is all there is to thought and conduct. Such a truism is both specious and misleading. If all man's activities are behavioral, then the term "behavior" becomes either meaningless or superfluous; just as, if the only color in the universe were red, "red" would have no meaning. Terms assume meaning only as they can be distinguished from other terms.

Inclusion within the behavioral rubric of activities such as thinking, willing, pondering, judging, imagining, and the like calls for a careful and thoroughgoing reassessment of the concept of behavior itself. Just as moral controversies today are seldom resolvable in terms of an old-fashioned either-or, good-or-bad dichotomy, but, rather, involve different and competing conceptions of the good, so controversies concerning the nature of behavior are least fruitful when they center merely upon the question of what is and what is not behavioral. Our important concern is better phrased when questions are raised, not about whether thinking, for example, is or is not a form of behavior, but about how thoughtful behavior differs from thoughtless—and other—kinds of behavior. Simply to lump all human activities in a general catch-all of behavior, as though to do so settled once and for all the whole matter of what constitutes thought, is both naïve and deceptive. Acts of charity and acts of murder, it may be granted, both represent forms of behavior. But it scarcely follows that, because both kinds of acts are behavioral, there is no qualitative difference between them.

Nevertheless, there are those in education today whose enchantment with behavior is such that, in their zeal to reduce every aspect of life and thought to a "performance" level, they would ignore certain subtle yet highly significant distinctions within the gamut of human learnings and human activities. In the crass demand for "Performance! Performance!" there is danger of neglecting to account for the subtle nuances, the speculative hypotheses, the spiritual aspirations, and the philosophic thrusts that are characteristic of the nature and history of man and that defy captivation and classification within the confines of systems. In the words of the late Justice Felix Frankfurter, "Life, with its exuberance and irony, has a way of making mockery of such systems."[1] Man is, in the phrase of Aldous Huxley, a "multiple amphibian," compelled to move and act in several incompatible realms—biological, spiritual, emotional, cerebral, social. The infinite depth and complexity of human nature must serve to make us wary of the notion that its superficial aspects represent all the being there is and that every human quality is reducible to its quantitatively measurable counterpart. As Stanislav Andreski has stated it:

[1] Felix Frankfurter, "The Meaning of Dewey to Us All," *John Dewey at Ninety*, ed. H. W. Laidler. New York: The League for Industrial Democracy, 1950, p. 11.

When the psychologists refuse to study anything but the most mechanical forms of behavior—often so mechanical that even rats have no chance to show their higher faculties—and then present their most trivial findings as the true picture of the human mind, they prompt people to regard themselves as automata, devoid of responsibility or worth, which can hardly remain without effect upon the tenor of social life.[2]

The behavioral argument is sometimes used to defend the notion that, since thought, reflection, and imagination are forms of behavior, then all forms of behavior must be thoughtful, reflective, and imaginative. Again, there is a parallel between this notion and the presumption of earlier "progressive" teachers that, since learning is an activity, then all activities must involve learning. The fact that many activities can be miseducative was rather conveniently overlooked. Yet, the connection between thought and activity needs to be preserved. In his *The Concept of Mind*,[3] Gilbert Ryle undertakes to destroy what he calls the myth of the dogma of the ghost in the machine—the Cartesian notion that an inner mind is separable from outward behavior. Descartes, it will be recalled, was an out-and-out dualist, believing that mind and body exist in two separate realms, each governed by its own, independent principles. The Cartesian myth, according to Ryle, is responsible for an indefensible dichotomy between mind and body, between thought and action.

Dewey, likewise, rejected Cartesianism, adhering to the view that thought is continuous with action; nevertheless, he retained a pointed distinction between the two. Ryle, however, argues that action is not simply an extension of thought but that thought is identical with action. Here, again, we are moved precariously close to equating the two, with the unfortunate result that action can easily be mistaken for thought, in which case we are in difficulty again. When, however, we qualify certain kinds of action as thoughtful and others as thoughtless, we are in effect recognizing a distinction which the mere equation of thought and action fails to account for.

That attitudes and feelings are themselves forms of behavior is likewise open to question. In the words of Stanley Elam:

while performance-based instruction eliminates waste in the learning process through clarity in definition of goals, it can be applied only to learning in which the objectives sought are susceptible of definition in advance in behavioral terms. Thus it is difficult to apply when the outcomes sought are complex and subtle, and particularly when they are affective or attitudinal in character.[4]

The poet Keats's insight that "heard melodies are sweet, but those unheard are sweeter" and Browning's reference to "all, the world's coarse thumb and

[2] Stanislav Andreski, *Social Sciences as Sorcery*. London: Andre Deutsch, 1972.
[3] Gilbert Ryle, *The Concept of Mind*. New York: Barnes & Noble, 1949.
[4] Stanley Elam, *Performance-Based Teacher Education: What Is the State of the Art?* Washington: American Association of Colleges for Teacher Education, 1972, p. 17.

finger failed to plumb" remind us that not every human thought and feeling rises to the surface level of perceptibility. Even the noted behaviorist B. F. Skinner concedes that ". . . many feelings have inconspicuous behavioral manifestations."[5]

IV

Whereas the Deweyan conception of the relationship between thought and action is holistic, the present emphasis in performance behavior appears to be merely analytic. It tends to isolate performance from thoughtful and long-range purposes, of which it is only a representation and to which it is properly subservient, thus dignifying the trivial and denigrating the important. It suggests the sort of analytic definition of education that Professor C. J. Ducasse formulated when he wrote:

Education is activity of one or another particular kind A, by a person T (teacher); activity A being motivated by T's desire to cause in a person P (pupil)—who may or may not be the same person as T—a response of kind R, which T believes will immediately or eventually result in acquisition by P of some capacity C, which T desires P to acquire; activity A being shaped by T's belief (i) that the existing circumstances are of a certain kind S; and (ii) that, under circumstances of kind S, activity of kind A by T would more or less probably cause or contribute to cause directly or indirectly in P acquisition of the desiderated capacity C.[6]

Involved in such an analysis is an attempt to tease out the several ingredients of the teaching-learning process, presumably under the impression that the juxtaposition of these separate elements is all that is required for learning to take place. But no competent teacher guides learning in such terms. If he attempted to do so, his endeavors would be limited to a mechanical process of sheer indoctrination. What provision, for example, is made for an exchange and interchange of ideas? How is the emergence of problem or novel situations provided for? What regard is taken of the interests, nature, or aptitudes of the learner? It is significant, also, to recognize that the only activity mentioned is lodged with the teacher, while the key words describing the role of the pupil are "response" and "acquisition."

Authoritarianism can present itself in many guises. What the indoctrination or conditioning thesis presumes is that there is no essential difference between the training of an animal and the education of a child. Because an animal is incapable of decision making on the basis of principle, the outcomes of animal training must be predetermined. The seeing-eye dog will halt at every curb, with the result that—*but not in order that*—its master is

---

[5] B. F. Skinner, *Beyond Freedom and Dignity*. New York: Alfred A. Knopf, 1971, p. 106.

[6] C. J. Ducasse, "On the Function and Nature of the Philosophy of Education," *Harvard Educational Review*, XXVI (Spring, 1956), 103–111.

better able to avoid stumbling or walking into traffic. But there is no evidence to support the contention that it acts out of a sense of moral purpose; its behavior is strictly a matter of conditioning. As Professor Harry Broudy has remarked, "Skinner quite rightly doesn't worry about whether his pigeons understand what they are doing so long as they do it."[7] Because human beings are capable of formulating, altering, and abiding by principles, the outcomes of learning that is distinctively human must be open-ended. To say that education involves a continual reorganization of experience is another way of saying that education enables the learner continually to reconstruct himself, his outlooks, his ways of viewing himself and his world. Subtle attempts to blur over or compromise the distinctions between training and education had best be viewed with suspicion. One of the most forthright attempts to bring in the conditioning technique under the guise of democracy is found in the following passage from the writings of the American educational sociologist Ross L. Finney:

> Ours are the schools of a democracy, which *all* the children attend. At least half of them never had an original idea of any general nature, and never will. But they must behave as if they had *sound* ideas. Whether those ideas are original or not matters not in the least. It is better to be right than original. What the duller half of the population needs, therefore, is to have their reflexes conditioned into behavior that is socially suitable. And the wholesale memorizing of catchwords . . . is the only practical means of establishing bonds in the duller intellects between the findings of social scientists and the corresponding social behavior of the masses. Instead of trying to teach dullards to think for themselves, the intellectual leaders must think for them and drill the results . . . into their synapses.[8]

Mere employment of the Pavlovian technique—producing anything from the simple salivation of a dog to the complex moral and social dilemmas raised by Anthony Burgess's *A Clockwork Orange*—fails to meet head on the fact of the basic, irreconcilable cleavage between the democratic conception of man as a free, choice-making individual and the authoritarian notion of man as an object of behavior manipulation and thought control.

V

In our urgency to emphasize skills and knowledge, we have neglected to attend to a consideration of the ends toward which skills and knowledge are to be directed. We have failed to distinguish between what might be called the necessary and the sufficient conditions of education. Our attempts to achieve a scornful detachment have resulted in an obsession with manners and surfaces. In our concentration upon mere performance, we are likely to

[7] Harry S. Broudy, *A Criticism of Performance-Based Teacher Education.* Washington: American Association of Colleges for Teacher Education, 1972, p. 11.

[8] Ross L. Finney, *A Sociological Philosophy of Education.* New York: Macmillan Publishing Co., Inc., 1928, p. 395.

turn out teachers who—like one of those audioanimatronic robots at Disneyland—are perfect facsimiles of teaching until you get close and hear the gears whirling. Unaccompanied by a cultivation of taste, mere ability to read is no guarantee that what is read will not be limited to the pornographic, the trivial, and the useless. Mere ability to write can be used for the purpose of demanding a bank teller to hand over his money. Mere knowledge of chemistry, unrelated to a reflected-upon system of values, can result—indeed, has resulted—in the production of bombs, napalm, and other devices for the destruction of human lives. Unless we are willing to pay the price, mastery of the fundamental skills cannot be separated from the moral, ethical, and humane ends that education is ultimately designed to serve.

The current tendency to concentrate upon efficiency and methodology is apparently predicated on the notion that, once a method has been perfected, the use to which it will be put is of no great consequence. In the later years of his life, Albert Einstein remarked, " Perfection of means and confusion of goals seem—in my opinion—to characterize our age." The need to chart our course before embarking upon it has been pointed out by Boyd Bode, who wrote: " There is little comfort, when we don't know where we are going, in being assured that we are on our way and traveling fast." A similar observation has been voiced by Lewis Mumford, who has said that "If society is paralyzed today, it is not for lack of means but for lack of purpose." That education is inescapably a value-ridden undertaking has been pointed out by John L. Childs. In his words: ". . . anyone who is conducting the education of the young should realize that he is involved in that basic philosophic enterprise of trying to distinguish the better from the worse in modes of human living."[9]

Nor is the centrality of theoretical ends limited to education. The pleading of cases in a court of law is an activity that demands a kind of "performance" competency. But it hardly follows that prospective lawyers need have no prior understanding of theoretical concepts of individual rights, of equity, or of the basic values of human life. What distinguishes the shyster from the respected jurist is his philosophy of law. Although both have available to them the same legal techniques, it is the principles and values in terms of which techniques are directed that make the difference. Similarly, a physician may be ever so competent in diagnosing an illness, in prescribing medicine, or in administering an anaesthetic. He may be ever so skilful in knowing how to perform an abortion, how to perform euthanasia, or how to perform a lobotomy. Yet, knowing how to perform such operations is obviously no substitute for a viable and reflectively formulated code of ethics, without which procedural decisions cannot responsibly be made.

[9] John L. Childs, Foreword to Frederick C. Neff, *Philosophy and American Education.* New York: The Center for Applied Research in Education, Inc., 1966, p. v.

Whether in law, in medicine, or in education, the ends to which an enterprise is geared determine the direction it takes and the basis for its evaluation. Ends without means are poor indeed; but means without ends are poorer still. The inspiration, the zest, and the excitement that are associated with education as a noble calling come not from methods and techniques but from the values it seeks to foster.[10] But we miss the whole purpose of education when, in the words of Santayana, we merely redouble our effort, having forgotten our aim. If success in education is not very different from success in life, we might do well to recall the words of Walter Pater:

The service of philosophy, of speculative culture, [of education] toward the human spirit, is to rouse, to startle it to a life of constant and eager observation. . . . Not the fruit of experience, but experience itself, is the end. A counted number of pulses only is given to us of a variegated, dramatic life. How may we see in them all that is to be seen in them by the finest senses? How shall we pass most swiftly from point to point, and be present always at the focus where the greatest number of vital forces unite in their purest energy? . . . To burn always with this hard, gemlike flame, to maintain this ecstasy, is success in life.[11]

VI

It is important to bear in mind that the performance-based approach to teaching and learning represents, after all, but one among many theories regarding the purposes of education. Once instituted and "officialized," however, it—like a state religion—is likely to become a new orthodoxy, deviation from which will be viewed as heretical. Essentially a learning theory, it, ironically, lays claim to being nontheoretical. At present it can be assessed only in terms of its hypotheses and anticipated results, for it has yet to prove itself in regard to long-range effectiveness. To the extent that it is exclusively a learning theory it cannot properly be construed as an educational theory. In so far as its methods can serve contrary and mutually incompatible ends, it has no built-in or self-corrective philosophy to guide it. Concerned primarily with skill and subject-matter proficiency, it is conceivably adaptable to a complete and successful mastery of the wrong things. It seems to be focused, not upon educational values, but exclusively upon specific teaching and learning objectives. One gathers the impression that occasional references to innovation and creativity represent attempts to placate critics more than they reflect a genuine ingredient of performance-

[10] According to Lillian Weber, associate professor of early-childhood education at City College of New York: "Our view is that good learning is accompanied by zest and energy. But there can be no set pattern, because one child may need structured help while another needs utmost freedom to explore. In fact, we urge teachers to retain whatever of the old traditions they need. . . . The main thing is to try to restore the human dimension to education."

[11] Walter Horatio Pater, *The Renaissance*. New York: Mentor Books, 1959, pp. 157–158.

based teaching itself.[12] What few references there are to theoretical aims, goals, and values appear to be "hitched on" as afterthoughts, not guidelines for procedure. Because performance-based teaching is primarily a technique, in no sense does it qualify as an educational philosophy. Finally, one cannot but raise the question whether such a method would not be as applicable and effective—perhaps more so—in a totalitarian setting as within the framework of democracy.[13]

The overriding task of education today relates to a revitalization of its service in the realization of humane ideals, a reformulation of its professional identity, a recapturing of its sense of direction. It is precisely because methods of teaching and learning can be geared to questionable and conflicting ends that a reinstatement of the crucial role of principles, purposes, and values is our most urgent educational need.

---

[12] Albert Shanker, president of New York's United Federation of Teachers, says: "Actually, the creative teacher is the one who has the greatest chance of being fired by outsiders. Who will be the evaluators? What are their values? How do they propose to improve or dispose of teachers?" It might also be asked how a person with a strongly developed aesthetic sense, a passion for innovation, a desire for reflection, or a strongly marked independence could possibly be happy within the strictures of performance-based teaching.

[13] If, as many educators believe, "quality education" hinges upon the values of the nation as a whole, perhaps the American "success motif" is itself in need of re-examination. Says Harvard Sociologist Seymour Lipset: "In the United States the thing that matters is who wins, no matter how. There is more emphasis on accomplishing something, no matter what means are used."

20

Education: Schooling and Informal

Joe Park

Informal education has been the traditional way by which the human race has educated its young. Schools are a recent development in the long history of mankind. Our present inclination, however, is to overlook this historical reality and to overestimate the importance of schooling. The truth of the matter is that schooling and informal education now both compete with, and supplement one another, but informal education likely remains more influential in the life of any human being. When compared with certain other agencies and avenues, schooling probably is, and always has been, relatively superficial, ineffective and irrelevant. Indeed the mounting criticism of our schools during the past two decades appears to have stemmed in part, at least, from the increasing effectiveness of certain competing means of informal education, and from the continued schism between what is learned in school, and what is going on and learned outside of school. However, there does not appear to have been any decline in academic attainment in schools during this period. In fact, the level of general academic accomplishment may never have been higher.

Joe Park is Professor of Education at Northwestern University. Joe Park, "Education: Schooling and Informal", *Educational Theory*, Vol. 21, No. 4 (Fall 1971), pp. 371–385. Used by permission of *Educational Theory*. Presidential Address at the Twenty-seventh Annual Meeting of the Philosophy of Education Society; April 4, 1971; The Adolphus Hotel; Dallas, Texas.

As Dewey[1] noted more than a half century ago, one of the weightiest problems with which the philosophy of education has to cope is keeping a proper balance between informal education and schooling, the more incidental and the more intentional modes of education. To avoid a split between what we learn by a specific job of learning in school and what we unconsciously know because we absorbed it by intercourse with others, becomes an increasingly delicate task with every development of special schooling and he should have added, with every development in the means and opportunity for informal education.

If the situation is as described, and if Dewey is correct, then a re-examination of the roles of schooling and informal education is in order. Let us try to set forth what we mean by these terms and then go on to consider some possible alternatives with respect to the accommodation or separation of the two forms of education.

I. SCHOOLING

"Schooling" probably is a candidate for extensive philosophical analysis but it is not the purpose of this paper to present such an analysis. As used here, "schooling" simply means instruction given, or attempted, under the auspices of an institution called a school. The institution may be public, private or parochial, and it may be an elementary school, a secondary school, or a college.

In the hierarchy of American values, schooling resides in the vicinity of God, country, and motherhood. But the relative high place it holds among our avowed values is not necessarily a true indication of our willingness to support it, either with adequate funds or with appropriate amounts of interest and effort.

A rather humorous illustration of this point recently occurred in Nevada. In a small town a "narrow-minded" and "moralistic" resident complained, of all things, because a schoolhouse and a house of prostitution stood side by side! The problem was widely discussed and the local newspaper editorialized "Don't move the house. Move the School," with the result that the school was moved. Some schooling is generally thought desirable, but a whorehouse is undoubtedly a necessity.[2]

Most Americans probably are convinced that our schools have served us well in the past and will, along with a belief in God and the preservation of the family, serve us in the future. Although this faith may be somewhat naïve, it cannot be denied that schooling has been a successful means for teaching the rudimentary skills of reading, writing, and arithmetic to many

---

[1] John Dewey, *Democracy and Education* (New York: Macmillan Publishing Co., Inc., 1916), pp. 10–11.

[2] *The Milwaukee Journal* (Sunday, July 13, 1969).

millions of American children. In addition, many hundreds of thousands have been prepared for vocational and professional roles necessary to the operation of a complex industrial society such as ours. Above all, perhaps, it has taught generation after generation of American youth the virtues of the American form of government, and the so-called American way of life. Schooling has become more effective over the years and may never have been better than it is at present, especially with respect to the training provided in mathematics, sciences, and technology. This is more of a conjecture than a statement of fact, however, as conclusive evidence is not available.

Even if one is willing to grant the schools a large measure of success, one is, at the same time, forced to admit that there has grown up in America a concurrent opinion that schooling has somehow failed us and paradoxically that its failure is in part due to its successes. We have known for a very long time, although we haven't done much about it, that schooling has been a failure if it was intended to educate all Americans. We have denied formal educational opportunities to certain segments of the population at particular times in our history. Unfortunately, we provide quite inferior formal education to a large proportion of American youth today, particularly in our inner cities and in the rural areas. But the point to be made here is that in all our schools many of our students, and particularly our brighter students, find too much of their school experience to be bookish, boring and disconnected from life outside of school, and the desire to find purpose or meaning in life, a philosophy of life, if you please. In the words of Whitehead, schooling is frequently the purveying of inert ideas. H. Rap Brown brings out both the comedy and the tragedy of schooling when he discusses his education in *Die Nigger Die*.[3] Writing of his high school experiences, he recalls that he saw no sense in reading Shakespeare for it was obvious that Shakespeare was a racist and a faggot. Brown would interpret things one way and his teachers would say he was wrong. He concluded that something was amiss, unless the teachers had a monopoly on truth or were communicating with the dead.

Of course, the tendency is to discount these remarks as the fulminations of a recognized black radical who is against all parts of the establishment including schooling. To dismiss his remarks on these grounds is to miss the point entirely; for even dutiful, energetic, bright, and academically successful students like the late Edward Lee Thorndike have similar complaints to make about schooling. Thorndike saw the school as a battleground where teachers and pupils were constantly at war. The teachers made it their duty, Thorndike remembers, to oppress the pupils and the pupils made it their business to annoy the teachers. And of his college work, he recalled that he elected several extra courses, but was of the opinion that unlimited cuts

---

[3] H. Rap Brown, *Die Nigger Die* (New York: The Dial Press, 1969).

would have been a blessing, since the classes were neither interesting nor challenging. Consequently, he usually occupied a rear seat for the purpose of doing other work.[4] No doubt these recollections of Thorndike are not dissimilar to those of most of us. The hostility and open strife between the student and teacher sub-cultures is no secret to anyone who has ever crossed the threshhold of a school. One might speculate that the destruction of school property to the tune of more than 200 million dollars a year and rising steadily, is attributable to some extent to a deep-seated hatred for what schools stand for.

It is paradoxical that part of the failure of schooling in America stems from its successes. As was pointed out above, our schools have served as one effective avenue for the transmission of our cultural heritage. But they have tended to pass on this heritage in too unexamined and closed manner. Now that our values and cultural patterns have come under somewhat closer scrutiny in recent years the schools have had to face the charge of indoctrination. Thus not only has schooling been called irrelevant, it allegedly has produced perverse effects. For example, each of our parochial schools has taught its own brand of dogma, as if it were truth, forgetting or conveniently overlooking, that when two or more dogmas are in conflict all cannot be true and possibly none are true. Teaching that which is open to question as if it were absolute truth stultifies the mind and breeds intellectual dishonesty. Thus, as the schools succeeded they also failed.

All our schools, but particularly our public schools, have taught the superiority of the American way of life in all respects.[5] "More than any other present-day nation," writes Harold Taylor, "the United States has produced an educational system so intimately connected with the going values of the society and so powerful in its effects as a socializing instrument that it creates a nationalism strong enough to support the basic policies of whatever government is in power."[6] When one stops to think that there are infinite possible ways of life, it is quite unlikely the American people alone have hit upon a way of life superior in all respects. History is replete with instances of people who have entertained a similar opinion of themselves; but subsequent evaluations have uncovered appalling flaws. Thus, while schooling has been successful in contributing to national uniformity and stability, it has failed, in that many areas have remained closed to critical study, e.g., communism, capitalism, the United Nations, and sex, to mention only four.

Unfortunately the way we prepare our teachers has contributed to successful failure, and as a result may also be classified as one itself. Our

---

[4] Geraldine Joncich, *The Sane Positivist: A Biography of Edward Lee Thorndike* (Middletown, Conn.: Wesleyan University Press, 1968), pp. 45, 76–77.

[5] Neil Gross, *Who Runs Our Schools?* (New York: Dryden Press, 1958).

[6] Harold Taylor, *Students Without Teachers: The Crisis in the University* (New York: McGraw-Hill Book Company, 1969), p. 6.

colleges and universities turn out teachers to man our classrooms; but the preparation of our teachers resembles a model for training faithful civil servants. There is a kind of circular effect at work in teacher education. A boy or girl who is going to be a teacher and thus will be in a position to break the hold of intellectual rubbish and apathy, is taught to accept the competitive academic, social, economic, and national systems through his elementary and high school years. He is then given what is essentially four more years of the same thing in college, and then fed back into the schools where he is expected to keep it all going pretty much in the same way. Thus, teachers are prepared to offer schooling that is confined to a narrow orbit of national self-acceptance. Professor Herbst has stated the problem clearly.

Much talk and many manifestoes to the contrary, American teachers as a group do not impress the observer as constituting a profession conscious of its self-chosen objectives, standards, and aspirations, and committed to uphold and improve these. Rather teachers resemble more what was once called "the hired clergy," a corps of specialists, ready to sell their talents, know-how, and skill to the highest or least demanding bidder, and ready, likewise, to adjust not only standards and aspirations, but also convictions and orientation to the demands of their employers. Proficiency in knowledge and skills are valued higher than the ability to judge discriminately in the choice of educational objectives, and to affirm one's choice in one's teacher.[7]

You may wish to argue that there is much or only some truth to the contentions made above, that schooling is of various sorts and quality, and that some teachers have succeeded in making schooling relevant and a source of counterinfluence to America's mass culture. Granted! But these teachers are the exception and the job mortality rate among them probably is appreciably higher than among those of whom Herbst is speaking. But, there is currently in America a questioning of the *status quo*, and a discontent with schooling, especially on the part of the young. Is the source of this questioning and discontent to be found alone in our schools? This is very much to be doubted. In all probability, it rises quite as much, possibly more so, from the influences of informal education.

II. INFORMAL EDUCATION

As some recent writers have reminded us, the history of American education is biased in that it deals chiefly with schooling while giving relatively little attention to informal education. By informal education is meant that planned or deliberate instruction a tutor may provide, or a parent may give a child, or a master impart to an apprentice. But more than that it includes self education a person may seek through a planned course of

[7] Jurgen Herbst, "The Anti-School—Some Reflections on Teaching," *Educational Theory* (Winter, 1968), pp. 13–22.

reading in a library, or secure through conversation with friends, or obtain by travel or general observation or by use of one or more of several mass media now so freely at hand. Thus informal education may be planned or deliberately imposed on another, or it may result from self-motivation and be self imposed. Sometimes it may result more from chance than from design. What distinguishes it from schooling is that there is no institution especially provided in which it takes place, although informal education may occur in a school even during regular class time. Throughout history informal education, rather than schooling, has been the primary avenue by which the young have been initiated into the adult culture. Even today in a city such as Evanston, Illinois, which is, or was, recognized for its good schools, the child spends far less time in school than outside it. The children of Evanston are required to attend school for five hours per day for only 180 days in each calendar year. This amounts to a total of 900 hours each year. Assuming that each child sleeps an average of ten hours per night, there remains for each boy and girl about 4200 waking-hours which are not spent in school. In other words, about twenty per cent of the pupil's time is spent in school. This percentage may increase in junior and senior high school but it will drop again during the college years. These figures may appear surprising to one who has not given the matter much thought, but they do not tell the whole story by a long shot. A child spends much of his early life learning at his mother's knee, so to speak, and, following college, he will have about forty-five to fifty years of life in which he will continue to learn, chiefly through informal channels. While it cannot be categorically stated that we all learn more through informal means of education, it is incontrovertible that the opportunity to learn in terms of time, is vastly greater outside of school than within. Recent research[8] tends to confirm the importance of informal education especially in the early months and years of a child's life. Children may be much more aware of their surroundings than scientists have heretofore surmised, which may explain the speed with which they apparently develop ideas about the world. Most child psychologists assert that the child's general intellectual capacity and outlook have been established even before he reaches school. If this is the case then, the impact of informal education in the early days of the child is crucial.

But informal education does not begin and end with early childhood, and the influence of informal education during school and after school years undoubtedly is greater now than ever. Contrast, for example, the means for continuing one's education that are at hand today with those at the time William Byrd sat in the House of Burgesses in Virginia. In the series of diaries he kept, Byrd recorded instances of conversation with neighboring plantation owners, noted newspapers and books purchased and read, made

---

[8] Maya Pines "Why Some 3-Year-Olds Get A's—And Some Get C's," New York Times Magazine (July 6, 1969), pp. 4–5, 13–17. See also Jean Piaget and Barbel Inhelder, *The Psychology of the Child* (New York: Basic Books, Inc., 1969), p. 3.

accounts of some of his travels and the like. Even then his position, curiosity, and intellectual pursuits were most uncommon when compared with the general population. A contemporary American today, on the other hand, has the benefits of many means of transportation and communication that were not available to Byrd. By the time an affluent American youth has completed high school he has viewed television for thousands of hours and has been sped about the countryside, if not around the world, in high speed cars, buses, railroads and airplanes. By the time he has graduated from college he has seen a score of films for every book he has read, and has had the opportunity to read an extensive assortment of magazines, newspapers, and paperbacks. Sandwiched in somewhere are hundreds of hours of listening, made more accessible than ever, by the ubiquitous transistor radio. It is not unlikely that he has engaged in some sort of political action or has performed some kind of social service such as tutoring. As a consequence he has first-hand acquaintance with the problems, concerns, and points of view of persons in different climes and circumstances from that into which he was born. Just what the total influence of this has been is difficult to say, but two results in particular bear directly on schooling.

First, it is not at all uncommon for students to know as much, if not more, than their instructors about certain aspects of subjects taught in school, especially in the areas of the social sciences and humanities. As a result some of the mystery has gone out of schooling and the instructors have lost some of their aura of authority. Peter Schrag put it bluntly, "Teach an ordinary seaman to use a sextant, and he begins to lose respect for the officers; now he too can determine where the hell he is. . . . What printing and the Bible did for the church, mass media are doing to the University."[9] If a political science professor lectures about civil rights and law and order he may be interrupted by one of his students who was in Selma or at the Democratic Convention in Chicago, who will remind him that it really wasn't that way at all. If a high school teacher discusses the moon landing with his class he will have been no closer, nor will he have seen any clearer, than many of his wards who probably saw it in color while he had to view it on his black and white set. Not only is the teacher's authority directly challenged by informed and sophisticated students, he must also constantly stand in the heat of unfavorable comparison with movie stars, and radio and television personalities. As a chemist of some prominence, and a man known for his skills as a teacher, put it, "The students think of me as a performer. They boo and hiss when a demonstration fails or they applaud when it works, or when I get off some clever remark." It is the extremely exceptional teacher who can come across to his class in English literature like Richard Burton, and a most unusual high school social studies teacher who can outshine Edward P. Morgan in analyzing the news.

[9] Peter Schrag, "The End of the Great Tradition," *Saturday Review* (February 15, 1969), pp. 94–95, 103–104.

But there is another, and doubtless more important result, which must be apparent from what has already been said. The issues and problems of the age have become more apparent and real while schooling has remained behind the times and often out of touch with the realities of the world. Our students are discovering from their travel, social involvement, and the various mass media that not all is well with the world, but yet, at the same time, schooling seems to remain largely unchanged as if nothing catastrophic faced the human race. There are curriculum revisions, of course, but to a considerable extent they are made to accommodate just enough change so that the school can go on about its business pretty much in the same old way. In the meantime, many students sense an arms race between the West and East, particularly between the United States and Russia. They see a massive nuclear deterrent being constructed that is sufficient to destroy both countries and threaten the existence of the entire human race. They realize that two-thirds of the population of the world lives under conditions of hunger, disease, deprivation and misery. They understand the gap between the rich and the poor at home and abroad. They have observed the pollution of our atmosphere and streams and lakes, the destruction of our wildernesses and the merging of our trash heaps. They see these developments and they ask questions. They want to know what older people who are supposed to run this nation, and those who are supposed to be running other nations, are doing about these problems. "In short," editorializes Harrison Brown in the *Saturday Review*,[10] "our actions and our inactions present to younger people a picture which, to put it bluntly, is ugly." The picture is one of an insensitive and selfish people who are more concerned with themselves than with their fellow man, and who either don't attempt to solve their domestic problems and international problems at all, or prefer to solve them by the use of force. In the meantime schooling seems to go on much as before. And the youth ask, "Why can't schooling deal with these realities of life?"

Having said all this about the possible effects of informal education, a word of warning is in order. It must not be overlooked that many avenues of informal education are used, just as schooling has been used, to preserve and protect what is, rather than to evaluate and to change what we value, and how we live our lives. This is particularly true of the press and mass media. Thus, it may be that the ferment we sometimes observe, especially among the young, comes more from first-hand social involvement of our young than from any other one source. Furthermore, it should be admitted that the sources of informal education are not always used to their fullest advantage. A very great deal is simply not absorbed because of ineffective presentation, or fatigue, boredom, and inattention produced by a constant exposure to their influences.

In any event, the threat of common catastrophy on one hand, and the

---

[10] Harrison Brown, "Editorial," *Saturday Review* (July 19, 1969), pp. 20–22.

tendency for schools to serve, albeit effectively, rather conventional and perhaps narrow ends on the other hand, has led some to embrace what Professor Herbst has called anti-schooling. Instead of the informal and the more intentional modes of education assuming some kind of purposive supportive roles, they appear to be working, at least part of the time, at cross purposes. What should be done about this?

III. Some Alternatives

Should we eliminate informal education? Born helpless, the human offspring is completely dependent upon others for his care and survival. But more than this, he is born into a complex cultural stream which he cannot escape assimilating during an extended period of childhood. It is as certain as anything can be that learning is an unavoidable and continuous aspect of human existence. As Shakespeare wrote in *Love's Labour's Lost*

> Learning is but an adjunct to ourself,
> And where we are our learning likewise is.

There seems no way of completely eliminating all informal education and controlling all learning through schools. The very first years of a child's life do not lend themselves to schooling. Even if every child could be born and reared in a school it is inconceivable that all his learning for his entire life could be restricted to schooling as we have defined it.

Can schools be eliminated? It is logically and technically possible to eliminate schooling but it seems unlikely that this will occur for at least three reasons. First, our schools perform an escape-valve and service function. Many frustrated parents look forward to the opening of school, when they can avoid some of their responsibilities of child rearing, and can find time to renew their energies and construct new perspectives for still further encounters with their young. Some use the school as a convenient repository for their children when they go off to work to support the family, to supplement the family income, to escape the drudgery of housekeeping, or to pursue some consuming interest.

By means of compulsory attendance laws we hold most all our young below the age of 16 from the labor force, thus keeping down the rate of unemployment. Our economy has been so productive that the hands of all are not needed in agriculture, services, or industry. Many can be provided with the leisure necessary to the pursuit of learning. Paradoxically, even though our economy has been quite affluent, not all have benefited equally. As a consequence, it has been necessary to dispense welfare to millions in the form of clothing, food and preventive and curative medicine, and this has been rather conveniently and effectively done, at least in part, through the schools.

Second, it is unlikely that the various kinds of professional and technical training necessary to maintaining an advanced technological society can be most economically and effectively provided through informal means of education at a time when there appears to be a greater reliance than ever upon intellectual abilities and skills. Tutorial education is impractical, for it assumes a tutor for every child, and we have nearly 40 million children of elementary school age alone. With the explosion of knowledge of the past decades, it is equally impractical to suppose that parents can or will carry the entire burden of educating their young. The truth of the matter is that many parents, perhaps most parents, are not themselves well enough educated to provide a high level of learning even in the more fundamental subjects of composition, mathematics, and reading. If each family were intellectually equipped to give all necessary instruction, it is to be doubted that it would have the time or equipment to do the job. Only a minority of our homes would have adequate library facilities, and fewer still, the laboratory equipment necessary to the teaching of the natural sciences. Of course, public and private libraries and industrial laboratories could be used, or homes equipped at government expense, but this is neither as convenient nor as economically feasible as the present arrangements.

Third, the school serves a socializing function that would be difficult to replace. Children are sent to school to learn to live with others; to have the harsh, rude and disagreeable edges of their personalities smoothed. Moreover, schools socialize in the sense we discussed earlier. Whether for better or for worse, each culture has certain values, knowledges, and skills, a cultural heritage, if you prefer, which it expects to have impressed upon the young. The school has developed as an organized and controlled way of doing this, and regardless of what one may think of aspects of the process, it is unrealistic to believe this or any other nation is likely to discontinue it. In fact, national survival is thought to depend upon the efficiency of the process.

Given the reasons set out above, it seems quite unlikely that schools will be discontinued. Instead, we shall have at our disposal both formal and informal means of education. Since this is the case, the question is, How, then, should we use these two forms of education? Several alternatives appear open to us. Let us consider some of them.

First, we may choose the course of extended liability. Here the aim would be to rigidly control both means of education in order to use their combined powers to attain certain specific societal goals. In some degree, every society attempts this, but if carried to extremes, it results in the kind of education Professor H. J. Eysenck of the London Institute of Psychiatry appears to be advocating. Professor Eysenck believes most of us are emotionally bound and lacking in innate intelligence. As a consequence we fall prey to superstitions. In order to prevent this, he advocates the use of techniques of emotional conditioning to inculcate attitudes favorable to rational behavior. He equates these with the scientific way of looking at things. He admits that his proposal will offend many, but that we will all have to face up to this necessity unless we wish to abjure all claims of effectiveness. In response to the charge that his is brainwashing, he declares:

> In the first place, such conditioning is all-pervasive and inevitable; it is inherent in the difference in size, maturity, and intelligence of parents and children, and the dependence of the latter on the former; the question is not whether to employ emotional conditioning, but in relation to what ends it should be employed. And my second point would be that even if we could avoid emotional conditioning completely, we would simply create a void; our children would not grow up as socialized human beings, but as selfish asocial monsters. It is difficult to see how this would increase human dignity.[11]

It would seem that the most likely result of employing this alternative would be a kind of education, call it indoctrination if you prefer, in which ordinary men and women might be expected to be docile, industrious, punctual, contented, and favorably inclined toward the rule of an intellectual elite who handle all matters in a coldly scientific or rational way, supposedly for the benefit of all.[12]

This approach to education can be observed on a more limited scale among certain religious denominations such as the Seventh-day Adventists. Beginning with the premise that they have the Truth they set forth a blueprint for building character like an architect might blueprint a skyscraper. Combining the forces of the home, school and church, and rigidly screening out, so far as possible, all other worldly influences, they seek to rear and educate their youth in a sterile atmosphere. If one does not accept the basic premise, he may judge these efforts as narrow, dogmatic and anti-intellectual. Thus, from our illustrations, there seem to be at least two prices likely to be paid if one selects the option of extended liability. One is the rule by an elite (hopefully benevolent) and the other is a national or religious dogma. History is replete with instances where the choice of this alternative has been catastrophic.

The second alternative is based on the notion of schooling assuming a limited liability. The more informal aspects of education are kept apart, so far as possible, from schooling. In this instance the school divorces itself, or pretends to divorce itself so far as it can, from the problems and issues of the times, and confines its activities to imparting a body of content and/or a

---

[11] H. J. Eysenck, "This Is How I Live," *The Humanist* (July/August 1969), pp. 19–21.

[12] See for example, Bertrand Russell, *The Scientific Outlook* (New York: W. W. Norton & Company, Inc., 1931), pp. 243–50. This alternative might work well under a benevolent and saintly regime but saints, like mules, usually do not reproduce themselves.

mass of skills. Sometimes schooling is conceived of in terms of training the mind. Somehow, schooling is neither thought of as a part of life nor intended to be immediately and directly related to the business of living. One is first educated and then goes forth into the world.

Hegel appeared to be advocating this alternative when he wrote that education was a moral enterprise in which the animal nature of the child was to be trained off, for the transformation of the mind alone was worthy of the name of education. The child's mind was to be brought to relinquish its peculiarities, and to grasp that which was common knowledge. The classics, so Hegel thought, were the best instruments for this important and delicate task, for they were an endless store of notable thoughts and ideas, affording guidance, inspiration, and *intellectual training.*[13]

A more contemporary instance of this alternative is to be found in the St. John's College curriculum which, in spite of recent changes, still places major emphasis upon the study of Western cultural heritage through the medium of the great books. Here the intent is first to train and liberate the mind and then to turn these trained and liberated minds loose in the world to tackle the manifold, and supposedly reoccurring, problems of mankind.

Certain kinds of vocational and professional education are not unlike this. Note the highly rigid and narrowly specialized curriculums sometimes found in engineering, business, the arts, and even in schools of education. In these instances the intent may not be to train the mind, but it certainly is intended to store the mind with skills and knowledges which can be transferred or used once one leaves school. Whether education has been broad enough to relate to the totality of life is often of little concern either to the instructors or the instructed. Whether measures should be taken to change the society are largely ignored or relegated to a place of secondary importance.

Like our first alternative this too has its advantages. It tends to preserve the cultural heritage, and it tends to insure the preparation of persons skilled and knowledgeable in their vocations and professions. Furthermore, it often goes at education in a somewhat more contemplative, leisurely and critically detached manner rather than in the emotional and frantic way sometimes characteristic of adherents to certain other alternatives.

But also like the first alternative, this too has its disadvantages. In the first place it assumes a high degree of automatic transfer. In the second place it seems unsuited for many students, as it turns off or alienates them. In the third place it runs the risk of racial suicide, for the problems of our time may be so enormous and so pressing that they must be attacked head-on.

A third alternative, devised to counteract the drawbacks (particularly

---

[13] Millicent Mackenzie, *Hegel's Educational Theory and Practice* (London: Swan Sonnenschein & Company, 1909).

the last one) of the previous position, may be called the world-problems approach. It is based upon the premise that the human race has reached a stage in which it has become necessary, for purposes of assuring continued survival, to surrender our parochialism and to extend our loyalty to the entire human race. It follows from this, or so it is argued, that schooling must shift its goals from serving narrow national ends, training minds, passing on a cultural heritage, or preparing for some profession or vocation to a conjoint student-teacher effort to study and find solutions to our survival-threatening problems of war, pollution, over-population, and the like. In order to do this the lines between informal and formal education have to be broken down and the world brought into the classroom, and the classroom taken out into the world. Implicit in this alternative is the need for continued education and a new social function for schooling, but most especially the university. Some who would defend this alternative have proposed again, as it was proposed during the early years of the League of Nations, that a world university be instituted with the world's knowledge as its curriculum, the world's problems as its responsibilities, and the world's best scholars and students as its members. This is not to say, however, that all existing institutions should be dismantled. Quite to the contrary. They too are to be de-nationalized on the one hand, and made problem orientated on the other.[14] The Friends World College might serve as a kind of paradigm here, for it sends its students around the world in a four-year program in which students largely determine their own course of study built around current problems.[15] Others have suggested that, where it is impossible to attend a world university or travel about the world, schooling must be made to focus on the most serious problems of our time. One writer has gone so far as to recommend that ultimately all instruction, formal and informal, must have as its goal the survival of the human race.[16] This alternative has the merit of focusing attention upon the issues of the time, and it brings the world and the classroom together. Furthermore, it is a means of motivating certain students. It harbors the disadvantage, however, of over-emphasizing the here and now, and of over-estimating the immediate impact students and faculty can have on events. Thus it runs the risk of producing a mood of pessimism and eventual withdrawal. Moreover, it may denigrate the more leisurely and detached critical assessment of ideas, and may foster a more emotional and immediate do-goodism. Lastly, it could easily evolve into alternative number one.

Fourth, there is the alternative of individual-centered education. As one student put it, "Education exists to serve the individual, the student, and not the educator. Each individual should be able to learn what he feels is

---

[14] Harold Taylor, "Editorial," *Saturday Review*, (Oct. 11, 1969), pp. 24 and 52.

[15] Leah Karpen, "Letter to the Editor," *Saturday Review*, (Nov. 8, 1969), p. 27.

[16] See for example Harold Taylor, *The World as Teacher* (Garden City, New York: Doubleday & Company, Inc., 1969). Also *Students Without Teachers, op. cit.*

relevant to life and should not be forced to spend time on subjects for *which he has no use.*"[17] Another student wrote

If we as educators can accept the idea that Anthony should be the one to decide which changes he wants in himself, and if we are willing to make a real effort to meet those needs—provide agencies to assist him—then the distinction between out of school and in-school learning becomes unimportant. The child takes a look at his world; he decides what he needs in terms of skills and pleasures to cope with the world. Adults whom he trusts involve themselves in his decision. One of several kinds of schools should be available to instruct him.

Letting children determine their own educational destinies is not so drastically different from the reality of schooling today. The disenchanted and the discontent tune out while they put in their classroom year. If they are designated as educational chaff they become the nonreaders and eventually the dropouts.[18]

Apparently what is offered through school, or by informal avenues of education, is to be viewed as a smorgasbord from which students choose or do not choose as they think best. One student's interest is considered as worthy as the next. The role of the relatively more mature teacher as a resource for opening up new concerns is not particularly emphasized.

This alternative is usually quickly dismissed by many as intolerably romantic, *laissez faire*, and anti-intellectual, for it is supposed that if it were acted upon systematically it would produce chaos. In matter of fact, however, some degree of intellectual respect for existing conditions and consequences would operate as a control factor in the formation and pursuit of pupil interests. But, in any event, this quick disposal should be avoided for, in reality, this alternative too has its merits. We early learn to pretend to be doing what our parents, teachers, and society expect of us. The pretense satisfies, for the most part, the expectations others hold for us. Thus, having appeared to satisfy the demands of others we are free to do many of the things that please and interest us. If parents and educators were to admit this and simply place their faith in the interests and self-motivations of the students, perhaps learning would not be diminished in the least. The results claimed for the First Street School[19] and Franconia College[20] seem to bear this out.

On the other hand, this position appears to reflect a high degree of self-centered pessimism. The pessimism may stem from the fact that our problems are so enormous and are increasing at such a rate that they cannot be adequately contended with, and that one had best retreat pretty much into a search for some kind of personal meaning and satisfaction in life.

[17] Jeff Filman, "Philosophy of Education," (unpublished paper, 1969).
[18] Gloria Randall, written preliminary examination, (Northwestern University, 1970). See also Rousseau's, *Emile*, and A. S. Neill's *Summerhill.*
[19] George Dennison, *The Lives of Children* (New York: Random House, 1969).
[20] *The Milwaukee Journal* (November 30, 1969).

Having completed this cursory treatment of some of our possible alternatives, and assuming they represent viable choices, where are we left? It has been shown that informal education is impossible to eliminate and that schooling will undoubtedly be continued for several rather compelling reasons. Thus, our choices are reduced to some kind of accommodation or forced separation of the two forms of education. In the examination of our alternatives, we have found each to have its advantages and its shortcomings. Perhaps the choices before us may be summarized as follows:

1. If you wish to promote the rule of an elite or perpetuate a particular way of life or preserve a religious dogma, then rigidly try to control both the formal and informal means of education and bring their combined powers to bear upon the particular end in view.

2. If you conceive of education in terms of training and storing the mind first and using it in practical affairs later, then elect to separate formal and informal education insofar as this can be done.

3. If you accept the premise that the human race is facing immediate catastrophy, and that all the combined efforts of man and all the forces of education must be brought to bear upon our common problems in order to save us from racial suicide, and if you are willing to take such risks as an over-emphasis upon the present, a suspension of the more leisurely and detached assessment of ideas, and a de-emphasis of the cultural heritage, then select the world-problem alternative.

4. If you believe that schooling and informal education, in whatever state they exist, should serve the individual, that each pupil's interests should be trusted, and if you are willing to accept the apparent self-centeredness and pessimism this may imply, then choose the alternative of individual-centered education.

If, however, no one of these alternatives is completely satisfactory to you, then you have the right, if not the obligation, of arriving at some kind of compromise from among them.

It must be admitted, however, that, whatever choice one exercises, it will be based primarily upon feeling, principle, and belief, and not upon any compelling body of experimental knowledge. This is the case because the problem we have been pursuing is essentially normative in character, and because our hard data are so limited.

As for myself, my inclination is to choose an eclectic alternative. But let it be clear that I reject entirely alternative one and draw my stand from elements within alternatives two, three and four. There is stressed in each of these primarily one dimension of the task of educating. Advocates of alternative two, and most especially of alternative three, may wish to argue that their alternative encompasses all that I shall have to say. Be that as it may, the dimensions as I see them, are:

(1) the cultural heritage, information, knowledge, skills, values, traditions, etc. (this looms largest in alternative two),

(2) realistic and vital issues and problems worthy of serious study as contrasted with a body of information to be mastered and repeated (this is most pronounced in alternative three), and

(3) student interest, concern, and personal growth (this is the principal element in alternative four).

No one of these is sufficient. All are necessary.

Homo sapiens has accumulated a heritage which has its worth and which we cannot entirely escape transferring to our young. This is not to say, however, that the heritage should be imparted unexamined and unchanged, for through time it becomes encumbered with flotsam and jetsam. Like it or not, its place must be determined in relation to other dimensions of education. A cultural heritage which is not used to identify problems and issues or to provide perspective and intellectual tools, but which is mastered with the faint hope of use later on in life, promotes the continuation of the *status quo* and evinces a contempt for the learner. Finally, the cultural heritage and the problems would not even exist without persons, for education is a distinctly human activity. While the heritage and the problems of our day have their proper place and their peculiar importance, neither should nor can be divorced from the learner and his powers and interests. The place of the learner may be exaggerated in alternative four, but the truth contained in the exaggeration shoud not be lost.

Thus, I opt for a view of the uses of informal education and formal means of education that would employ the cultural heritage as both a source and an object of change. I would wish both informal and formal means of education to be at the same time problem-oriented and student-centered. I would, however, wish to avoid the evils likely to attend alternative one. Just how this can be satisfactorily arranged, if at all, is the subject for another paper.

I am prepared to suggest, however, that what is likely to happen in our society is that we shall follow most closely alternatives one and two but that at the same time, we shall continue to hear from advocates three and four. This state of affairs will result, from an effort on the part of the silent majority, to keep things running pretty much as they are, while others will become increasingly alarmed and vocal over the prospects for survival with each passing day. As H. G. Wells said many years ago, we are in a race between education and catastrophy, and the latter appears to be winning.

B. Religion in Education

Since the founding of this nation, the place of religion in the school curriculum has been debated. Schools in the colonies were largely dominated by Protestant religious interests. During the first half of the nineteenth century, Catholics found the public school curriculum unsatisfactory and set about building schools of their own free from Protestant influence in which catholic religious instruction could be integrated. The number of Catholic schools has increased over the past hundred years until they now represent the largest number of religious affiliated schools in the United States. Parochial schools today are faced with many of the same problems that confront public schools, and many parochial schools have been discontinued for educational as well as financial reasons. Somewhat ironically, but nevertheless understandably, at a time when parochial schools are being closed for lack of funds, legislation has been passed on both the federal and state levels to aid these schools. In this nation, with its tradition of separation of church and state, this has again raised the question of the proper place of religion in education.

The next chapter presents a recent, official statement of the Ecumenical Council of the Catholic Church toward religious education. This is followed by a statement prepared by Allan Hart Jahsmann, which puts forth the philosophical underpinnings of the schools operated under the aegis of the Missouri Synod of the Lutheran Church, the largest group of Protestant parochial schools. In the following chapter, C. D. Hardie presents an opposing view, holding that the teaching of religion usually leads to indoctrination and anti-intellectualism.

246

21

Declaration on Christian Education

THE SACRED ECUMENICAL COUNCIL

INTRODUCTION

The Sacred Ecumenical Council has considered with care how extremely important education is in the life of man and how its influence ever grows in the social progress of this age.

Indeed, the circumstances of our time have made it easier and at once more urgent to educate young people and, what is more, to continue the education of adults. Men are more aware of their own dignity and position; more and more they want to take an active part in social and especially in economic and political life. Enjoying more leisure, as they sometimes do, men find that the remarkable development of technology and scientific investigation and the new means of communication offer them an opportunity of attaining more easily their cultural and spiritual inheritance and of fulfilling one another in the closer ties between groups and even between peoples.

Consequently, attempts are being made everywhere to promote more education. The rights of men to an education, particularly the primary rights of children and parents, are being proclaimed and recognized in public documents. As the number of pupils rapidly increases, schools are multiplied and expanded far and wide and other educational institutions are established. New experiments are conducted in methods of education and teaching. Mighty attempts are being made to obtain education for all, even

The translation of the "Declaration on Christian Education" is taken from *The Documents of Vatican II*, published by Guild Press, America Press, and Associated Press and copyrighted 1966 by America Press. Used by permission of the National Catholic Welfare Conference and Guild Press, Inc.

though vast numbers of children and young people are still deprived of even rudimentary training and so many others lack a suitable education in which truth and love are developed together.

To fulfill the mandate she has received from her divine founder of proclaiming the mystery of salvation to all men and of restoring all things in Christ, Holy Mother the Church must be concerned with the whole of man's life, even the secular part of it insofar as it has a bearing on his heavenly calling. Therefore, she has a role in the progress and development of education. Hence this sacred synod declares certain fundamental principles of Christian education especially in schools. These principles will have to be developed at greater length by a special post-conciliar commission and applied by Episcopal conferences to varying local situations.

1. The Meaning of the Universal Right to Education

All men of every race, condition and age, since they enjoy the dignity of a human being, have an inalienable right to an education that is in keeping with their ultimate goal, their ability, their sex, and the culture and tradition of their country, and also in harmony with their fraternal association with other peoples in the fostering of true unity and peace on earth. For a true education aims at the formation of the human person in the pursuit of his ultimate end and of the good of the societies of which, as man, he is a member, and in whose obligations, as an adult, he will share.

Therefore, children and young people must be helped, with the aid of the latest advances in psychology and the arts and science of teaching, to develop harmoniously their physical, moral, and intellectual endowments so that they may gradually acquire a mature sense of responsibility in striving endlessly to form their own lives properly and in pursuing true freedom as they surmount the vicissitudes of life with courage and constancy. Let them be given also, as they advance in years, a positive and prudent sexual education. Moreover they should be so trained to take their part in social life that properly instructed in the necessary and opportune skills they can become actively involved in various community organizations, open to discourse with others and willing to do their best to promote the common good.

This sacred synod likewise declares that children and young people have a right to be motivated to appraise moral values with a right conscience, to embrace them with a personal adherence, together with a deeper knowledge and love of God. Consequently it earnestly entreats all those who hold a position of public authority or who are in charge of education to see to it that youth is never deprived of this sacred right. It further exhorts the sons of the Church to give their attention with generosity to the entire field of education, having especially in mind the need of extending very soon the benefits of a suitable education and training to everyone in all parts of the world.

2. Christian Education

Since all Christians have become by rebirth of water and the Holy Spirit a new creature so that they should be called and should be children of God, they have a right to a Christian education. A Christian education does not merely strive for the maturing of a human person as just now described, but has as its principal purpose this goal: That the baptized, while they are gradually introduced to the knowledge of the mystery of salvation, become ever more aware of the gift of faith they have received, and that they learn in addition how to worship God the Father in spirit and truth (cf. John 4:23) especially in liturgical action, and be conformed in their personal lives according to the new man created in justice and holiness of truth (Eph. 4:22–24); also that they develop into perfect manhood, to the mature measure of the fulness of Christ (cf. Eph. 4:13) and strive for the growth of the Mystical Body; moreover, that, aware of their calling, they learn not only how to bear witness to the hope that is in them (cf. Peter 3:15) but also how to help in the Christian formation of the world that takes place when natural powers viewed in the full consideration of man redeemed by Christ contribute to the good of the whole of society. Wherefore, this sacred synod recalls to pastors of souls their most serious obligation to see to it that all the faithful, but especially the youth who are the hope of the Church, enjoy this Christian education.

3. Authors of Education

Since parents have given children their life, they are bound by the most serious obligation to educate their offspring and, therefore, must be recognized as the primary and principal educators. This role in education is so important that only with difficulty can it be supplied where it is lacking. Parents are the ones who must create a family atmosphere animated by love and respect for God and man, in which the well-rounded personal and social education of children is fostered. Hence the family is the first school of the social virtues that every society needs. It is particularly in the Christian family, enriched by the grace and office of the sacrament of matrimony, that children should be taught from their early years to have a knowledge of God according to the faith received in Baptism, to worship Him, and to love their neighbor. Here too they find their first experience of a wholesome human society and of the Church. Finally, it is through the family that they are gradually led to a companionship with their fellowmen and with the people of God. Let parents, then, recognize the inestimable importance a truly Christian family has for the life and progress of God's own people.

The family which has the primary duty of imparting education needs the help of the whole community. In addition, therefore, to the rights of parents and others to whom the parents entrust a share in the work of education, certain rights and duties belong indeed to civil society, whose role is to direct what is required for the common temporary good. Its function is to promote the education of youth in many ways, namely: To protect the duties and rights of parents and others who share in education and to give them aid; according to the principle of subsidiarity, when the endeavors of parents and other societies are lacking, to carry out the work of education in accordance with the wishes of the parents; and, moreover, as the common good demands, to build schools and institutions.

Finally, in a special way, the duty of educating belongs to the Church, not merely because it must be recognized as a human society capable of educating, but especially because it has the responsibility of announcing the way of salvation to all men, of communicating the life of Christ to those who believe, and, in her unfailing solicitude, of assisting men to be able to come to the fulness of this life. The Church is bound as a mother to give to these children of hers an education by which their whole life can be imbued with the spirit of Christ and at the same time do all she can to promote for all peoples the complete perfection of the human person, the good of earthly society, and the building of a world that is more human.

3a. Various Aids to Education

In fulfilling its educational role, the Church eager to employ all suitable aids, is concerned especially about those who are her very own. Foremost among these is catechetical instruction, which enlightens and strengthens the faith, nourishes life according to the spirit of Christ, leads to intelligent and active participation in the liturgical mystery and gives motivation for apostolic activity. The Church esteems highly and seeks to penetrate and ennoble with her own spirit also other aids which belong to the general heritage of man and which are of great influence in forming souls and molding men, such as the media of communication, various groups for mental and physical development, youth associations, and, in particular, schools.

4. Importance of Schools

Among all educational instruments the school has a special importance. It is designed not only to develop with special care the intellectual faculties but also to form the ability to judge rightly, to hand on the cultural legacy of previous generations, to foster a sense of values, to prepare for professional life. Between pupils of different talents and backgrounds it promotes friendly relations and fosters a spirit of mutual understanding; and it establishes as it were a center whose work and progress must be shared together by families, teachers, associations of various types that foster cultural, civic, and religious life, as well as by civil society and the entire human community.

Beautiful indeed and of great importance is the vocation of all those who aid parents in fulfilling their duties and who, as representatives of the human community, undertake the task of education in schools. This vocation demands special qualities of mind and heart, very careful preparation, and continuing readiness to renew and to adapt.

5. Duties and Rights of Parents

Parents who have the primary and inalienable right and duty to educate their children must enjoy true liberty in their choice of schools. Consequently, the public power, which has the obligation to protect and defend the rights of citizens, must see to it, in its concern for distributive justice, that public subsidies are paid out in such a way that parents are truly free to choose according to their conscience the schools they want for their children.

In addition it is the task of the state to see to it that all citizens are able to come to a suitable share in culture and are properly prepared to exercise their civic duties and rights. Therefore, the state must protect the right of children to an adequate school education, check on the ability of teachers and the excellence of their training, look after the health of the pupils, and, in general, promote the whole school project. But it must always keep in mind the principle of subsidiarity so that there is no kind of school monopoly, for this is opposed to the native rights of the human person, to the development and spread of culture, to the peaceful association of citizens, and to the pluralism that exists today in ever so many societies.

Therefore, this sacred synod exhorts the faithful to assist to their utmost in finding suitable methods of education and programs of study and in forming teachers who can give youth a true education. Through the associations of parents in particular they should further with their assistance all the work of the school but especially the moral education it must impart.

6. Moral and Religious Education in All Schools

Feeling very keenly the weighty responsibility of diligently caring for the moral and religious education of all her children, the Church must be present with her own special affection and help for the great number who are being trained in schools that are not Catholic. This is possible by the witness of the lives of those who teach and direct them, by the apostolic action of their fellow-students, but especially by the ministry of priests and laymen who give them the doctrine of salvation in a way suited to their age and circumstances and provide spiritual aid in every way the times and conditions allow.

The Church reminds parents of the duty that is theirs to arrange and even demand that their children be able to enjoy these aids and advance in their Christian formation to a degree that is abreast of their development in secular subjects. Therefore, the Church esteems highly those civil authorities and societies which, bearing in mind the pluralism of contemporary society and respecting religious freedom, assist families so that the education of their children can be imparted in all schools according to the individual moral and religious principles of the families.

7. CATHOLIC SCHOOLS

The influence of the Church in the field of education is shown in a special manner by the Catholic school. No less than other schools does the Catholic school pursue cultural goals and the human formation of youth. But its proper function is to create for the school community a special atmosphere animated by the Gospel spirit of freedom and charity, to help youth grow according to the new creatures they were made through Baptism as they develop their own personalities, and finally to order the whole of human culture to the news of salvation so that the knowledge the students gradually acquire of the world, life, and man is illumined by faith. So indeed the Catholic school, while it is open, as it must be, to the situation of the contemporary world, leads its students to promote efficaciously the good of the earthly city and also prepares them for service in the spread of the Kingdom of God, so that by leading an exemplary apostolic life they become, as it were, a saving leaven in the human community.

Since, therefore, the Catholic school can be such an aid to the fulfillment of the mission of the People of God and to the fostering of the dialogue between the Church and mankind, to the benefit of both, it retains even in our present circumstances the utmost importance. Consequently this sacred synod proclaims anew what has already been taught in several documents of the magisterium, namely: The right of the Church freely to establish and to conduct schools of every type and level. And the Council calls to mind that the exercise of a right of this kind contributes in the highest degree to the protection of freedom of conscience, the rights of parents, as well as to the betterment of culture itself.

But let teachers recognize that the Catholic school depends upon them almost entirely for the accomplishment of its goals and programs. They should, therefore, be very carefully prepared so that both in secular and religious knowledge they are equipped with suitable qualifications and also with a pedagogical skill that is in keeping with the findings of the contemporary world. Intimately linked in charity to one another and to their students and endowed with an apostolic spirit, may teachers by their life as much as by their instruction bear witness to Christ the unique Teacher. Let them work as partners with parents and together with them in every phase of education give due consideration to the difference of sex and the proper ends Divine Providence assigns to each sex in the family and in society. Let them do all they can to stimulate their students to act for themselves and even after graduation to continue to assist them with advice, friendship, and by establishing special associations imbued with the true spirit of the Church. The work of these teachers, this sacred synod declares, is in the real sense of the word an apostolate most suited to and necessary for our times and at once a true service offered to society. The Council also reminds Catholic parents of the duty of entrusting their children to Catholic schools wherever and whenever it is possible and of supporting these schools to the best of their ability and of cooperating with them for the education of their children.

8. DIFFERENT TYPES OF CATHOLIC SCHOOLS

To this concept of a Catholic school all schools that are in any way dependent on the Church must conform as far as possible, though the Catholic school is to take on different forms in keeping with local circumstances. Thus the Church considers very dear to her heart those Catholic schools, found especially in the areas of the new churches, which are attended also by students who are not Catholics.

Attention should be paid to the needs of today in establishing and directing Catholic schools. Therefore, though primary and secondary schools, the foundation of education, must still be fostered, great importance is to be attached to those which are required in a particular way by contemporary conditions, such as: Professional and technical schools, centers for educating adults and promoting social welfare, or for the retarded in need of special care, and also schools for preparing teachers for religious instruction and other types of education.

This sacred Council of the Church earnestly entreats pastors and all the faithful to spare no sacrifice in helping Catholic schools fulfill their function in a continually more perfect way, and especially in caring for the needs of those who are poor in the goods of this world or who are deprived of the assistance and affection of a family or who are strangers to the gift of faith.

9. Catholic Colleges and Universities

The Church is concerned also with schools of a higher level, especially colleges and universities. In those schools dependent on her she intends that by their very constitution individual subjects be pursued according to their own principles, method, and liberty of scientific inquiry, in such a way that an ever deeper understanding in these fields will be obtained and that, as questions that are new and current are raised and investigations carefully made according to the example of the doctors of the Church and especially of St. Thomas Aquinas, there may be a deeper realization of the harmony of faith and science. Thus there is accomplished a public, enduring, and pervasive influence of the Christian mind in the furtherance of culture, and the students of these institutions are molded into men truly outstanding in their training, ready to undertake weighty responsibilities in society and witness to the faith in the world.

In Catholic universities where there is no faculty of sacred theology there should be established an institute or chair of sacred theology in which there should be lectures suited to lay students. Since science advances by means of the investigations peculiar to higher scientific studies, special attention should be given in Catholic universities and colleges to institutes that serve primarily the development of scientific research.

The sacred synod heartily recommends that Catholic colleges and universities be conveniently located in different parts of the world, but in such a way that they are outstanding not for their numbers but for their pursuit of knowledge. Matriculation should be readily available to students of real promise, even though they be of slender means, especially to students from the newly emerging nations.

Since the destiny of society and of the Church itself is intimately linked with the progress of young people pursuing higher studies, the pastors of the Church are to expend their energies not only on the spiritual life of students who attend Catholic universities, but, solicitous for the spiritual formation of all their children, they must see to it, after consultations between Bishops, that even at universities that are not Catholic there should be associations and university centers under Catholic auspices in which priests, religious, and laity, carefully selected and prepared should give abiding spiritual and intellectual assistance to the youth of the university. Whether in Catholic universities or others, young people of greater ability who seem suited for teaching or research should be specially helped and encouraged to undertake a teaching career.

10. Faculties of Sacred Sciences

The Church expects much from the zealous endeavors of the faculties of the sacred sciences. For to them she entrusts the very serious responsibility of preparing her own students not only for the priestly ministry, but especially for teaching in the seats of higher ecclesiastical studies or for promoting learning on their own or for undertaking the work of a more rigorous intellectual apostolate. Likewise it is the role of these very faculties to make more penetrating inquiry into the various aspects of the sacred sciences so that an ever-deepening understanding of sacred Revelation is obtained, the legacy of Christian wisdom handed down by our forefathers is more fully developed, the dialogue with our separated brethren and with non-Christians is fostered, and answers are given to questions arising from the development of doctrine.

Therefore, ecclesiastical faculties should reappraise their own laws so that they can better promote the sacred sciences and those linked with them and, by employing up-to-date methods and aids, lead their students to more penetrating inquiry.

11. Coordination to Be Fostered in Scholastic Matters

Cooperation is the order of the day. It increases more and more to supply the demand on a diocesan, national, and international level. Since it is altogether necessary in scholastic matters, every means should be employed to foster suitable cooperation between Catholic schools, and between these and other schools that collaboration should be developed which the good of all mankind requires.

From greater coordination and cooperative endeavor greater fruits will be derived particularly in the area of academic instituions. Therefore, in every university let the various faculties work mutually to this end, insofar as their goal will permit. In addition, let the universities also endeavor to work together by promoting international gatherings, by sharing scientific inquiries with one another, by communicating their discoveries to one another, by having exchange of professors for a time and by promoting all else that is conducive to greater assistance.

The sacred synod earnestly entreats young people themselves to become aware of the importance of the work of education and to prepare themselves to take it up, especially where because of a shortage of teachers the education of youth is in jeopardy.

This same sacred synod, while professing its gratitude to the priests, religious men and women, and the laity who by their evangelical self-dedication are devoted to the noble work of education and of schools of every type and level, exhorts them to persevere generously in the work they have undertaken, and, imbuing their students with the spirit of Christ, to strive to excel in pedagogy and the pursuit of knowledge in such a way that they not merely advance the internal renewal of the Church but preserve and enhance its beneficient influence upon today's world, especially the intellectual world.

22

What's Lutheran in Education?

ALLAN HART JAHSMANN

Every human being has a philosophy, a basic outlook, a *Weltanschauung*, a point of view, through which he sees his world and finds its meanings and purposes and values.

As Aristotle said long ago: "Whether we want to philosophize or whether we do not want to philosophize, we must philosophize." To the extent to which the human mind functions, to that extent it forms notions, hypotheses, theories, ideas, and judgments of the world and what goes on in it, especially insofar as the individual himself is involved in it.

And even though most people make no systematic effort to gain a true and unified picture of the world and their part in it, and are often inconsistent "split" personalities in that they do not apply their philosophy to life, yet a man adds content to his philosophy and becomes an organized, integrated human being to the extent to which he applies his philosophy to the issues and problems of life and living.

What is a philosophy of education? In the light of what has just been said, it is one's philosophy, one's world view, and one's way of thinking, applied to education. Strictly speaking, there are as many philosophies as there are individuals, and if you don't think Mrs. Schmidt has a philosophy of education, just ask her what her idea of education is or how *she* thinks school ought to be conducted and why.

Allan Hart Jahsmann is executive editor of the Board of Parish Education of the Missouri Synod. Allan Hart Jahsmann, *What's Lutheran in Education?* (St. Louis: Concordia Publishing House, 1961), pp. ix–xii. Used by permission of the author and publisher.

What is a Lutheran philosophy? There are some men in the Lutheran church who deny that one can properly speak of a *Lutheran* philosophy of life and of education. Because a Lutheran takes as his basic assumptions the doctrines of Holy Scripture, and because his primary or first principles are established by revelation instead of by reason, they say that one can speak only of a Lutheran *theology* and not of a Lutheran *philosophy*.

We readily acknowledge that to the extent that theology determines a person's point of view, it is a part of his philosophy. And when a Lutheran applies Lutheran theology to the questions of education or systematizes his educational thinking in harmony with his theological principles, to that extent his theology is the basis of his educational philosophy, the foundation on which he builds his structure of thinking.

But the very nature of philosophy suggests that there is a Lutheran philosophy and, from one point of view, *many* Lutheran philosophies, for though Lutherans accept the doctrines of Holy Scripture as inspired divine truth and their standard of faith, yet this does not mean that they must cease to think. Rather, they have the philosophic task of thinking consistently in harmony with their theology and of critically evaluating their educational theories and practices in the light of their philosophy or, as we might call it, historical Lutheran faith.

Again the question: What is a *Lutheran* philosophy? When is a point of view, an approach, an idea, a system, a product, a person, truly and distinctly Lutheran? The answer isn't simple ... but this much can be said at the outset: One of the distinguishing features of a genuine Lutheran is that he accepts the Bible as the primary source and basis of his faith. Hence, truly Lutheran thinking flows from, or is in harmony with, Biblical theology.

Krauth summed up the nature of Lutheran theology and thereby also identified and described a basic essential of anything intrinsically Lutheran when he said in his classic book, *The Conservative Reformation and Its Theology* "It is a fundamental principle of the Reformation that God's Word is the sole and absolute authority and rule of faith and life, a principle without accepting which no man can be truly Evangelical, Protestant, or Lutheran."[1] This is called the formal principle of Lutheranism.

There are, of course, other principles, factors, qualities, and character-istics that are essential to Lutheranism and typical of anything classifiable as Lutheran. For example, Lutherans emphasize that Christ is the focus of the Scriptures and that justification by faith in Him is the central doctrine.[2] This is called the material principle. The effect of this material principle on the nature of Lutheran thinking and practice will be indicated.

Here let it simply be said that truly Lutheran *educational* philosophy is

---

[1] Charles P. Krauth, *The Conservative Reformation and Its Theology*. Philadelphia: General Council Publication Board, 1899, p. 17.

[2] Article IV of the Augsburg Confession.

Biblical theology and Lutheran thinking applied to education. To say (as it has been said) that Lutherans do not have a philosophy (or theory) of education is to maintain that their theology does not influence their educational program. This certainly is not true.

THEOLOGICAL ASSUMPTIONS AND ACCENTS*

1. God is. We believe He exists. The physical world, man's conscience, the history of His people, the inspired Scriptures, and especially the Person Jesus Christ reveal God. But we must humbly keep in mind that though human beings can learn to know Him, human understanding of Him is always limited and faulty. "O the depth of the riches both of the wisdom and knowledge of God! How unsearchable are His judgments and His ways past finding out!" (Rom. 11: 33).

2. God caused the Scriptures to be written so that man might hear His Word, the revelation of His judgment and grace (Law and Gospel). In the Bible we have the God-inspired record of His acts, His will, His plans, and His promises. Thereby God revealed Himself and continues to do so. But God's judgment, grace, and power have been revealed not only in His past actions and in the words of Sacred Scripture. The Word of God is incarnate in Jesus Christ. And God continues to act and to reveal Himself through His Spirit and particularly also through the witnessing actions of Christ's body, His church, alive in the present.

3. God, the Creator of every good gift, intended that all things should find their ultimate completion in Him. This applies in a special sense to human beings, whom God creates to live in loving, harmonious, and joyful relationship to Him and with power to subdue and rule the earth. The accent of Christian education must be on the fact that God's purpose for man involves life, joy, hope, and the unity of all things in Christ (Eph. 1: 10). Because all of God's creations are good in their essence and intended use, the new materials will affirm the essential goodness of God's world even while acknowledging starkly its corruptions.

4. Man sins. Through sinning man has disrupted his relationship with God and has brought death to himself and to the world. Today's society shows this separation particularly by violence, materialism and greed, feelings of alienation, and the misuse of God's creations. Man's great dilemma is that he has alienated himself from God and is unable to restore his broken fellowship with God. This is the main reason why sin is such a desperate reality. But this problem can be truly seen only by the person whom Jesus Christ has set free from the bonds of sin. Also sin must be dealt with

* The following is from *Design for Mission: Life.* St. Louis: Concordia Publishing House, 1970, pp. 30–43. Used by permission.

evangelically and not legalistically. A Christian's use of Law must serve the purposes of the Gospel of God's redeeming grace in Jesus Christ.

5. God restores human beings to a perfect relationship with Him through Jesus Christ. Through Christ's life, death, resurrection, and living spirit God redeems, justifies, reconciles, and saves sinners and unites all things in Him (Eph. 1: 10). In Christ God took the initiative to accomplish the redemption of His world. God's initiative is expressed today through the Christian who proclaims and lives the Gospel of Christ. The Gospel is always the prevailing power and mood of truly Christian education. The Law is to be used mainly to make all men equal in their need of Christ and His salvation. And though we must acknowledge that a Christian is in every act and instance a sinner as well as a saint, everything we say about the twofold nature of the Christian ought to help him appreciate the worth and dignity that is his as a redeemed and continuously forgiven child of God.

6. Man receives God's redemption and salvation through faith in Jesus Christ. But Christian education endeavors must emphasize that faith is trust more than it is knowledge or assent. Intellectual knowledge is important only to the extent that it contributes to such trust, and assent must be the assent of the heart to the heart and spirit of God. Our teaching must emphasize that such faith is entirely a gift of God's Spirit. It is the Spirit who calls us to reconciliation and new life in God's eternal kingdom.

7. The context in which man's restoration takes place is the church, which includes children and youth. The church is the body of Christ, all its members. A fundamental truth regarding the church is that teaching is an essential function of the church (Matt. 28: 19–20). This teaching consists not merely in transmission of information but especially in relationships and in the fostering of the doing of God's Word (1 Cor. 12; Eph. 4, etc.) As God's people study and learn the Word of the Scriptures, declare their faith to one another, and apply the Gospel to their present life and world, Christian education is in process.

8. Christian education must be sacramental and liturgical. By sacramental we mean that God graciously sends His Spirit through the Sacraments of the church—that these too are the Word of the Gospel and means of grace. By liturgy we mean the structures and forms of Christian response to God's Spirit both in worship and loving actions. These things are not to be done because the Christian ought to do them. Rather, they are to be educational experiences through which people learn to know and appreciate what God is like and what Christians do.

9. The Christian lives in the assurance of an eternally ongoing relationship with God. In the spirit and life of God's kingdom he has an intimation of his heavenly inheritance. The Christian can live out his life on earth in joy because he confidently believes that in Christ he will attain the full realization of the relationship with God that he now knows imperfectly. But the *now* of eternal life deserves emphasis, not just our future hope.

SPECIAL ACCENTS

While all theological principles are interrelated, accents of the new curriculum relate especially to the truths concerning the church of God, the Spirit of God, and the Word of God. These could, of course, be considered in a different order. They are inseparably related to the doctrines of God, man, and Jesus Christ.

THE CHURCH AND EDUCATION

In developing the Mission: Life program the planners saw Christian education as the church's basic mission and task and also considered it to be the function and life of the church as church. This is what the name of the program implies. In other words, when church groups function as the church of Jesus Christ, they are educating. The church's mission and life consist in the various parts of the body building one another up in Christ (Eph. 4) and teaching to make disciples of other human beings on earth. (Matt. 28: 19).

This means that when a local congregation calls itself a church (i.e., a part of the church of Jesus Christ), it has assumed the responsibility to teach, educate, feed, or nurture its members, the people of God. This obligation of a congregation to help its members grow toward maturity in Christ extends to *all* the members at every age. And any group in the church must see itself as a living, healing, and nurturing part of Christ's body, also when it is engaged in other than formal study activities.

When a Christian congregation and individual parents and teachers teach as the church of Christ, they do so as the people of God made alive (called, gathered, enlightened, sanctified) by the Spirit of God. They acknowledge Christ as their Lord and Savior and practice mutual forgiveness and love in the fellowship that is theirs through Jesus Christ. Without undue concern for personal status and legal authority, teachers and students led by God's Spirit become mutual worshipers and learners of Christ in a truly democratic and Christian process.

THE SPIRIT AND THE WORD

Lutheran theology maintains that the Spirit of God comes into human life and society only through the Gospel of God's love in Christ and not through laws. Therefore authoritarian uses of power and methods of imposed teaching conflict with the very nature of Christian education. The church needs an evangelical and spiritual type of educational process that actually depends on God, who is a spirit, working through the Gospel and through people who in love become the servants of one another.

Such a process or style of operation requires that there be a right understanding of what is meant by the Gospel, the Word which Lutherans believe is the means of grace. Much has been written about this Word in recent years. We can all agree that the Word of God, the Word of truth and life, the saving Word of Christ, is something more than the human sounds or signs we call words. It is the Word of reconciliation, of love and peace and life and joy. It is the Word of the spirit who is God.

This Word, though conveyed and revealed by the words of Scripture, can be communicated in many other forms, both verbal and nonverbal—by art, poetry, drama, ritual, human example, to name but a few. A denial of this principle can readily lead to Biblicism and literalism—a magical use of Bible words and an insistence on a given form. Always we must be primarily concerned with the substance or meaning of the Word in whatever form it is before us, and always we must bear in mind that the meaning of any word or message is ultimately in its spirit.

The Mission: Life materials will be thoroughly Biblical by being based on Biblical content and doctrine, but the program must tap the riches of Christ also in present-day human life and in the arts, both past and present. Simply to teach the narratives of Scripture is not enough. One must interpret these narratives in terms of present-day personal and social meanings in order to help another person to hear the Word as the voice of a living God. More than that, through the Gospel and a Christian faith we can also see present-day ordinary happenings and human expressions as signs of God's presence and actions or as the absence of His light and spirit.

MAJOR ELEMENTS OF CHRISTIAN EDUCATION

Looking theologically at the major elements in Christian education, we might note that the context of Christian nurture must be the church functioning as the church. The content and power of Christian education is to reveal the need for the forgiving, accepting love of God. Only in the spirit of God's grace and freedom can the Word of God, particularly His imperatives, serve as evangelical instruction and guidance. Law imposed as law upon children of God who have been freed by Christ from living according to law puts them back under the curse of law.

In the light of this cardinal principle of the Christian faith, there is reason to believe happily that modern educational theory is in many respects more suited to the purposes of Christian education than authoritarian, law-oriented, formally disciplined, largely didactic verbal procedures. Let us consider, then, some of the present-day educational trends that have direct and promising application to Christian religious education.

The Education Process

In 20th-century education there is a distinct shift from a more or less passive receiving and parroting of teacher-transmitted content to active inquiry, expression, and doing by the student. More and more the process is becoming a mutual exploration and dialogue by both student and teacher. This is not simply the activity method and techniques of what was called progressive education in the earlier decades of the 20th century. That activity was mainly workbook exercises, assignments, and pupil activity for its own or the teacher's sake.

Today the concern is for insight into a significant issue of life and openness to discovery of new aspects of truth. The personal interest and active involvement of the learner in the matter under study is valued and fostered, and a greater variety of approaches to a question or subject is likely to be used.

Awareness of the importance of the individual as a person also has grown in recent years. This has led to a growing interest in the psychology of interpersonal relations, the personal touch, and group dynamics.

Are these trends applicable to religious education? Very much so. The God-intended nature of the church calls for a focus on the Word of truth, especially the Gospel-life significance of that which is being studied. It also requies the personal interest, involvement, understanding, and participation of the learner in the meaning of the Word under consideration.

The Mission: Life materials are being shaped by the assumption that our teaching of religion in the decades ahead must become less autocratic and more democratic, less stereotyped and more open. The spirit of the times calls for education that is less codified and more contemporary and arresting, less transmissive in the imposed sense and more dialogical and personal. Such teaching employs a variety of material (media) as resources and references and a variety of individual and group methods for student learning and doing.

PRINCIPLES RELATED TO MATERIALS

There are, of course, other educational principles that the church dare not ignore in her mission and ministry to her members or to the world. The following principles are related to materials:

Certainly there is a continuing need for Biblical content in the traditional sense—Bible history, the church year and its liturgy, and Christian doctrine taught through Biblical events, Bible verses, and creedal formulations. The Mission: Life program will continue to include Biblical history and systematic doctrinal (catechism) study in various age-level and agency programs. But the focus of concern must be on the significant Word of Law-Gospel meaning, the Word of God's judgment and grace. Factual details are important only as means of gaining an understanding of God's *truth.*

Present-day Christians are living in an increasingly secular, scientific, more educated, but at best largely humanistic world. They need to be able to think theologically on the basis of a broad and rich background of Christian education and experience. They need more than a little remembrance of some Bible story facts told and drilled by a question-answer method that neither calls for nor permits any personal thinking or creative expressions of Spirit-filled faith.

In the future perhaps more than in the past, God's people will need a serious in-depth study of the Bible and the Christian faith. They will have to be ready to give *personal* answers to contemporary personal and social issues. If these responses are to be Christian, Christians will have to give thought to the present meanings of God's truths of life.

In the church there must also be an awareness of how children and youth grow religiously. Today, for example, all educators know how important it is to have graded materials. Laws of learning and human development apply to Christian education just as much as to any other kind of human communication. This principle applies to content as well as vocabulary. As the priority of concerns and values in Christian education shifts from subject-matter goals to the learner and his spiritual life and growth, the demand for materials distinctly appropriate to the age of the learner grows.

OTHER PRINCIPLES AND CONCLUSION

The planning committee of the Mission: Life curriculum identified the following other educational principles as noteworthy:

1. Learning depends largely on the quality of relationships.

2. The leader, teacher, communicator, and his expressions and responses are highly important in Christian education.

3. Feeling and behavioral responses of a learner are as important as cognitive ("purely" intellectual) learning.

4. The arts (both their products and their activities) are powerful modes of communication.

5. For a Christian, life experiences and secular materials can be revelations of God (His presence, activity, and nature) in present, concrete forms. When used as such, they become valid content for Christian education.

6. Learning results from the process (the method and procedure) as well as the content of a lesson.

New programs are to reflect a greater concern for the learner and the workings of God's Spirit—within the learner as well as through the Word of the Scriptures. We have also said that Christian education takes place only in teacher-learner relations and actions that are in keeping with the Spirit of God and the God-intended nature of the church. This is why the Mission-

: Life materials will emphasize administrative procedures and teaching methods that lead toward the study of God's Word by both the students and the teachers.

Finally, materials are more interesting when they employ many types of media and learner-involving methods. This is why the Mission: Life program will provide many types of material. It is also a reason why guides will suggest mainly inductive, exploratory, discovery, learner-response, and expressive methods of teaching. Through such methods new materials will be more or less open-ended to allow the Spirit of God to lead the learner as well as the teacher—both by means of His Word in the materials and by the Word of faith in the learner and the teacher.

23

Religion and Education

C. D. HARDIE

INTRODUCTION

The relations between religion and education have undergone many changes in the course of the christian era. At the present time the prescription that no public funds should be used for any religious education governs the situation throughout the United States, and this means both that education in church schools must not be subsidized from public funds and that the public schools must not give religious education. At the same time it is important to remember that this has come about largely through disagreement and hostility among the churches themselves. They have been teaching inconsistent doctrines, and as at most one of a set of mutually inconsistent propositions can be true (while they may all be false), it follows that either all the churches, or all but one, are teaching some falsehoods. Now it is difficult to justify spending public money on the teaching of falsehoods, so most people are willing to accept that no public money should be spent on religious education.

This position, however, is not very satisfactory. Where there is greater religious homogeneity, as in Great Britain with an established church, the tax supported schools do give religious education and religious bodies are

C. D. Hardie is Professor of Education at the University of Tasmania. C. D. Hardie, "Religion and Education," *Educational Theory*, Vol. 18, No. 3 (Summer 1968), pp. 199–223. Used by permission of the author and *Educational Theory*.

I should like to express my warm thanks to Mr. Peter Baldino for making a number of helpful suggestions.

aided by public funds in their conduct of schools. Moreover, as a result of a growing movement towards unification among the leading churches, the climate of opinion may change in the United States. It seems to me important, therefore, that the case against religious education should be stated apart altogether from agreement or disagreement among the different churches, and I propose to argue not only that religion should have no place in education, but that it is, in a clear sense, anti-educational.

I. SUPERNATURAL RELIGION AND EDUCATION

Blessed are they that have not seen, and yet have believed.
—Gospel according to St. John

Probably religion is most often thought of as being concerned with man's thoughts, feelings and behavior in relation to the supernatural, and, as a consequence, religious education is thought to involve inculcating truths about the supernatural, and evoking right attitudes and securing appropriate behavior towards the supernatural. This clearly supposes not only that it is sensible to talk about the supernatural, but that in some sense the supernatural exists. Let us consider in more detail what this can mean.

At first we tend to think of the supernatural in the way in which it occurs in children's stories—miraculous happenings, ghosts, Santa Claus—and it is perhaps significant that so many of the churches try to start influencing children about the same time as the latter first listen to such stories. Now what meaning do children attach to Santa Claus and on what grounds do we say he doesn't exist? Most young children are quite happy to think of him as a kind old gentleman who leaves gifts for them in a stocking on Christmas morning, and the meaning they attach to God at the same age is often not very different. It is probably less specific, but He may be thought of as a kind old man who gives them what they want if they ask nicely. Now in spite of sometimes bitter disappointment, most children come to accept that Santa Claus does not "really" exist. What convinces them? It is surely just the fact that everything that happens can be explained without him.

Ghosts are a little more intractible. But stories of haunted houses have a way of dissolving into a series of ordinary, if unusual, occurrences; and I do not suppose any educated person now considers such alleged events to be unexplainable by existing knowledge.

Can any meaning then be given to the supernatural? There are, certainly, many occurrences for which at present no explanation is available in terms of our present knowledge of the facts, laws and theories of the natural sciences. Striking examples are the high energy associated with some radiation from outer space, the abnormal behavior of some human beings whom we lock up in institutions, the crossing-over of chromosomes which sometimes produces a mutant variety, and so on. If we define "natural knowledge" to be our existing knowledge of all laws and theories known in all the sciences together with the facts on which they are based, then it is true to say that there are events which at present are outside our natural knowledge. Shall we then define these events to be the region of the supernatural, and shall we say that they have to be given a supernatural explanation?

We can easily define the supernatural in this way, but there are two reasons for not allowing the use of the word "explanation." The first is that our present natural knowledge has been built up precisely by assimilating unexplained events into its structure. This may be done in various ways that are described in detail by books on the nature of the various sciences (ways such as the discovery of new laws, or the relating of previously unrelated facts by new theories). If, at the present moment, we are to say that our natural knowledge is complete and that what is unexplained is supernatural and must be given a supernatural explanation, then we should be setting up a barrier beyond which the sciences would not be allowed to progress. The second reason is, however, more fundamental. It is that such a supernatural explanation would not in fact be an explanation at all. What we have done is simply to classify events as those that are at present explainable by our existing natural knowledge, and those that are not. The latter we have then pigeonholed as suitable for supernatural explanation. But the meaning of "explanation" is in terms of the existing procedures and structures of the sciences. No meaning has been attached to "explanation" outside of this. Thus to say that some events must receive a supernatural explanation is merely to say that at present they have not received an explanation, and is a misleading way of saying this.

It follows that even if there should be some events that are essentially unexplainable by the sciences, this does not justify the use of the phrase "supernatural explanation." For example, events such as the high energy associated with some radiation from outer space may well be brought into the realm of natural knowledge before many years or even months have passed. But it might be argued that there are still, and always will be, some events that will fall outside the range of the sciences. What these events are or may be would be dangerous to say, for many events which in the past have been thought to be far beyond the range of the sciences, however advanced (for example, many of the phenomena associated with life) have already been shown to be included in our natural knowledge. But even if it is admitted, and I do not believe any grounds have been produced for admitting it, that there will always be some events essentially unexplainable by the sciences, it does not help the least little bit to talk of a supernatural explanation for them. For all this can mean is that they are not explained by the sciences, and it is surely much less misleading just to say so.

As far as man's attitude and behavior toward the supernatural are concerned, I believe that it should be at least one of respect and one even of reverence. It is not wise to be casual about what one does not understand, and therefore I agree entirely with those scientists who, although claiming to be atheists, say they have reverence for the "mystery of the universe." The amount in the universe that we cannot explain is still so colossal that it may legitimately be called a mystery and an object of reverence. But this is not to say that we should stop our efforts to understand, or that what is at present in the supernatural pigeonhole will not gradually be transferred to the natural knowledge pigeonhole.

Consequently if we think of religion as being concerned with man's thoughts, feelings and behavior in relation to the supernatural, we will have to come to the conclusion that it is a very different sort of thing from religion as it is usually described. Man's thoughts about the supernatural will all be concerned with how to include it in natural knowledge, or how to extend our existing principles of natural knowledge so as to include it. His feelings and behavior in relation to it may well be, and I think should be, humble, reverent, yet at the same time inquiring and exploratory. Indeed it can be said that the ordinary descriptions of religion are based on a mistake—the mistake of supposing that there is a domain of knowledge, feeling and behavior that is basically different from the domain of science, and not different merely in that it is in a different pigeonhole from that labeled "natural knowledge" and may at any moment be transferred to it. It is also clear that there is no case for some special subject called "religious education." For if man's thoughts, feelings, and behavior in relation to the supernatural are as I have described, then they will be trained most suitably and adequately in the classrooms and laboratories of the science teachers.

At this point it may be argued that I have defined the supernatural in a way that would be unacceptable to most Christians. Let us then forget that Christian education has traditionally linked it with unexplained events such as miraculous happenings, visions, etc., and start afresh with what the Christian calls "faith." The existence of the supernatural in the shape of a God or Gods is then one of the facts which, it is alleged, we know through faith. Faith is one of the seven cardinal virtues, and one of the three great Christian virtues of faith, hope and love. In view of its importance one would imagine that some clear statement would be available about its meaning and nature, but if so, I have failed to discover it. St. Thomas Aquinas, whose teachings are still accepted by the Roman Catholic Church as the official account of Christianity, held that lack of faith was such a serious sin that heretics and apostates should be compelled to conform—the nature of the compulsion being the threat of torture and death. The test of whether a person had faith or not seemed to be merely whether he was prepared to utter certain sentences or not.

In ordinary usage the word is closely connected with belief, particularly the favorable beliefs which we may hold about people. I may say "I don't believe it is going to rain tomorrow, for I have faith in the weather forecasters and they have prophesied a dry day." This means that, in general, I believe the weather forecasters to be accurate. Similarly, I may lend money to Smith because I have faith in him, meaning thereby that I believe Smith is a man who pays debts, and so on. We do not generally use the word in connection with unfavorable beliefs about people. If I do not believe that a released convict has reformed, I am unlikely to say that I have faith he will land back in jail. Thus having faith in someone is believing a set of propositions about him which reflect favorably on his ability or character.

Can we apply this to the religious usage? Can we say that having faith in God is believing a set of propositions about God, and because propositions about God necessarily testify to His goodness and power, the use of the word is highly appropriate? There are two reasons why this is unsatisfactory. First of all, when I talk of having faith in the weather forecasters, the beliefs which I hold about them have only a certain degree of probability. If over a long period of time I were to take note of the forecasts and were to correlate them with the weather which actually occurred, then I might be disposed to change my opinion. Under such circumstances I should say that I had lost faith in the forecasters because of the empirical evidence that I had collected. Similarly, if Smith sometimes does not pay his debts, or is slow in paying them, I may change my mind about him and say I have lost faith in him. Having faith in someone is thus holding beliefs about him which have been rendered probable by evidence from the past, but which may be rendered improbable by additional evidence. But this is not what the Christian wants at all. He thinks of faith as having beliefs independently of any evidence for them or even if there is evidence against them. Indeed, it is sometimes suggested that it is a greater virtue to have faith against the evidence than to have faith when the evidence is favorable. For example, it may be said of a Christian, whose life has always been lived in pleasant circumstances, that it is easy enough for such a person to have faith. But it is considered a much greater virtue if someone whose life has been hard and miserable has nevertheless retained his faith throughout. When, therefore, the Christian talks of faith, he does not mean belief which has been rendered probable by evidence. But what sort of beliefs are independent of evidence? Normally we call a person irrational if he holds beliefs to a degree that is not warranted by the evidence, and if the irrationality is sufficiently marked we call him insane.

What about belief in mathematical truths? Most people would now agree that mathematical propositions are independent of all empirical evidence. Does our attitude to mathematics throw any light on the Christian attitude to faith? I do not see how it can. For we know mathematical propositions to be true because they are analytic; that is, they are true in virtue of the way they have been constructed in accordance with the rules of a symbolic system. But the Christian does not mean that the knowledge he has through faith is analytically true. This can be seen easily enough by asking him if an alternative symbolism is possible. There is no necessity for us to accept mathematical propositions if we do not use the system of which they are a part. They are necessary within the system, that is all. But we could construct a different system in which the symbols are used according to different rules. But the Christian would not allow this as far as faith is concerned. Any other system would indeed be idolatrous, and, as Aquinas said, everyone should be forced to accept the system. Thus, the truths of faith are not analytic.

It seems therefore that the propositions or truths of faith are neither grounded in empirical evidence nor demonstrable from the properties of a symbolic system. This should be sufficient for them to be rejected as propositions, and if the Christian still wants to call them propositions, he has a clear obligation to indicate in what way or ways they can possibly be true or false. No one, as far as I know, has done this.

But there is a second difficulty, which seems to be equally fatal, confronting the Christian when he attempts to explain the meaning of faith in God as equivalent to believing a set of truths about God. This centers on the word "God" rather than on the word "belief." It is hardly possible to discuss religious education or the relations between religion and education without asking what role is to be assigned to propositions involving the word "God," or, to put it another way, how is the word "God" to be taught?

Just as there are two ways in which the truth or falsity of a proposition can be decided—by showing its place in the structure of a symbolic system or by empirical means—so there are two corresponding ways for teaching words to children. We may show how a word functions inside a system, or we may point to some object or event that can be perceived. For example, in the sentence "the cat sat on the mat" we can easily point to objects that the child sees for the words "cat" and "mat," and the words "sat on" can be explained in a similar way. Even the two occurrences of the word "the" in the sentence can be given a meaning, using several cats and several mats and indicating which is "the cat" and which is "the mat." All the words children learn to begin with are learned in this way. Even words like "not" and "and" can be given meaning in this way. For example, we may say to the child at tea time "the bread, not the cake" and "bread and butter."

But once children have a small stock of words then other words can be introduced by using the words they already know. Thus if the child already knows "father" and "mother," "parent" may be introduced as meaning "father or mother." Similarly, if the child already knows "brother," "uncle" can be introduced as "brother of father or brother of mother." Simple symbolic systems such as this one for dealing with relatives or the number system for dealing with counting may then be explained.

Now how is the word "God" to be taught? It is evident from what was said earlier that the teacher cannot explain it by any perceptual means. For the Christian is not prepared to tie his experience of God to any event in the natural world. Whatever may or may not be perceived is in the end irrelevant to him. Can the word be introduced by means of other words? It is clear that this can be done using traditional phrases like "the most perfect Being," "a perfectly loving and all-powerful Being," and so on. But if the word is introduced in this way, then the existence of God becomes dependent on the type of existence assigned to the defining phrase.

The real trouble facing the Christian is that he wants the defining phrase to be not only part of a symbolic system, but to have also some link with the natural world. It is easy enough to construct a language, which we can call the theological language, with a vocabulary and syntax. The vocabulary would contain, for example, words like God, spirit, grace, trinity, heaven, and the syntax would permit "God is a trinity," for example, as a correct sentence. But how is this language to have any relation to the natural world? If we say it need not have any, then theology becomes an idle game to be indulged in only by those who find it amusing. If, on the other hand, we say it has some relation, then we must link the words and sentences of the theological language with our experience of the natural world. The situation could be similar to theories in the different sciences, which are formulated in this kind of way, that is, they have a vocabulary and syntax governing the "theoretical entities." But they have also rules which if they do not link these entities directly to observable quantities in the natural world, at least show how a sentence in the theoretical language is to be correlated with what can be observed. But it is this correlation of the two languages that has always been fatal to the language of theology. Because once a scheme of correlation has been prescribed, then what happens in the world is of immediate relevance to the acceptance or rejection of the theology.

Thus the attempt to explain faith as the belief in certain propositions about God runs into fatal objections both about the word "belief" and about the word "God." Indeed there seems no way at all by which one could teach someone else what it is to have faith. Now the Christian may, as a last resort, admit this, and say that it is something which must just happen to a person. In this connection he may point out that the accounts that have been given of notable conversions, such as those of St. Paul and of St. Augustine, read indeed as if this were the case. But even this will not do. For the statement that something has just happened to him is itself meant as an empirical statement, with its own criteria for being accepted or rejected. But what are the criteria? Whatever ones are proposed the Christian would not be prepared to accept, for again they would link the experience of faith with the natural world.

We started off this section by considering religion as concerned with man's thoughts, feelings and behavior in relation to the supernatural. Religious education must then be concerned with teaching truths about the supernatural and evoking emotional and behavioral patterns appropriate to the supernatural. But two different attempts to explain this have run into hopeless difficulties, and I believe that any scheme to base religious education on such a concept of religion is doomed to failure.

At the same time I think we should go farther, and make it clear (if it is not already clear) that positive harm will accrue if religious education is planned on such a basis. For it is almost inevitable that children will be left with the idea that there are two distinct realms, the natural and the supernatural, and that whereas the former may not transgress into the latter, the latter can on occasions intrude on the former. Moreover, while the former is available for exploration both intellectually and experimentally, the latter is beyond exploration, and when known, is known by faith, revelation, insight, etc., all of which are processes of which no intelligible account has been given. The harm that this can do, and has done, to children is immense. For it encourages them to remove certain experiences from the field of publicly testable knowledge and this prevents the rational and consequently peaceful solution of many conflicts. The tragic history of religions, and particularly of Christianity, bears ample testimony to this. It is for this reason that I have called religion anti-educational.

Finally, it is perhaps desirable to point out that atheistic and agnostic teaching is subject to the same kind of difficulty. For the atheist believes that it is at least probable that God does not exist, and such a belief is open to the same sort of objections as have been argued against the belief in God's existence. The agnostic, on the other hand, is unable to make up his mind whether to believe or not to believe that God exists. It is a question on which, in his opinion, it is wise to keep an open mind. But the arguments above are just as conclusive against this position, for not only is it not a question on which we should keep an open mind, it is just not a question. The theist, the agnostic and the atheist are thus, to a certain extent, all in the same boat. What they say is not true, but it is not false either. Thus the rejection of religious teaching, when it is understood in the sense explained, does not result in a justification for atheistic or agnostic teaching.

II. NATURAL RELIGION AND EDUCATION

If we are to assume that anybody has designedly set this wonderful universe going, it is perfectly clear to me that he is no more entirely benevolent and just, in any intelligible sense of the words, than that he is malevolent and unjust.

—T. H. Huxley

There is, however, a concept of religion very different from the concept so far considered, and I want now to consider the relation of religion in this new sense with education. In this new sense the natural world is not only highly relevant but is essential to religion. It is maintained that it is from observation of features of that world that man has evolved this concept of religion and therefore it is appropriate to call it "natural religion." There are many different forms of natural religion and I shall consider only three.

In the first form it is claimed that certain objects in the natural world have characteristics that enable them to satisfy men's desires and purposes. Obvious examples are overcoats, clocks, washing machines, ball-point pens, etc. Now when any of these have been investigated, it has been found that they have been constructed sometime in the past by intelligent action. It has never been found that matter by itself, that is, without the intervention of some guiding intelligence, has taken up the form of, for example, a ball-point pen. Consequently, it is argued that the existence of what might be called "design" in the world always implies the existence of an intelligent designer. Now some things in the world exhibit design, for example, the human eye, but we know that no human intelligence has designed them. Therefore, the argument runs, we are entitled to conclude that some non-human intelligence exists and to such an intelligence we can give the name "God." The existence of God is then an inference from the existence of design in the natural world.

This argument is formally quite unsatisfactory. It consists of three interdependent arguments, one inductive and the other two deductive. The inductive one is: A, B, C, . . . exhibit design and have been found to be constructed by intelligent action. Therefore, all objects exhibiting design have been constructed by intelligent action.

The first deductive argument accepts this conclusion as a major premise, and combines it with the minor premise "x exhibits design" to give the conclusion "x was constructed by intelligent action." The second deductive argument then combines this conclusion with the empirical statement "x was not constructed by human intelligent action" to give the conclusion "x was constructed by non-human intelligent action." Now it is obvious that the empirical statement "x was not constructed by human intelligent action" is relevant to the premise on which the original inductive argument was based. This should, therefore, be reformulated as follows: Some things A, B, C, . . . exhibit design and have been found to be constructed by human intelligent action; other things x, y, z, . . . exhibit design and have been found not to be constructed by human intelligent action. But from such a premise it is clear that the required inductive conclusion cannot be drawn.

The invalidity of the argument must have been apparent to almost everyone, and yet the argument still continues to appeal to some people. I think the reason for this can be understood if I quote a kind of parable, which was originally suggested by John Wisdom, but was put into the present form by A. G. N. Flew.

'Once upon a time two explorers came upon a clearing in the jungle. In the clearing were growing many flowers and many weeds. One explorer says "Some gardener must tend this plot." The other disagrees, "There is no gardener." So they pitch their tents and set a watch. No gardener is ever seen. "But perhaps there is an invisible gardener." So they set up a barbed wire fence. They electrify it. They patrol with bloodhounds. . . . But no shrieks ever suggest that some intruder has received a shock. No movements of the wire ever betray an invisible climber. The bloodhounds never give cry. Yet still the believer is not convinced. "But there is a gardener, invisible, intangible, insensible to electric shocks, a gardener who has no scent and makes no sound, a gardener who comes strictly to look after the garden which he loves." At last the sceptic despairs. "But what remains of your original assertion. Just how does what you call an invisible, intangible, eternally elusive gardener differ from an imaginary gardener or even from no gardener at all?"[1]

Thus there is no factual difference between the believer and the sceptic, but they use two different pictures of the world. Because we know that some things that have been designed have also been intelligently constructed, the believer says that he is going to picture the construction of everything that exhibits design in the same way. It is clear that the believer is happier with this anthropomorphic picture of the world, and is prepared to adhere to such a picture even when it has become a kind of Picasso production whose representational function is zero.

The task of religious education with this type of natural religion will then be to draw attention to objects and situations in the world which appear to further man's desires and purposes. The careers of successful individuals, for example, are often pointed to, both by the individuals and by other people, as examples of designs for living. Sometimes even the disasters that befall the prodigal and the evil are regarded as part of God's plan for educating the human race. The trouble with religious education of this sort is just, of course, that it gives a very misleading picture of the world, if the picture is thought of as having any representational value. When the career of an evil Mussolini ends with a public hanging in the market place, then it is possible to say that there is a design governing human lives. But many a poor, good-living Negro has had his life ended in the same way in Mississippi. Has our world picture to show the same designer at work?

The appeal which this kind of natural religion has exercised is probably steadily diminishing at the present time. Most of the examples of objects or events that have apparently been designed, but are known to have no human designer, come from or are associated with living organisms. But ever since 1859, when Darwin first published *The Orgin of Species*, it has been possible to understand, through the ideas of random variation and natural selection, how organisms highly adapted to their environment could have evolved without the intervention of any intelligent action. The existence of an object such as a human eye, which appears to be marvelously designed for seeing, is

[1] A. G. N. Flew, "Theology and Falsification" in A. G. N. Flew and A. Macintyre (editors) *New Essays in Philosophical Theology* (Student Christian Movement Press Limited, London, 1955).

to be explained not as the product of non-human intelligent behavior, but as the product of natural selection working for hundreds of thousands of years on chance variations that occur in the genetic material that controls the development of eye cells. There is no harm in drawing the attention of children to the existence of objects and events that apparently exhibit design; this is almost bound to be an important feature of almost all early childhood education. But the very use of the term "design," which it is virtually impossible to avoid, does suggest the world picture which the believer in natural religion envisages, and this picture can be adhered to only if it is realized that it has no representational value as far as many of the "designed" objects are concerned. Moreover, when it has no representational value, then children should be encouraged to discover the factors that have been at work to produce the appearance of design.

A second form of natural religion has been based on certain feelings human beings have about their own behavior. Sometimes this is called the phenomenon of conscience; conscience being thought of as a kind of wise voice that pronounces judgment on the behavior of the body which encompasses it. Even if the phenomenon of conscience is doubted or denied, however, most people are willing to admit that they have often had feelings of, for example, remorse on looking back at periods of their own history. It may then be claimed that such feelings are directly caused by something outside of the individual which must be morally and intellectually superior to man, as it causes feelings in man that make him criticize himself. This something that is outside of man but superior morally and intellectually to him can be taken then as the definition of God.

Again this must be regarded as a weak argument. If we ask how it is known that such feelings are directly caused by something outside the individual that is morally and intellectually superior to him, the usual answer is that this is known intuitively or by instinct. This, however, is an extraordinary claim to make. The whole idea of cause and effect is notoriously vague and perhaps even unintelligible, and the more advanced sciences have long ago discarded it as an explanatory device. But even when it is retained, as it is, for example, in medicine, the establishment of the claim that "x causes y" is made only after a long series of observations and very often only after controlled experiments have been made. To claim that we know "x causes y" by some intuitive process is again to revert to an anthropomorphic picture of the world. Moreover, there is some evidence that such feelings as are associated with conscience are, if not "caused" by, at least related to environmental factors. I do not wish particularly to defend the work and theories of the psychoanalysts, nor to attribute to them opinions which may be held by only a small minority of them. But at least some of them believe, as a result of empirical evidence, that such feelings are related to the attitude which the parents exhibit towards the child in its early years. The fact that this attitude tends to follow a certain pattern in family life, at least in European and American countries, has resulted in the phenomenon of conscience being widely observed, but they would claim that it is by no means universal. In particular it has been noted that when children have been reared from an early age in a non-human environment, they exhibit no signs at all of having these feelings about their own behavior that we associate with conscience. This was true, for example, of Amala and Kamala,[2] the two Indian girls who had been suckled and brought up for some years by wolves. The frequency with which such feelings do occur among the human race may therefore be merely a reflection of the obvious fact that most children are influenced in their early lives by the attitudes of their parents. It is these, which are both loving and critical, which eventually result in the individual having those feelings about the rightness and wrongness of his behavior that we call conscience. Now whether this is an accurate account of what some psychoanalysts believe, and whether, if it is accurate, it is also true is not of particular importance for our present purpose. What is important is that it is the kind of thing which clearly could be true, and whether it is true or not could be decided only after a great deal of observation and of what is possible in the way of experiment. There is no ground at all, therefore, for saying that the phenomenon of conscience must have been caused by some moral and intellectual being, although it is true to say that it may have been caused by one or both parents who at the time were intellectually and morally superior to the child.

In any event this view of natural religion does not render possible any serious practice of religious education. For if the way to arrive at God is by instinct or intuition from our feelings of conscience, then presumably either we arrive at Him or we do not. It may be that by suitable lessons in the home and in the classroom we can provide the occasion for and aid the functioning of intuition and instinct, but in the long run there is not much we can do if a child claims to have no such intuition. The situation is rather similar to that of the geometry teacher in the old days. As Sir John Adams used to say, if after repeated assertions by the teacher, a child refused to admit that when equals are added to equals the results are equal, then all that could be done was to send the child home with a polite note to the parents informing them of the sad fact.

A third type of natural religion has been based on ethics. Ever since Plato made a study of the " Idea of the Good " the highest stage in the education of the rulers of his Republic, there have been many attempts to formulate what is often called " the supreme or ultimate Good for man." While there have been wide disagreements about the alleged nature of this Good, it has been argued that nevertheless there must exist something that is the supreme Good for all men insofar as they are rational beings. If this is so, God can be defined to be this supreme or ultimate Good, and religious

[2] A. Gessell, *Wolf Child and Human Child* (Harper, 1941).

education will then be devoted to its discovery and to the means by which individuals can realize it in their own lives.

The main argument for the existence of the supreme Good rests on the distinction, which again is at least as old as Plato, between those things that we value as a means to something else, and those things that we value for themselves. For example, it would appear as if we value an overcoat for the warmth which it gives us on a cold day; we value a soft chair for the comfort we get in sitting; we value a set of golf clubs insofar as they enable us to play golf well, and so on. But we do not value an overcoat in summer for we do not need its warmth. Thus it is not a good in itself, or good as an end, or an ultimate good. It is only a good as a means to something outside itself. On the other hand, it might be claimed that there must exist at least one thing that we value for itself and not merely as a means to something else. For if nothing existed of value in itself, then nothing could have value as a means to what is of value in itself, and we have just seen that we value many things as means. Love, for example, has at least a *prima facie* claim to have value in itself, although, of course, it sometimes has value as a means to other things such as power and wealth. Now it may be the case that if there is more than one thing which has value in itself, then all such things have some property in common. This property could be identified with God.

It is probably true that if religion is interpreted in this way, it could lead to a clear and well-defined concept of religious education. The traditional seven cardinal virtues, wisdom, courage, temperance, justice, faith, hope, and love, may all plausibly be claimed, for example, to have value in themselves and not merely as a means to something else. Lessons and exercises designed to train children in the practice of these can then be devised.

The crucial question, of course, which must be satisfactorily answered before this can properly be called religious and not merely moral education, is whether all the things that are valued in themselves have some property in common which could thus be called the supreme Good and identified with God. Some people certainly think that such a property exists and that it is this which gives meaning or purpose to life. Many educationists also who have written on the aim of education have identified it with the end for man or the supreme purpose of life. For example, Phenix defines religion as "the pattern of organization of life in relation to values regarded as ultimate,"[3] and considers that there can be no question but that everyone must have a religion. But the lack of agreement that is apparent among those who have written about such supreme or ultimate Goods must make us wonder if there is any reason to suppose that there is something common to all those things that have value in themselves. If there is, how is it supposed to be discovered? It cannot be by tracing the consequences of those different

---

[3] P. H. Phenix, "Religion in American Public Education," *Teachers College Record*, 57 (1955).

Goods, for, by hypothesis, these are things that have value in themselves, that is, apart from their consequences. It seems, therefore, that it must be by some kind of mental inspection.

But if, as may well be claimed, mental inspection shows nothing common to all those things which have been claimed to have value in themselves, then do we deny that there is a God, or do we set up many Gods, each identified with a particular Good? (For example, "money is a God to him.") I think the basic trouble with this whole approach is that the original distinction between those things that have value in themselves, and those things that are good as a means to something else, is interpreted as a classification of things in terms of properties. Having "value in itself" is regarded as a property which something may or may not possess, but if it does possess it, then it must share something in common with other things that also possess it. The analogy, which is often used, is to compare "this is good" with "this is red." It seems legitimate to say that, if we judge "x is red" and "y is red," both x and y have the same property which we call redness. Can we not similarly say that if we judge "x is good" and "y is good" that x and y share the same property "goodness"?

This view was first seriously challenged, as far as I am aware, by Ogden and Richards in *The Meaning of Meaning*. They suggested there that when I use a sentence such as "this is good," I am not using language in a descriptive or (as they said) scientific sense at all. Thus I am not attributing a property to this. Rather I am using language in an emotive way which indicates my attitude to this. The concept of emotive language, as Ogden and Richards conceived it, has probably never been adequately clarified, but for our present purposes it is sufficient to follow them in rejecting the descriptive function of "this is good." To see this, we need only ask how is such a sentence used? It is clearly used, not to state some fact which describes the world and which may be of use in science, but to indicate the result of a choice or judgment. I am asked what I think of x, how I value it, and I reply "x is good." I am not saying that x has this or that property, but I am judging it and expressing satisfaction with it.

In ordinary discourse we do not normally use such phrases as "x is the good," and once we realize this, we no longer are inclined to ask "what is the good"? or "what is the supreme Good"? We use value words like "good" to indicate that I would choose this rather than that, to show that I recommend or approve something. Now it may be objected at this point that even if this is so, I surely commend or approve something in virtue of some property it possesses and is not that property goodness? The answer to the second part of the question is in the negative. I may approve an object in virtue of some property in it, but the statement that the object has that property is a descriptive statement subject to the ordinary empirical tests of truth and falsity, while the statement that "this is good" is not subject to these empirical tests, but expresses a value judgment by me.

One of the ways in which we come to approve things or value them is by means of their effects or consequences. Indeed it is sometimes maintained that this is the only way in which we can come to make value judgments. But whether this is so or not, the original distinction that was drawn between things that have value in themselves and things that are good as a means to something else is clearly inappropriate. We express our valuations by means of sentences like "x is good," and we may give reasons for these valuations by describing the effects which follow from x or we may not. But there is no property of x described by this value judgment, and consequently any attempt to find some property common to all things that are approved is necessarily doomed to failure. *A fortiori* it must be impossible to base a religion on the existence of such a property, and we must also conclude that moral education, insofar as it may be possible, will not merge into religious education.

We have now considered three attempts to base religion and religious education on what can be observed in the natural world: (1) from the existence of design, (2) from the existence of conscience, (3) from the existence of moral judgments. We have seen that all these attempts have failed, and this may make us suspect that the task is impossible. There is one important consideration which I think shows this to be so.

All concepts of religion and of religious education, as far as I am aware, do involve judgments of value. Certain things are pronounced to be good or bad, certain actions to be right or wrong, and so on. Indeed, if the inculcation of a set of beliefs about the universe did not at the same time impose some evaluative judgments, it would not be called religion. Nor would an education which did not attempt to prescribe certain ways of behaving and forbid other ways of behaving be called religious education. But if this is so, then any attempt to define or explain religion and religious education by means of properties of the natural world must involve what has come to be known as the naturalistic fallacy.

This arises in the following way. Most of the statements that human beings make can be classified broadly in three ways: (a) as logical, (b) as descriptive, (c) as evaluative. The character of a logical statement is such that it is formally true; that is, it is true because of its form or structure and not because of its content. Statements of this kind may be taken to include not only traditional statements of logic like "no unmarried men are married" and "if all men are mortal, and Socrates is a man, then Socrates is mortal," but also the more complicated statements of pure mathematics. The truth of a descriptive statement, on the other hand, depends on its content as well as on its form. Another way of putting that is to say that its truth depends on the existence of the facts or the state of affairs which it describes. It is clear then that "truth" as applied to logical and descriptive statements means two quite different things. In the sense in which descriptive statements are true, logical statements are not true—nor, of course, are they false—for no facts are relevant to them at all.

Now what about an evaluative statement? Does it also have a special sense of truth attached to it? It is now fairly clear, I think, that it cannot be true or false in the way in which logical and descriptive statements are. For it is not true independently of its context, as are logical statements. Further, since the time of David Hume, it has been widely recognized that it is not descriptive of any state of affairs. "In every system of morality which I have hitherto met with I have always remarked that the author proceeds from time to time in the ordinary way of reasoning, and . . . makes observations concerning human affairs; when of a sudden I am surprised to find, that instead of the usual copulation of propositions, *is* and *is not*, I meet with no proposition that is not connected with an *ought*, or an *ought not*. This change is imperceptible; but is, however, of the last consequence. For as this *ought* or *ought not*, expresses some new relation or affirmation, 'tis necessary that it should be observed and explained, at the same time that a reason should be given, for what seems altogether inconceivable, how the new relation can be a deduction from others, which are entirely different from it."[4]

After the publication of G. E. Moore's *Principia Ethica* in 1903, any attempt to explain an evaluative statement (for example, an *ought* statement) by means of a descriptive statement (for example, an *is* statement), or to answer a question concerning an evaluative statement by the method of answering a question concerning a descriptive statement, has been called the naturalistic fallacy. It is a fallacy which occurs often enough not only in ordinary life, but also among workers in the social sciences. Lawyers, for example, have to be careful that the discovery and description of facts in a case are sharply separated from an evaluation of them. Teachers have to distinguish a description of a child's performance in a test from an evaluation of that performance. Psychologists should, but often do not, distinguish the descriptive and evaluative meanings of ambiguous words like "need," "guilt," "normal," "adaptation," "character." Now we can avoid the naturalistic fallacy fairly easily if we always keep in mind that an evaluative statement is essentially practical; that is, it is concerned with our choices. It functions, therefore, in an entirely different way from a descriptive statement. It may be used to commend, to command or to forbid, to express an attitude, and so on. Consequently the way of answering an evaluative question is entirely different from the way of answering a descriptive question, for there is no factual or scientific way of answering it.

Let us introduce the term "prescription" for an evaluative statement, and this will perhaps help to remove the temptation to talk of them as either true or false. Once a group of people or a society has accepted certain prescriptions, it can then be described, to some extent, by these prescriptions. Thus certain facts, such as modern warfare, may be judged as murder by a Christian community, but not by a non-Christian community, and clearly we may describe differences between communities by enumerating

<hr>

[4] David Hume, *A Treatise of Human Nature*, Book III, Part I, Section I.

the prescriptions which have been accepted by them. There is then a new temptation to ask how we judge the prescriptions themselves. We want to know, it may be said, which prescriptions are true, or what is absolutely or ultimately right? But this is a misleading question. Evaluating is a legitimate and serious business in education, in the law courts, in art galleries, and so on, but it makes sense only because a set of prescriptions has been accepted. If we try to get beyond any prescription, and ask which of them is true or what is the meaning of absolutely or ultimately right, we are forgetting the nature of an evaluative question and we fall into the naturalistic fallacy.

Now all religions which are based on properties of the natural world in the end commit this mistake. For they define God by means of features exhibited in the natural world, or at least link his Being and Attributes to such a world. Moral concepts are then defined by means of God's Attributes, and moral prescriptions become descriptive statements about God and hence about the natural world. But no prescription can be that. Thus we come to the same conclusion about religious education, when religion is interpreted as natural religion, as we did when it was interpreted as supernatural religion. Not only is it based on a mistake, but positive harm may accrue from it. For if moral prescriptions are understood as descriptive statements, then when the latter are shown to be false, the prescription is rejected. This rejection in turn is likely to influence personal and social behavior, and may lead to the kind of moral anarchy which many people claim to be characteristic of the present time.

III. CHRISTIAN ETHICS AND EDUCATION

You have made for yourself something you call a morality or a religion or what not. It doesn't fit the facts. Well scrap it. Scrap it and get one that does fit.

—Shaw

We saw in the previous section that questions of value have to be carefully distinguished from questions of fact, and consequently that questions about what is of supreme or ultimate value are misleading questions in that they assume the answer lies in some characteristic or property (natural or supernatural). But surely, it may be said, this does not mean that we cannot question value judgments. Clearly we often do question them. A non-Christian today may well question a Christian's prescription that divorce is wrong. How then do we judge between one prescription and another. We cannot say that one is more true than another, for this would mean that one describes the world more accurately than the other, but there must be reasons why we accept some prescriptions and reject others.

In one sense of the word "reason" the answer lies, of course, in the moral education we have received. The vast majority of prescriptions which we accept throughout our lives are those accepted by the majority of the community in which we live and which we have been taught to accept. But most of us do from time to time question some of these, and we probably reject some and substitute others. Occasionally people will change radically, perhaps by some "conversion," and then they may discard almost all the prescriptions that they have accepted until that time, and accept new ones. In such cases they adopt, as we say, a new way of life. Now is the questioning of prescriptions, with the subsequent rejection of some and acceptance of others, a reasonable process? Can our choices, in other words, be rationally justified?

The answer to this depends on what we are prepared to allow as rational justification. The rational justification of logical and mathematical statements is the proof by which they are connected to the postulates in some symbolic system. The rational justification of factual statements is empirical evidence. It is certainly not obvious that either of these is appropriate to the acceptance and rejection of prescriptions. Nevertheless we do often talk of wise and foolish choices. Is there any rational basis for this?

I think there are two ways in which we often attempt to justify some prescription. One way is by showing that it is in accord with some more general prescription which is itself acceptable, and the other way is by showing what the consequences will be if we act on it. For example, if A dislikes B, I may say to A that he ought to be kind to B, and justify this prescription on the ground that we ought to love our enemies. Alternatively, I may attempt to justify it on the ground that if he does show kindness to B that may result in a change in B's behavior and attitude, so that A may in fact come to like him. Both these procedures provide what may reasonably be called "justification." If a principle, which is really just a more general prescription, is appealed to, then it must in turn be one that is accepted; similarly the alleged consequences to which appeal is made must be welcomed. If A does not want to like B under any circumstances, there is little point in urging him to do something that will have the consequences of making him like him.

Now although there are these two ways of justifying our acceptance of prescriptions, the second, or the appeal to consequences, is the more fundamental. If we appeal to a principle, that is, a more general prescription, then we can be asked why do we accept it? We may then appeal to a still more general prescription, but in the long run we have to justify it also by an appeal to consequences. It is this working out of the consequences of an action which has been prescribed that provides for the place of reason in moral choice. Our choices are "reasonable" then, in this second sense of "reason" if the prescriptions which we accept lead, when applied, to consequences that we accept.

We are now in a position where we can consider a third possible account of religious education. This makes no attempt to base it on the properties of either the supernatural or the natural world. Instead it bases it on the Bible, and in particular on the New Testament. Moreover, it ignores large parts of these and concentrates solely on the ethical teaching given. If such teaching is called Christian Ethics, then this view says that religious education should consist in the teaching of Christian Ethics. It should be admitted, I think, that such teaching may not be regarded by many Christians as the most important message of the Bible, for they would consider it to be merely a consequence of the theological revelations disclosed therein. But in view of the arguments in the first section, we cannot accept such a basis for religious education. But we can now examine the questioon whether, if religious education is identified with the teaching of Christian Ethics, there are grounds for including it in the school curriculum.

There are two preliminary difficulties that I must first say something about. There seems little doubt that as far as ethical teaching is concerned, the Bible is sometimes inconsistent. In particular, some of the teaching in the Old Testament is inconsistent with some of the teaching in the New Testament. Let us assume, therefore, that where there is inconsistency the New Testament account is the one that is to be accepted. A second difficulty is more serious. It may be questioned whether there is anything that could be called an ethical system in the Bible or in the New Testament. This may surprise some people, for we often hear or read things which would make it appear as if everyone knows what Christian Ethics are. It may be said, for example, that Christian Ethics are being threatened today by atheism, by humanism, by secularism, by the advance of science, by communism, by the welfare state, by public education, by psychiatry, and perhaps by a dozen other things. It may well be that any or all of these are true, but what is it that is being threatened?

Is it even correct to say that the Bible, or the New Testament, does teach a system of ethics? It seems to me very doubtful if it is. The New Testament is primarily, I take it, a record of the life, and of some of the effects of that life, of a very exceptional individual. But Jesus clearly did not regard himself as teaching a system of ethics. He was undoubtedly a teacher, but he regarded his teaching as teaching about God, and what he said about man's behavior is, in general, consequential to that. What makes some people so confident that there is a system of Christian Ethics is that they identify it with what they claim to know by their conscience or by intuition or by instinct. But all that the latter can tell a man, if anything, is the set of prescriptions which he is prepared to accept. It cannot tell him anything about other people; still less can it tell him what is recorded in the New Testament. Thus the only basis for asserting that there is a system of Christian Ethics is study and investigation of the New Testament itself, and as far as I can see it is somewhat doubtful if the ethical teaching in it is sufficiently clear and comprehensive to be called a system.

Having expressed these doubts, let us nonetheless assume that there is a system of Christian Ethics to be obtained from the New Testament, and that this is to be the content of religious education in schools. Can we accept this entirely, or only with some qualifications, or not at all? The reasons for the acceptance of any such system—the system being a set of value prescriptions—are, I have suggested, either more general prescriptions or the consequences that are likely to follow the implementation of the prescriptions.

What then are the most important prescriptions that we find in the New Testament? Different people will have different opinions on this, and such disagreement is evidence for doubting that there is any system at all, but I am going to propose the following ten principles or prescriptions as representative. I do not wish for a moment to suggest that they exhaust the ethical teaching of the New Testament, nor do I wish to suggest that they are mutually independent.

(1) We ought to love our fellow man, even to the extent of loving our enemies. "Love your enemies, do good to them that hate you, bless them that curse you, pray for them that despitefully use you." (Gospel according to St. Matthew, Chapter V.)

(2) We ought to be merciful, gentle, humble. "Blessed are the merciful, for they shall obtain mercy"; etc. (Gospel according to St. Matthew, Chapter V.)

(3) We ought to be generous. "Give to everyone that asketh thee, and of him that taketh away thy goods ask them not again." (Gospel according to St. Matthew, Chapter V.)

(4) We ought to treat other men as ourselves. "As ye would that men should do to you, do ye also to them likewise." (Gospel according to St. Matthew, Chapter VII.)

(5) We ought to be tolerant and forgiving. "How often shall my brother sin against me, and I forgive him? As many as seven times?" Jesus said, "I do not say to you seven times, but seventy times seven." (Gospel according to St. Matthew, Chapter XVIII.)

(6) We ought not to be critical or to judge other people. "Judge not, that ye be not judged." (Gospel according to St. Matthew, Chapter VII.)

(7) We ought to repent for our sins. "Repent, for the kingdom of heaven is at hand." (Gospel according to St. John, Chapter IV.)

(8) We ought not to be deterred in anything we believe right by the disapproval of others. "Blessed are ye when men shall revile you, and persecute you, and shall say all manner of evil against you falsely." (Gospel according to St. Matthew, Chapter V.)

(9) We ought not to resist evil with force. "To him that smiteth thee on the one cheek, offer also the other, and from him that taketh away thy cloak, withhold not thy coat also." (Gospel according to St. Matthew, Chapter V.)

(10) We ought to be poor. "Blessed are the poor." (Gospel according to St. Matthew, Chapter V.) "Do not lay up for yourselves treasures upon earth." (Gospel according to St. Matthew, Chapter V.)

The reasons Jesus gives for accepting these prescriptions are, in the main, theological and are therefore not valid for us. But it may still be wise to accept them, even if the original reasons given for them are invalid. Can we find reasons for accepting them, and for admitting religious education if defined as the teaching of these ten? To do this I have suggested that we should consider the consequences if the prescriptions were acted on in our present society and then judge if these consequences are acceptable.

As far as my own choices are concerned, I should be prepared to accept (1) and (2) without reservation if the terms are understood in any ordinary sense, and I shall say no more about them. I should say that (3), (4), and (5) can be accepted with some slight reservations; that (6), (7), and (8) can, with some slight reservations, be rejected; and that (9) and (10) can be rejected without any reservation.

As far as (3) is concerned, while I accept that it is good for everyone to be generous, I should draw the line somewhat before " Give to everyone that asketh thee." Sometimes the worst thing we can do for a person is to give him what he asks.

(4) is often called the Golden Rule, and is in general an excellent prescription to accept. On the other hand, there must be some limitations imposed in its application. If A and B are both in love with the same girl and are competing for her favors, A may wish that B would treat him as the victor and retire, but I do not see that that imposes an obligation on A to retire.

(5) is also a good prescription, but I should again draw the line somewhat before the time recommended, or at least be prepared to consider drawing the line earlier if the circumstances seemed to demand it.

My opposition to (6) is based on the fact that in our society at the present time, some people must be critical of others. Our standards of health, education, justice, for example, can be maintained only if some of us are trained to criticize and judge others, and are also given the power to enforce our criticism. Again, improvement of standards in most of the arts is dependent on active and informed criticism. Thus, I should reject this prescription, although I agree that there is a limited sphere of experience in which it could be usefully accepted.

On the whole, I think that (7) should be rejected. If we interpret a sin as the violation of some of the prescriptions which we have accepted, then I agree that some remorse and self-examination is a good thing, and if this is all that is entailed, I should have no quarrel. But if repentance, as it often is, is regarded as an exaggerated form of remorse, accompanied perhaps with some public admission, then I should reject the prescription.

My ground for rejecting (8) is that, if it is assumed that most people can be regarded as reasonable beings, then there must be some plausibility that their disapproval in any given case is soundly based. I agree with the prescription that the disapproval of others should in the end not *prevent* a man doing something which he judges to be right, but it should make him have second thoughts on the matter, and to that extent should *deter* him.

Probably few prescriptions from the New Testament or from anywhere else have been debated more frequently than (9). Because some form of Christianity has become the official religion in many countries, or if it is not the official religion, is at least the religion of the governing classes, it appears to be inconsistent for such countries to wage even a defensive war. On the contrary, however, the history of many of these countries is a terrible record of offensive as well as defensive wars, and these have continued almost unbroken from the earliest times up to and including the present. In Great Britain, for example, the sovereign is head of both the Church of England and the armed services, and no one has satisfactorily explained how she can be both, if the Church of England accepts this prescription. For the only justification for the existence of the armed services is acceptance of the prescription that evil, in the form of aggression, and particularly "unjustified" aggression, should be resisted with force. There have been attempts to "reinterpret" the prescription, so that, for example, it applies to individuals only and not to national states. But again no one has explained how it is possible for a state to resist evil with force, while no individual in the state uses force. In any event, reinterpretation of the New Testament prescriptions cannot be allowed. For what is to guide the reinterpretation? If we are to be allowed to reinterpret what is in the New Testament in accordance with our own conscience or intuition, then why not rely on these in the first place? There is clearly no need for the New Testament if what it says is to be judged and interpreted in the light of prescriptions that have some other source. Thus if religious education is to mean the teaching of the prescriptions that are in the New Testament, then our source of these must be the New Testament, and not some individual's reinterpretation of it.

If we take the prescription as it stands, then it seems to me we should reject it. This does not mean that I am opposed to pacifism in the national or international sphere. The acceptance or rejection of that is surely an extremely complicated matter, and one about which it is probably best to make no prescriptions at all, but to decide each separate issue on its merits. Gandhi's non-resistance movement, for example, triumphed against the British in India, but it could well be disputed that it would have triumphed against Hitler or Stalin. Whether a similar movement by the Negroes in the southern states of the USA will eventually succeed is also a matter of doubt, although it has probably already done more for them in five years than had been accomplished in the previous fifty. But the prescription as it stands, while it certainly endorses pacifism and to that extent I am not opposed to it, goes much farther. For it says that no act of evil should be resisted with force. This to me is incredible, and should at once be rejected. Should we make no attempt to force a bully to stop torturing a young child? Should we allow any criminal to commit what acts of violence he chooses, without even any attempt to prevent or resist him? The only argument that I know of which supports the prescription is that when confronted with non-resistance the aggressor will be shamed into changing his behavior, and that this effects a permanent change in his character. If, on the other hand, we merely force him to stop, we do not succeed in changing him at all, and merely defer the outbreak of aggression to some more suitable time and place. In some cases I believe this is a true analysis. But there are many individuals, unfortunately, who would not be shamed when confronted with non-resistance, but who would instead grasp the opportunity to inflict more cruelty unimpeded. The amount of cruelty inflicted on children and animals throughout the world is surely sufficient proof of that. Thus I can see nothing to justify the acceptance of this prescription.

The prescription enjoining poverty (10) I should also reject. With the possible exception of the previous one about non-resistance to evil, I think this one has caused more argument and more soul-searching than anything else in the New Testament. Again, as with the previous one, attempts have been made to reinterpret it, but these must be rejected for the same reason as before. Indeed there is probably no theme to which Jesus returns more often than this one—that a good life can be lived only in the absence of material wealth.

To some extent this need not be regarded as peculiar to Christian teaching. When Plato described his ideal state in the *Republic*, he insisted that the best people in it, who were to be the administrators, must live together in a small communistic type of community. In this not only would they not possess private property, but wives would be held in common, and they would not know their own children. These drastic regulations indicate the danger of corruption which Plato believed attached to any form of ownership. Similarly, the early revolutionaries in Russia believed that if they could abolish private property, then the most important step would have been taken to create the conditions necessary for a good life. What certainly impressed Plato, and what may well have impressed Jesus is that it is about our personal belongings that our emotions are most easily aroused. Plato considered emotions to be dangerous at any time, and so dangerous for people in positions of power that he was prepared to take all the precautions he could think of to prevent his rulers being exposed to situations where they could be aroused. In furtherance of this, he was even prepared to expel Homer from their education and to ban all artists from the state. While this was proably quite logical for Plato, who valued reason above everything else, it is not so easy to understand why Jesus should distrust the emotions, for he taught that love was the most important virtue. But whatever the reason, there is no doubt at all that Jesus insists on poverty as a condition of the good life.

Such a prescription has, I think, to be rejected. It is clear that if it were put into practice by anything more than a small minority of our present population, not only would our existing way of life be destroyed, but many people would die of starvation. This would be so not only in Europe and America, but throughout large parts of Asia and Africa as well. If everyone were to resolve to be poor, then the demand for all goods and services, not directly involved in providing food, clothing and shelter, would wither and die, so that almost all our industrial and commercial enterprises would collapse. Now the proportion of our population, who are directly involved in producing food, clothing and shelter, is quite small, so that a large proportion would be thrown out of work and be unable to buy even the necessities of life. The situation would be much grimmer than the worst economic depression imaginable. Whether it is a good thing or not, the fact is that our existing way of life depends very much on the stimulation of consumption, so that people buy more and more goods and thereby create the demand for more and more production. But this creates an affluent rather than an impoverished society. The devout Christian may say that this is all wrong, and that it would be a good thing if our present form of civilization was destroyed. But few people at the present time genuinely accept that, and I think wisely so. For a prescription that would lead to such a revolution and to such destruction of life is surely to be rejected.

Even if we were to agree that our present civilization is thoroughly bad, and shut our eyes to the loss of life that would ensue in the change to such a radically different kind of life, it still seems to me that the New Testament prescriptions about wealth are wrong. "Take no thought for the morrow." This is consistent with the prescription that we should be poor, and suggests that not only should we not try to avoid poverty, but that we should be deliberately improvident. How Jesus imagined that everyone in a community could live in this way is hard to understand. Some individuals may accept the prescription and survive in our present society, but they do so because other individuals do not accept the prescription and create wealth which supports them. But why should we attempt to justify what amounts to a parasitical life?

Most Christians, at least in comparatively recent times, have apparently just ignored this prescription. Practically all the Christian Churches, and particularly the Roman Catholic Church, are enormously wealthy, and in most European and American countries church members tend to come from the middle and upper classes in an economic sense rather than from the poorer classes. How this is reconciled with the New Testament teaching about poverty is never explained.

It will be obvious from the last few paragraphs that, as far as my own choices are concerned, there is about as much to be said against the ten prescriptions as in favor of them. If, therefore, religious education is identified as the teaching of Christian Ethics, and if the latter can be identified, or at least represented by the prescriptions I have listed, then I can see little in balance to favor it.

It is true that some of its prescriptions are of great value, while others appear to be definitely harmful. But there is, in addition, one great disadvantage to this whole approach to religious education. It assumes, implicitly, if not explicitly, that all moral teaching is a matter of what is laid down in the New Testament. I agree that this need not be so. But few Christians would be willing to assert that Christian Ethics are not competent to deal with modern social and personal problems, and if they are competent then the solution to our ethical problems today must be obtained from reading the New Testament. Now the New Testament just does not give prescriptions that can, in any honesty, be said to deal with things like gambling, communism, capital punishment, birth control. How then are moral problems about these to be decided? I have suggested earlier that we make our decisions, insofar as they are rational, in two ways. Either we bring our judgment under some more general prescription which we accept, or we work out the consequences of acting on any proposed prescription. But if children are taught that the way to decide moral issues has been laid down in the New Testament, they are then left unprepared and unable to reach a wise decision in such situations. It seems clear that children should be taught from the beginning how to solve their moral problems, and they should be taught to apply this method in judging the prescriptions laid down in the Bible as in any other book.

This brings me to what is, I think, the worst feature of Christian Ethics—it attaches very little value to the use of reason. Indeed it would not be unfair to say that it attaches no value at all. This was probably deliberate on the part of Jesus, who attempted instead to show the value of Faith. It is nowhere made clear, as I indicated earlier, what this means, but it has been taken to imply at least that we should accept uncritically the prescriptions laid down by Jesus and not attempt to use our reason to decide moral problems. It is little wonder then that many Christians today find themselves completely bewildered in trying to resolve problems that are arising all the time in their personal, social and political lives. Even the Roman Catholic Church is, if one may judge from newspaper reports, confused and uncertain on the morality of contraception.

Our examination of religious education has thus brought us to a completely negative conclusion. Although it has been interpreted in three quite different ways, we have not been able to find any justification for it in even one of these three ways. There remains, however, what might be called a thoroughly pragmatic argument for it, although I do not want to suggest that such an argument has in fact been advanced by those who profess to be pragmatists.

It is sometimes claimed that religious education (in which sense is not specified, but for the argument it does not matter) has brought immense comfort to millions of people, and it is, therefore, not only foolish to attempt to do without it, but also wicked. The question whether it has brought such comfort or not is clearly an empirical question, and the answer may be affirmative, although I think it is important to remember the other side of the picture as well. For certainly an immense amount of suffering and cruelty has also been inflicted on the world by religious education, both the Roman Catholic and Protestant churches having imposed drastic penalties on those who refused to conform to the education prescribed.

But suppose we shut our eyes to the other side and consider only the comfort which has been brought. This does not seem to me to provide justification at all, for I do not accept that the provision of comfort is a valid aim in teaching. Socrates is alleged to have described his function as a teacher as being to "arouse, persuade and rebuke," and in this there is no mention of providing comfort. Nor does Jesus suggest at any time, so far as I know, that his teaching is likely to do so. Still less, surely, can the provision of comfort be regarded as a teacher's aim, if it is achieved by falsehood or error of any kind. Now if the arguments which I have tried to outline are sound, it could only be achieved in this way. Indeed the very proposal that religious education should be retained because of the comfort which it may bring to people is unworthy, and degrades it to the level where it deserves the jibe of Marx about being the opiate of the people.

C. Ends

Throughout the course of Western thought, the goals or aims of education have been of concern to philosophers. Although philosophers are probably not better able than others to define the course that education should take, philosophers, from Socrates to the present, have nevertheless offered ends for education or have criticized the goals that others have advocated or accepted. Yet, in spite of this long and continuous debate, complete agreement has not been reached on the ends of education and it is not likely that agreement will be reached for the reasons discussed in Part Three. The selection of ends for education thus remains as yet another recurring normative issue.

The final chapters consider the ends of education from three different viewpoints. Robert Maynard Hutchins describes the educated man as he is viewed by a classical humanist. In a far more pragmatic vein, Daniel J. Coffey catalogues the activities of those persons who survive and thrive in our society. In the last chapter, Rosecranz Baldwin humorously discusses the possible influence that a broad general education might have on business management in this nation.

24

Locksley Hall:
A College of the Future

ROBERT MAYNARD HUTCHINS

I have thought that instead of presenting an article of my own, I might offer here the annual report of the Chairman of the Faculty of Locksley Hall for the year 1988–89.

The report begins:

To the Board of Visitors of Locksley Hall:

As the elected representative of the faculty, I have the honor to submit its report for the year 1988–89. At this time, which marks the expiration of my five-year term and the end of the first 25 years of the College, it seems appropriate to review the history of the College since its foundation. This will necessarily involve some account of the origins and progress of the state of Rancho del Rey.

As is well known, the state of Rancho del Rey originated in the gift to the public by the owners of the King Ranch in Texas of 100,000 square miles. The reason for the gift was that the owners of the ranch had become convinced that the development of people was more important than that of animals. They therefore determined to provide a refuge for those who could

Robert Maynard Hutchins is Chief Executive Officer of the Fund for the Republic. Robert M. Hutchins, "Locksley Hall: A College for the Future," *School and Society*, Vol. 87, September 12, 1959, pp. 334–338. Used by permission.

Address to the Conference on the Shape of a College for the Future, Miami University, Oxford, Ohio, April 18, 1959.

not face the prospect of having their children go through the American educational system, but who did not wish to secede from the Union. Two conditions were attached to the gift. First, the land was to be organized into a state in accordance with the provisions of the treaty between the Republic of Texas and the United States. Second, American women of child-bearing age who had children under 12 were to have priority in gaining entrance to and owning land in the new state. Those who were married were permitted to bring their husbands with them if they wished.

The financial resources of the donors were such that they easily persuaded the legislature of Texas to see the merits of their plan, and since both houses of Congress had for many years been controlled by residents of Texas, no difficulty was experienced in Washington. President Stevenson signed the measure on Christmas Day, 1964, and Rancho del Rey was admitted to the Union on January 1, 1965. Immigration began at dawn the next day, and our state, which was formerly occupied by a few cowboys and a couple of million cattle, is now the most densely populated in the Union, having passed Rhode Island in 1975. As loyal Americans we hope that the depopulation that has taken place in other states will prove to be only temporary.

It cannot be too often emphasized that Locksley Hall is only one unit in the educational system of Rancho del Rey and that its dependence on the other units in the system is complete. For example, the average student at Locksley Hall finishes his formal liberal education at the age of 18. This would not be possible in the three years ordinarily spent here if it were not for the organization of the six-year elementary schools and three-year high schools of this state. On the other hand, 50% of our graduates go on to the University, and this would not be possible if it were not for the recognition by the University that liberal education is the best preparation for professional study and research. If I may be pardoned a personal word, I may say that one of the most moving experiences of my life was that day 1967 on which the Cosmological Faculty of the University, at the insistence of the sub-faculty in medicine, voted down special requirements in mathematics and science for entrance to medical work and decided to admit applicants on the basis of their fulfillment of the requirements of Locksley Hall in liberal education.

First, then, Locksley Hall has flourished because of the excellence of the educational system of which it is a part. A second reason for its success is that there never has been any doubt about its own role in the system. It is devoted solely to liberal education, the education that every citizen ought to have. In the schools and colleges of Rancho del Rey vocational training is unknown. The constant acceleration of technology since the '50's and the steady reduction in the working week to the present 20 hours have made direct preparation for earning a living in the educational system an obvious absurdity. In this state young people are trained for jobs on the job. The object of the educational system is to teach them what they cannot learn on the job—how to be citizens and human beings. As the Commanding Officer of the United Nations Police Force, Chief John Eisenhower, has nobly said, "The one certain calling is citizenship; the one certain destiny is manhood."

Locksley Hall has no departments. All members of the faculty are expected to be able to give instruction in all the subjects studied in the College. It has, however, three divisions. In addition to the division devoted to the instruction of youth, it has a division for the preparation of teachers and one for the education of adults.

Among the many blessings conferred upon us by the Founding Fathers of Rancho del Rey, the constitutional prohibition against academic degrees must come high on the list. The statutory prohibition of schools of education has proved equally valuable. The two together have meant that in this state it has been possible to educate teachers. In the early days there were fears of a teacher shortage; but they did not materialize. Every intelligent man and woman teaching in the United States started for Rancho del Rey as soon as the state was opened up to settlement. In the effort to establish their priority, many of these teachers adopted children under 12, and I regret to say that one distinguished male scholar from Columbia was detected at the border disguised as a pregnant woman. Candor compels me to add that teachers' salaries in Rancho del Rey have always been somewhat higher than elsewhere. This is because of the constitutional provision known as the General Motors Index, which stipulates that the compensation of teachers must always be equal to that of junior executives in that great corporation.

A powerful inducement to teachers to join the faculty of Locksley Hall is the complete independence and freedom that we enjoy. Locksley Hall has no president and no board of trustees. The Board of Visitors has no power; the faculty of the College has the legal as well as the moral responsibility for its management. The faculty is aware, however, that all bodies of privileged persons inevitably tend to deteriorate and therefore welcomes the public and private criticism that the Board has lavished upon it in the last 25 years. The faculty knows that its rejection of many of the recommendations of the Board would have provoked, in lesser men, some feelings of resentment. The principle that management is the function of the faculty and criticism the function of the Board is now established, and all parties are agreed that it must remain forever inviolate.

It must be added that the freedom we enjoy is accompanied by a responsibility we did not expect. It is very convenient to have somebody else to blame. Here at Locksley Hall we of the faculty can blame nobody but ourselves. We cannot evade the consequences of our weakness and self-seeking by relying on the President or the Trustees to save us from them, and we are denied the consolation of attributing whatever anybody in or out of the College does not like about it to the arrogance of the administration and the stupidity of the Board. In the early years of the College some of my older brethren, who had been brought up under a different system, felt so uncomfortable when called upon to cast votes for which they would be held responsible that they echoed the cry of the ancient Israelites, "Give us a King to rule over us." Fortunately, wiser counsels prevailed. We have been much assisted by the fact that we have no departments and no academic ranks. These fruitful sources of group bickering and individual animosity being absent, we have been able to think for an increasing part of the time when we are together about what is good for the College and for the community. But it is no use denying that the path has been a hard one. We record again our gratitude to the Board of Visitors for helping us to be better than we otherwise would have been.

The number of teachers required in Rancho del Rey was small in proportion to the population because the number of subjects taught was somewhat less than a third of the number taught in other states. My great predecessor, the first Chairman of the Faculty, had emblazoned on the walls of the senior common room as a constant reminder to us all the words of Sir Richard Livingstone: "The good schoolmaster is known by the number of valuable subjects he declines to teach." The excellence of the elementary and secondary schools and the fact that students do not come to us until they have passed the examinations in these schools mean that Locksley Hall never has had to offer remedial work in Greek or Latin, to say nothing of mathematics or English. The students arrive at our gates prepared to go on with these subjects and to add to them the exploration of the world of ideas, which is, of course, their main business with us. These limitations on the number of subjects taught have made possible the level of teachers' salaries that the General Motors Index requires.

Of course, a good deal of re-training was necessary to permit our educational system to absorb the teaching immigrants to whom I have referred. Most of them never had had any liberal education. By the use of films, television (open and closed circuit), and the teaching machines invented by B. F. Skinner, we were able to expedite this process.

Today prospective teachers at Locksley Hall get a liberal education. They then go on to the University to study one or more of the three fields to which the University confines itself—theology, cosmology, and law. Thereafter, they work here as apprentice teachers with the more experienced members of the staff. Every seminar and discussion group at Locksley Hall has two teachers—a senior and a junior member of the faculty. The teachers learn to teach by teaching.

The constitutional prohibition of academic degrees has had one incidental benefit: commencement exercises are unknown in Rancho del Rey. At no time, therefore, is a citizen of this state given the impression that he has completed his education. The state is a community learning together, and the citizen is expected to keep on learning throughout his life. This is why the curriculum of Locksley Hall could remain simple and clear: the

College has been under no pressure to teach every young student everything that he might need to know at later stages of his career. The aim of the College is to teach the student what he needs to know in order to keep on learning, to awaken his interest in continued learning, and to train him in the habits that will help him to learn whatever he wants to learn.

Locksley Hall is the realization of the ambition that Woodrow Wilson expressed just 80 years ago. He said, "Here is the key to the whole matter: the object of the college . . . is not scholarship . . . but the intellectual and spiritual life. Its life and discipline are meant to be a process of preparation, not a process of information. By the intellectual and spiritual life I mean the life which enables the mind to comprehend and make proper use of the modern world and all its opportunities. The object of a liberal training is not learning, but discipline and the enlightenment of the mind. . . . What we should seek to impart in our colleges, therefore, is not so much learning as the spirit of learning. You can impart that to young men; and you can impart it to them in the three or four years at your disposal." Having acquired this spirit, the 50% of our graduates who do not go on to the University are expected, like the other citizens of this state, to enroll in discussion groups in which their intellectual interests and capacities may develop. The faculty of Locksley Hall organizes such groups for adults of this community who wish to continue their liberal education.

In the educational system of Rancho del Rey, time-serving and the accumulation of credits are unknown. Goals are set up for the students to reach. The examinations determine whether or not he has reached them. The student may present himself for the examinations whenever he is ready to do so. If he fails, he may take them again. The chronological age of students and what used to be called their "adjustment to the group" are matters of supreme indifference to everybody, including the student himself and his contemporaries. I have said that in Rancho del Rey the elementary school takes six years and the high school and the college three years each. But these are statements of averages. The goals having been set by the teaching staff, it was found that in the ordinary case six years of instruction prepared the pupil for the examinations of the elementary school, three years for the high school, and three years more for the college. As far as Locksley Hall is concerned, 10% of our students graduate in less than three years, and 10% in more. Eighty per cent take the average time.

The goal that was set for the students of Locksley Hall was the acquisition of that education which in the opinion of the faculty was necessary for a free man in a free society. It cannot be too strongly insisted that the educational program of Locksley Hall was designed for everybody and that experience has shown that it can be mastered by everybody, though at different rates of speed. If there is one thing that the history of Locksley Hall demonstrates, it is that the ancient American doctrine that the course of study must be trivial and the life of the student frivolous because most young people cannot be interested in anything important is as fallacious as it was popular. The Latin motto of the Students' Association of Locksley Hall is *sero sed serio*—we may be young, but we are in earnest.

All citizens of Rancho del Rey are expected to achieve the education that is offered by Locksley Hall. Although the intellectual attainments of the people of this state are clearly higher than those of any other, there is no evidence that their native capacities exceed those of persons born elsewhere. Since the founding of this country, experience everywhere has shown that the young American will respond to the best that can be offered him. The reason he has been offered in some places less than the best is that his elders do not want to take the trouble to find out what the best is or to find out how it may be effectively offered. We have known, moreover, since the time of Plato that what is honored in a country will be cultivated there. The state of Rancho del Rey was established in honor of the human mind. It was to be a community learning together. The culture of this state, therefore, supports at every point the serious intellectual purpose of the educational system of this state.

To descend to a more practical level, consider, if you will, the effect upon the interests and, hence, upon the development of the young of a system in which everybody has studied or is studying the same things and has a common language and a common stock of ideas. At Locksley Hall, for example, the faculty and all the students have followed or are following the same prescribed curriculum and are discussing the issues it raises throughout their waking hours. The multiplication of the power of the individual through the support of the academic community is added to the multiplication of this power that comes from the support of the larger community outside. We are perfectly prepared to believe that students who have succeeded with us would have failed elsewhere. We suggest, as Edward Gibbon did long ago, that like conditions produce like effects.

The conditions obtaining in Rancho del Rey have made it, as everybody knows, the cultural center of the world. The head of the Chinese delegation to the United Nations remarked last year that Peking even today had not achieved the beauty, serenity, and vitality of our capital, and the President of Greece has applied to our state the words in which Pericles described his native city. The principal newspapers, publishing houses, magazines, dramatic groups, film studios, and television networks now have their headquarters here. The leading artists, writers, musicians, scientists and scholars of the world now reside among us.

But it would be selfish of us to be concerned only with the happiness of our own state. In every walk of life the citizens of Rancho del Rey and the graduates of Locksley Hall—the oldest of whom are now about 40—are making a world-wide contribution. It often has been remarked that it is fortunate the graduates of Locksley Hall are not much interested in making money, because their equipment is such that if they wanted to, they would make all the money there was. In the professions, in politics, and in business they have distinguished themselves, earning the affection of their alma mater and the admiration of their fellow citizens.

The period through which we lived in the '40's, '50's, and early '60's of this century is now commonly called the Age of Illusion. It was a period in which things were not what they seemed, or at least not what we said they were. At this epoch Americans were in the habit of saying one thing and believing another and thinking one thing and doing another. Numerous efforts were made to repeal the Law of Contradiction. The fact was that our situation had changed too fast for our ideas. The result was that we could offer no rational explanation for much that we did. For example, we had an economic theory built on the mindless mechanism of the market and a political theory based on the conception of the night watchman state. When these theories appeared inapplicable and unworkable in an advanced industrial society, we had no guide to intelligent action. The educational system of those days was suitable to the production of consumers, jobholders, objects of propaganda, and statistical units. The universities were not centers of independent thought. They appeared designed for vocational certification and highly specialized research. In their never-ending quest for money, they felt compelled to sell themselves to the highest bidder. Instead of enlightening the society, particularly about its own shortcomings, they flattered it. Hence, they flattered and perpetuated its illusions.

The era that now seems to be dawning will be called, we hope, the Age of Reason. The change began with the end of the Cold War and the transfer of all weapons to the United Nations 15 years ago. That made it possible for us to begin to think what we were doing and to reflect at last in a rational way about how we might use our resources for the benefit of our fellow citizens in America and throughout the world. The change has been accelerated by the example of the State of Rancho del Rey and by the work of its people. In this change, Locksley Hall is proud to have played a modest part.

25

The Function of Education in Our American Democracy Today: A Point of Departure

DANIEL J. COFFEY

An American with some teaching experience and a passing penchant for improving education is likely to subject his friends to periodic, well-meaning, pious platitudes about what education in our society should be. He is also likely to codemn himself to sporadic periods of depression as a result of thinking about setting goals for our schools. For even a few steps into this arena leaves the participant sinking into a morass of learning theories, personal insights, biases, bureaucratic mazes, myths, and political maneuverings.

But despite the difficulties involved, it is becoming increasingly clear that we must (albeit humbly) try to make sense of our education and give direction to our schooling operation. The most immediate reasons for such an endeavor are:

(a) The operation of schooling devours much of our time, money, and irreplaceable human energies.

Daniel J. Coffey is Vice-President, Educational Research, Kenneth Boyer Associates, Inc., Deerfield, Illinois and Director of Institutional Research at Central YMCA Community College, Chicago. Especially prepared for this edition.

(b) Formal education has an impact (albeit less than we have sometimes thought) upon individuals in that it help to decide who will enjoy the good life and what the good life will mean.

(c) We recognize intuitively that schools can help individuals to become participating members in our democracy.

(d) We are awakening to the fact that the schools should be accountable to the larger population usually referred to as "the community," and we must decide what we will ask them to be accountable for.

But two grave problems face anyone trying to get beyond his own platitudes:

(a) Where should one begin to generate goals that will define the function of education?

(b) How can one find a practical (leading to action) point of departure that is also global? Our schools do form a system where each part impacts all the others; so one is forced to take on the whole system at once if he wants to change it.

The second problem is especially crucial if you wish your ideas to be more than dust collectors. Our present system of education is a tight ecosystem of interlocking parts that easily rejects any radical change of any one of its elements.

My point of departure for this article is from the existing practice of those outside the schools. Stated most succinctly, I have catalogued and organized into a system what it is that persons do who survive and thrive in our society.

This starting point avoids a long meandering through all the logical combinations possible to educational goals. It is practical because it begins where people are already operating. It is global in relation to the school system because it begins from a wider horizon in which the schools are only a part of a larger system.

My data is the information that I have gathered as a participant observer for the last five years in the professions of teacher (college and graduate), Ph.D. student and dissertation writer, Chicago grass roots political worker (both machine and independent), urban planner, environmental studies analyst, institutional researcher for a thriving urban community college, and vice-president of an active Chicago elementary school community council. What follows is my systematization of how successful scientists, academic researchers, engineers, planners, managers, businessmen, politicians, staff assistants, school administrators, concerned parents, and children actually behave.

All of these methodologies are reduced to five models or cycles of problem-solving:[1]

(1) Myth: Nonmeaning
(2) Random: Chance
(3) Common sense: Intuitive
(4) Technological
(5) Scientific: Academic

MYTH: NONMEANING PROBLEM SOLVING[2]

The basic steps in this cycle are:

(1) Concrete problem as felt.
(2) Concern.
(3) Myth and ritual performance.

---

[1] I will not be treating all the processes that lead to the success of those I have observed. Most noticeably absent from consideration are the basic language skills of reading, writing, speaking, and mathematics.

Secondly, I will not be treating the function of the liberal arts in the achievement of the good life.

These are shortcomings to the present project that will be remedied at some future date.

Another apparent shortcoming of my approach is that arguing from what *is* to what *ought to be* is caught in the *status quo* and leaves little room for reform or improvement.

It will become clear to the reader when we have finished with the treatment of the technological model that the models presented in this article are meant to be used as a part of the "theoretical fund" for technological problem-solving. Models are used in technology to raise questions, not to give "canned answers." Therefore the method is not so tied to the present as it seems upon first glance.

[2] I am using myth in the anthropological sense of such authors as Mircea Eliade and Bronislaw Malinowski. For this article myth means: the performance of a ritual that is familiar to the participants and justifies some action, occurrence, or even by an appeal (through the ritual) to some sacred reality.

Mircea Eliade defines myth:

Myth narrates a sacred history; it relates an event that took place in Primordial Time, the fabled time of the "beginnings." In other words, myth tells how, through the deeds of Supernatural Beings, a reality came into existence, be it the whole of reality, the Cosmos, or only a fragment of reality, . . . Hence myths describe the various and sometimes dramatic breakthroughs of the sacred (or the "supernatural") into the World. It is this sudden breakthrough of the sacred that really established the world and makes it what it is today. Furthermore, it is as a result of the intervention of Supernatural Beings that man himself is what he is today, a moral, sexed, and cultural being. Mircea Eliade, *Myth and Reality* (New York: Harper & Row, Oublishers, Inc. 1963), pp. 5–6.

Malinowski says:

Studied alive, myth, . . . is not symbolic, but a direct expression of its subject matter; it is not an explanation in satisfaction of a scientific interest, but a narrative resurrection of a primeval reality, told in satisfaction of deep religious wants, moral cravings, social submissions, assertions, even practical requirements. Myth . . . expresses, enhances, and codifies belief; it safeguards and enforces morality, it vouches for the efficiency of ritual and contains practical rules for the guidance of man. Myth is thus a vital ingredient of human civilization: it is not an ideal tale, but a hard-worked active force; it is not an intellectual explanation or an artistic imagery, but a pragmatic charter of primitive faith and moral wisdom. Bronislaw Malinowski, *Magic Science and Religion* (New York: Doubleday & Company, Inc., 1954), p. 101.

(4) Decision.
(5) Trial action.
(6) Results.
(7) Problem not felt—end cycle or problem still felt—recycle to step one.

An example of this kind of problem-resolution process would be some of the ecology activities that are arising to meet the current pollution problems.

The *problem as felt* would be the actual experience of dirty air, the stench of alewives, an oil-blackened beach, a blighted neighborhood photographed for the local papers, or the like.

The *concern* would be the anguish that becomes conscious every time the problems enter consciousness. It is usually articulated by a vague statement such as: "We have to do something about this mess."

The *myth justification* would be mass meetings, complete with either rock or apple-pie liturgical songs (the academic liturgies are in terms of cocktail parties, speeches, and endless discussions), and the emergence of new symbolic acronyms, CAP, EPA, IEQ, ECB, and so on. The desired results of all these mythical rituals is not an answer but rather reassurance; we reaffirm by rituals and reference to myths that we are still good people and that we live in a world that is safe and friendly to good people.

Decisions come when some few people begin to recognize that, despite all of the concern and ritual hooplah, the air is still dirty, the alewives still stink, the beach is still closed, and houses are still falling down. Something concrete that can pass for ecological action must be initiated.

Trial Actions are generated faster than the human eye can watch or the mind count. Magazines publish articles for housewives, listing all the soaps they are to buy and bottles to avoid. Groups of citizens scream about noise reduction, the City puts through antipollution ordinances, and the government decides that a one-degree heat pollution in the lake is its standard, and so on. No one feels certain that his actions will resolve the problem, but each comforts himself with the position: "At least I am doing *something* to stop pollution and restore ecological homeostasis. If it does not work, I will try something else."

The *results* are evaluated as successful if the problem is no longer felt; as unsuccessful if the problem is still apparent. For example, if the alewives are no longer stinking up my beach the issue is considered closed. Lake Michigan is safe and its ecological balances are restored. But if the beach still stinks, the cycle begins again—concern, myth, decision, and so on.

COMMENTS

The limitations of the method are obvious. The *problem* as felt is an extremely narrow appreciation of any situation.

The *myth justification*, whether it be in terms of liturgy or the formation of new symbols is still justification and not explanation.[3] Even when these mythical systems are used to form young peoples' morals (Sunday School, Girl Scout Camp, and the like), all the activity has little or nothing to do with rationally deciding what will resolve the problem.

The *decision* and *trial actions* resolve problems only by chance except for the fact that mythically based, traditional answers have been gradually perfected through trial and error.

Difficulties arise with myths because:

(a) People think that the ritual itself will resolve the problem.

(b) Participants become so enamored with the ritual that they believe that any suggested action is good and hence run after a lot of naïve trail actions that fail.

(c) Participants fail to recognize what rituals are acceptable to the others involved and begin to miscommunicate (e.g. the college administration forgets that decisions must float up very slowly through long discussions and tries to force through what the students actually want, but are not ready to accept that the ritual has not yet been completed).

BEST USES

As many authors have explained, the mythical approach to problems serves man in areas where rational answers cannot be generated (e.g., social stratification, sex, adolescence) or where the greatest human *anomalies* occur (death, serious sickness, chance accidents).

Recently, we have come to recognize that myth works well in the academic world. It was used successfully by many administrators to quiet students during the turbulent years at the end of the 1960s and must be used again by colleges if they hope to deal with student demands in the future. There must be a ritual (usually endless talks with the very top of the administration in the best office or conference room in the school) within which conversation can take place and by which all parties are guaranteed that they are putting themselves into contact with the sacred and that the world is still good—in the sense of the Book of Genesis, this defines goodness.[4]

In summary, myth has two functions:

(a) To justify an action occurrence or custom that reason cannot deal with.

---

[3] As the quoted passage from Malinowski explains, myth does not deal with scientific reality. It is a justification of what happens, not a consideration of what is true or what the facts are.

[4] Gen. 1, 2 : 1–3.

(b) To accompany human problem-solving by providing a security background while difficult decisions are being made.

RANDOM: HIT AND MISS APPROACH

The basic steps to this approach are:

(a) Concrete hindrance or promise of immediate satisfaction.
(b) Playing around.
(c) Results.
(d) Short, unsystematic memory of what happened.

A good example of this method is when a child first encounters a "busy board" with its myriad knobs, cranks, and clocks (*promise* of immediate satisfaction). The child *plays around* until music begins, a mirror moves, or some other pleasant result occurs.

Another, more adult example, is when one of our urban geniuses finds himself on his first vacation out in the woods with an outboard motor that will not start (*hindrance*). He pushes, pulls, chokes, tilts, and kicks, with no idea of what he is doing (*playing around*) until the motor suddenly starts (*results*).

Both the child and the urban genius have some *post facto* idea of what action led to desirable results and remember the sequence between action and results for a short time thereafter. Thus they can bring about the result without a long trial and error sequence. (On the other hand, they usually have several useless steps in their process because they are not quite sure of what causes what). But neither makes an attempt to store this information solidly in his/her memory. Hence, if they get away from the "busy board" or outboard motor, they will forget what they have learned.

COMMENTS

This kind of problem-solving is most relevant to early childhood education and is the base of environment-rich learning centers used in open-classroom schools. The question for these schools is whether students should progress out of this method and how a teacher or atmosphere can encourage the student toward common sense or technology.

BEST USES

The random or chance approach is fun for life's trivial problems and is important for very early child learning. It also is the only method available to a person approaching totally new environments. One has to inject several stimuli (playing around) to detect some pattern or response (results) before he can begin to work from a more systematic base.

COMMON-SENSE: INTUITIVE[5]

The basic steps of this approach are:

(1) Problem as vaguely understood.
(2) Questions that arise from the vague understanding and practical experience.
(3) Specific answers.
(4) Rational decision.
(5) Action.
(6) Results.
(7) Problem no longer sensed—end cycle or problem still there— recycle to step one.
(8) Unsystematic feedback to practical experience.

We can trace the steps of this cycle through the same ecology example used earlier.

The problem as *vaguely understood* not only means that we feel the dirty air but that we also recognize certain causal relations between the air and coal, air and automobile emissions, and air and temperature inversions. We also have some idea of the synergistic effects of particulate matter, toxic gases, wind currents, and the like. In short, we understand how diverse elements come together to produce alewife stink, filthy beaches, a dying lake, or polluted air.

Based on this vague and unsystematic understanding and on practical experience with similar problems, the intuitive person begins to ask *questions* about what causal relations are most relevant and what changes he can make to rid himself of the problem.

The *answers* are specific. For example, to control air pollution, we should: prohibit the use of low-sulfur coal, force antipollution devices to be put on cars, or reduce industry production when temperature inversion occurs. These answers, and the questions as well, grow out of both the present problem and the fund of common sense and practical experience (memories of what happened in the past) of the person or community attempting to resolve the problem.

The *rational decision* is reached as a result of selecting certain actions based on the comprehension of causal relations.

The *feedback* loop occurs because the *action and results* are seen not only as resolving a present problem but as also being valuable for some future date. Thus, for example, people involved in reducing air pollution keep files and clippings labeled "for future use" stacked away in their

---

[5] My ideas on common sense and intuition have been developed from direct observation and from the ideas in Chapters VI and VII of Lonergan's *Insight*. B. J. F. Lonergan, *Insight A Study of Human Understanding* (New York: Philosophical Library, 1958), pp. 173–244.

apartments, but more importantly, in their minds. But they do not consciously integrate their findings into any systematic fund that is unified, logical, and coherent.

Another example of this method, from education, is the process used by administrators to plan a registration process. The problem as *vaguely understood* is to get the students registered for courses within some reasonable amount of time, get them into the right classroom, and tell the teachers which students are coming.

Usually, the dean or vice-president in charge will get his staff together to *raise questions* about what needs to be done to take the students from the front door into the proper classrooms. (Coffee and . . . usually provides the minimum ritual). Out of these meetings, at which each person brings up his questions and suggestions, a set of possible ways (*answers*) to handle registration are put on the table and either the group or the chief administrator picks one (*decision*) of the processes and advises his staff that " this is the way we are going to handle registration."

The *action* is the resulting signs, stations, and forms that are set up for registration plus the registration itself. If there are no complaints, the system is a success. If there are a few complaints, the system is still a success, but there will be minor problems to consider before the next registration. If there are many complaints, then the cycle begins with the entire registration procedure open for questions and suggestions.

The feedback occurs in some minutes of meetings that are filed, but more importantly in the experience that each of the administrators gets from his plan and its relative success. The staff, after two or three of these registrations, becomes experienced—i.e., it has built a fairly large base of practical experiences that will help them raise the right questions for problems about registration in the future.

COMMENTS

This method is perhaps the most common approach to problem-solving. It is the one we use for making home repairs, deciding what car to buy, picking out a suit, choosing a spouse, fixing a leaky faucet, planning a party, and the like. It is distinguished from the first two cycles by the fact that it begins with some ideas of how things fit together (i.e., we are not just playing around—we grasp immediately that relations exist between cars and toxic gases or between good registration forms and short waiting periods), and by the fact that there is a conscious attempt to ask questions and grasp meaning. The questions arise from the problem itself and from the storehouse of practical experience that the individual and his community have about similar issues. (The term " common-sense " means that wisdom that is commonly available to the group for approaching a problem.)[6]

[6] Ibid., pp. 209–214.

This method is best used in those parts of our life where the community has familiarized itself with the issues, where short-range problems are involved, and where technology is not yet developed enough to meet the decision-making deadlines.[7]

TECHNOLOGY

The basic steps of this cycle are:

(1) Concrete problem as vaguely understood.
(2) Questions arising from vague understanding, common-sense experience, technical practical experience, and scientific funds.
(3) Professional answers.
(4) Rational decisions.
(5) Action.
(6) Results.
(7) Problem no longer sensed (or solution sensed)—end cycle or problem still sensed—recycle back to step two.
(8) Feedback to practical experience, technical practical experience, and sometimes to sciences.

This process differs from common sense in that it utilizes two additional funds for raising questions. It takes advantage not only of the problem itself and common sense experience but also draws from the records of previous technical studies and from relevant theoretical journals and experiments. The prime analogate for technology is the engineer, who has a sufficient theoretical background to make him comfortable in theoretical physics and chemistry (*theoretical funds*), has worked on various similar engineering problems, (technical practical experience), and has good common sense of his own.

If we return to our ecology example, the technological approach would be that of Bolt, Baranek and Newman, Inc. (the consultants who drafted the first noise legislation for the city of Chicago in 1970–71). These technical experts considered (raised questions about) the issues of Chicago (*current* problem), plugged into the practical experience (*common sense*) of Chicago and other cities (by a review of legislation), consulted other technological

[7] I have been continually challenged when discussing this point, to define the difference between problems with "short range" implications. There is no easy formula that I have discovered and I am usually reduced to reciting examples and anecdotes. Thus, for example, a short range problem of registration might be the decision about whether to use black or blue ink to print up signs. But even the examples I use are problematic, since we now recognize that the different kinds of paper, colors of ink, and the like will have unexpected ecological impact on our environment. It is my own position that we will be more and more forced to use technological methods in all activities of our life and that the age of common sense is slipping away.

studies of noises (*technical*), and referred to the latest theoretical studies (*scientific fund*) on sound. Then they presented a series of recommendations (professional answers).

With the help of staff persons from the city, a set of *decisions* was made with the *result*ant legislation that was passed by the City Council in the spring of 1971.

The feedback occurred to the practical experience of the city and the professional files of Bolt, Baranek and Newman (who have since gone on to do similar studies for other cities). It is to be supposed that some of the insights (e.g., regarding continued versus intermittent noise) will find their way back to the theoretical physicists, but this is only of incidental interest to the Bolt firm which is paid for resulting legislation (action) rather than for any contributions made to physical science.

Reverting to our educational example of planning for a registration, the starting point of a technological process would be the same concrete problem as *vaguely understood*, except that there would be a commitment to do more than just work with the common sense of the staff.

The *questions* arising out of the *theoretical and technical* funds will more than likely come from an outside consultant who brings to bear the wisdom of his trade regarding paper-moving processes and traffic flow patterns as well as some acquaintance with the fields of psychology, sociology, and statistics as these bear on how to lay out the registration, what kind of information to seek, and how to learn what is happening from the registration results.

To the chagrin of those using common sense to solve the problem, the technological planning process will include much documentation and many flow charts about what is happening not only during the registration week but also in the weeks previous to the time when the students arrive so that each element of the system fits together neatly and every piece of information arrives where and when it should.

The *professional answers* will be presented in writing and with the reasons why each step is being taken. The decision (if it is a technological decision) will be in terms of these reasons. Spurious (i.e., ideas that do not fit the pattern of reasoning established by the technologist) will be rejected as not to the point. This again will distress the men and women of common sense who enjoy their anecdotes and cannot see why they are not pertinent.

COMMENTS

This method has been in use in engineering, architecture, medicine, and law for some time, and is also used in management and information systems design and educational institutional research.

Within this model, three kinds of technologists can be identified according to the procedures they use. *Technologist A* is the fellow who has not read a book since finishing school and relies totally on common sense. *Techno-crat B* is a man with good common sense who is well versed in the practical experience of his fellow engineers, doctors, or law partners. *Practitioner C* can cull the best insights and questions from the latest theoretical journals, makes good use of the practical experiences of his colleagues, and brings his own good common sense to bear on the issue at hand. *Technologist A* is quite adequate for run-of-the-mill jobs in familiar surroundings. *Technocrat B* is valuable for jobs that require a bit more sophistication. *Practitioner C* brings the most penetrating (because the most extensive and adaptable) set of tools to bear on the problems at hand. He is the fellow to work on innovative projects.[8]

BEST USES

The age of ecology with its new insights into the long-range (time) and geographically extensive (space) effects of seemingly trivial projects is urging us to use technologists rather than just men of common sense in projects that alter our environment. In education, for example, we see the need for planning our registration processes to give us accountability and marketing information as well as to help students get the courses they need. It is safe to conclude that for any actions that might have impact beyond the immediate future, the technologist is the best man for the job.[9]

THEORETICAL SCIENCE: ACADEMIC RESEARCH

The steps in this process are:

(1) Problem (concrete or theoretical) vaguely understood and having some relevance to a discipline or scientific field.

---

[8] "Familiar surroundings" means that range of activities where we have experience, can react from habit, and can immediately anticipate the majority of consequences. In terms of an example, it means the kind of architecture design needed to design and construct a house within the general framework used to design and construct many other houses.

"More Sophistication" refers to the problem solving necessary in those dimensions of our lives where we do not have much experience and readily available models. An example would be in the design of town houses that make efficient use of land and yet generate the feeling of privacy.

The area of "innovative projects" is that set of problems where there are no ready-made models to be copied or worked around nor has there been much systematization of theoretical information. The need is to design a conceptual framework that will at once generate the right kinds of questions and quickly dismiss items that will not be significant. An example of this area of concern would be the architectural and engineering design of new personal rapid transit systems to replace automobiles in the central districts of our urban centers.

[9] "Immediate future" is a term similar to "short range." Basically, I am saying that we will need the services of a technologist for all problem-solving that goes beyond the most elemental problems we face in our present and future ecosystem. Common sense is a very limited approach to problem-solving, which becomes less and less adequate as we come closer to the limits of the finite energy in our world.

(2) Questions—primarily systematic and related to a specific discipline.
(3) System related (analog, new instance of old theory, basic challenge to existing theory) answers that are generalizations.
(4) Laboratory verification.
(5) Feedback and integration into theoretical fund.

This process can begin with a concrete *problem* (the environmental problems cited) or with some theoretical concern (e.g., the ontological status of relations or the logical dilemmas of set theory). But irrespective of the way in which the problem starts, it is immediately converted into an issue that relates to a specific science or academic discipline. This means that the problem is converted into an atemporal, aspatial concern where the questions begin with some logical anomaly or curiosity (not from the pressure of some time space located problem or promise) and cease only when the logical exigencies (defined by a science or academic field) have been met.

Secondly, although some *questions* arise from practical experience (common sense or technology) the principal concern of the scientist is to formulate *questions* that are clearly articulated and related to his own discipline. Hence the physicist would not raise any questions about sound based on city legislation, but he would be concerned with decibels, pressure, wave lengths, and the like.

When seeking *answers*, the scientist strives for a statement that will apply not only to Chicago, in particular, but to all cities. He seeks generalizations that are, as far as possible, valid independent of time and space. He also couches his answers in a framework that is determined by his discipline in which he shows how his findings are a new instance of something already known, a slight variation (analog) of some known hypothesis or a *basic challenge* to the established field.

Verification is also a process that is different from anything found in the previous cycles. The scientist sets up this step very carefully to control all extraneous stimuli, to stipulate exactly what is to be measured (in terms of dependent and independent variables), to structure the experiment in a manner so that others will be able to repeat his work, and to follow the accepted canons of the discipline in question.

There is no *action* or *result* phase to this cycle. The process ends when the logical questions cease.

COMMENTS

It is obvious that the procedures and goals of this approach are quite distinct from any model that has thus far been discussed. The scientist works in an abstract world (i.e., a world that is atemporal and aspatial) where his every method is conscious. His operation begins because of some intellectual curiosity and keeps going until the intellectual puzzle or enigma is logically resolved. The scientist is not concerned with action in our concrete world. Finally, the scientist limits his investigation to a selected segment of reality (such as physics) and ignores the other aspects of reality so that he can be exact in his methods and come up with generalizations.

BEST USES

This method functions exceptionally well for the sciences and academic disciplines that seek to construct generalized laws within the context of models, theories, and an over-all science.

More important for us to understand, however, is that it is *not* a method suited for dealing directly with the concrete world that is unique, historical, and not amenable to piecemeal consideration. A physicist is not a good engineer, a political scientist does not win elections, and a research psychologist is not a good school consultant.[10]

SOME GENERAL COMMENTS ABOUT ALL THE METHODS AS PRESENTED

These five cycles or models of problem-solving are only skeletons. More work needs to be done in defining how commonsense and technological practical experiences are constructed and utilized. The feedback system for all the cycles must be more fully explicated. In technology, we need to discover how complete families of technologies might be molded into a coherent whole so that interdisciplinary studies might become less chaotic and technologists might increase their vocational and economic mobility in a future marked by ever changing job markets and problem foci.

On the positive side, these five models offer a conceptual framework for setting educational goals that are based on what is already happening.

One of the intriguing observations in my analysis of problem-solving operations of various persons was that one can list certain occupations under each method and establish that a particular method dominates the problem-solving processes of several vocations, as demonstrated by the following breakdown:

Method	Used by
THEORETICAL: ACADEMIC	Pure research in physical sciences Laboratory-oriented work in the social sciences Library research of academic scholars

[10] Obviously, there are examples that disprove this statement, but I would maintain that good scientists become good technologists only if they change their methods. A method designed to give abstract generalizations will not provide concrete answers.

TECHNOLOGY	Engineers
	Architects
	Lawyers
	Medical doctors
	Planners (urban, city, environmental)
	Some business consultants
	Some teachers
	Some businessmen
COMMON SENSE	Management (especially at the decision-making level)
	Politicians
	Most businessmen
	Most teachers
	Blue-collar trades
	White-collar workers
	Skilled and semiskilled workers
MYTH	Politicians
	Teachers
	Organized religion
	Media producers
	Advertisers
RANDOM	Children
	Anyone forced into a totally new environment
	Leisure and fun activities

What is most interesting about these classifications is that the politicians and top management (the two groups who make the majority of long-range decisions about our world) use common sense. It has been pointed out that common sense is ill-equipped for this type of problem-solving. It is no wonder that our environmental homeostasis is threatened and our urban centers are a hodgepodge of pragmatic, gerrymandered ecosystems that serve only a very few.

But we cannot be too hard on the decision-makers who use common sense. For both technologies and the sciences, because of their emphasis on logical completeness and conscious methods, require more time (in fact time cannot rule their lives because they must serve logic whose every step can consume twice or thrice the projected time) to reach answers than does common sense.

I have witnessed occasions where the best intentioned politicians and technical personnel have failed to come up with the technical answers in time to meet deadlines, thus forcing the decision-makers to revert to common sense. And there have been many instances in which managers hired top-flight scholars and scientists to attack concrete problems only to be rewarded with a late, abstruse, and undecisive report. This is not so surprising in the light of our analysis, which demonstrated that science is not geared to deal directly with the concrete.

I sympathize with the mayors who have complained, "What do the scientists know about running an urban center?" These practical fellows are not only venting their own ego vapors but are also registering a true disillusionment in the ability of the experts to say anything directly meaningful about the big cities.

What neither the mayors nor the scientists have recognized is that the role of the academic is critical for our daily life *not because of the answers* that the scientists and scholars may give in learned journals but *because of the theoretical* funds of information, insights, and skills they establish. For it is from these funds that the technologist is able to develop penetrating *questions* that will lead to answers that are applicable to "the real world."

To cut back on any of the sciences would not disturb the immediate operation of our world, but it would take away the tools we need to operate on the future.

The final general comment that needs to be made about these various methods is that communication between any two methods (more properly between any two persons using a different method) usually becomes miscommunication. The man of common sense has a great deal of difficulty understanding the scientist because common sense seeks action rather than logical completeness. The academic "looks down his nose" at common sense because it is irrational. Technologists and scientists are like babes in the woods when it comes to dealing with politicians who use myth to justify their actions. Politicians, on the other hand, end up wasting a lot of money to hire "staff" because the information and answers generated by these technologists presuppose a technological and theoretical background and are thus unintelligible to the politicians.

It is possible, of course, for a scientist of *methods* (sometimes called a philosopher) to analyze what procedures each person is using and facilitate communication.[11] However, if he is truly a scientist, he will be more interested in understanding and conceptualizing the *methods* than in actually getting people to talk to one another.

The technologist, with some philosophy, seems to be the man who is most ideally suited to break the communication barriers, because he understands logical background and yet is committed to action.

These problems to communication also apply to what happens in the schools. The basic methods used by teachers (academic), students (*common*

---

[11] Lonergan, pp. 385–594 and John Dewey, *Democracy* and *Education* (New York: The Free Press, 1966), pp. 321–332.

sense), and administration (common sense), block both personal growth and communication unless someone steps in to translate and explain. Needless to say, curricula designed for scientists will hardly interest students of common sense.

WHAT COMBINATION SHOULD THE SCHOOLS FACILITATE

We started out to discuss the function of formal education and have listed various methods that persons actually use in their lives. The questions now arise:

(a) Is any one method the best?
(b) Should we concentrate on some combination of methods?

It is clear from what we have said that no one method is best. Each method covers a different part of our daily living needs.

However, some recommendations can be made about which combination of methods should be the goal of our schools. This issue can be approached from two distinct viewpoints:

(a) That of the individual
(b) That of the community and the self-survival of our ecosystem.

INDIVIDUAL

It is my observation that three kinds of people are thriving and surviving in our world:[12]

(a) The man of common sense and myth.
(b) The man of technology and myth where problems have shown common sense to be inadequate.
(c) The man of science where myth supports his position.

Hence my most honest recommendation for those who want to enjoy the material and spiritual benefits of our world and participate in the direction of our world should decide which of these kinds of persons he wishes to be and proceed to acquire the proper skills.[13] The breakdown of jobs and methods used could serve as a starting point for deciding what combination a person will need for the various vocations.

---

[12] This judgement is based on my five years of participant observation.

[13] Spiritual is meant to include all the nonphysical; the cultural and social interactions as well as power, prestige, and control.

From the viewpoint of the survival of our world, which is most properly the viewpoint for determining the combination that the schools should produce, the primary need will be for:

(a) Men of common sense and myth in those areas where short range actions are involved.[14]

(b) Men of technology and myth for the future because almost all actions will have ecological impact.

(c) Men of science in the established disciplines as they logically evolve.

But we must decide which of these has a higher priority and which is properly the function of the schools to help create.

From what I have seen in environmental studies, the primary need in the United States at this time is for men of technology and myth. This has the highest priority.

Since we live in an ecosphere of finite energy, we will have to limit the amount of resources that we devote to science, and this limit will have to utilize information from the technologists about what are the most serious needs of our concrete world and what sciences seem to be moving in the direction of meeting these needs (i.e., generated funds from which valuable questions can arise). Thus, we must not eliminate science, but limit its expenditures in terms of concrete needs.

This proposal is not so different from what is actually happening today in the United States. Scientists work in areas in which they can get government money, which is supposedly tied to the action priorities of the nation. The only change I would advocate is that we should be more careful to base our decision of the use of finite resources on technology and not myth.[15]

The lowest priority is assigned to training men of common sense and myth because I think that a school is not the best place to learn how to become a man of common sense and myth. Once we recognize that the graduate schools control the myth rituals of our schools and the certification processes that place students in life, we can see why schools do not deal with common sense.[16] For the graduate schools are scientifically oriented and have created spaces (classrooms and laboratories) and programs that are proper for the development of logic and controlled experimentation, not action-oriented practical intuitions.

Furthermore, what we are just beginning to rediscover is that all of the

---

[14] See footnote 7 for explanation of *short range.*

[15] Analyses of presidential speeches and legislative defenses of huge expenditures in the United States makes clear how many of our decisions about scientific research are based on mythical justification rather than hard-nosed technology.

[16] This notion about the importance of graduate schools is an insight that was brought home to me by a group of students in a Philosophy of Education Class in the fall of 1972 at Northwestern University, Evanston, Illinois.

methods of problem-solving are, in fact, learned by an apprenticeship. The scientist becomes a theoretical master in the laboratory and classroom because these are apprenticeship spaces and programs. The technologist does so by actually working in the field because he is learning by doing. The man of common sense learns by doing. And the myth-maker becomes good by practice.

The logical conclusion that is drawn is that a great deal of time is wasted in school for those who wish to pursue a life of common sense and myth.[17] The only reason we can truly give these persons for remaining in school is that they will be fulfilling the mythical requirements of our society by acquiring the proper certificates that link them with the sacred, so that they will have a right to do what they would have been able to do all along.

Of course, we cannot hope to take common-sense learning out of the classroom unless we construct an acceptable myth (set of rituals) other than the schools.[18]

DECIDING WHETHER THE SCHOOLS ARE ACHIEVING OUR GOALS

The thrust of proposing our five descriptions of problem-solving has been to provide the first part of an answer to the question: "What should we expect and demand from organized (school) education?"

We have not addressed the issue of measuring whether people served by the schools actually perform according to the models that are appropriate for the life problems they face. This will be a long, complex process of random sampling, correlations, checks, null hypotheses, debates about the adequacy of evidence collected, and the like. But it is a process that can be carried out once we decide that this is what we want to look for.

The only insight I have for the issue of measuring output is a reminder that our system supposes that the goals of education are achieved *after* a person leaves school in the normal process of surviving and thriving in the economic, social, political, and cultural arenas of our world. Thus the evaluations should be made totally outside the schools.

CONCLUSION

The reader will be somewhat confused if he tries to place this article in one of my problem-solving categories. Insofar as the article creates logical models that apply to more than one space-time reference, it is a scientific

---

[17] This is not a new idea. It parallels the work of Ivan Illich and Everett Reimer. See Ivan Illich, *Deschooling Society* (New York: Harper Row Publishers, Inc., 1970) and Everett Reimer, *School is Dead: Alternatives in Education* (New York: Doubleday & Company, Inc., 1971).

[18] The need for a mythical structure in the movement for alternatives to the present school education cannot be underestimated. Unless there is some new way of connecting nonschool education with the sacred, we will not be able to construct lasting alternatives.

treatise. Insofar as it is addressed to the issue of where to go with our formal education in the United States at this juncture in history, it is a technological article. Insofar as this article addresses not just one discipline of science but cuts across many fields, it fails to accede to the demands of a known theoretical fund. It is, in the terms of Lonergan, Dewey, and Whitehead, a philosophy. Just how philosophy differs from these models is the topic for a future treatise, but for the present reader, Chapters XI–XVII of B. J. F. Lonergan's *Insight: A Study of the Human Understanding* will give some basic directions.[19]

Finally, everything in this article can be described as an Inductive Empirical Theory.[20] It begins with assumptions, plunges into observation of what is happening, systematizes what is observed, and ends with a conceptual framework that can be used for further questions and observations, and in the hands of a technologist—action.

[19] See John Dewey, *Democracy and Education*, and Alfred North Whitehead, *The Function of Reason*.

[20] A fine treatment of this kind of modeling is contained in an article by David G. Ryans. David G. Ryans, "Theory Development and the Study of Teacher Behaviour," *Contemporary Thought on Teaching*, ed. Ronald T. Hyman (Englewood Cliffs, N.J.: Prentice Hall, Inc., 1971), pp. 99–103.

This approach does not quite fit into the "Model for Evaluating Philosophies of Education" by Dr. Frankena reproduced elsewhere in this volume because it gives more importance to empirical observations and generalization than does Frankena.

26

A Lot of Learning
Is a Dangerous Thing

ROSECRANZ BALDWIN

I have just returned, considerably amused and more than a little dismayed, from one of our Alumni Luncheon Round Tables. Except for two of my colleagues, the group consisted entirely of businessmen, and, as usual, the conversation turned to the question of the kind of education a young man planning a business career ought to receive. As an academician, I would have guessed that the businessmen who were there would have been vociferous champions of vocationalism in education, as opposed to the humanities, but amazingly enough, this was not the case. Almost to a man, they fell all over each other in their eagerness to affirm the cardinal importance of the liberal arts—Greek, philosophy, history of art, and all the rest. These are the subjects which they all seemed to think are essential to business success.

As I look back on our two-hour session, I find myself disturbed about the near-fanaticism with which so many businessmen have taken up the slogan, "Humane education for a humane executive." In fact, the more I reflect on this notion, the more I am convinced that it is not only fallacious, but downright dangerous. I realize, of course, that the powers that be in my old university will not thank me for what I am about to say here, because businessmen, like those in the group I have just lunched with, are the source of all our new buildings and endowments. Nevertheless, I feel so strongly

W. Porter Chandler, III, "A Lot of Learning Is a Dangerous Thing," *Harvard Business Review* March–April 1972, pp. 122–31. Used by permission of *Harvard Business Review* and the author.

This article first published under a pseudonym.

about the points I propose to make that I am impelled to record my views plainly, even if the immediate result is a telephone call from the Chancellor.

New School of Thought

First of all, let me state positively that today's luncheon conversation could not have occurred ten years ago. Back in those pre-hippie days of honesty and plain speaking, the successful executive made no bones about his belief that the only form of education that was worthwhile was a four-year curriculum in business administration—"Biz Ad," as it is sometimes called—packed full with accounting, finance, marketing, and other such useful subjects. Not for him were the *Dialogues* of Plato, the *Meditations* of Descartes, or the poetry of Ezra Pound. And not for anyone on his payroll, either.

Of course, when he found himself in academic circles he had more sense than to come right out with his views in front of the professors. But, when he sent his company's recruiter out to the campuses each spring, he made certain that this persuasive individual had been very clearly instructed to grab the Biz Ad graduates and forget the English or Philosophy majors. After all, the president of the company had been a Biz Ad major himself and knew what was what.

But that was ten years ago; today the successful executive operates in a rather different environment from the one in which he operated then. The heightened social awareness that one finds in today's corporation board room guarantees that he will find himself attending out-of-office gatherings of one "cultural" genre or another, where the conversation is likely to stray into areas in which he feels uninformed—areas where he feels (or is made to feel) something of an oaf.

When he essays a sally, say, on the success his Model 101 is enjoying over the competing Model A-22 in the Duluth market, he is likely to detect a lack of interest among his hearers, accompanied by a modicum of scorn. They may want to talk about Charles Ives's music, eighteenth century French literature, or the painting style of Modigliani, and he will not be able to keep up. Worse, he probably doesn't really *want* to keep up, but he has a strong feeling that he *ought* to want to. And worst of all, he feels that he ought to be *able* to keep up, whether he wants to or not. The result is a combination of heartburn and frustration.

A Case of Overcompensation

If this experience had happened to only a few individuals, nothing would have resulted from it. But when thousands of top-flight businessmen repeatedly find themselves conversationally equipped with only thumbs, it should not surprise us that they develop a cultural-inferiority complex. Indeed, it is small wonder that in recent years there has been a gradual but pronounced change in the thinking of corporate executives about the educational needs of fledgling businessmen. On all sides, they are now proclaiming that the only way for a young man to achieve business success is to become "broadly grounded in the deep wellsprings of the humanistic traditions of Western civilization."

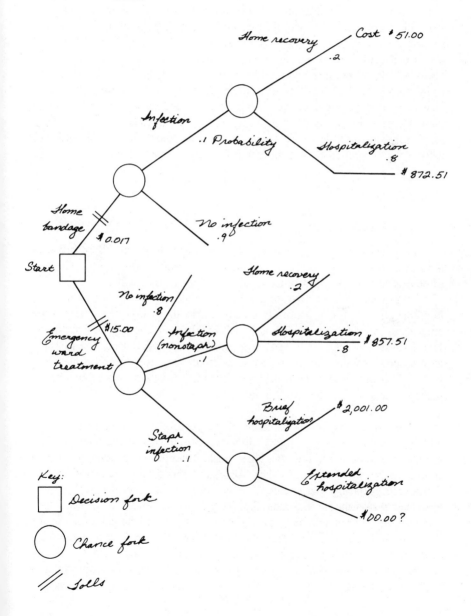

In other words, he should eschew Biz Ad and instead pump himself full of English literature, French, History, Philosophy, and even the Classics. *These* are what he needs, so they say, to be the well-rounded, all-purpose guy that will inevitably rise to direct the affairs of Consolidated Flypaper Corporation.

Of course, once he has his BA and is liberally educated, the young man must also secure an MBA from a graduate school of business to stock up on a few business basics and, more importantly, to learn the new and essential scientific techniques (i.e., simulation models, linear programming, decision theory, decision trees, operations research, systems analysis, and the rest) that are absolutely indispensable for the modern corporation manager. This vocational frosting on the educational cake must not, however, be permitted to interfere with the broad intellectual and humanistic grounding which is so essential to corporate success, especially in the expanding universe of business. He must know about such things as decision trees (see the diagram on page 321) and be able to use them, but, more importantly, he should also comprehend them in their proper place in the stream of Western thought and culture.

A Scientific Tool for Managing Difficult Decisions

The decision tree is currently the rage at leading schools of business administration. This tree is rooted in a schematic methodology whereby difficult decisions are laid out for solution diagrammatically.

For example, a mother might have to determine whether to apply a bandage to her child's profusely bleeding arm or to take the child to the emergency ward of the local hospital ($15.00 cover charge) for treatment. Her first step would be to get paper and pencil and outline the possible consequences of these alternatives and calculate the costs of each consequence. . . . The advantages she would derive from this new management tool in making her best decision are obvious.

I believe this is a fair statement of the position (if you can call it that) which the alumni group at today's lunch espoused with so much fervor. And the idea is indeed a stirring one. How grand it would be to have a twentieth century Immanuel Kant at the helm of a giant corporation or a modern-day Voltaire negotiating merger after merger for a conglomerate! And it may even seem reasonable that, as the complexity of business continues to increase, the greater will be its need for men who have been educated in the broad humanistic tradition. Hence the battle cry, "We want Educated Men (even though they have to know some accounting too)" which is being shouted by the silver-haired gentry who control the nation's industrial and financial machine.

On paper this all looks fine—but is it? Has Biz Ad been downgraded too much? Are the liberal arts being too highly touted? And if they are, has the new trend progressed to the point where it is irreversible?

As I shall show in a moment, the answers to these questions are of crucial importance to the economic life of our country; for if by some wild chance the notion of giving the embryo business executive a liberal education should take hold, we shall have a major crisis on our hands: the executive class, as we know it today, will die.

But before I go into that, I must first make clear what I mean by "business executive." Who is he? What is he like? What does he do? Let me draw him for you, so you can judge the wisdom of giving him what was once called a gentleman's education.

A Portrait Drawn from Life

First of all, he is *not* the classic entrepreneur, the risk-taker, the inventor, the genius who takes a bright idea or an inherent ability and blows it up into a large and prosperous enterprise. Such individuals still exist, thank heaven, but each one is an atypical businessman, a maverick whose departures from the norm are the chief reasons for his success.

It is not these oddballs with whom I am concerned, but with the typical denizen of the management of the large publicly held corporation; the man who lives in the confines of one or more of these empires virtually from graduation to grave. He is the *professional* manager, the reluctantly anonymous member of the management team. Or, in less romantic terms, he is the ruthlessly ambitious man of not inconsiderable ability who somehow claws his way up the ladder of a big company and finally achieves a post of command.

His Origins and Emergence

Where does this man come from? Usually, he is—or was—a member of a middle-class family, either in a small town or in an equivalent metropolitan neighborhood. A product of public schools, both elementary and high, he has a consistently good scholastic record. His IQ probably tests at 125 or better. He is prominent in his high school class, although he seldom excels in athletics or the more frivolous nonacademic pursuits. He studies industriously and, whether his family is hard up or not, works part-time after school and in the summer.

A thoroughly virtuous and intelligent person, and seemingly possessed from birth with all the attributes of success, he nevertheless lacks certain qualities which might have led him ultimately into fields of achievement outside the business world. Specifically, he is uncreative.

Until a few years ago, of course, most psychologists believed that a person with a high IQ was necessarily also endowed with commensurate creative ability. He could reason; ergo he could create. This assumption is now being widely challenged; educators are gradually coming to the conclusion that it is possible for a person to be extremely smart without being creative. If Pablo Picasso, André Malraux, and the Chairman of International Glue Corporation have the same IQs—as one must assume—it seems clear that Pablo and André have something, some additional quality, to which the glue king can never aspire, despite his brains and his salary. Should he then waste his time in college trying to master subjects for which creativity is a prerequisite?

His 'Higher' Education. After high school, our executive probably attends a state university (rather than Harvard, Yale, or Princeton), where he takes large doses of accounting, finance, and the like. He may or may not go on to acquire an MBA at the same or another institution.

Throughout his university years he probably maintains grades of As and Bs, and when he graduates, he has little difficulty in getting a job. During his senior year—even in a recession year like 1971—he is literally besieged by recruiters from the large corporations who tell him over and over what a great guy he is and who lure him to their respective headquarters in New York or Chicago for further blandishment.

Inundated with dazzling literature and importuned with money, he at length chooses his employer and so begins his management career. What does he do first in his new life?

HE FINDS HIS FEET

In his first job the larval executive is probably classified as a trainee, and as such is shuttled around with a hundred or more other young men to get a quick exposure to company sales, accounting, and production. He may even don blue overalls and go out into the plant for a year or two, to better fit the Horatio Alger formula. In a couple of years, however, he is back in the office, industriously working away as a junior accountant, marketing coordinator, or production planner. This initial period may last three or four years.

Next comes his period of mobility. After his initial orientation has been completed—that is, after he has been broken to the company way of life—he may be made a branch manager (private office, vinyl tile floor, black telephone) in Des Moines, Atlanta, or Butte. Or he may become an assistant plant manager or assistant divisional controller (with the same perquisites) in Houston, Duluth, or Syracuse.

By this time he has married and had children, but he is still merely a piece on the corporate checkerboard, to be moved from place to place at the whim of the corporate management. And woe betide him if, at the end of his fifth move, he protests! It is of no consequence that his own family or his wife's have had their roots in Boston since the Revolution, or that his children have become emotionally unstable through constant adjustment to new schools and changing environments. He is a "member of the company team" and it is not for him to reason why—at least not out loud. If the boss says "Move," he moves—and his wife had better shut up and pack.

So long as he stays out in the provinces, away from company headquarters, he can still call his soul his own to some extent. He can still get home most nights and may reasonably expect to have an occasional Saturday away from the office. All this changes, however, when he finally leaves the provinces for the home office to become an assistant to a vice president or some such. When this happens, he knows that he has become one of the elect, that his star is ascendant, that he may have what it takes.

And he has signs that tell him so. For one thing, he finds himself in a carpeted office, rather small, but in the immediate vicinity of executive row. He also finds a green telephone on his desk, instead of the more menial black one, a symbol of preliminary beatification.

Also, since his responsibilities expand at this stage, he now finds larger figures on his paycheck—at least, *enough* larger so that he can maintain a life style that is suitable, in the company's eyes, to one in his position. Specifically, he is now able—and "strongly encouraged"—to live in a house in a new suburb inhabited largely by young men who are similarly on their way up. And he is now allowed the status of a station wagon, though probably a relatively inexpensive one, such as a Ford or Chevrolet.

He Toes the Line

That the company can dictate to him in this way may sound ridiculous, but actually, in the executive world, the type of car a man owns or the house he lives in is as important a social index of status as the color of his desk telephone. If his car is too cheap a model, he is looked down on; if it is too expensive, he is deemed presumptuous. Many companies are absolutely frank about their censorship of their executives' habits of living.

I recall that a few years ago, a friend of mine—a lawyer—was debating whether to give up professional practice and join a large well-known corporation as its general counsel. When the president interviewed him for the job, he said, unblushingly, "Mr. Jones, as our general counsel you will hold the equivalent rank of vice president and must comport yourself accordingly. This means, let us say, that you may drive a Buick, although it would be unwise for you to own a more costly car."

My friend looked Big Brother squarely in the eye and turned the job down. But many—in fact, *most*—would have toed the line without even worrying about it. May I question the utility of equipping the morally subservient with an education in transcendental ethics?

HE STARTS TO RUN

When the young executive joins headquarters' management, another (and far more significant) change takes place in his life: he surrenders the last of his free time, and hence whatever part of his soul has hitherto remained free.

The company does not dictate this change, but rather *induces* it in ways that are no less effective for being inexplicit and indirect. For example, our hero is bound to note that his successful competitors are first to the office in the morning and last out at night, an institutional practice that receives unspoken blessing from above. He quickly follows suit; whether or not he has work to do, he realizes his best strategy is to stay at his desk until at least 10 p.m. two or three nights a week, looking as busy as possible.

Saturday attendance is, of course, mandatory, and if he has a shrewd political sense, he starts appearing on Sundays at least often enough to encourage commendation from his superiors.

The acid test comes, however, when his vacation is due. What matter if his wife wants to take the children to the seashore, or that the whole family is bone weary? If the young man is smart, he will sigh ruefully and announce to the boss that his work is too pressing for him to go, for there is an absolute law in business which Parkinson has yet to discover, but which is nonetheless valid: the more liberal the company's vacation policy, the less time off the junior executive can take—if he wants to get ahead in the company.

What does this total commitment mean to the young man's home life? What sort of life does he live?

We know the answers. His home life is largely nonexistent. Leaving early in the morning and arriving home late most nights, he perforce relegates to his wife the job of managing the home and bringing up the children. Even on weekends, if by chance he is not working, he usually finds it politic to arrange a Sunday game of golf (or "gawlf" as it is usually called in business circles) with men of equivalent or (preferably) higher rank in the corporation. He has learned by this time that golf is the thing to do in the executive set, and that if he does not wax enthusiastic over the game, he may become suspect.

So out on the links he goes, whether he plays well or badly, simply because it is *expected* of him. The fact that his family has to wait at home for him all day Sunday is of little consequence by comparison with his all-important company career.

HE MAKES THE FINAL HEAT

Up to now our young man has been a sort of executive-in-waiting, but at age 35–40 he may make the second big breakthrough. He may become a vice president or, in a very large organization, an assistant vice president. If he does, he has now cracked "top management," and his life abruptly changes again.

First of all, its tempo increases; he must defend himself against a narrowing and more vigorous competition by putting in even longer hours and developing an even more assiduous devotion to company business.

Second, he must get rid of his less successful friends and acquire new, more successful ones. He accomplishes this by moving from the "on-the-make" suburb to a "made" one. He buys a larger house and achieves the supreme status accomplishment of joining a club. It may be a downtown city club where he will nervously eat his lunches in company with the local business greats. Or he may go into a country club—not, of course, the one the really top executives frequent—where he will also associate with other, equally nervous young men who are climbing the same ladder.

At this stage in his career, he will almost certainly buy his wife a mink stole—the symbol of executive success everywhere. She, for her part, will hire help for the house and the children, to free her time for thoroughly publicized good works and (more or less) subtle social maneuvering on behalf of *his* career.

At about this time our executive will begin to see the need for more social polish. Brooks Brothers clothing will suddenly loom on his horizon, and he will begin to acquire proficiency in the executive name-dropping process, which will eventually end, he hopes, by his knowing nobody but successful executives, to all of whom he will refer only by their first names.

But socially he will still be all thumbs, as in fact he will probably continue to be. At mixed functions he will still tend to join the men in one corner and talk business, while the wives congregate in another and talk clothes and children. When compelled to mix with intellectuals (college professors, professional people, and so on) he will either be mute or else will become excessively hearty. Hearty, that is, about what *they* do, for the art of general conversation will be largely foreign to him.

He Breaks the Tape

The ultimate goal for which he has been striving so desperately is, of course, the presidency of the corporation. By now he is an adept politician; he has privately been cultivating members of the board of directors, and most important of all, he has ingratiated himself with the company's bankers.

If he has done his politicking with the proper finesse, and if his devotion to duty has been impeccable, he will in due course be named president, and then, in corporate parlance, he will have "arrived." He will now wear a gray homburg and tailor-made clothes, his wife will buy suitably large jewels, and they will both immediately start the friend-sloughing process all over again by the same convenient device of moving.

This time they will gravitate to whatever the local executive heaven may be—Greenwich or Bloomfield Hills—where they will buy a very large house, probably quasi-French or Tudor. His wife will move up to a full-length mink. His car (or cars) will be a Cadillac, Lincoln, or European equivalent, and the company may provide a chauffeur-driven limousine as well. His office is now large and sumptuous, with better fittings than those of the lower officers, including, variously, plate glass and/or paneling, a deep sofa and easy chairs, a private shower, and an original (or nearly original) Wyeth on the wall. He may even get an airplane. He will *certainly* get a white telephone for his private calls.

And at last he will be able to take vacations, although he will usually refer to them as business trips and ostentatiously break them off in the middle for a few days to show that his physical presence in the office is necessary to the company's welfare. These vacations, however, will in all probability be spent at a very select executive club in the Bahamas where a golf course has somehow been coaxed out of the sand. Here, the conversation will still be about business and "gawlf," but the sun and the ocean will be lovely. He will be able to identify them from childhood memories.

More importantly, as a newly elected president of a corporation, the executive will immediately receive what is known as the "buildup" from the company's public relations counsel. A campaign will automatically be started to "develop his image" so that, by degrees, he will be "elected" to the boards of the local Community Chest, the local Red Cross drive, and a few carefully screened welfare agencies which will not require much of his time, but whose letterheads are well studded with executive names. A bank directorship will fall into his lap; he will find himself making speeches (ghosted) before civic groups; and thus, almost overnight, the "civic personage" will emerge.

And if a Republican Administration is in office, that will add just one more fillip to his image—he will be able to make frequent and satisfyingly mysterious trips to Washington.

He Wins the Ultimate Accolades

Most important of all, our executive now joins The Club. This may not necessarily be the best club in the area, although he will think it is. It certainly will have the most top executives in it, and it will unquestionably be the most lavish. Golf will naturally reign supreme among the members, but in the winter the newly arrived executive will find that curling is also socially acceptable among the set. The same excessive heartiness and slightly spurious bonhomie will prevail.

Our executive will still be a social disaster, but since his fellow members are likely to be disasters on an equal scale, he and they may never notice it.

The successful executive's final triumph will come when, in exchange for a company-endowed professorship, or perhaps for funds for a new library, he will be awarded an honorary doctorate by some reasonably prominent college, where he will make the usual commencement address about the importance of liberal education for executives. Then, and then only, will he have fully arrived in business. He has at last reached the summit. From then on, the road can lead only downward.

Sic Transit Gloria Mundi

And the descent is indeed precipitous. As he approaches 65 and compulsory retirement, he finds the younger wolves in the top-executive pack snapping ever closer at his heels. His authority begins to dwindle and, in self-defense, he adopts an increasingly elder-statesman attitude toward business affairs.

Finally, the day of retirement arrives. The company gives him a huge dinner where the mayor and other dignitaries heap eulogies on him. He receives a scroll; he responds with a gracious little speech. Then, oblivion. Five years later some of the secretaries in the office may know him by sight, but don't bet on it. For him, the race is done.

So here we have the U.S. executive—the man who is henceforth to be given a humanistic education in college, the man who is to be changed into a broader-gauged individual, a devotee of literature and the arts, a leader who is vibrantly concerned with national and world problems. Should we do this to him or not?

If broader education will help this man better to play his appointed role in life—even if it will only make him happier—then by all means let us steep him in Schopenhauer, Goya, and Mozart. If, on the other hand, too much exposure to the humanities and arts will have a deleterious effect on his performance in business—and this, I believe, is a real danger—then let us indeed proceed warily.

Why Gild the Lily?

It is often said that nothing is perfect in this world, and certainly this maxim is as applicable to the performance of the U.S. businessman as to anything else.

Even so, it is hard to imagine how the typical executive could do much better at his job than he is doing today. Never has his devotion to duty been more assiduous; never has so-called scientific management been practiced more widely; and never—even in 1971—have our corporations made more money.

And what of the much-touted U.S. standard of living—the envy of the world? Americans live better than anybody else: they eat better, and they have more possessions than anybody else. And there can be little doubt that this extraordinary achievement is due to the diligence and managerial acumen of our executive class. Doubtless this record can be bettered, and doubtless it will be. It would seem rash, however, to conclude on the basis of their performance that U.S. executives drastically need improvement.

But suppose they *could* stand some improving. Would having a broader cultural background contribute toward this end? I am convinced that the answer is negative. In fact, the results would be the exact opposite of those hoped for.

If his college courses developed in him a love for good reading, say, or for historical study, or for music, or for painting, would the executive be content to abandon these extrabusiness pursuits for the company grindstone? Would he be willing to work long hours during the week and sacrifice his weekends to the office and the golf course? Would he be willing to leave his friends and associations in Boston, and move to East Lockjaw, Texas, just to satisfy the whim of some superior? To put it in a nutshell, would he not demand to have a life apart from his business to which he would be free to devote a reasonable part of his time? Of course he would.

Consider, also, some of the other aspects of the life of the typical executive. As the game is played today, he must abdicate his responsibility for bringing up his children; a broad-gauged man would resent that fiercely. He must live in an all-executive suburb, miles away from orchestras, theaters, and museums; our broadened man would have an acquired need for these things, and he would insist on having them. He would abhor the social life he has to live—with its segregation of the sexes and total dearth of amusing and exhilarating conversation.

And suppose that his augmented background led him to develop a sincere interest in social welfare—say, boys-club or settlement-house work. Suppose he preferred to spend his Sunday afternoons in such pursuits, instead of groggily watching the Green Bay Packers on TV. Would he be able to satisfy his humanitarian desires and inclinations merely by having his name on the letterhead of the National Council for the Prevention of Childhood Diseases? No. He would start to cheat on his insatiable mistress, the company.

THE DANGERS OF SOPHISTICATION

If the executive did have all these outside interests to which he wished to devote time, and if he found his life in the office and the company of his business associates intellectually unsatisfying, the inevitable result would be a substantial diminution in his work output. No longer would he labor late into the night and no longer would he show up on Saturday and Sunday.

A reduction in his workweek from, say, 65 hours to 40 hours would decrease his contribution to the welfare of the company by as much as 40%, and the effect on its profits would almost certainly be comparable. This, of course, would not be so bad if only one individual or one company were involved, but if all the executives in the U.S. industrial complex get broadened, the results will be little short of catastrophic. . . .

The Threat of National Economic Crisis

Empirical reasoning first led me to the conclusion that any significant decrease in executive productivity would doom the nation. Because the conclusion might seem unduly alarmist to some, I sought statistical confirmation by enlisting the services of two of my mathematical colleagues at the Reichenbach Institute, Professor James Moriarity and Dr. Sebastian Moran.

These men mailed a questionnaire to some 500 top U.S. executives, requesting data on their work habits. Analysis of the replies they received shows a striking correlation between the executives' per-hour output and the performance of the U.S. economy, the curve for which is shown in the graph below.

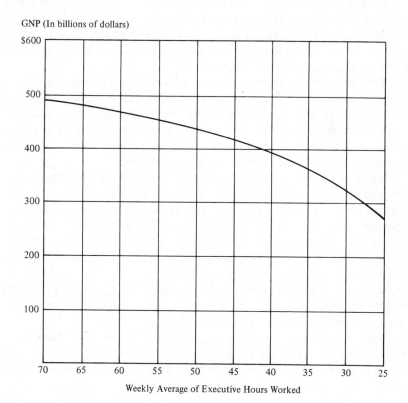

GNP (In billions of dollars)

Weekly Average of Executive Hours Worked

Given the downward slope of this curve, one begins to wonder whether the change in curriculum that is being suggested and, in some cases, already effected in executive education is not already having evil results. This change may be responsible in part for the economic slump that has occurred in the last two years. If this is in fact the case, the downward trend of the economy may be expected to accelerate sharply, unless the proponents of the "new education" are curbed.

For the mathematically curious, the equation of the curve developed by Messrs. Moriarity and Moran may be written as

$$\sqrt[4]{G} = \sum_{n=0}^{\infty} \frac{n^{n-1}(E + \infty^n)}{(n^{n-1})!}, \; G \geq n, E,$$

where

G = gross national product,
E = executive hours worked,
$\sum$ = the quantitative derivative,
n = hours devoted to extrabusiness activities,
∞ = coefficient of effectiveness (a constant).

Instead of growing at the hoped-for rate of 5% per year, the national economy will shrink, and unemployment will soar. Most serious of all, the United States will rapidly fall behind in its race with the Soviets and the Chinese for world leadership, until eventually the free world will slide helplessly into the arms of Communism.

This possibility is alarming enough in itself, but it becomes doubly so when one considers the side effects that may be expected to ensue if executive work output is in a permanent decline. For example, if the executive's interest in business affairs decreases, so will his interest in golf. If this occurs, one can expect a succession of country club bankruptcies (in fact, a number of prominent clubs have recently closed their doors).

Again, if the dissatisfied executive insists on moving from Darien to a city townhouse or apartment in proximity to concerts and museums, suburban real estate values will collapse. And as he also acquires a distaste for executive status symbols, the effect on the wall-to-wall carpet and furniture industries will be prompt and disastrous. General Motors' Cadillac Division will, of course, fold, throwing thousands of people out of work, and the Bahamas will once again revert to sand spits.

Ironically enough, even education will suffer, because the newly broadened executives will no longer be willing to trade new libraries, gymnasiums, and stadia for honorary LLDs.

Such would be the results of sophistication. If we were successful in grafting "culture" onto the executive, we would derange the fabric of his existence and wreck society in the process. Since he is doing so well for us now, and since, deep down in his existential being he knows no kinship for the life of liberal education, why tamper with his cultural naïveté? No, let us be as diabolical as Machiavelli, as scheming as Metternich—let us forgo this folly-ridden delusion that an executive must be a man for all seasons.

The lesson of the insects: Of course some will argue that all of this is merely supposititious and might easily not happen. Perhaps this is so, but the question I ask is: Can we afford to take a chance? If the executive is doing finely as he is, why run the risk of changing him? After all, he is entirely content with his own ghastly form of monasticism, and no one can argue that he is not being amply paid for what he does. Moreover, it is certain that the technical education he has traditionally received fits him perfectly for his destined role. One may recall the lunar insects in H. G. Wells's *The First Men in the Moon*, who were raised from birth in confined jars so that only those parts—claws, antennae, and so on—which they would need for their future industrial jobs would be permitted to grow. Have we not the same situation here in this matter of executive education?

Let us Harden Our Hearts

That about concludes my arguments, but before I finish, I must express one last caveat.

I have argued that too much (or possibly *any*) humanistic education will impair the performance of the men who are destined to manage the private sector of our nation's economy. The harshness of this concept may well arouse compassion within the hearts of many readers of this article, who may logically ask, "Why should these talented men be intellectually stunted merely to ensure their performance in the drab world of commerce? Why should they be singled out for special treatment, when their fellows on the highway of life are left free to achieve the fulfillment of each one's capabilities?"

My answers to these pleas are stern but, I think, reasonable. First, if our modern corporation executives lived unhappy lives in their chosen careers, we might be justified in feeling sorry for them. But they do not! Look at what we pay them. Look at the luxury in which they live. Look at the prestige they enjoy in the circles in which they move. No, these are by no means unhappy men in terms of their own aspirations and horizons.

And even if this were not so, the country's greater good must take precedence over sentimental considerations. The United States needs its executives, and it needs maximum performance from them. If their education must be truncated to ensure this performance, then let us harden our hearts and give them only the educational tools they need to fill their appointed roles in life. The future welfare of the United States is far too

important for us even to consider any alternative course of action, however
well motivated it may be.

Soap and education are not as sudden as a massacre,
but they are more deadly in the long run.
　　　　　Mark Twain (1835–1910), *The Facts Concerning the Recent Resignation*

Annotated Bibliography

This Annotated Bibliography is not intended to be exhaustive. It is comprehensive enough, or so it is hoped, that it will introduce the serious student of philosophy and the philosophy of education to some of the most important publications in the field. Through the reading of these works, and noting the bibliographies contained in some of them, the student can move on to certain other related and more technical works. For the most part textbooks have been excluded, except in certain instances where it was thought they contained material of sufficient importance to warrant inclusion. With a few exceptions, all the books were published in this century and deal with the more contemporary aspects of Western philosophy. Finally many of these books are in paperback. By a judicious selection of titles from this bibliography the student can begin to build for himself a personal library of some consequence at a modest cost.

Philosophy

AUSTIN, J. L., *How To Do Things With Words*. Cambridge: Harvard University Press, 1962. Pp. x + 167.

A collection of lecture notes used by the author in his William James Lectures at Harvard in 1955. This book will be of special interest to linguistic analysts. It provides a program for what might be done with words.

AYER, ALFRED JULES, *Language, Truth and Logic*. New York: Dover Publications, Inc., 1946. P. 159.

An avowed logical positivist writes on the elimination of metaphysics, the function of philosophy, the nature of philosophical analysis, the *A Priori*, truth and probability, ethics and theology, the self and the common world, and solutions of outstanding philosophical disputes. Ayer holds that our sentences express (1) genuine empirical hypotheses, (2) tautologies, or (3) metaphysical expressions that are neither true nor false but "literally senseless."

————, *The Origins of Pragmatism*. San Francisco: Freeman, Cooper & Company, 1968. Pp. xii + 336.

Ayer ignores the writings of others on Peirce and James and instead has tried to make up his own mind about what these men were saying. Also, he has developed some of his own theories on issues these two founders of pragmatism have raised.

————, *The Problem of Knowledge*. London: Macmillan & Company, Ltd., 1956. Pp. x + 258.

The author begins by raising the question, "What is meant by knowledge?" He then deals with the questions of skepticism and certainty. From this, he passes on to a detailed analysis of the philosophical problems of perception, memory, and "Myself and Others." Very well written.

————, *et al., The Revolution in Philosophy*. London: Macmillan & Company, Ltd., 1957. Pp. vi + 126.

A collection of lectures on outstanding figures in British philosophy from F. H. Bradley to Wittgenstein. Traces the origins of mathematical logic, logical atomism, the Vienna Circle, and linguistic analysis.

336

BARKER, STEPHEN F., *The Elements of Logic*. New York: McGraw-Hill Book Company, Inc., 1965. Pp. xiv + 336.
Covers the traditional topics in logic in concise and clear language.

BARRETT, WILLIAM, *What Is Existentialism?* New York: Grove Press, Inc., 1964. P. 218.
This volume is intended primarily to provide a comprehensive exposition of Heidegger's thinking.

———, *Irrational Man*. New York: Doubleday & Company, Inc., 1962. P. 314.
This is one of the more popular volumes on existentialism. It opens with an account of the advent of existentialism, traces the sources of existentialism in Western tradition, provides lengthy chapters on Kierkegaard, Nietzsche, Heidegger, and Sartre, and closes with a discussion of integral versus rational man. Very readable.

BLACK, MAX (ed.), *Philosophical Analysis—A Collection of Essays*. Ithaca, N.Y.: Cornell University Press, 1950. P. 429.
In his introduction to this book, Black cautions the reader against naïvely believing that there is but one school of philosophical analysis. The essays, which range from the mechanics of philosophical analysis to introspection, aesthetics, and ethics, substantiate Black's thesis.

BLANSHARD, BRAND, *Reason and Goodness*. New York: Macmillan Publishing Co., Inc., 1961. P. 451.
Blanshard sets out to defend the position of reason in ethics, which has come under recent philosophical attacks. He discusses tensions between reason and feeling, stoicism, subjectivism, deontology, instrumentalism, emotivism, the linguistic retreat from emotivism, goodness, thought and desire, reason and politics, and the rational temper.

BOBIK, JOSEPH (ed.), *The Nature of Philosophical Inquiry*. Notre Dame, Indiana: University of Notre Dame Press, 1970. Pp. x + 303.
Five different views of the nature of philosophy prepared by distinguished philosophers: Stephan Korner, Martin Versfeld, A. J. Ayer, Stephen Pepper, and O. K. Bouwsma.

BRANDT, RICHARD B., *Ethical Theory, The Problem of Normative and Critical Ethics*. Englewood Cliffs, N.J.: Prentice-Hall, Inc., 1959. Pp. xvi + 538.
Ranges over the main problems in ethics such as tests of ethical principles, science and ethics, noncognitivism, things worthwhile in themselves, justice, human rights, retributive justice, and determinism.

BUBER, MARTIN, *Between Man and Man*. London: Kegan Paul, 1947. Pp. viii + 210.
A collection of five works by Buber brought together in one volume for English readers. The first work, *Dialogue*, is intended to clarify the "dialogical" principle presented in Buber's I-Thou philosophy. The second work relates to politics and the third and fourth relate the dialogical principle to education. The book closes with a discussion of the essence of man.

———, *I and Thou*. New York: Charles Scribner's Sons, 1958. Pp. xviii + 137.
A presentation of the famous I-Thou and I-It categories. Buber sees man's relation with God as the basis for true humanity. God he sees entering relations with men in "creative, revealing and redeeming acts."

CASSIRER, ERNST, *An Essay on Man: An Introduction to a Philosophy of Human Culture*. New Haven: Yale University Press, 1944. Pp. xii + 237.

An examination of man's effort to understand himself and to deal with the problems of his universe through the creation and use of symbols. The book is broken down into two parts: "What Is Man?" and "Man and Culture." Excellent chapters on religion, language, art, history, and science.

CHAPPELL, V. C. (ed.), *The Philosophy of Mind.* Englewood Cliffs, N.J.: Prentice-Hall, Inc., 1962. Pp. xii + 178.

A collection of essays that deal with the main issues concerning mind, such as the problem of other minds, mind and body, concept of the person, and private and public behavior. This book will be of most help to the advanced student in philosophy and education.

COPI, IRVING M., *Introduction to Logic.* New York: Macmillan Publishing Co., Inc., 1972. Pp. xii + 540.

One of the standard textbooks in logic. It is divided into three sections: language, deduction, and induction.

COPLESTON, FREDERICK, S. J., *A History of Philosophy.* Garden City, N.Y.: Doubleday & Co., Inc.

An eight volume paperback history of philosophy written in an interesting and very instructive manner. Volume 8, (in two parts) published in 1966, is of special interest to students in education as it covers British Empiricism, American Pragmatism, and British and American Idealism.

DEWEY, JOHN, *Art as Experience.* New York: Minton, Balch & Company, 1934. Pp. xii + 348.

A series of lectures delivered at Harvard in 1931. Dewey relates art to his concept of experience and discusses the act of expression, the substance of art, the human contribution, and art and civilization.

———, *Experience and Nature.* New York: Dover Publications, Inc., 1958. Pp. xvi + 443.

The method of empirical naturalism is seen as the "only way" by which one can freely accept the standpoint and conclusions of modern science and yet maintain cherished values, provided they are critically clarified and reinforced.

———, *How We Think.* Boston: D. C. Heath and Company, 1933. Pp. x + 301.

In this well-known book Dewey discusses the problem of "training thought" in the schools and provides an analysis of what he calls the complete act of thought.

———, *Logic, the Theory of Inquiry.* New York: Holt, Rinehart and Winston, Inc., 1938. Pp. x + 546.

In Dewey's basic work in logic, he discusses the problem of logical subject-matter; the structure of inquiry and the construction of judgments, propositions, and terms; and the logic of scientific method.

———, *Problems of Men.* New York: Greenwood Press, Inc., 1968. P. 424.

Except for the introduction, this is a collection of essays reprinted from periodicals to which Dewey contributed in the 1930s and 1940s. The essays are grouped under "Democracy and Education," "Human Nature and Scholarship," "Value and Thought," and "About Thinkers."

———, *Reconstruction in Philosophy.* New York: Mentor Books, 1950. P. 168.

A series of lectures delivered in Japan in 1919 in which Dewey tried to "exhibit the general contrast between older and newer types of philosophical problems ..." He covered a broad range of subjects including science, logic, ethics, and social philosophy.

DRAKE, DURANT, et al. (eds.), *Essays in Critical Realism: A Cooperative Study of the Problems of Knowledge.* New York: Peter Smith, 1941. Pp. x + 244.

A collection of essays by Drake, Arthur O. Lovejoy, James B. Pratt, Arthur Rogers, George Santayana, R. W. Sellars, and C. A. Strong on such topics as pragmatism, knowledge, the problem of error, proofs of realism, and the nature of datum.

DUCASSE, CURT J., *Art, The Critics, and You.* Indianapolis: The Bobbs-Merrill Company, Inc., 1944. P. 170.

Describes the enterprise of esthetics and outlines the essentials of the author's philosophy of esthetics. Chapter 6 calls attention to the importance of education of human feelings and suggests that "the work of the various free and decorative arts have a role to play analogous to that of scientific treatises in education of the mind for activity in the fields of science."

EDIE, JAMES E. (ed.), *What is Phenomenology?* Chicago: Quadrangle Books, Inc., 1962. P. 191.

A translation of four essays written by Pierre Thevanez with an introduction by the editor and a preface by John Wild. Wild states that he knows of no brief introduction to phenomenology that is as accurate as this series of essays.

EDWARDS, PAUL (Editor-in-Chief), *The Encyclopedia of Philosophy.* New York: Macmillan Publishing Co., Inc., and The Free Press, 1967.

More than 1,500 articles on philosophical theories, concepts, and individual thinkers written for the most part by distinguished United States, British, and Canadian scholars.

————, and ARTHUR PAP (eds.), *A Modern Introduction to Philosophy.* New York: The Free Press, 1965. Pp. xviii + 797.

A collection of readings on seven problems: determinism, induction, mind, morals, existence of God, perception, *a priori* knowledge, and meaning. Noted for its excellent bibliographies to be found at the end of each section.

EWING, ALFRED CYRIL, *The Idealist Tradition: from Berkeley to Blanshard.* Glencoe, Ill.: The Free Press, 1957. Pp. xxii + 369.

Chapters on Berkeley, Kant, Hegel, Schopenhauer, Green, Bradley, Bosanquet, Royce, Croce, Blanshard, and others. A section on the critics of idealism.

FEIGL, HERBERT, and MAY BROADBECK (eds.), *Readings in the Philosophy of Science.* New York: Appleton-Century-Crofts, 1953. Pp. x + 811.

The editors define philosophy of science as a way of talking about science and classify it as a specialized part of analytical philosophy. The readings cover the natural, biological, and social sciences.

FEIGL, HERBERT, and WILFRED SELLERS (eds.), *Readings in Philosophical Analysis.* New York: Appleton-Century-Crofts, 1949. Pp. x + 626.

Readings arranged under the headings of Language, Meaning and Truth, Meaningfulness and Confirmation, The Nature of Logic and Mathematics, *A Priori* Knowledge, Data, Reality and the Mind-Body Problem, Problems of Description and Explanation, and Problems of Theoretical Ethics. All selections are from the writings of well-known philosophers.

FRANKENA, WILLIAM K., *Ethics.* Englewood Cliffs, N.J.: Prentice-Hall, Inc., 1963. Pp. xvi + 109.

The author seeks to do moral philosophy and not just talk about it. He clearly marks out the differences between judgments of moral obligations, judgments of

moral value, and judgments of nonmoral value. An excellent introduction to the
subject of ethics by an analyst much interested in education.

GOROVITZ, S., R. WILLIAMS, et al., *Philosophical Analysis: Introduction to Its Language and Techniques*. New York: Random House, Inc., 1965. Pp. xii + 137.

A very helpful reference prepared by Stanford University graduate students.
Chapters on elementary logic, predicate calculus and sets, assertions, sentences
and propositions, extensional and intensional sentences, the Analytic-Synthetic
and *a priori* and *a posteriori* distinctions, definitions, reading and writing philosophy, and divisions of philosophy.

HAMPSHIRE, STUART, *Thought and Action*. London: Chatto and Windus, 1959. P. 276.

Written for the layman, this book has been called a philosopher's essay in unphilosophical thinking. The book invites its readers to consider what it means to be
one's self. Discusses such topics as freedom of the will, moral philosophy, philosophy of the mind, and the relation between knowledge and action.

HARE, R. M., *The Language of Morals*. London: Oxford University Press, 1952. Pp. viii + 202.

Recognized as one of the most important studies in analysis and morals. The
author conceives of ethics as "the logical study of the language of morals." The
book is divided into three sections dealing with "the imperative mood," "good,"
and "ought." Must reading.

HOCKING, WILLIAM ERNEST, *The Lasting Elements of Individualism*. New Haven:
Yale University Press, 1937. Pp. xiv + 187.

Dedicated to John Dewey, this little book is called by its author ... "a study in
the philosophy of history—looking forward." Hocking is hostile to "mere pragmatism" but not to "pragmatism" for he believes it is ... "destined to transform
itself into a version of the 'dialectic method' whereby mere groping takes on
a rational direction and destination." He discusses the individual as a unit of
social order, liberalism, two necessities for future societies, and the Co-agent
state.

HOLT, EDWIN, et al., *The New Realism: Cooperative Studies in Philosophy*. New
York: Macmillan Publishing Co., Inc., 1912. Pp. xii + 491.

A collection of essays on the historical significance of realism, the emancipation
of metaphysics from epistemology, a realistic theory of independence, a defense of
analysis, truth and error, illusory experience, and some implications of biology
for realism. Note especially R. B. Perry's essay on "A Realistic Theory of
Independence."

HOSPERS, JOHN, *An Introduction to Philosophical Analysis*. Englewood Cliffs, N.J.:
Prentice-Hall, Inc., 1953. Pp. xii + 532.

An extremely interesting and readable book. The first four chapters are exceptionally helpful to beginning students in philosophy and education. These deal
with words and the world, necessary knowledge, empirical knowledge, law, cause,
and freedom.

JAMES, WILLIAM, *Pragmatism and Four Essays from The Meaning of Truth*. New
York: Meridian Books, Inc., 1955. P. 269.

A series of lectures delivered at the Lowell Institute in Boston and at Columbia
University in which James admits that he does not like the name pragmatism but
goes on to explain what he means by the term. He discusses truth, religion,
humanism, and several other philosophical problems. An American philosophical classic.

JASPERS, KARL, *Reason and Existenz.* New York: The Noonday Press, 1955. P. 157. Translated with an introduction prepared by William Earle, this collection of lectures in existential philosophy covers the origin of the contemporary philosophical situation, basic ideas for the clarification of reason and existenz, and possibilities for contemporary philosophizing.

JOHNSTONE, HENRY W., Jr. (ed.), *What is Philosophy?* New York: Macmillan Publishing Co., Inc., 1965. P. 118.

A collection of essays by modern philosophers on the nature of philosophy. The editor has prepared a most helpful introduction to his book in which he states that there is no general agreement among contemporary philosophers as to just what the role of philosophy is or should be. Provides a wide range of views including those of Maritain, Dewey, Russell, Husserl, and Heidegger.

JONES, WILLIAM THOMAS, *History of Western Philosophy.* New York: Harcourt Brace Jouanovich, Inc., 1952. Pp. xviii + 1036.

Jones concentrates upon the main figures in Western philosophy, presents extensive quotations from each, and sketches in a cultural background for each. The key passages quoted are connected in the text by comment, criticism, and interpretation.

KAUFMANN, WALTER, *Existentialism from Dostoevsky to Sartre.* New York: Meridian Books, Inc., 1956. P. 319.

A collection of writings from Dostoevsky, Kierkegaard, Nietzsche, Rilke, Kafka, Jaspers, Heidegger, and Sartre. An excellent introduction and short biographical sketches tie the selections together.

LANGER, SUSANNE K., *Feeling and Form.* New York: Charles Scribner's Sons, 1953. Pp. xvi + 431.

Langer developed her theory of art from her theory of symbolism set forth in *Philosophy in a New Key.* She discusses her philosophy of art under three headings: The Art Symbol, The Making of the Symbol, and The Power of the Symbol.

———, *Philosophy in a New Key.* New York: Mentor Books, 1948. P. 248.

A study in symbolism, the key "to all humanistic problems. In it lies a new conception of 'mentality', that may illuminate questions of life and consciousness, instead of obscuring them as traditional 'scientific methods' have done." Chapters on logic of signs and symbols, language, sacrament, myth, music, art, and meaning.

LEWIS, CLARENCE IRVING, *An Analysis of Knowledge and Valuation.* LaSalle, Ill.: The Open Court Publishing Company, 1946. Pp. xxii + 568.

A naturalistic conception of valuation is based upon a careful study of meaning and analytic truth and empirical knowledge. A sophisticated study of empiricism and naturalistic ethics and esthetics by one of our most noted philosophers.

———, *The Ground and Nature of the Right.* New York: Columbia University Press, 1955. Pp. x + 97.

Delivered as Woodbridge Lectures at Columbia in 1954. The lectures cover the subjects of "Modes of Right and Wrong," "Right Believing and Concluding," "Right Doing," "The Right and the Good," and "The Rational Imperatives."

———, *Our Social Inheritance.* Bloomington: Indiana University Press, 1957. P. 110.

Points up the complex requirements that must be met if man is to be prepared to live a civilized life. Quickly traces the social inheritance of twentieth-century Americana, discusses some of the principal ingredients in the human mentality, and concludes with a treatment of critical judgments.

MARCEL, GABRIEL, *The Philosophy of Existentialism.* New York: The Citadel Press, 1961. P. 128.
A collection of three papers written by a famous Catholic Existentialist. The first explains the main points in Marcel's position, the second is a critical survey of Sartre's philosophy, and the third seeks to define the doctrine that Marcel holds. "An Essay in Autobiography" concludes the book.

MEHTA, VED, *Fly and the Fly-Bottle.* Baltimore: Penguin Books, Inc., 1965. P. 223.
A collection of essays based upon interviews with British philosophers and historians. Exciting account of contemporary British philosophy destroying several erroneous American notions about British philosophy and history.

MOORE, GEORGE EDWARD, *Principia Ethica.* Cambridge: Cambridge University Press, 1959. Pp. xxviii + 232.
One of the most influential books of this century covering such topics as the subject matter of ethics, naturalistic ethics, hedonism, metaphysical ethics, conduct, and the ideal. The discussion revolves about two principal questions: What kinds of things are intrinsically good? and What kinds of acts ought we to perform?

MURRAY, JAMES A. H., HENRY BRADLEY, W. A. CRAIGIE, and C. T. ONIONS, *The Oxford English Dictionary.* Oxford, England: The Clarendon Press, 1961.
A twelve volume dictionary that presents in alphabetical series "the words that have formed the English vocabulary from the time of earliest records down to the present day, with all the relevant facts concerning their form, sense-history, pronunciation, and etymology." A primary source for those doing concept analysis.

NAGEL, ERNEST, *Sovereign Reason and Other Studies in the Philosophy of Science.* New York: The Free Press, 1954. P. 315.
Sixteen essays built around four themes: the relation of abstract theory to ordinary experience, the nature of reliable knowledge, the expendable nature of metaphysical systems, and the impact of new ways of thinking developed by scientific research.

——, *The Structure of Science: Problems in the Logic of Scientific Explanation.* New York: Harcourt Brace Jovanovich, Inc., 1961. P. 618.
An examination of logical patterns in scientific knowledge and the logical methods of modern science. Sections on social sciences and history especially interesting.

NOWELL-SMITH, PATRICK H., *Ethics.* Great Britain: Billing & Sons, Ltd. Guildford-London, Penguin Books, Inc., 1954 and 1957. P. 283.
In the first part of his book, Nowell-Smith develops the principles of linguistic analysis implicit in moral language. These tools are applied to the general moral behaviors of choosing, advising, duty, and obligation. The book concludes with a brief epilogue cautioning against unwarranted generalizations and stressing the necessary individuality of morality.

OGDEN, C. K. and I. A. RICHARDS, *The Meaning of Meaning.* New York: Harcourt Brace Jovanovich, Inc., 1938. Pp. xxxii + 544.
A study of the scope and task of the Science of Symbolism. Chapters on thought, words and things, the power of words, sign-situations, signs in perception, canons of symbolism, definitions, meaning of beauty, meaning of philosophers, the meaning of meaning, and symbol situations.

OTTO, MAX, *Science and the Moral Life.* New York: Mentor Books, 1949. P. 192.

Otto maintains that the impulse of our time is "life more abundant." He reminds us, however, that the crucial question is "What meaning shall we give to life more abundant?" The author is convinced that the scientific method must be put to work in man's search for the good life—"the good life richly and profoundly conceived."

PARKER, DeWITT H., *Human Values. An Interpretation of Ethics Based on a Study of Values.* New York: Harper & Row, Publishers, 1931. Pp. x + 415.

Parker maintains there is no separate moral interest or value but that . . . "morality is indissolubly connected with every branch of human activity." Beginning with this presupposition the author then discusses the fundamental principles of value—the values of "real life" and the values of "imagination."

PARKINSON, G. H. R. (ed.), *The Theory of Meaning.* Glasgow, Scotland: Oxford University Press, 1968. P. 188.

This is one of a series of books published under the general editorship of G. J. Warnock of Magdalen College, Oxford. The aim of the series, "Oxford Readings in Philosophy," is to bring together important recent writings in major areas of philosophical inquiry. This particular book includes chapters on verification, verifiability, referring, uses of language, meaning, and the like.

PASSMORE, JOHN, *A Hundred Years of Philosophy.* London: Gerald Duckworth & Co., Ltd., 1957. P. 523.

Traces the history of philosophy from John Stuart Mill down to the present. Excellent chapters on pragmatism, logic, the new realism, logical positivism, Wittgenstein, and existentialism.

PEPPER, STEPHEN C., *The Sources of Value.* Berkeley: University of California Press, 1958. Pp. xiv + 732.

Pepper recognizes a common problem running throughout the study of value, "how to make well-grounded decisions in human affairs?" Drawing heavily upon psychology he sets forth the contextualists' view of the source of our values. His discussion of the legislation among values is insightful.

PERRY, RALPH BARTON, *Realms of Value. A Critique of Human Civilization.* Cambridge, Mass.: Harvard University Press, 1954. Pp. xiv + 497.

A book written to bring "unity and order" into the fields of the natural and social sciences, aesthetics, philosophy of education, and philosophy of religion by "adhering constantly to a fundamental definition of value . . . a thing—anything—has value, or is valuable . . . when it is the object of an interest—any interest. Or, whatever is object of interest is ipso facto valuable."

The Philosopher's Index. Bowling Green, Ohio: Philosophy Documentation Center.

An international subject and author index, which includes abstracts of all major American and British philosophical periodicals and selected journals in other languages and related interdisciplinary publications. Published quarterly. A most useful guide to publications in philosophy and in education.

PITCHER, GEORGE, *The Philosophy of Wittgenstein.* Englewood Cliffs, N.J.: Prentice-Hall, Inc., 1964. P. 334.

Pitcher bases the need for this simplified and rather lengthy introduction to *The Tractatus* and *Philosophical Analysis* on two premises: that Wittgenstein is a great philosopher and that his writings are deceptively simple. One must agree with these premises to appreciate this book. His analysis is an effort to provide a general and uncritical framework within which to understand Wittgenstein's process of thought. The more obtuse sections of Wittgenstein's philosophy are untouched.

POPPER, KARL R., *Conjectures and Refutations*. New York: Basic Books, Inc., 1962. Pp. xiii + 405.

A collection of essays and lectures designed to develop a theory of knowledge and its growth. Discussions of three views of human knowledge and the demarcation between science and metaphysics are particularly valuable.

RATNER, JOSEPH, *Intelligence in the Modern World: John Dewey's Philosophy*. New York: The Modern Library, 1939. Pp. xvi + 1077.

An excellent introduction of more than two hundred pages precedes more than eight hundred pages excerpted from Dewey's writings on such diverse subjects as science, social philosophy, law, education, psychology, logic, religion, aesthetics, and meaning. An excellent collection from Dewey's major works.

REICHENBACH, HANS, *The Rise of Scientific Philosophy*. Berkeley: University of California Press, 1957. Pp. xii + 333.

The author states that his purpose in writing this book is to show that philosophy has proceeded from speculation to science. The book is divided into two parts: The Roots of Speculative Philosophy and The Results of Scientific Philosophy. The final chapter compares the speculative with the scientific philosophy.

RICE, PHILIP BLAIR, *On the Knowledge of Good and Evil*. New York: Random House, 1955. P. 299.

The author holds that the language of ethics has two main functions, first to guide conduct and second ". . . to do this with the aid of knowledge, or reflective awareness of the natural and human world."

ROYCE, JOSIAH, *Lectures on Modern Idealism*. New Haven: Yale University Press, 1919. Pp. xii + 266.

Lectures delivered at Johns Hopkins University on Kant's conception of the nature and conditions of knowledge, Kant's conception of the self, the dialectical method, later problems of idealism, and so forth.

RUSSELL, BERTRAND, *A History of Western Philosophy*. New York: Simon and Schuster, 1945. Pp. xxiv + 895.

Russell's purpose is to exhibit philosophy as an integral part of social and political life. As a result it contains more general history than is usually found in such treatments. The book covers the period from ancient philosophy to the time of its publication. Very entertaining reading.

————, *Human Knowledge: Its Scope and Limits*. New York: Simon and Schuster, 1948. Pp. xvi + 524.

Russell recognizes that skepticism is " logically impeccable " but " psychologically impossible." He sets out to examine the relation between individual experience and the body of scientific knowledge we possess. The book is divided into sections on the world of science, language, science and perception, scientific concepts, probability, and postulates of scientific inference.

————, *The Problems of Philosophy*. New York: Oxford University Press, A Galaxy Book, 1959. P. 161.

Russell confines himself ". . . in the main to those problems of philosophy in regard to which I thought it possible to say something positive and constructive . . ." The major emphasis in this book is upon epistemological issues rather than upon metaphysical matters.

RYLE, GILBERT, *The Concept of Mind*. New York: Barnes & Noble, Inc., 1949. P. 334. This is one of the more important recent books in philosophy. It is intended "... not to increase what we know about minds, but to rectify the logical geography of the knowledge we already possess." This is the book in which Ryle identifies what he calls "the ghost in the machine."

SARTRE, JEAN-PAUL, *Existentialism and Human Emotions*. New York: Philosophical Library, Inc., 1957. P. 96.
The author sets out to defend existentialism against charges that have been brought against it. He moves on to the chief focus of his work, which is that man is personally responsible for what he is and what he does; that there are no values external to man, and no given human nature he is destined to fulfill.

SCHILPP, PAUL ARTHUR (ed.), *The Philosophy of John Dewey*. New York: Tudor Publishing Company, 1951. Pp. xvi + 718.
Brief biography of Dewey, articles on aspects of Dewey's philosophy by noted philosophers, and a reply by Dewey. An extensive bibliography of Dewey's works.

———, *The Philosophy of Bertrand Russell*. Evanston, Ill.: The Library of Living Philosophers, 1944. Pp. xvi + 815.
Russell's autobiography, descriptive and critical essays on his philosophy, and Russell's reply to his critics and bibliography of his principal writings.

———, *The Philosophy of Alfred North Whitehead*. Evanston, Ill.: The Library of Living Philosophers, 1941. Pp. xx + 745.
This is another in the series, "The Library of Living Philosophers," edited by Professor Schilpp. This volume on Whitehead contains Whitehead's autobiography, descriptive and critical essays on the philosophy of Whitehead by a number of authorities, and an extended bibliography of Whitehead's writings. Chapter 17 deals with Whitehead's views on education.

SCHNEIDER, HERBERT W., *A History of American Philosophy*. New York: Columbia University Press, 1963. Pp. xviii + 590.
Traces the history of American philosophy from puritan times to the "emergence of naturalistic realisms in the twentieth century." Many references to education throughout.

———, *Three Dimensions of Public Morality*. Bloomington: Indiana University Press, 1956. P. 166.
A very general and elementary moral treatise exploring the interrelations and correlation of our traditional ideals of "Liberty, Equality, and Fraternity."

SELLARS, ROY WOOD, *The Philosophy of Physical Realism*. New York: Macmillan Publishing Co., Inc., 1932. Pp. xvi + 487.
Sellars rejects "probable realism" and Kantian Noumena, and defends physical realism.

SPIEGELBERG, HERBERT, *Phenomenological Movement: A Historical Introduction*. The Hague: Martinus Nijhoff, 1965. Pp. xxvi + 765.
Volume 1 defines the phenomenological movement and traces its development from Brentano to Nicolai Hartmann. Volume 2 traces the French phase of the movement, discusses phenomenology at midcentury, and concludes with the essentials of the phenomenological method.

STEVENSON, CHARLES L., *Ethics and Language*. New Haven: Yale University Press, 1944. Pp. xii + 338.

The author's object is to clarify the meaning of ethical terms and "to characterize the general methods by which ethical judgments can be proved or supported." A very influential book in American philosophy.

TOULMIN, STEPHEN EDELSTON, *An Examination of the Place of Reason in Ethics*. Cambridge: Cambridge University Press, 1958. Pp. xiv + 228.
The author examines the traditional approaches to ethics, the relation of logic and life, the nature of ethics, and the boundaries of reason. He contends that the common weakness of all traditional ethical theories is that they give no adequate account of ethical reasoning.

ULICH, ROBERT, *The Human Career: A Philosophy of Self-Transcendence*. New York: Harper & Row, Publishers, 1955. Pp. xvi + 255.
The author examines modern civilization, views man as a self-transcending being, and declares that if our opinions are to be of worth they must be based upon criteria gained from a new understanding of the human being. This understanding lies in the direction of a restless search for new meanings.

URMSON, J. O., *Philosophical Analysis: Its Development Between the Two Wars*. Oxford at the Clarendon Press, 1956. Pp. x + 203.
A discussion of philosophical analysis and logical atomism, logical positivism and the downfall of logical atomism, and the beginnings of contemporary philosophy.

WARNOCK, G. J., *English Philosophy Since 1900*. London: Oxford University Press, 1958. Pp. x + 180.
A study of the evolution of English philosophy in this century. Separate chapters on Moore, Russell, Wittgenstein, logical positivism, logic, metaphysics and philosophy, and belief.

WARNOCK, MARY, *Ethics Since 1900*. London: Oxford University Press, 1960. Pp. viii + 207.
A study of the different kinds of moral philosophy current during the past sixty years. The book begins with Bradley's metaphysical ethics, proceeds through Moore, intuitionism, the emotive theory, and moral psychology and closes with a lengthy chapter on "Existentialism: J. P. Sartre."

WHITE, MORTON, *The Age of Analysis*. New York: Mentor Books, 1955. P. 253.
Commentaries on the writings of leading twentieth-century philosophers: G. E. Moore, Croce, Santayana, Bergson, Whitchead, Husserl, Sartre, Peirce, James, Dewey, Russell, Carnap, and Wittgenstein. Selections from the writings of each are included.

————, *Foundations of Historical Knowledge*. New York: Harper & Row, Publishers, 1965. Pp. xii + 299.
A discussion of fact, law, and value in history; explanatory arguments and explanatory statements; causal interpretations; reasons; historical narration; and ethics and free will. An excellent analysis of what history is and what the historian does.

————, *The Origins of Dewey's Instrumentalism*. New York: Octagon Books, Inc., 1964. Pp. xvi + 161.
An essay on Dewey's ideas of the nature of inquiry. Dewey's intellectual conversion from idealism to instrumentalism is traced in a chronicle covering the years 1879 to 1903.

————, *Science and Sentiment in America*. New York: Oxford University Press, 1972. Pp. x + 358.

A study of American philosophical thought from Jonathan Edwards to John Dewey with especial attention to the responses to the challenges posed by natural science.

WHITEHEAD, A. N., *Adventure of Ideas*. New York: Mentor Books, 1955. P. 302. Whitehead states that this book " is a study of the concept of civilization, and an endeavor to understand how it is that civilized beings arise." One point emphasized throughout is the importance of adventure for the promotion and preservation of civilization. The book contains four parts: " Sociological," " Cosmological," " Philosophical," and " Civilization."

————, *Science and the Modern World*. New York: Mentor Books, 1948. P. 212. Perhaps Whitehead's most widely read publication. A series of eight lectures delivered at Harvard in 1925 covering such topics as the origins of modern science, relativity, quantum theory, science and philosophy, abstraction, God, religion and science, and the requisites for social progress.

WIENER, PHILIP P. (ed.), *Values in a Universe of Change: Selected Writings of Charles S. Peirce*. New York: Doubleday & Co., Inc., 1958. Pp. xxvi + 446. The editor of this book has been guided by two considerations: the introduction of the reader " to the many sides of the most versatile, profound, and original philosopher that the United States has ever produced " and to include " unpublished and inaccessible material in which Peirce presented the cultural or humanistic aspects of science and philosophy . . ." Sections on the philosophy of science, materialism, religion, and education.

WILD, JOHN, *The Challenge of Existentialism*. Bloomington: Indiana University Press, 1959. Pp. viii + 297. The author's aim is "to present the reader with a critical exposition of this phenomenological philosophy of existence." He gives the background of this way of thought, develops some of its basic doctrines, and discusses some of the advantages and defects of these doctrines.

WITTGENSTEIN, LUDWIG (trans. by G. E. M. Anscombe), *Philosophical Investigations*. Oxford: Basil Blackwell, 1953. Pp. xii + 232. A highly influential publication in Western analytic philosophy. These "remarks," as Wittgenstein called them, were published to contrast his newer philosophical thought with that contained in *Tractatus Logico-Philosophicus*, a work he came to believe contained " grave mistakes."

Philosophy of Education

ARCHAMBAULT, REGINALD D. (ed.), *John Dewey on Education: Selected Writings.* New York: Modern Library, 1964. Pp. xxx + 439.

This book is intended to promote a new look at Dewey's educational theory. Selections from his major writings in education and some basic statements of his philosophical position are included. The material is grouped under the rubrics: philosophy and education, ethics and education, aesthetics and education, science and education, psychology and education, society and education, and principles of pedagogy.

———, *Philosophical Analysis and Education.* New York: The Humanities Press, 1965. Pp. xii + 212.

A collection of essays by British authors designed to define the philosophical study of education. The essays are arranged under four headings: the nature and function of educational theory, context of educational discussion, conceptions of teaching, and the essence of education. Many will find the editor's introduction quite helpful in explaining the present status of educational theory and the place of philosophy in it.

ARNSTINE, DONALD, *Philosophy of Education: Learning and Schooling.* New York: Harper & Row, Publishers, 1967. Pp. x + 388.

A study of education using the tools of psychology and philosophy. Chapters on method, learning, schooling, curriculum, aesthetics, and curiosity.

BANDMAN, BERTRAM, *The Place of Reason in Education.* Columbus, Ohio: Ohio State University Press, 1967. P. 200.

The purpose of this study "is to determine what, if anything, qualifies as a rational argument to help us decide what should be taught." The author discusses the two senses of argument, the use of metaphysical and moral arguments in education, and the place of metaphysical and moral reasons in education.

BANDMAN, BERTRAM, and ROBERT S. GUTTCHEN (eds.), *Philosophical Essays on Teaching.* Philadelphia: J. B. Lippincott Co., 1969. Pp. x + 326.

There has been a great deal of philosophical work done on the concepts of teaching, learning, and knowing during the past decade. Much of that work is included in this anthology.

348

BAYLES, ERNEST E., *Democratic Educational Theory*. New York: Harper & Row, Publishers, 1960. Pp. xii + 266.

The author works out what he sees as the logical consequences of the national democratic commitment and states what ought to be the major tenets of a genuinely democratic educational program. He reports on experiments with reflective thinking, discusses value theory, religion and character education, educational purposes, evaluation of pupil progress, and concludes with chapters on Dewey, progressivism, and the present status of educational theory in the United States.

———, *Pragmatism in Education*. New York: Harper & Row, Publishers, 1966. Pp. xii + 146.

Written to promote an understanding of pragmatism and its meaning for educational practice. Chapters on relativity; the nature of man; truth, value, and existence; the nature of culture; educational purpose and program; and illustrative units.

BELTH, MARC, *Education as a Discipline: A Study of the Role of Models in Thinking*. Boston: Allyn and Bacon, Inc., 1965. Pp. xviii + 317.

A logical analysis of the structure of education with attention given to the concept of education, scope of the study of education, elements of education, educational thinking, organization of elements in the discipline, models of education, self-corrective procedure, and the curriculum.

BEN-HORIN, MEIR, *Common Faith—Uncommon People: Essays in Reconstructionist Judaism*. New York: Reconstructionist Press, 1970. P. 245.

These essays are divided into three groups: Dimensions of Judaism, Dimensions of Jewish Education, and Dimensions of Zionism. Of these three, the section on education is the longest. This book definitely reflects the Reconstructionist position and cannot, therefore, be said to represent the thinking of all Jews on the matters discussed. A strong case is made for faith in intelligence in face of a trend toward antirationalism.

BEREDAY, GEORGE Z., and JOSEPH A. LAUWERYS, *Education and Philosophy*. New York: World Book Company, 1957. Pp. xiv + 578.

One of the few books in the field that provides insights into the nature of philosophy of education in countries outside of Western Europe and North America. Sections devoted to "The Great Traditions," "Determinants of Policy," "National Systems," "Historical Examples," "Experimental Institutions," and "The Teaching of Philosophy of Education."

BIGGE, MORRIS L., *Positive Relativism: An Emergent Educational Philosophy*. New York: Harper & Row, Publishers, 1971, Pp. x + 182.

Bigge describes positive relativism as an extension and refinement of the educational implications of John Dewey. His book is intended as "a development of a systematic, normative educational philosophy-positive relativism-supported by a coordinate, apposite educational psychology-cognitive field psychology."

BRAMELD, THEODORE, *Education as Power*. New York: Holt, Rinehart and Winston, Inc., 1965. Pp. xiv + 146.

A series of lectures delivered in Korea. Readers will find Chapter 4 a clear outline of the author's position. The charter for educational leadership, given in the appendix, sets forth eight guiding concepts to which Brameld is committed and to which he would have us commit ourselves.

————, *Education for the Emerging Age.* New York: Harper & Row, Publishers, 1965. Pp. xii + 244.

Brameld sees the task of education as embracing "the whole complex of human dynamics through which every culture seeks both to maintain and to innovate its structures, operations, purposes." In no sense should education and schooling be considered synonymous. The author discusses the philosophical foundations of education with particular emphasis upon his reconstructionism, indicates the need for an interdisciplinary approach to educational problems, treats three current controversial issues in education, and points up the kind of education needed to bring about a "cultural renaissance."

————, *Patterns of Educational Philosophy: Divergence and Convergence in Culturological Perspective.* New York: Holt, Rinehart and Winston, Inc., 1971. Pp. xx + 615.

Brameld draws upon three disciplines: education, anthropology, and philosophy, as he discusses education in an age of crisis. The author examines progressivism, essentialism, perennialism, and reconstructionism. He is known, of course, as a foremost advocate of reconstructionism.

BUTLER, J. DONALD, *Idealism and Education.* New York: Harper & Row, Publishers, 1966. Pp. xiv + 144.

This little book explains what idealism is and attempts to view it critically within the context of present events. Chapter 3 focuses upon "Idealism as a Philosophy of Education."

CHAMBLISS, J. J., *Boyd H. Bode's Philosophy of Education.* Columbus, Ohio: Ohio State University Press, 1963. Pp. xii + 98.

This essay places emphasis upon Bode's criticism of various points of view in educational theory and practice, his concern for the common man, and his efforts to draw meaning from pragmatism for the purpose of humanizing education. Extensive quotations from Bode and well documented.

————, *The Origins of American Philosophy of Education.* The Hague: Martinus Nijhoff, 1968. Pp. viii + 114.

Traces the development of philosophy of education in the United States from Joseph Neef's, *Sketch of a Plan and Method of Education* (1808) to Paul Monroe's, *Cyclopedia of Education* (1911–1913).

DEARDEN, R. F., P. H. HIRST, and R. S. PETERS, *Education and the Development of Reason.* London: Routledge & Kegan Paul, 1972. Pp. xiv + 536.

A collection of essays on the nature of education and its aims; the nature of reason and its relationship to feeling, willing, and acting; and the development of reason in an educational context. Most of the articles prepared by British philosophers.

DEIGHTON, LEE C. (Editor-in-Chief), *The Encyclopedia of Education.* New York: Macmillan Publishing Co., Inc., and the Free Press, 1971.

A ten volume work containing more than 1,000 articles on education. A helpful general reference that purports "to offer a view of the institutions and people, of the processes and products, found in educational practice."

DEWEY, JOHN, *The Child and the Curriculum and The School and Society.* Chicago: The University of Chicago Press, Phoenix Books, (n.d.). Pp. xii + 159.

Two of Dewey's more important works are published in one volume. The discussion of psychologizing materials of instruction is quite valuable. There are illustrations of children's work in the Dewey School at the University of Chicago. These essays are reproduced elsewhere; see: Dworkin, *Dewey on Education.*

————, *Democracy and Education.* New York: Macmillan Publishing Co., Inc., 1916. Pp. xiv + 434.

Intended as an introduction to the philosophy of education, this is Dewey's magnum opus on education. Must reading for all serious students in the field.

————, *Experience and Education.* New York: Macmillan Publishing Co., Inc., 1938. Pp. xvi + 116.

Nearly eighty, Dewey looks back upon progressive education to point out what he considers to be the difference between progressive education and traditional education. He issues warnings to those disposed to think in either-or terms and clearly states wherein he believes progressive education, or at least some of its exponents, have failed. The book closes on an optimistic note.

————, *Moral Principles in Education.* New York: The Wisdom Library, 1959. Pp. xii + 61.

Selections from Dewey's essay on "Ethical Principles Underlying Education," which was originally published in the *Third Yearbook of the National Herbart Society for the Study of Education.*

Subjects covered include the moral purpose of the school, moral training supplied by the school community, social nature of the course of study, and psychological aspects of moral education.

DUNKEL, HAROLD B., *Whitehead on Education.* Columbus, Ohio: Ohio State University Press, 1965. Pp. xvi + 182.

A comprehensive study of Whitehead's philosophy and his writings on education. The book is intended to establish relationships between the two as well as to offer criticisms of Whitehead's work in education.

DWORKIN, MARTIN S., *Dewey on Education.* New York: Bureau of Publications, Teachers College, Columbia University, 1959. P. 134.

A handy reference for those who wish to read John Dewey's "My Pedagogic Creed," "The School and Society," "The Child and the Curriculum," and "Progressive Education and the Science of Education." The last named is particularly pertinent today. This collection closes with the last published work on education by Dewey, an introduction to a book by Elsie Ripley Clapp, *The Use of Resources in Education.*

EBEL, ROBERT L. (ed.), *Encyclopedia of Educational Research.* (4th ed.) New York: Macmillan Publishing Co., Inc., 1960. Pp. xx + 1522.

This work presents a critical evaluation, synthesis, and interpretation of reported studies in educational research. A brief selected bibliography follows each article. Another handy reference.

Educational Theory. JOE BURNETT, Editor, Editorial Office, 276 Education Building, University of Illinois, Urbana, Illinois.

Published quarterly by the John Dewey Society and the Philosophy of Education Society. The purpose of this journal is to foster the continuing development of educational theory and to encourage wide and effective discussion of theoretical problems in education.

EHLERS, HENRY (ed.), *Crucial Issues in Education.* New York: Holt, Rinehart and Winston, Inc., 1969. Pp. xvi + 357.

A collection of readings on a broad range of topics such as national unity, poverty, segregation, excellence, religious education, instructional strategies, and the teaching profession. The readings are carefully selected and well arranged.

Encyclical Letter, *Divini Illius Magistri of His Holiness Pope Pius XI*. New York: The American Press, 1936. P. 35.

Pius XI clarifies the position of the Roman Catholic Church on Christian Education. Discusses aims of education; responsibility of family, state, and Church for education; and coeducation and sex education. Now somewhat out of date.

FORD, G. W. and LAWRENCE PUGNO (eds.), *The Structure of Knowledge and the Curriculum*. Chicago: Rand McNally & Co., 1964. P. 105.

An examination of the nature and structure of knowledge with special reference to the natural sciences, mathematics, English, and the social studies.

FRANKENA, WILLIAM K., *Philosophy of Education*. New York: Macmillan Publishing Co., Inc., 1965. P. 116.

Selections from the writings of Dewey, Whitehead, Maritain and R. S. Peters are arranged under two major headings: Education, its nature, aims, and principles; and education, its kinds, methods, programs, and problems. More important, however, is the introduction that provides a model for analyzing a philosophy of education.

GAGE, N. L., *Handbook of Research on Teaching*. Chicago: Rand McNally & Co., 1963. Pp. xiv + 1218.

Quick reference to theoretical orientations, methodologies in research and summaries of research on teaching at various grade levels and subject matters. Unfortunately a bit out of date but still useful.

GREEN, THOMAS F., *Activities of Teaching*. New York: McGraw-Hill Book Company, Inc., 1971. Pp. xiv + 234.

One of the more important publications in the field because of its emphasis in each chapter on philosophical method.

GUTTCHEN, ROBERT S., and BERTRAM BANDMAN (eds.), *Philosophical Essays on Curriculum*. Philadelphia: J. B. Lippincott Co., 1969. Pp. x + 388.

Students interested in some of the most important philosophical writings on the curriculum (sciences, social sciences, literature, and the arts) will find this book a most helpful place to begin.

HARDIE, CHARLES D., *Truth and Fallacy in Educational Theory*. New York: Bureau of Publications, Teachers College, Columbia University, 1962. Pp. xx + 156.

This is a landmark volume in the philosophy of education for it is the first book in which linguistic analysis was applied to education. This edition contains a most enlightening preface prepared by James E. McClellan and B. Paul Komisar.

HENRY, NELSON B. (ed.), *Modern Philosophies and Education*. Chicago: The University of Chicago Press, 1955. Pp. x + 374.

The fifty-fourth yearbook of the National Society for the Study of Education. One of the better known books in the field with chapters prepared by some of America's noted philosophers: Wild, Maritain, Greene, Geiger, Feigl, and Feibleman.

HOLLINS, T. H. B., *Aims in Education: The Philosophic Approach*. Great Britain: Manchester University Press, 1964. P. 135.

In the Spring of 1961, the School of Education of Manchester University invited a number of philosophers and educators to rationally analyze the general topic of "Aims of Education." This volume contains six of those lectures. The subject-matter ranges from Neo-Thomism to education and indoctrination, but the approach through-out is that of logical and linguistic analysis.

HOOK, SIDNEY, *Education for Modern Man, A New Perspective.* New York: Alfred A. Knopf, Pp. iii + 236.
A former student of Dewey surveys the contemporary scene in education; examines the ends of education; discusses the content of education; and investigates problems of method, program, and the relation of education to society.

HULLFISH, H. GORDON, and PHILIP G. SMITH, *Reflective Thinking: The Method of Education.* New York: Dodd, Mead & Co., 1961. Pp. xiii + 273.
Designed to help teachers understand how the methods of thinking can be applied. Written in a lucid style. It should be especially helpful to teachers who wish to see how Dewey's ideas may be implemented.

JAHSMANN, ALLAN HART, *What's Lutheran in Education?* St. Louis: Concordia Publishing Company, 1960. Pp. x + 185.
This is the most recent and most complete attempt yet made by a member of the Missouri Synod—Lutheran Church to state a philosophy for the schools of this synod. Reflects the strong influence of thelogy on philosophical and educational thinking.

KANT, IMMANUEL, *Education.* Ann Arbor: Ann Arbor Paperbacks, The University of Michigan Press, 1960. P. 121.
A collection of Kant's lecture notes edited by one of his students. Unfortunately this volume does not have an introduction and, for that reason, should be supplemented by such a work as William K. Frankena's *Three Historical Philosophies of Education* or Kingsley Price's *Education and Philosophical Thought.*

KILPATRICK, WILLIAM HEARD, *Philosophy of Education.* New York: Macmillan Publishing Co., Inc., 1951. Pp. x + 465.
This is a summing up, as it were, of the author's thinking in connection with his life work of teaching philosophy of education. He sets forth in detail his philosophy of life and his philosophy of education. This is "Mr. Progressive Education's" major work in philosophy of education.

KNELLER, GEORGE F., *Existentialism and Education.* New York: Philosophical Library, Inc., 1958. Pp. xvi + 170.
The first full-length book published on the subject. Written for the layman and educator, it is not highly technical. The author suggests educational theory and practice.

———, *Introduction to the Philosophy of Education.* New York: John Wiley & Sons, Inc., 1964. Pp. x + 137.
A brief outline of "those elements of philosophy that are relevant to a proper understanding of education and the task of teaching." Sections on philosophy and education, traditional philosophies of education, newer modes of thinking, and contemporary educational theories. Designed for the general reader and for those who wish a quick summary of the field.

———, *Logic and Language of Education.* New York: John Wiley & Sons, Inc., 1966. Pp. x + 242.
An attempt to relate logic to education. Chapters on the nature of logic, modes of logic, formal analysis, informal analysis, and the relation of logic to psychology, teaching, and learning.

LAWRENCE, NATHANIEL M., and ROBERT S. BRUMBAUGH, *Philosophers on Education:*

Six Essays on the Foundations of Western Thought. Boston: Houghton Mifflin Company, 1963. Pp. x + 211.

These essays deal with Plato, Aristotle, Rousseau, Kant, Dewey, and Whitehead. The final chapter cites some contemporary problems and develops a prologue to future philosophies of education.

LUCAS, CHRISTOPHER J. (ed.), *What is Philosophy of Education?* New York: Macmillan Publishing Co., Inc., 1969. Pp. 167–75.

A collection of essays.

MAGEE, JOHN B., *Philosophical Analysis in Education*. New York: Harper & Row, Publishers, 1971. Pp. xii + 189.

This book shows the usual concerns of analytic philosophers. Chapter II, "How Analysts Do Philosophy," will be rewarding to the beginning student who wishes to learn to do philosophy in this vein. Other chapters on teaching, learning, educating, curriculum, values, and democracy.

MARTIN, JANE R., *Explaining, Understanding & Teaching*. New York: McGraw-Hill Book Company, Inc., 1970. Pp. viii + 248.

A sophisticated discussion of explaining, understanding, and the various roles explaining and understanding play in education. Very worthwhile for the serious student of education.

MARTIN, WILLIAM OLIVER, *Realism in Education*. New York: Harper & Row, Publishers, 1969. Pp. x + 198.

This study is a search "for those philosophical truths in terms of which all educational means (i.e., practice) should be guided." Inquiries into the nature and structure of the learning-teaching activity and finds four basic causes in that activity: material, formal, efficient, and final.

MCCLELLAN, JAMES E., *Toward an Effective Critique of American Education*. Philadelphia: J. B. Lippincott Co., 1968. Pp. x + 324.

A critical and sometimes humorous evaluation of the educational thought of Conant, Brameld, Barzun, Skinner, and Goodman. The last chapter has proven prophetic.

MORRIS, VAN CLEVE, *Existentialism in Education: What It Means*. New York: Harper & Row, Publishers, 1966. Pp. xii + 163.

Morris states that existentialism is a theory of individual meaning that asks each person to ponder the reasons for his existence. From this, he moves on to discuss existentialism as a philosophy and to indicate its meaning for education.

NAKOSTEEN, MEHDI, *The History and Philosophy of Education*. New York: The Ronald Press Company, 1965. Pp. xii + 746.

This book begins with ancient educational theory and moves on to contemporary problems, issues, and trends. Students of the philosophy of American education will find it particularly valuable to consult the last two sections of this book.

NASH, PAUL, *Authority and Freedom in Education: An Introduction to the Philosophy of Education*. New York: John Wiley & Sons, Inc., 1966. Pp. x + 342.

Rejecting the school's approach, which he feels is "vestigial and anachronistic," Nash uses the analytical approach, coupled with a wide use of methods and materials from several disciplines, to develop a particular theme. His avowed goal is clarity as to ideas and commitment as to courses of action and choices among belief.

O'CONNOR, D. J., *An Introduction to the Philosophy of Education*. New York: Philosophical Library, Inc., 1957. Pp. viii + 148.

Writing from the viewpoint of philosophical analysis, the author presents a remarkably fine discussion of the relation of philosophy and education, the justification of value judgments, explanation, and theory, and closes by commenting upon questions of morals and religion.

PETERS, RICHARD, *Authority, Responsibility, and Education*. London: George Allen & Unwin, Ltd., 1959. P. 137.

The last part of this book is of particular interest to educators. Peters raises the question, "Must an educator have an aim?" This has become a rather widely discussed subject in American circles. The chapter on aims has been reproduced in William Frankena's *Philosophy of Education*.

PETERS, R. S., *Ethics and Education*. Chicago: Scott, Foresman and Company, 1967. P. 235.

A somewhat abridged edition of a book that appeared in England in 1966. It deals with the application of ethics and social philosophy to problems in education: equality, worthwhile activities, interest, freedom, respect for persons and fraternity, authority, discipline, punishment, and democracy.

PHENIX, PHILIP H., *Education and the Common Good*. New York: Harper & Row, Publishers, 1961. P. 271.

The author maintains that "the focal point around which the entire argument of this book revolves is that the cardinal goal of instruction in whatever field . . . should be the development of loyalty to what is excellent, instead of success in satisfying desires." Sections deal with intelligence, creativity, conscience, and reverence.

————, *Realms of Meaning: A Philosophy of the Curriculum for General Education*. New York: McGraw-Hill Book Company, Inc., 1964. Pp. xvi + 391.

This book states that there are six basic realms of meaning that are characteristically human. The fundamental patterns of meaning in these six realms are set forth, and an attempt is made to draw some conclusions regarding curriculum.

Proceedings of the Philosophy of Education Society. Francis Villemain, Editor, School of Education, Southern Illinois University at Edwardsville, Edwardsville, Illinois. Contains the minutes of the society, reports of its major committees, and the papers delivered before the membership at the annual conventions.

REID, LOUIS ARNAUD, *Philosophy and Education*. London: William Heinemann, Limited, 1962. Pp. xvi + 203.

A brief survey of philosophy of education with emphasis upon the nature of philosophy, values, application of theory to practice, the self, freedom, discipline, teaching, and professional education of teachers.

RICH, JOHN MARTIN, *Education and Human Values*. Reading, Mass.: Addison-Wesley Publishing Co., Inc., 1968. Pp. xii + 163.

To a very large extent, education is a value laden enterprise. Rich examines some of the value issues in education today and proposes possible solutions to these problems. He organizes the book around cultural, organizational, moral, and aesthetic values.

RUSK, ROBERT R., *The Philosophical Bases of Education*. Boston: Houghton Mifflin Company, 1956. Pp. viii + 176.

A statement of the philosophy of education from the idealistic standpoint. Chapters on the need for a philosophy of education, materialism, realism, naturalism, pragmatism, instrumentalism and experimentalism, and, of course, idealism, which is treated in much greater depth.

RUSSELL, BERTRAND, *Education and the Good Life*. New York: Boni & Liveright, 1926. P. 319.

Russell presents his aims for education and relates them to his idea of the good life. Early childhood education and what he calls "intellectual education" are treated in depth.

————, *Education and the Modern World*. New York: W. W. Norton & Co., 1932. P. 245.

This is Russell's second and last book devoted exclusively to education. He reflects upon the social implications of education under such headings as a negative theory of education, heredity, emotion, discipline, and the individual versus the citizen.

SCHEFFLER, ISRAEL, *Conditions of Knowledge*. Chicago: Scott, Foresman and Company, 1965. P. 117.

An extended discussion of a definition of propositional knowledge with implications drawn for education.

————, *The Language of Education*. Springfield, Ill.: Charles C. Thomas, Publishers, 1960. Pp. x + 113.

The purpose of this book is to apply certain philosophical methods to education in order "to clarify certain pervasive features of educational thought and argument." Chapters on definitions, slogans, and metaphors in education as well as two chapters on teaching and teaching and telling.

SMITH, B. OTHANEL, and ROBERT H. ENNIS, *Language and Concepts in Education*. Chicago: Rand McNally & Company, 1961. Pp. x + 215.

A collection of essays that are focused upon neglected meanings, conceptual blunders, the removal of pseudo-questions, and the logical inconsistencies in educational writing. The essays cover such topics as learning and experience, needs and the need-curriculum, explanations, and the logic of slogans.

SMITH, HUSTON, *Condemned to Meaning*. New York: Harper & Row, Publishers, 1965. P. 94.

As the ancestral order decays and the ancient religious certainties are dissolved by science, how can modern man find meaning that binds his experience and engages his faculties and passions? The author discusses this poignant question under such pertinent headings as meaning, meaning in the academic discipline, the meaning of life, and "Import for Education."

SOLTIS, JONAS F., *An Introduction to the Analysis of Educational Concepts*. Reading, Mass.: Addison-Wesley Publishing Co., Inc., 1968. Pp. xii + 100.

The author begins with a brief introduction to the work of the philosophical analyst in education and then turns his attention to the analysis of several concepts including knowing, teaching, learning, explaining, and understanding. About one fourth of the book is made up of an annotated bibliography of more advanced analytic writings and an unannotated bibliography of the sources used in preparation of the book.

Studies in Philosophy of Education. Francis Villemain, Editor, School of Education, Southern Illinois University, Edwardsville Campus, Edwardsville, Illinois.

One of the two journals in the field of philosophy of education published in America. Excellent source of information on current thinking in the field.

ULICH, ROBERT, *Crisis and Hope in American Education*. Boston: Beacon Press, Inc., 1951. Pp. xiv + 235.

This book deals chiefly with secondary education but includes chapters on the education of teachers, higher education, and adult education. In Chapter II Ulich describes the kind of school he desires for the future.

————, *Philosophy of Education*. New York: American Book Company, 1961. Pp. xiv + 286.

The author's intent has been to "present substantial material concerning the basic philosophic issues and aspects of education which every prospective teacher should, sooner or later, think about." He has arranged his material under two main rubrics, "The Theoretical Groundwork" and "Education in Action." The former section deals with aims, conception of man, and ethical views, whereas the second is concerned with religion, art, method, and curriculum.

VAN DUSEN, HENRY P., *God in Education*. New York: Charles Scribner's Sons, 1951. P. 118.

Van Dusen argues against the negativism, doubt, and vain elevation of human reason ushered in by Descartes. A reaffirmation of our religious faith and the restoration of religion to a position of necessary and unchallenged centrality must be the foundation of both life and education. The last chapter is a summarization of the dissenting opinions on the Supreme Court's decision of the McCollum Case.

WHITEHEAD, ALFRED NORTH, *Aims of Education and Other Essays*. New York: Macmillan Publishing Co., Inc., 1929. Pp. viii + 247.

The general idea behind this great book is, in Whitehead's words, "The students are alive, and the purpose of education is to stimulate and guide their self-development." This protest against inert ideas deals with the aims of education, the rhythm of education, technical education, classics, mathematics, and the function of universities as well as with certain scientific ideas.

WIRSING, MARIE E., *Teaching and Philosophy: A Synthesis*. Boston: Houghton Mifflin Company, 1972. Pp. xiv + 226.

This book attempts to directly relate teaching methods and philosophy of education. The author has used these materials in her classes at the University of Colorado, Denver Center, as she has worked with elementary and secondary school teachers. Her main point has been to get across to teachers that they can do exactly the same thing in a classroom for entirely different reasons. Students of a more practical turn of mind may enjoy this book.

WIRTH, ARTHUR G., *John Dewey as Educator: His Design for Work in Education* (1894–1904). New York: John Wiley & Sons, Inc., 1966. Pp. xviii + 322.

The purpose of this book is to answer the fascinating question, "What did Dewey stand for when he directed his Laboratory School at the University of Chicago?" The book is divided into two parts: theory, psychological and philosophical, and curriculum and method.

Index

Index